Teaching Public Issues

in the High School

DONALD W. OLIVER, *Harvard University*

JAMES P. SHAVER, *Utah State University*

Utah State University Press

Original Publication of
Houghton Mifflin Company • Boston
Reissued 1974 by
Utah State University Press
Printed in the U.S.A.

CONTENTS

Appendix

An Experimental Curriculum Project Carried Out Within the Jurisprudential Framework

TABLES

PREFACE

Too often reports of curricular work in the social studies are fragmented. Questions about the nature of American society are raised, with perhaps a few general implications for the curriculum; or the objectives of social studies instruction are discussed, again with a few curricular implications; or, after a brief touching on objectives, a course of instruction is described. Occasionally some experimental results with a course may be presented, usually without carefully setting the course in the context of objectives. This book presents what the authors believe is a rather unusual attempt to follow through a total sequence of curriculum development. The nature of the society, especially the implications of pluralism, is discussed; objectives of instruction are based on that discussion; curricular implications are developed; and detailed reporting of the experimental evaluation of the resulting curriculum is included, in the Appendix.

Because this volume reports a rather comprehensive effort at curriculum development and evaluation, different audiences may find various parts of the book more or less relevant to their own professional or civic interests. Parts Two and Three should be of most interest to the apprentice teacher who is exploring various approaches to the social studies or the experienced teacher who is seeking specific techniques and intellectual strategies to enrich his presentation of public issues in the schools. Part One might be especially appropriate for either the apprentice or the experienced teacher who has developed a successful classroom approach, but who wishes to examine in some detail the ethical basis of this approach and to compare it with what we suggest here. (For the apprentice teacher struggling to keep order in the classroom, Part One will probably appear somewhat "academic" and "theoretical.")

Graduate students in social studies education are more likely to find the whole book of interest, including the technical research reported in the Appendix. It is written from a particular point of view and in this sense is deliberately meant to stimulate controversy and further research. And research at three quite different levels is much needed: investigations into the philosophical premises of curriculum; sophisticated curriculum development programs in which philosophical premises are applied to classroom practice; and empirical research into the effectiveness of particular content or teaching procedures. It should also be noted that the work reported in the Appendix moves into two neglected areas of educational research: the assessment of learning outcomes and the relationships between teacher style and student personality. Insofar as graduate students and their advisers find either the philosophical and curriculum work or the empirical investigations provocative, we hope they will be stimulated to work in similar directions.

We also hope the book will have a wide audience among professional and lay people interested in the future of social studies education in America. It is our conviction that the social studies have reached a crucial juncture in the schools. The book is meant to be an open challenge to current efforts to redefine the social studies in narrow academic terms. What we conceive to be the major issues in the present controversy over an adequate conceptualization of the social studies are presented in Chapter Twelve, which might well be read first.

Although the reader will note that the curricular materials developed by the authors were tried out initially in junior high school, in no sense is the approach to be construed as limited to this level. We are in fact now extending our work into the senior high school and see a six-grade sequence encompassing Grades 7 through 12. Our decision to begin our work at the junior high school level was based as much on chance factors as on theoretical considerations. It is important that the reader see that our so-called "jurisprudential approach" can be translated into materials and instructional strategies at various age levels and with various curricular structures. The particular materials and procedures reported in the Appendix were fitted into a conventional junior high school United States history course. Much of the same type of material could also be worked into a ninth-grade civics course, an eleventh-grade United States history course, or a twelfth-grade problems of democracy course. Work is currently being carried out at Harvard to develop an integrated social studies sequence which is intended to *replace* the existing required course structure in the high school rather than "fit in" to such a structure. In whatever way one views where and how this approach might be used in the schools, we would suggest that the rationale and conceptual structure of our work have broad utility and should not be pegged at a particular course or grade level.

This book is, in a real sense, a progress report based on the first five years of the Harvard University Social Studies Project, from 1956 to 1961. The work reported here was made possible by generous financial support from a number of sources as well as the intellectual and moral support of our colleagues and associates. The Project was first sponsored by a private grant from Mr. Monroe Gutman of New York City. This was later augmented by support from the School-University Program for Research and Development, and still later by the Cooperative Research Branch of the United States Office of Education. It should be clear that the major support came from the initiative and resources of a private university.

The authors are indebted to all who helped to develop and clarify the basic ideas behind this book as well as to the teachers and administrators who provided a working context within which to test these ideas. We would like to acknowledge especially the three teacher-researchers who, with us, constituted the teaching staff for the major part of the experiment: Harold Berlak, Leonard Godfrey, and Ernest Van Seasholes. Moreover, the experiment would not have gone beyond the first six months without the unflinching administrative and moral support provided by Morton Seavey, former Principal of the Emerson Junior High School in Concord. Nor would we have been able to compare the work in Concord with that of other schools without the cooperation of the teachers and administration at the Weston Junior High School in Weston, Massachusetts, the Bigelow Junior High School in Newton, and the Wheatley School in Old Westbury, New York.

Much of the statistical work was done at the Computation Center at The Massachusetts Institute of Technology, Cambridge, Massachusetts. We are indebted to International Business Machines, Inc., and to MIT for making this facility available.

Finally, we owe a major debt to the Harvard Graduate School of Education and especially to Judson Shaplin for enlightened policies and able administrative leadership which made our work both possible and easier. It was he who advocated with such zeal the concept of school-university cooperation, the creation of the teacher-researcher role, and uncompromising support for able graduate students whose primary focus was on the improvement of school practice.

DONALD W. OLIVER
JAMES P. SHAVER

PART ONE

The Social Studies as

General Education

CHAPTER ONE

The Selection of Content in the Social Studies

The selection of appropriate content for the social studies program in the public schools should be the first order of business for social studies teachers and other curriculum people responsible for instruction in this area. Unfortunately, the rather static condition of the social studies for the last fifty years or so (since the report of the 1916 Commission on the Social Studies)[1] indicates that if educators have been actively involved in this selection process it has not seemed necessary, at least among those who finally control the curriculum, to make any significant changes. As with any generalization, there are, of course, exceptions to such a statement: In some school systems the curriculum structure of the social studies has undergone considerable change. But in the main, whether because of reliance upon conservative, commercially produced textbooks, reluctance to depart from past practice, or firm convictions about the validity of the traditional social studies pattern, the status quo has prevailed.

To those concerned with content selection, however, the problems have become increasingly acute in recent years. There are several reasons: The first has to do with history and historians. There is growing sophistication regarding the fact that historians must select the data upon which to base their narratives and interpretations of the past, and that further selection is made by the teacher — either deliberately or by default. This aspect of the problem is becoming more pressing as decades of history add up and as historical works accumulate dealing with the past in greater breadth and depth. It is not comfortable to fall back on the textbook and its historical selection when one recognizes the amount of time that could be spent, for example, teaching only that period of American history covering World War II to the present,[2] or when one thinks of the flood of historical material on the Civil War alone that has become available in the last hundred years.

But the expansion of knowledge problem is not confined to history. The methodology and accumulated findings of the various social sciences[3] have mushroomed since the beginning of World War II. A relatively new branch of social science, the behavioral sciences, has developed a methodology and approach to human and societal problems that is influencing other disciplines, such as political science and economics, which traditionally have been historical or philosophical studies.

Moreover, in the last few years the pendulum has swung again, and the indifference of the social scientists to the social studies curriculum of the secondary school has changed to active concern. Social scientists have been seeking a greater part in the shaping of the secondary school curriculum — following on the heels of notable involvement in curriculum development on the part of physical and biological scientists. They are also seeking greater acceptance of methodology and theory from the social science disciplines in the secondary school curriculum. Some want to insure preservation of the integrity of their disciplines in the social studies curriculum; others want to do away with "social studies" and teach the social sciences as courses. But in general, most are willing to discuss how the social sciences might best fit into the social studies program of the high school. And many are even willing to carry on this discussion in the context of citizenship education.[4] This reinvolvement of the social scientist has had a healthy effect. Social studies educators are being forced to rethink more rigorously the relationships between the social sciences and social studies objectives. But the pressure of time — and the concomitant need to select — is the specter peering over the shoulder of the discussants.

Another factor adding to the problem of selection should not be overlooked. With increased world-wide ideological competition,[5] Americans have become more self-conscious with regard to their own values and value commitments. As a result, people are suggesting strongly that history as well as the newer social sciences should be used as vehicles by which the student can learn what is right and what is wrong (particularly the former) about himself, his community, and his national society. When forces in society act to mold the social studies curriculum according to the belief that morality should be taught directly through historical or social science content, or when, more in line with our commitments to rationality, it is maintained that such content should be used to clarify social issues, expansion into the areas of political and ethical theory is inevitable. This expansion should be thought through clearly and not be a haphazard appendage to an already poorly justified social studies curriculum.

But where should one start in rethinking the social studies field? It is an axiom of education that curricular decisions should be made on the basis of objectives. That is, course content, teacher behavior, and the means used to evaluate student progress are appropriate, or valid, to the extent that they are derived from the aims of the course. Course objectives are to be consistent with the objectives of the school and, more broadly, with the goals of the society.

There is much evidence that objectives do not actually play this esteemed role in curricular decision-making in the social studies. Despite the espousal of objectives having to do, for example, with the development of the reasoning abilities of students, both teacher-made and published tests all too often call mainly for the recall or paraphrasing of "factual" material.[6] The fragmented nature of the social studies curriculum in many schools has often been noted. Frequent lack of sequential relationship between social studies courses, and even between parts of individual courses, suggests that an overall structure for the social studies has not evolved from a consideration of objectives.

Various elements that should constitute the basis of an integrated social studies program in American high schools — i.e., history, ethics and law, social science concepts and generalizations, analytic concepts, and exposure to societal problems — are commonly listed in curriculum guides. The vital interaction between such elements as ethics and legal principles and between legal principles and legal procedure, as presented, for example, in Cahn's *The Moral Decision*[7] and on the television series *The Defenders,* is rarely the focus of the classroom. By the same token, the tendency is to present abstract descriptions of societal problems along with various bland recommendations for their solutions, rather than involving the students in the emotion-laden situations underlying the problems. But most important is the practice of having the student learn *about* the various elements in the same fragmentary and disconnected way they are listed in the curriculum guides. The student "learns" a series of historical concepts. He *may* "learn" a set of ethical-legal concepts, but, as just noted, these are more often ignored. He may be "taught" a selection of social science concepts applied to simplified or contrived historical situations but seldom to the great problems facing our civilization. He *may* "learn" a series of specific critical thinking skills and something of their application, but usually not in terms of basic strategies of analytic thinking. Educators imagine that these fragments will somehow become ingredients in a complex intellectual process which will enable most, if not all, students to think more intelligently, or rationally, about man and the society in which they live. The problem, we suspect, is that, like the curriculum, the elements remain fragments, rather than becoming assimilated by the student into a working intellectual framework. This general failure to relate the various fragments of the existing curriculum undoubtedly accounts in part for the current trend toward deriving structure for the social studies from the social science disciplines, rather than from a consideration of the nature of citizenship in the modern democratic state.

This book, then, is an attack on two related problems: first, the problem of dealing with the substance of the social studies in the high school in such broad and abstract terms that the student is, at best, an observer of the thinking and conclusions of others (whether it be the teacher, the textbook, or the latest historical interpretation in paperback); and second, the problem of curricular fragmentation. We assume that structure can be provided for the social studies by a careful consideration of the role of the citizen in the community, rather than by resorting to arbitrarily selected, and still fragmented, university disciplines. Consequently, we shall first consider the nature of democracy and democratic commitments, then present a conceptual framework for a curriculum based on such considerations. The selection of problem areas for study and the evaluation of learning will also be dealt with in this context, as well as the results of an experimental curriculum built within this conceptual framework.

CRITERIA FOR THE SELECTION OF CONTENT

Before dealing explicitly with the framework according to which content might be selected for the social studies, we should make two preliminary points of clarification. One involves the distinction between the social sciences and the social studies; the other involves the definition of "content."

Social Studies as General Education

The terms *social science* and *social studies* are often used interchangeably.[8] However, to many educators the terms do have different referents, and it is thought that keeping them distinct helps to make thinking less muddled. Wesley first put in writing definitions that have come into common usage among those in the field. He defined the social sciences as scholarly fields "concerned with the detailed, systematic, and logical study of human relationships." The social studies, on the other hand, were called "those portions or aspects of the social sciences that have been selected and adapted for use in the school or in other instructional situations."[9] Actually, the increasing concern with the criteria by which selection will be made from the social sciences has been accompanied by the idea that there might be a certain unity to the social studies. Some have even argued for consideration of the social studies as a discipline.[10] And educators have begun to say "the social studies is" rather than "the social studies are," indicating a feeling of integrity of subject matter organized around central goals. That the social studies does not yet deserve the rubric "discipline" is perhaps evident from our discussion of lack of structure and concern for relating instructional choices to objectives. But to some extent this book can be viewed as a contribution to building the social studies into a unified curriculum area.

The distinction between the social sciences as the study of man in his social environment and the social studies as the pedagogical application of the results of this study has some important implications for content selection. One may choose to teach a social science as a discipline or to use social science content to contribute to the general intellectual competence of all the citizenry, but each choice will lead the teacher to a different curricular decision because the criteria for content selection will be different. The following example should make this point clear: What reply might a university scholar of the Jacksonian period of American history make if asked why he wishes to teach students about Jackson? It would not be surprising if he simply said that it happens to be his field of scholarly competence. From a disciplinary point of view, need he answer more? His rationale for presenting certain data to students and for not presenting other data bearing on the Jacksonian period need rest only on the premise that a particular selection of "facts" will represent the most accurate interpretation of the period. That is, his criterion for content selection is basically that of choosing historical data and interpretations that meet his own scholarly requirements, and perhaps those of his academic colleagues in history.

As a professional historian, the teacher might also include in his justification the hope that a permanent spark of interest about the period may be generated in his students — if it is not already there. Some of them will then perhaps pursue the subject of Jackson for the sake of knowing — for scholarship or personal interest. But basically, justification rests on the straightforward assumption that a particular social science discipline should be taught as an attempt to perpetuate scholarship and "truth."

The same reasoning might be used to justify teaching introductory courses in any of the basic disciplines to large numbers of able college (or, for that matter, high school) students.[11] Although only a small percentage of those introduced to a particular content area will actually enter training in a scholarly field, the decision might well be defended on the ground that one is not only passing on knowledge but recruiting academic personnel who may make significant contributions to the discipline and to the culture as a whole.

Such criteria are not adequate for the selection of specific content for the general education high school social studies program. Here the personal predilections of the teacher, or even the perpetuation of truth-seeking within a discipline, has at most second priority. The interests of the community, and of the student who will live within the community, become the most essential factors. Because of this obvious fact, curriculum-developers in the social studies often begin with a statement of objectives such as "selecting content to help the student understand his community, his country, and the world."

As a basis for content selection, such a general statement is unrealistic because it provides no guidelines. And educators are becoming increasingly aware of, and disturbed by, the scope and complexity of the potential curriculum required to attain this objective. Trends in the present secondary school curriculum suggest that social studies educators and teachers are seeking to solve the "increasing complexity" or "explosion of knowledge" problem either by introducing courses covering a wider and wider range of content at successively higher levels of generalization[12] or by developing new and more specialized fragments. We note, for example, the yearly extension of United States history courses to include contemporary history; the current popularity of "world history" courses which literally attempt to cover recorded history from the first caveman to the last atom; and the inclusion of specialized African and Asian area studies in world civilization courses.

It is certainly possible to extend the scope of existing courses, but this does not solve the problem of selecting particular content to put into the exhaustive chronological or geographical scheme which must still "fit" into the same amount of instructional time. Perhaps teachers feel that because the chronology covers the full range of time, or because the instructional plan includes geographical areas over the whole globe, the content selected to parallel the totality of the earth's known time and space is complete. This notion is, of course, absurd. After this recognition we will, perhaps, use our time more profitably to seek out more specific criteria for curriculum development.

Two Meanings of Content

The second point that should be clarified concerns an ambiguity in the use of the term *content*. It is commonly assumed that *content* refers to materials describing the world, or the ways in which data about the world might be interpreted or classified under "topics." In the social studies, *content* generally refers to the data and interpretations of data within such disciplines as history, geography, economics, government, sociology, and psychology. Each of these content areas is, of course, subject to finer slicing: e.g., ancient Babylonian history, ancient Egyptian history, ancient Greek history, ancient Roman history, and so on.

There is, however, a second kind of content requiring analysis and selection: that describing the intellectual processes the student is to use in dealing with data and the interpretation of data, e.g., how he is to ground his beliefs or justify the conclusions he reaches about a particular topic.[13] What, for example, is the student expected to do with the information presented as part of a topic? Bloom's *Taxonomy of Educational Objectives*[14] is one example of a scheme for classifying teacher expectations about what students are to do with information. A student might simply "know" information; he might "comprehend" or "paraphrase" it; he might "apply" it; he might "analyze" or "synthesize" it; and/or he might "evaluate" it. Obviously, complex intellectual operations like "evaluating" can be broken down into many more specific processes, such as testing a set of beliefs for logical consistency or using direct observations to support a general conclusion. Since Dewey's *How We Think*[15] was first published, intellectual operations and strategies for dealing with problems have been analyzed with varying degrees of complexity and usefulness. The "proof process" literature includes such noted works as Larrabee's *Reliable Knowledge*[16] Cohen and Nagel's *Logic and Scientific Method,*[17] and, more recently, Hullfish and Smith's *Reflective Thinking.*[18]

Selecting content, then, should be a matter of deciding not only to which data the student should be exposed but what he will be taught to do with the information, if anything. We must justify not only the selection of informational topics but also the selection of intellectual operations which will allow the student to deal with the information in some constructive fashion.

Position on Criteria

The social studies as a general education school subject, then, demands that the criteria for content selection — or, in a broader sense, curriculum development — be derived from a consideration of the needs of society rather than from concern for the needs of social science disciplines. Beard[19] emphasized some thirty years ago that one cannot discuss the objectives of education without considering the objectives of the society in which the education is to operate. This is especially pertinent to the social studies.

The basic theme of this book is that the multiplicity of purposes in American society can be summarized in one very abstract phrase: to promote the dignity and worth of each individual who lives in the society.[20] This statement of central commitment in our society is not unique; on the contrary, it is common, and it is not likely to be disputed at least as an ideal, even though it presents some problems in translation into practice.

We find it basically impossible to justify or rationalize in any ultimate sense *why* individual freedom and human dignity *should* be the central objective of the society. Not only does such rationalization on a philosophical level inevitably become regressive and circular, but anthropological evidence suggests the extent to which the persuasiveness of "reasons" depends on the culture in which one is reared. There is no final proof of such a value; when one pushes to the heart of human values, he must invariably end up accepting some tenet on faith. Recognizing the impossibility of breaking loose entirely from the strictures of one's culture, even if one desired to do so, we see in the commitment to human dignity an inexplicable affirmation of the belief in man as an end in himself. We frankly accept the value of human dignity as a societal goal in a society in which that commitment is central.[21] (The sources of values and the justification of human dignity as a value will be discussed further in Chapter Three.)

To assert that our society is dedicated to the value of human dignity obviously is to say very little. The key term is vague, and nothing is said about the kind of behaviors which evidence this commitment or the type of curriculum that might produce these behaviors. We will not define dignity in very specific terms, although the rest of the present chapter and succeeding chapters will be concerned with values derived from and giving meaning to this central value. Chapters Two and Three will contain defenses, primarily pedagogical, for leaving our key term at a low level of specificity.

In considering criteria for curriculum development based on commitment as a society to this central value, we must be concerned with the perpetuation of the value. There are undoubtedly a number of ways in which a society that promotes and protects the value might be organized. We assume that, whatever way is chosen, the society will have one salient characteristic: A number of groups which have different points of view regarding how the basic problems of the society should be solved will exist more or less independently of governmental control. These groups represent subcultures in the society.

We are assuming, then, that if human dignity and one of its essential defining characteristics, the right to make important choices, are to exist there must be real freedom to choose among a variety of ways of life. There must be, therefore, a multiplicity of groups — subsocieties — to support alternative solutions to the problems men must face in their dealings with the world. There is no participation in choice-making in the totalitarian society, where the formal instruments of government, even though sometimes supported by the great majority of people, are used to define and enforce the one solution that can be contemplated for each major decision. A plurality of active groups — i.e., pluralism — is a necessary ingredient of a free society, because it is the only natural mechanism which can insure some freedom of choice. Pluralism, as we are using the term, implies the existence not only of different political or partisan groups within the society but of various subcultures which claim the mutual respect of one another, at least to the extent that there is free communication among them.[22]

If cohesion is to be maintained in a society which contains the desired multiplicity of competing subgroups holding a variety of views toward the adjustments man needs to make to his social and physical environment, several factors must be present: (1) Despite an inevitable degree of isolation among groups within the society, there must be recognition that many problems have to be handled by the community as a whole. (2) The members of all the subgroups must to some extent share value commitments and a normative vocabulary as a framework within which to deal with these common problems. And (3) this normative framework must include procedures for the mediation of interpersonal and intergroup conflict, especially as necessary to solve the societal problems.

A conflict model of society such as has been presented above is required also to take into account the most important pragmatic reason for maintaining society in the first place, i.e., the interdependence of men and groups within a societal setting as a necessary condition of human fulfillment. Initially, small groups of Europeans, mainly for economic or religious reasons, banded together and came to the New World. The gradual development of these groups into larger colonies and finally the uniting of the colonies into a single nation reflected the increasing development of economic and cultural interdependence which created a single society — at least in the political and economic sense — out of the separate and fairly distinct smaller societies. Smaller "societies" are still with us to maintain diversity and freedom within the national society; but the larger society is with us too. A national government is called for that can deal with the problems of the larger society and yet allow the broadest and deepest conception of personal freedom and human dignity to exist among the subgroups.[23]

One must also recognize that in many cases the manner in which national problems are resolved may well promote, disrupt, or destroy the values, or even the integrity, of subgroups. For example, the southern "solution" to racial problems has in large part been rejected by the larger community. How does this affect the concept of human dignity in the southern white community?

The commitment of the government, then, to the concept of human dignity has two components: protecting the autonomy of individual subsocieties or groups and developing a common standard which can be applied to conflicts within the national community. A national society is possible only if there is some conception of national ethical standards on which antagonists can find common ground to debate their differences.

Broad general concepts, such as the concept of human dignity, moreover, are too vague to be very useful as normative criteria for debating community problems. They must be translated into ideals with more concrete meaning. These more specific ideals are not difficult to discover in the political and legal documents which describe the ethical basis of our own society and government. The Declaration of Independence, for example, states that all men are created equal — that each is entitled to life, liberty, and the pursuit of happiness. The keynote is clearly political equality guaranteed by constitutional government. The Preamble of the Constitution enumerates the ideals of justice, domestic tranquility, common defense, general welfare, and the blessings of liberty. Liberty is further defined in the Bill of Rights to include freedom of speech, freedom of religion, freedom of assembly, the right to privacy within one's own home, and the right to the protection of personal property. Justice is defined in the Bill of Rights in terms of an explicit system of due process, as well as equal protection under the law (in the Fourteenth Amendment).

Myrdal calls these normative concepts or ideals the "American Creed."[24] They provide the national community with standards by which common problems facing the community can be described, debated, and evaluated.

The role of the government in handling the common problems of a free society is critical. Because of different standards of "right" or "good," men will not see the general welfare of the community or interpret the ideals in political and legal documents in the same light. And, insofar as the government accepts some responsibility for resolving societal problems, even by mediating between those who differ on solutions, it carries with it the power to tolerate or destroy various groups within the community. The government is thus in a very difficult position: It is obligated to protect the rights of men and groups, even though by doing so it fosters social and political conflict. It is obligated to invite rational contention and dispute, but it is also often the only instrument through which disputes that affect the whole community can be resolved, however temporarily. The paradox of tolerating, even encouraging, dispute, yet helping to resolve it, is a major challenge to the government in a free society. This paradox places special demands on the public school in its governmental function.

There are, of course, a number of possible ways for the government and the schools to approach the general problem of conflict control. One is to assume that man is basically tolerant; that even though the individual's own values or interests are threatened by other persons and groups, he can be educated or trained to understand and "love" them. This approach requires faith in the ultimate educability of man — faith that the antisocial impulses can be trained out of man, or that he can be reared in such a way that aggression will never develop into a serious problem.

There are ideologies, including both Christianity and Communism, that are based on this "ideal" solution and that also hold the protection of human dignity to be the highest purpose of society. People holding these ideologies assume that a true definition can be reached regarding the "good" man and the "good" society — and they claim to have this truth. They further assume that when all men see "the truth" and act in accordance with it there will be no aggression or intolerance. In these ideologies conflict is *ultimately* bad. The prophets of both Communism and Christianity have envisioned a state of man in which there is no conflict and hence no need for coercive institutions to control conflict; conflict is viewed as a temporary state of society, caused by, and causing, temporary imperfections in man's character.

Such ideological viewpoints may serve as long-range evolutionary goals for modern man. But in the light of history, as well as of the results of studies of socialization,[25] they are unrealistic bases upon which to erect curricula for the public schools of a democracy. The position taken in this book is that for most of the public decisions required of a pluralistic society men cannot define truth in such unequivocal terms that all will see it and grasp it in the same way. The variety of backgrounds provided by the multiplicity of subgroups precludes this. Moreover, one of the most important elements of the concept of human dignity in this society — freedom of choice — assumes that there is usually more than one legitimate alternative from which to choose in matters of public decision.

The implications of this position for general education in the social studies are important. First, since there is no revealed truth, the teacher is obliged to tolerate a variety of ideals, values, or creeds among his students. Furthermore, although the teacher may find a personal solution to ideological conflict, he must condone the constant battle among various groups within the society as they are represented in his classroom. The good society is not to be construed as one in which everyone behaves uniformly according to some agreed-upon substantive definition of right; rather the good society is one in which individuals and groups are allowed wide latitude in developing their own standards and tastes — i.e., their own definitions of human dignity. Progress from this point of view consists of longer and longer periods of non-violent conflict among groups of free men who have chosen a variety of modes of conduct as exemplifying the "good life."[26]

On the basis of these considerations about the pluralism and commonality of American society, two criteria for selecting content for general education in the social studies become salient. First, the student should be exposed to public problems within our society — situations over which individuals as well as the society are in conflict. And second, the student should be taught to analyze these public problems within some useful political and social framework. We are suggesting that initially the appropriate framework grows out of a Western constitutional tradition.

To teach this content adequately, however, the teacher must be able to assume that two prerequisites have already been met by the student's education. The student must have some familiarity, at both a descriptive and a conceptual level,[27] with his own culture and other cultures that impinge upon it. He must also be committed to the basic ideals of American society emerging from the democratic traditions of Western civilization.

Although no extensive or systematic review of the elementary school curriculum was carried out, a quick perusal of elementary social studies books was not encouraging in regard to the first prerequisite. Several inadequacies are apparent. First, the texts seem grossly unrealistic, both in substance (errors of fact) and in emphasis. Second, they contain much material that is irrelevant to the challenges and questions which American citizens at present and prospectively face. Third, there appears to be little effort to build a relationship between important historical and social science concepts and the concrete experiences that would make these concepts functional for the student. Concepts such as *mass production, slum, automation, labor union, corporation,* and *social class,* to select but a few, are rarely mentioned, much less illustrated with the wide range of exemplars required for the development of adequate concepts.[28] Of the many objectives of the elementary curriculum, the teaching of social science concepts necessary to understand contemporary American society should have high priority. A curriculum emphasizing the study of societal problems cannot teach the social science concepts simultaneously; both tasks are too complex. However, the public controversy curriculum should serve to expand the meaning of concepts introduced earlier.

The suggestion that the school teach commitment to the basic ideals of American society always creates problems. The red flag of "indoctrination," with its implications of unthinking obedience, is often waved. Nevertheless, we have already noted the need for societal cohesion based upon common normative commitments. The dilemma is a real one.[29] The solution lies in carefully distinguishing between the general values of the society to which all can reasonably be expected to be committed and the translation of these values into specific policy decisions about which there must be disagreement. In regard to the latter, the individual's freedom of choice must be firmly protected. This book is largely an explication of a position which provides for individual choice within a framework of societal values, as well as a curriculum based upon that position. The problem of how to handle values in the classroom will be treated extensively in the following pages.

SUMMARY AND PREVIEW

In summary, our position might be stated as follows. Despite the fact that different economic groups and different ethnic and racial groups have a variety of modes of life, in a society based on a commitment to personal freedom and human dignity such pluralism is tolerated and encouraged.

Many of the most important personal decisions each of us makes, however, are contingent upon the conduct of other groups within society which may have different interests and different standards of conduct from ours. This is a source of constant conflict and controversy. When the conflicts become salient for large segments of society, they move from the realm of private decision to public decision, because the government is the only agency which has sufficient coercive power to deal with such far-reaching issues. When a decision becomes public, all the citizens are involved directly or indirectly, and each citizen has a stake in the conflict. To debate public issues requires common standards, common principles of ethical and political conduct, and a common vocabulary of norms. Western civilization in general, and America in particular, has developed such standards to serve as a basic vocabulary for the debate of public issues. They include concepts such as *property rights, free speech, freedom of religion, freedom of personal association and privacy, rejection of violence and faith in reason as a method of dealing with conflict, the general welfare of all, equal opportunity, equal protection under the law, rule of law or constitutional limits on government, rule by consent of the governed, due process of law, separation of powers,* and *local control of local problems.*

Committing ourselves to public conflict and political controversy as the focus of general education in the social studies is, however, only the first step in selecting content. One must specify what the student is to do with the content once he has received it. The intellectual process, the acceptable standards of analysis by which the student is actively to relate the content to his own principles of conduct, and the criteria for defining when content is "understood" must be described. An attempt to describe an acceptable framework for analysis will be presented in succeeding chapters.

First, however, an extremely important point must be clarified. There is, we believe, an intimate connection between the way one conceptualizes the nature and structure of societal values and the process by which one clarifies an ethical position.[30] Whether one conceives of liberty, equality, and fraternity, for example, as each demanding equal allegiance from the citizen or as placed in a hierarchical order makes a fundamental difference in the way one uses them to justify his position on a particular controversial issue. We next, therefore, turn to social values and how they operate in the arena of public controversy.

References

1. See, for example, Willis D. Moreland, "Curriculum Trends in the Social Studies." *Social Education* (1962), 26:102.

2. Arthur S. Bolster, Jr., in "History, Historians and the Secondary School Curriculum," *Harvard Educational Review* (1962), 32:48-49, suggests that one

solution has been to cover history on a more superficial level, using generalizations that have successively less meaning to the students.

3. For the moment, we will not include history in the social sciences and thus avoid the wrath of historians who do not like such classification.

4. See Bernard Berlson *et al., The Social Studies and the Social Sciences* (New York: Harcourt, Brace & World, Inc., 1962); and Erling M. Hunt *et al., High School Social Studies Perspectives* (Boston: Houghton Mifflin Company, 1962).

5. The ideological conflict referred to here includes more than the present conflict between liberal democracy and state Communism. The success of Fascist regimes in Italy, Germany, and Spain as well as the Russian Revolution marked the beginning of a serious new challenge to modern democratic government. As suggested by Friedrich and Brzezinski, because of technological changes in communication and transportation, this challenge is far more radical than that of the older autocratic state. Carl J. Friedrich and Zbigniew K. Brzezinski, *Totalitarian Dictatorship and Autocracy* (Cambridge, Mass.: Harvard University Press, 1956).

6. That much of this material is not factual is documented by H. J. Noah, C. E. Prince, and C. R. Riggs, "History in High School Textbooks," *School Review* (1962), 70:414-436.

7. Edmond Cahn, *The Moral Decision: Right and Wrong in the Light of American Law* (Bloomington: Indiana University Press, 1956).

8. See, e.g., Berlson *et al., op. cit.*

9. Edgar B. Wesley and Stanley P. Wronski, *Teaching Social Studies in High Schools* (Boston: D. C. Heath & Company, 4th ed., 1958), pp. 3-4.

10. For example, Samuel P. McCutcheon, "A Discipline for the Social Studies," *Social Education* (1963), 27:61-65; and Stanley P. Wronski, "A Philosophy of the Social Studies," address delivered at a section meeting of the 1963 annual meeting of the National Council for the Social Studies in Los Angeles, p. 1 of a mimeographed copy.

11. However, for an interesting account of the attempt of college instructors of introductory economics courses to deal with the relationship of their courses to citizenship and other needs of their students see Kenyon A. Knopf, *The Teaching of Elementary Economics* (New York: Holt, Rinehart & Winston, Inc., 1960).

12. Bolster, *op. cit.*

13. The performance of an explicit intellectual process is commonly referred to as a skill. The dichotomy between skills and knowledge is not particularly logical, although it may be useful in clarifying issues in curriculum development. The "skills" actually consist of instrumental knowledge, i.e., information about how to obtain, describe, or validate other knowledge. The possession of instrumental knowledge is evidenced by the student's ability to perform specified intellectual operations (e.g., identify a point on a map using conventional coordinates), just as recall tests measure the retention of "topical" knowledge.

14. Benjamin S. Bloom (ed.), *Taxonomy of Educational Objectives* (New York: David McKay Co., Inc., 1956).

15. John Dewey, *How We Think* (Boston: D. C. Heath & Company, 1933).

16. Harold Atkins Larrabee, *Reliable Knowledge* (Boston: Houghton Mifflin Company, 1945).

17. Morris R. Cohen and Ernest Nagel, *An Introduction to Logic and Scientific Method* (New York: Harcourt, Brace & Co., 1934).

18. Gordon Hullfish and Philip G. Smith, *Reflective Thinking: The Method of Education* (New York: Dodd, Mead & Co., 1961).

19. Charles A. Beard, *The Nature of the Social Sciences* (New York: Charles Scribner's Sons, 1934).

20. May Edel and Abraham Edel, *Anthropology and Ethics* (Springfield, Ill.: Charles C Thomas, Publisher, 1959), pp. 91 ff., suggest that this value can be found in many primitive societies and may well approach being a universal value. However, Mehnert's treatment of Chinese culture and the extent to which the Chinese is "conditioned by his surroundings" casts doubt on the universality of a commitment to the individuality of man. Klaus Mehnert, "The Chinese and the Russians," *Annals of the American Academy of Political and Social Science* (1963), 349:2-4.

21. A word might be said here about the relationship between the operative values of the society (the commitments on the basis of which people actually behave), the ideals of the society (the values professed by the society), and the personal values of the individual teacher. It is our position that if the teacher is committed only to the operative values and/or is not committed to the ideals of the society he should not be in the classroom, where, presumably, the minds he is attempting to influence will be particularly receptive to his personal values and beliefs. From our point of view, the classroom is an inappropriate place to subvert the ideals of the society because of the problem created for the student who is not in an autonomous position to fight back. (It should be emphasized that we mean subversion of the ideals, not subversion of operative values or practices.) From both a practical and an ethical point of view, if the teacher cannot in good faith operate from the ideals of the society in which he lives, he should either leave the society and teach somewhere else or attempt to influence the adult community to change its value structure. (He might start a political movement, a subversive organization, etc.)

22. For a somewhat more detailed explication of the pluralistic position, particularly in relation to some traditional statements of goals for the social studies, see Donald W. Oliver, "The Selection of Content in the Social Studies," *Harvard Educational Review* (1957), 28:271-300.

23. See A. D. Lindsay, *The Modern Democratic State* (London: Oxford University Press, 1943), Chap. V.

24. Gunnar Myrdal, *An American Dilemma* (New York: Harper & Row, Publishers, 1944).

25. See, e.g., H. D. Schmidt, "Bigotry in Schoolchildren," *Commentary* (1960), 29:253-257. After presenting some very persuasive data demonstrating the extent to which social and political attitudes are beyond influence by the schools, except in the most superficial way, the author gives a convincing argument supported by experimental evidence that in-group feelings of allegiance are inextricably tied to out-group hostility. Facing this fact realistically, the author concludes:

"The problem of group hatreds is not one of how to loosen the hold of strong in-group feeling — that is impossible — but rather how to keep group loyalty and group antagonism within reasonable and safe bounds in a dangerous world. Friction and conflict of interests will always exist between groups as they will always exist between individuals, but they should not be allowed to lead to collective crimes. It is more honest — and indeed the only possible remedy on an individual level — to tell young people that political hatred exists in all of us and is a natural result of our history, but that it is one thing to harbor an intense feeling of hatred and quite another to translate that feeling into anti-social acts" (p. 257).

26. The conflict-tension model suggested here is nothing new in American political thought. In 1934 Beard, commenting on the relationship between social science and political ethics, wrote (*op. cit.,* pp. 170-171):

   "If, however, [empiricism in the social sciences] pushes its inquiry as far as possible toward the periphery of its subject matter, it must then examine and describe as accurately as possible these tensions of change and direction and the ideas of choice offered by human thought.

   "And when the social sciences discharge this obligation faithfully, they disclose the fundamental fact that the whole political system through which adjustments are made in the United States is founded upon the conception of a flexible frame of control and reference — the Constitution of the United States. Born of tension, it assumes the perdurance of tensions and the possibility of adjusting them by inquiry, discussion, proposal, and decision within the borders of law. The values for such adjustments are furnished by the cultural heritage of the nation and the ideas evolving out of and added to the heritage."

27. We are familiar with at least two general approaches for teaching the child a conceptual view of his own society and demonstrating its relationship to other societies. The approach developed by Paul Hanna of Stanford advocates organizing the curriculum on the basis of valid generalizations about the social world and sequencing them on the basis of the child's physical or psychological distance from the communities of which he is part — which Hanna assumes are linearly related: school, neighborhood, city and county, state, nation, etc. Joseph Grannis of Harvard (see ,e.g., Joseph C. Grannis, "The Framework of the Social Studies Curriculum," *National Elementary Principal* [1963], 42:20-27) has undertaken a curriculum development program which also is focused on the systematic development of societal concepts in children. Grannis' program does not, however, assume the physical-psychological linear relationship of communities which is at the center of Hanna's work. Moreover, there is greater stress placed upon training the child to perform different logical operations by which concepts can be related to one another.

28. It is instructive to look at topics such as "Cuba" in modern elementary school social studies texts. Pre-Castro Cuba is usually presented as a happy republic which was originally set "free" from Spain by the United States. Reforms guaranteed in the Cuban constitution (e.g., "Women have the right to vote") are commonly presented as facts rather than legal fictions. Little is said of the poverty among great masses of people. Nothing is said of the ruthless Batista dictatorship.

29. For a comprehensive treatment of individualism in the context of general values as "symbols of unity and cohesion," see Donald W. Oliver, "Educating Citizens for Responsible Individualism," in Franklin Patterson (ed.), *Citizenship and a Free Society,* 30th Yearbook of the National Council for the Social Studies, 1960, pp. 201-227.

30. Beard, *op. cit.,* pp. 182-183, 188-191, emphasizes the importance of a person's frame of reference in determining his behavior. He particularly stresses the influence on teacher behavior, including content selection.

|

CHAPTER TWO

Social Values in the Analysis of Public Issues

Perhaps the best introduction to our own conception of social values and the intellectual process by which their nature and function may be understood is provided in Appendix 1 of Myrdal's *An American Dilemma*. The essential points of Myrdal's thesis are reproduced below because of the clarity and strength of the writing. The few points on which we take issue with Myrdal and an elaboration of the process which he introduces will follow.

People have ideas about how reality actually is, or was, and they have ideas about how it ought to be, or ought to have been. The former we call *"beliefs."* The latter we call *"valuation."* A person's beliefs, that is, his knowledge, can be objectively judged to be true or false and more or less complete. His valuations — that a social situation or relation is, or was, "just," "right," "fair," "desirable," or the opposite, in some degree of intensity or other — cannot be judged by such objective standards as science provides. In their *"opinions"* people express both their beliefs and their valuations. Usually people do not distinguish between what they think they know and what they like or dislike.

There is a close psychological interrelation between the two types of ideas. In our civilization people want to be rational and objective in their beliefs. We have faith in science and are, in principle, prepared to change our beliefs according to its results. People also want to have "reasons" for the valuations they hold, and they usually express only those valuations for which they think they have "reasons." To serve as

19

opinions, specific valuations are selected, are formulated in words and are motivated by acceptable "reasons." With the help of certain beliefs about reality, valuations are posited as parts of a general value order from which they are taken to be logical inferences. This value hierarchy has a simple or elaborate architecture, depending mainly upon the cultural level of a person. But independently of this, most persons want to present to their fellows — and to themselves — a trimmed and polished sphere of valuations, where honesty, logic, and consistency rule. For reasons which we shall discuss, most people's advertised opinions are, however, actually illogical and contain conflicting valuations bridged by skewed beliefs about social reality. In addition, they indicate very inadequately the behavior which can be expected, and they usually misrepresent its actual motivation.

The basic difficulty in the attempt to present a logical order of valuations is, of course, that those valuations actually are conflicting. When studying the way in which the valuations clash, and the personal and social results brought about by the conflicts, we shall, moreover, have to observe that the valuations simply cannot be treated as if they existed on the same plane. They refer to different levels of the moral personality. The moral precepts contained in the respective valuations correspond to different degrees of generality of moral judgment. Some valuations concern human beings in general; others concern Negroes or women or foreigners; still others concern a particular group of Negroes or an individual Negro. Some valuations have general and eternal validity; others have validity only for certain situations. In the Western culture people assume, as an abstract proposition, that the more general and timeless valuations are morally higher. We can, therefore, see that the motivation of valuations, already referred to, generally follows the pattern of trying to present the more specific valuations as inferences from the more general.

In the course of actual day-to-day living a person will be found to focus attention on the valuations of one particular plane of his moral personality and leave in the shadow, for the time being, the other planes with their often contradicting valuations. Most of the time the selection of this focus of evaluation is plainly opportunistic. The expressed valuations and beliefs brought forward as motives for specific action or inaction are selected in relation to the expediences of the occasion. They are the "good" reasons rather than the "true" reasons; in short, they are "rationalizations."

The whole "sphere of valuations" — by which we mean the entire aggregate of a person's numerous and conflicting valuations, as well as their expressions in thought, speech, and behavior — is thus never present in conscious apperception. Some parts of it may even be constantly suppressed from awareness. But it would be a gross mistake to believe that the valuations temporarily kept in the shadow of subjective inattention — and the deeper-seated psychic inclinations and loyalties represented by them — are permanently silenced. Most of them rise to consciousness now and then as the focus of apperception changes in reaction to the flow of experiences and impulses. Even when submerged, they are not without influence on actual behavior. They ordinarily bend behavior somewhat in their direction; the reason for suppressing them from conscious attention is that, if obeyed, they would affect behavior even more. In this treatise, therefore, behavior is conceived of as being typically the outcome of a moral compromise of heterogeneous valuations, operating on various planes of generality and rising in varying degrees and at different occasions to the level of consciousness. To assume the existence of homogeneous "attitudes" behind behavior would violate the facts, as we must well know from everyday introspection and from observation and reflection. It tends to conceal the moral conflicts which are the ultimate object of our study in this book.

The individual or the group whose behavior we are studying, moreover, does not act in moral isolation. He is not left alone to manage his rationalizations as he pleases, without interference from outside. His valuations will, instead, be questioned and disputed. Democracy is a "government by discussion," and so, in fact, are other forms of government, though to a lesser degree. Moral discussion goes on in all groups from the intimate family circle to the international conference table. Modern means of intellectual communication have increased the volume and the intensity of such moral interrelations.

When discussion takes the form of moral criticism by one person or group or another, it is not that the one claims to have certain valuations that the other does not have. It is rather an appeal to valuations which the other keeps in the shadow of inattention, but which are assumed, nevertheless, to be actually held in common. This assumption, that those with opposing opinions have valuations in common, is ordinarily correct. . . . [C]ultural unity in America consists in the fact that most Americans have most valuations in common, though they are differently arranged and bear different intensity coefficients for different individuals and groups. This makes discussion possible and secures an understanding of, and a response to, criticism.

In this process of moral criticism which men make upon each other, the valuations on the higher and more general planes — referring to *all* human beings and *not* to specific small groups — are regularly invoked by one party or the other, simply because they are held in common among all groups in society, and also because of the supreme prestige they are traditionally awarded. By this democratic process of open discussion there is started a tendency which constantly forces a larger and larger part of the valuation sphere into conscious attention. More is made conscious than any single person or group would on his own initiative find it advantageous to bring forward at the particular moment. In passing, we might be allowed to remark that this effect — and in addition our common trust that the more general valuations actually represent a "higher" morality — is the principal reason why we, who are convinced democrats, hold that public discussion is purifying and that democracy itself provides a moral education of the people.

When thus even the momentarily inopportune valuations are brought to attention, an element of indecision and complication is inserted. A need will be felt by the person or group, whose inconsistencies in valuations are publicly exposed, to find a means of reconciling the inconsistencies. This can be accomplished by adjusting one of the conflicting pairs of valuations. If the valuation to be modified is on the less general plane, a greater moral harmony in the larger group is brought about. Specific attitudes and forms of behavior are then reconciled to the more general moral principles. If, on the other hand, an attempt is made to change or reinterpret valuations which are more general in scope and most of the time consciously shared with all other groups in society, the deviant group will see its moral conflict with other groups becoming increasingly explicit (that is, if the other groups are not themselves prepared to change their general valuations toward a moral compromise). This process might go on until discussion no longer becomes feasible. In the extreme case such a moral isolation, if the dissenting group is powerful enough, may break the peace and order of society and plunge a nation into civil war.

. . . .

The feeling of need for logical consistency within the hierarchy of moral valuations — and the embarrassed and sometimes distressed feeling that the moral order is shaky — is, in its modern intensity, a rather new phenomenon. With less mobility, less intellectual communication, and less public discussion, there was in previous generations less exposure of one another's valuation conflicts. The leeway for false beliefs, which makes rationalizations of valuations more perfect for their purpose, was also greater in an age when science was less developed and education less extensive. These historical differentials can be observed today within our own society among the different social layers with varying degrees of education and communication with the larger society, stretching all the way from the tradition-bound, inarticulate, quasi-folk-societies in isolated backward regions to the intellectuals of the cultural centers. When one moves from the former groups to the latter, the sphere of moral valuations becomes less rigid, more ambiguous and also more translucent. At the same time, the more general valuations increasingly gain power over the ones bound to traditional peculiarities of regions, classes, or other smaller groups. One of the surest generalizations is that society, in its entirety, is rapidly moving in the direction of more general valuations. The speed stands in some relation to, and can be gauged by, geographical mobility, the development of intellectual communication, the decrease of illiteracy and the funds spent on education.

During this process of growing intellectualization, people's awareness of inconsistencies in their own spheres of valuations tends to be enhanced. At the same time — if moral cynicism does not spread . . . — they are increasingly reconditioned to demand consistency in their own valuations and, particularly, in those of other people. They learn to recognize and to avoid the use of illogicalities and misconceptions of social reality for overcoming the incongruities in their valuations. The impatient humanitarian might find this process exasperatingly slow, and the results meager. The perspective of decades and generations, however — providing moral catastrophes do not interrupt the growth process — yields a more optimistic impression.

. . . .

If this educational effort meets with success, the illogicalities involving valuations become exposed to the people who hold them. They are then pressed to change their valuations to some degree or other. For if popular beliefs depend upon valuations, as we have shown, the valuations also depend upon the beliefs in our civilization bent upon rationalism. When supporting beliefs are drawn away, people will have to readjust their value hierarchies and, eventually, their behavior. As the more general norms in our culture are given supreme moral sanction, this means — if we assume that this "valuation of the valuations" is upheld, and moral cynicism counteracted — that the valuations on a more specific level (often called "prejudices") will yield to them. This is the reason, and the only reason, why we generally assume that improved knowledge will make for "better" citizens. Facts by themselves do not improve anything.[1]

We would emphasize as follows those parts of Myrdal's position which have central significance for us:

1. It is important to distinguish between factual issues or beliefs, which are subject to the methods of objective verification, and values or valuations, which require a different kind of analysis and justification.

2. Values operate at different levels of generality. Some apply to specific groups; some apply to all men; some apply to specific situations; some apply to all situations. The more specific values often contradict the general values.

3. We attempt to "rationalize" values by finding facts or beliefs which are affectively loaded in the same direction as our values. Factual distortion and repression take place when the affective loading of our facts is inconsistent with our values.

4. There are two kinds of inconsistencies with which we have to deal: (a) inconsistencies between the loading of a fact and a social value and (b) inconsistencies between specific values and general values.

5. General values, those which apply to all men at all times, have a higher and more permanent status, at least as Americans see them.

6. When we stand on the threshold of a value conflict, we tend to deal with it by leaving one value in the shadow of our consciousness and making salient the value which supports our immediate behavior. In this way we try to avoid recognizing and coping with inconsistency.

7. Open discussion tends to force society to have before it the total range of beliefs and values, even those which conflict with one another.

8. Most Americans share the basic values of the culture. There is cultural unity at the general value level, but different individuals and groups share these general values with different degrees of intensity as they apply to different issues.

9. Since most Americans share the same general values, when public discussion lays bare our inconsistencies we feel compelled to deal with them.

10. As a "public" becomes increasingly sensitive to the fact that many of the specific beliefs supporting its values are erroneous, it will be forced to alter the values. And as the public becomes aware of the inconsistency between the specific values and the more permanent and general values (e.g., liberty, equality, and Christian brotherhood), the specific values will gradually become modified and finally effect a change in behavior.

As an analysis of the way values and facts modify one another, and of the way specific values interact with general values, Myrdal's remarks have our general agreement. However, we do have some disagreement with his final point. Myrdal apparently assumes that values at the general moral level will be consistent with one another. Only the values of the narrow, unenlightened bigot will contradict the more general values. From our point of view, it is possible for the most fundamental and enduring values of the American creed to conflict with one another when applied to practical political situations. So while we agree that the initial step in the analysis of political controversy involves testing the factual assumptions behind the alleged violations of certain general values, or exposing inconsistencies between the narrow values of special interest groups and the more general values of the society, what Myrdal fails to note is that the narrow values of these groups are in themselves supported by basic values: personal freedom and cultural autonomy. Myrdal's preoccupation with brotherhood and equality, the values so salient in the race issue, probably accounts for his position. Even so, it is quite possible for these two values to conflict with each other: Christian brotherhood can be interpreted to mean discrimination in favor of a particular group within society — the weak and humble.

So while Myrdal assumes that the general values of the Creed are consistent with some more general notion of just relations among men, from our own point of view this is the case only when one sees these general values as abstract ideals. When one attempts to justify practical judgments about specific situations on the basis of the general values alone, he still faces problems of inconsistency. Our own solution is to regard what Myrdal calls "general valuations" as existing on two moral planes. The higher plane is denoted by a single "ultimate" value — human dignity. The second level consists of the values identified in Myrdal's American Creed. In this way we feel it is possible to avoid the difficulties Myrdal encounters when he considers the general values of the Creed final. If these values are final, permanent, and universal, what do we do when one of them contradicts another? If both are final, both must be accepted as right; it is impossible to choose between them as criteria for action. An important part of our own solution is to raise our thinking to a higher moral plane and posit the more general "ultimate" human dignity and look at the values of the Creed as both *defining characteristics of and instrumental to the final value.* Thus values such as consent or representation, due process, freedom of speech and conscience, and equal protection under the law can be conceived as containing some essential facet of man's idea of human dignity. In the sense that each contains a defining characteristic of dignity, these values are not contradictory; they are all criteria of a single concept and collectively describe how men should behave toward one another in an ideal society. Because the person committed to the democratic ideology believes that all of these social values are elements of human dignity, he construes political controversy in terms of the values, often without reference to the former. Many of these values or rights are guaranteed under law, it being assumed that support of such concrete aspects of dignity will lead to the promotion of the less tangible and more general value. Constitutional restraint, for example, can be conceived as a defining attribute of human dignity — the coercive power of government should be delegated to it by the men who are governed. Constitutional restraint also has instrumental value — when built into the concrete legal institutions of the society, it helps to insure that government will not infringe unduly upon those aspects of existence judged necessary to their dignity by the members of the society.

The social and political values, then, can be thought of both as the general values which help define an ultimate ideal concerning how men should treat one another and as instrumental values supporting practical public institutions which may enhance or promote the ideal of human dignity. As operative political or legal values, however, they take on concrete meaning and as such are often inconsistent; e.g., personal freedom sometimes does conflict with the general welfare of the majority. Nevertheless, whatever shortcomings Myrdal's analysis may have, we are in agreement that these general American values provide the normative rhetoric by which analysis and judgment of controversial public policies can begin.

Two further points of clarification must be added before we proceed to a fuller description of the intellectual process of our proposed curriculum. First, although he is not explicit on the point, it is clear that Myrdal is dealing with values as psychological facts, as "valuations." Yet when he talks about society's moving in the direction of more general values, he apparently considers this a good thing, at least for the humanitarian. If values are no more than psychological facts, why are general values to be weighted more heavily than specific ones in making a practical judgment? No appeal is made to metaphysical notions, such as Kant's rational faculty which makes certain truths logically "self-evident." Instead Myrdal simply treats the higher status of general values as an interesting ethical phenomenon characteristic of the American (or Western) mind.

Unlike Myrdal, we choose, as noted in Chapter One, to make our commitment to certain general values an explicit assumption. For us the most basic values of the Creed, as they relate to the function of the school in the society, are to be treated as more than psychological facts. They describe certain potentially universal characteristics of man which, at least from our particular cultural frame of reference, make him "human" — such as a quest for self-respect, a sense of sympathy and love, a concern for fairness and justice in his dealings with others. It is characteristics like these, conceived as generalized goods, that we are calling general "values."

Obviously some societies do not share our conception of what are the essential qualities of the "good" man. From our point of view, one must deal with the fact of cultural diversity by first recognizing that value commitments are necessary to normal human behavior and then searching deeply into one's own moral consciousness, re-examining one's own values, and finally moving toward a broader conception of the universal nature of man and/or rejecting those values of "alien" groups that seem the result of living under "abnormal" conditions. "Abnormal" conditions are evident, for example, when groups of men are forced to live under severe stress, as when living under constant threat of extermination in Nazi concentration camps. In these circumstances, men may very well develop standards of conduct which would be considered "wrong" within the Western tradition. From our point of view such standards may be necessary for animal survival, which may be the only kind of survival possible. Assuming that survival itself is good, one is likely to conclude that different standards may be appropriate to meet the exigencies of various kinds of stress situations. We would still maintain, however, that, within the limits of a politically stable and intellectually enlightened community of reasonable economic means, certain values in line with the Western concept of "humanity" should hold. Certainly, as emphasized in the first chapter, the teacher in this society has an obligation to use its culture as an operative basis for curricular decisions. We must, however, always be careful lest, through lack of introspection and cultural perspective, our commitment to the Creed become a rationalization for simple bigotry.

It is crucial to emphasize that the inability to provide a final proof for values should not lead one to consider the search for values a casual or trivial concern. Ultimate scientific truth is not available either, but we do not discontinue the search for a deeper and more penetrating interpretation of the natural world. We also test our beliefs against our perceptions of reality and base our actions on them, even though at best they have a high level of probability, not certainty. An ultimate definition of "man" and the range of social conditions necessary to man's fulfillment may be more difficult to approach than scientific truth. As Myrdal points out, valuations "cannot be judged by such objective standards as science provides." But this should not prevent us from making judgments about priorities of values, and from living by tentative conclusions about ultimate moral meaning. Nor could we refrain from doing so; behavior itself presumes norms upon which specific actions are predicated.

Our second point of clarification concerns two ways of using or thinking about social values. One may think of them either as "ethical ideals" (equality, freedom) or as dimensional constructs (equal — unequal, free — coercive). If we regard social values as ethical ideals, we judge behavior on an all-or-nothing basis: this behavior is either fair or unfair, lawful or unlawful. When we consider social values on a dimensional basis, our ethical problem is to determine at what point on a value dimension an action should be categorized as intolerable or bad or at what point it should be given priority over another competing value.

Both conceptions of value have particular strengths. Thinking of a value as an ethical ideal or ethical absolute tends to focus our attention on the essential defining characteristics of the value and prevents us from pretending that compromises with the value really don't matter. Thinking of the value as a dimensional construct, on the other hand, allows us to apply the value more flexibly in a broad range of situations and to deal more realistically with problems of value conflict.[2] Rather than simply saying that a value is or is not violated in a particular situation, we can describe degrees of violation and weigh the violations against other "goods" protected in the same situation. For example, separate-but-equal schools for Negroes are clearly not as extreme a violation of the equality concept as are separate-and-inferior schools. To treat both situations simply as examples of inequality tends to force us into a rigid moral posture which cripples our ability to compromise one value to protect or preserve another.

Freedom of speech can be used to illustrate the same principle. As an absolute value, freedom of speech is violated both by law and by custom in this country. We cannot libel or slander and plead free speech for a defense (although Justice Black has suggested that this rule be changed). In times of national emergency, many of us are restricted by legal censorship. One cannot speak so as knowingly to violate the peace and safety of large numbers of people in the community, e.g., incite to riot. These restrictions violate the unqualified concept of "free speech." If we think of free speech as an ethical absolute, we can rationalize these restrictions only by saying that what is restricted is really not an expression of free speech but an "excess," which is not, in fact, "free speech" at all. From our point of view this is a semantic dodge. Considered as a dimensional construct, the absolute value of free speech must be compromised to some extent to protect other values.

Ethical conduct in a particular conflict situation consists of the "right" compromise among the values by which the situation is conceptualized or construed. Extreme violations of the values can be considered ethically justifiable only under extreme conditions, e.g., restrictions on civil rights during wartime. Otherwise we attempt to protect each value from all but minimal violation. "Minimal violation," however, has meaning only if we maintain a clear image of and commitment to the ethical ideal as an ethical absolute. Otherwise time and conditions may obscure this standard until finally an extreme violation is condoned, not because the value is no longer held essential to human dignity, but because our basic conception of the value has become altered. Freedom of speech, for example, may gradually give way to censorship because each new generation allows a little erosion to take place. Perhaps the only antidote to such erosion is to maintain a powerful image of the positive end of the value continuum as an ideal value, recognizing that the ideal must not be compromised except in the interest of other competing values which also make demands upon the conscience of the individual and the society. Utopia, then, is not a community in which each value finds maximum expression. It is a society in which each value makes the proper claim upon the actions of the individual so that human dignity finds maximum expression.

The problem of maintaining a clear conception of social values is further complicated when we recognize the implications of regarding our final value, human dignity, as a composite of the values in the Creed. In a single situation, we may condone an action which can be justified as supporting one aspect of human dignity but condemn the same action because it violates another dimension of dignity. For example, suppose a speechmaker on a street corner incites a noisy crowd, which then threatens the safety of the speaker, innocent bystanders, and the crowd itself. At this point should a policeman who happens on the scene forcibly stop the speaker because the crowd is too large to be dispersed, or call for reinforcements, who may arrive too late to prevent injury and violence?

Let us suppose the policeman forces the speaker to stop. In the same act he is abridging free speech and protecting the safety of both the speaker and the people on the sidewalk. For purposes of clarification, we might imagine that such a value dilemma can be described as two value constructs or dimensions abstracted from a single situation. These constructs can be considered diagrammatically as a coordinate system,[3] lacking, of course, the preciseness of unitization implied by the mathematical terminology:

```
              Security of the
            speaker and crowd
                     +
                     |
Area of disagreement |     Area of agreement
                     |
                     |
Censorship  —_____|_____+  Free speech
                     |
                     |
Area of agreement    |     Area of disagreement
                     |
                     —
              Violence to the
            speaker and crowd
```

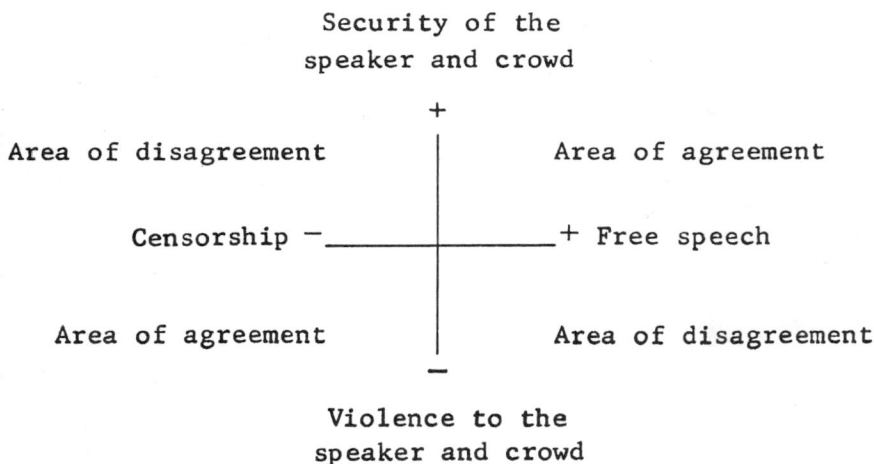

The "perfect" society is one in which rejecting actions which fall in the lower left-hand quadrant, where an action is bad on either dimension, or accepting actions which would obviously fall in the upper right quadrant are the only choices. The most difficult decisions are usually posed when men are forced to choose between courses of action which fall in either the lower right-hand or the upper left-hand quadrant. Of necessity, the support of one value is to the detriment of another. In real life these are the situations which are likely to cause ethical confusion and inner conflict because, as Myrdal points out, we have internalized the whole Creed, not simply the parts with positive connotations in each particular situation.

Our ethical position, which is the basis of our framework for the analysis of public controversy, is now in the open. But why so much concern over ethical clarity? Beard answered this question with great force some thirty years ago:

> Every human being brought up in society inevitably has in mind a frame of social knowledge, ideas, and ideals — a more or less definite pattern of things deemed *necessary,* things deemed *possible,* and things deemed *desirable;* and to this frame or pattern, his thought and action will be more or less consciously referred. This frame may be large or small; it may embrace an immense store of knowledge or little knowledge; it may be well organized with respect to categories of social thought or confused and blurred in organization; and the ideal element in it may represent the highest or lowest aspirations of mankind. But frame there is in every human mind. This is known, if anything is known. If the fact be denied, if a large, clarified, and informed frame of purpose is rejected, is deliberately and ostentatiously put out at the front door of the mind,

then small, provincial, local, class, group, or personal prejudices will come in at the rear door, occupy the background of the mind, and constitute the frame.[4]

Every teacher or other builder of social studies curricula has a frame of reference that, consciously or unconsciously, shapes the way he deals with ethical and political conflict — even if it is to ignore such controversy as too upsetting or as irrelevant to the more "pressing tasks" of the social studies classroom. It is crucial that each frame of reference be made explicit and critically examined if it is to serve adequately as a basis for curricular decisions in the social studies.

References

1. Gunnar Myrdal, *An American Dilemma* (New York: Harper & Row, Publishers, 1944), pp. 1027-31. Copyright © 1944, 1962 by Harper & Row, Publishers, Incorporated.

2. The question of whether to consider values as ideals or absolutes or whether to consider them as dimensional constructs — matters of degree — has been the focus of much debate in the Supreme Court, especially between Justices Frankfurther and Black. A book and two articles are most informative on this issue: Wallace Mendelson, *Justices Black and Frankfurter: Conflict in the Court* (Chicago: University of Chicago Press, 1961); Charles I. Black, "Mr. Justice Black, The Supreme Court, and the Bill of Rights," *Harper's* (1961), 222:63-68; C. Peter Magrath, "Nine Deliberative Bodies," *Commentary* (1961), 32:399-407.

    In the Charles Black article, Justice Black is quoted as follows: "It is my belief that there *are* 'absolutes' in our Bill of Rights, and that they were put there on purpose by men who knew what the words meant, and meant their prohibitions to be 'absolute.'" The alternative position, supported by Justice Frankfurter, is termed the "balancing" point of view. The rights of some are balanced against the rights of others or the interests of the community. The author argues that although there are no absolutes in any real sense, considering basic rights as absolutes (even though they must be weighed against other considerations) does make a difference in how one acts ethically. Our own distinction between ideals and dimensional values, we feel, to some extent clarifies this issue.

3. For simplicity of illustration, our example is presented on two dimensions. A particular decision may necessitate a multidimensional analysis. For example, equality of treatment may also be relevant.

4. Charles A. Beard, *The Nature of the Social Sciences* (New York: Charles Scribner's Sons, 1934), p. 181.

| CHAPTER THREE

Alternative Approaches to Value Conflict

Because of the number and variety of ethical positions that are either the implicit operative base of social studies teachers or the explicit dogma of curriculum planners, we will deal with some of them briefly in this chapter. It should be clear that no pretense is made of presenting here a comprehensive or systematic survey of various schools of ethical thought. We are more concerned with touching upon those specific points of view which might either challenge or clarify our own.

THE SUBJECTIVE-RELATIVIST POSITION

The subjective-relativist position has probably gained its greatest impetus from the studies of the social sciences, in particular psychology and anthropology. These disciplines suggest that one's values are contingent upon his cultural environment. The obvious fact that different sets of values arise in different environments leads the relativist to maintain that there are no ultimate standards of right or wrong by which to judge behavior. Each person's values are the product of his cultural conditioning, and one culture, one set of personal values, is as valid as another. The position is subjective because the final criterion for judging conduct is the individual's own personal preferences, which may or may not include regard for whether or not these preferences are good or bad for others. The position is relativistic because the goodness or badness of an act is always relative to one's purposes, and these, as noted above, are culturally determined subjective judgments. The ends of the community are simply the collective purposes of individuals within the community. The ethical worth of the means for achieving the ends is judged subjectively by each member of the community.

A major difficulty with this position is that it does not deal with the very real fact that there are operative *social* values within the society. As a society, we are committed to certain ethical principles. We have not always lived up to them, but, as Myrdal points out, most of us believe in them. More important, however, is the relativist's inability to debate issues of political controversy when they rest on social value premises. There is no debate because there are no "oughts" for the whole community.

Few serious advocates of any rational approach to political controversy have ever taken this position. It is, however, a trap into which iconoclastic teachers commonly fall. The teacher is sometimes encouraged to use a relativistic type of approach by educational committees and commissions that say we should not *teach* controversial issues, we should only teach *about* controversial issues. Opposing positions are to be described in some abstract manner without any implication that one or another is right. But how can the teacher do even this effectively if he is not willing to use the operative ideals and moral commitments of the society in his instructional framework? On this specific question the subjective-relativist position offers little guidance. The teacher, left without any viable context for dealing with debates over values, is torn between mouthing empty moralisms (how shameful it is to treat the Negro this way) and fear of being so dynamic that he may involve his students and the community in real controversy.

Whatever framework is applied to the analysis of controversy, it must deal with the fact of conflict of values within each citizen and among citizens and the necessity of making choices. Relativism is inadequate as a basis for the social studies curriculum because it fails to do this. It ignores the fundamental ethical basis of societal controversy: the desire of one individual or group to persuade the community that one decision is more consistent with the general values of the group than another. To ignore or refuse to deal with the problem of justifying decisions *vis-à-vis* the general values simply avoids the issue; it does not resolve it.

THE PRAGMATIC POSITION

A second position, commonly attributed to Dewey, states that social conflicts can be settled by evaluating the consequences of suggested policies scientifically. Ethical problems can be reduced to empirical problems. Some variations of this position even assume that disagreements over values are fundamentally not different from disagreements over factual claims. Hullfish and Smith stated this position as follows:

> It turns out, then, that believing, judging, and knowing with respect to value involve no elements which are basically different from those involved in situations in which values are not at issue. Statements concerning the extrinsic value of objects or events are grounded in the same way other synthetic statements are grounded. Knowledge of extrinsic value, being concerned with space time, factual affairs, is never absolute or final. Knowledge of intrinsic value, being concerned with the mediating structures in experience, could enjoy the formal certainty found within other conceptual systems. The "value" of such a system, however, like the "truth" of any system for structuring experience, is a matter of the long-range, objective (impersonal) usefulness in the conduct of human affairs.
>
> Competing political-social systems may be thought of, for example, as alternate formal conceptual schemes for structuring experience. There is a sense in which the American Revolution and the Copernican Revolution may be compared. How shall the solar system be conceived? How shall a political-social system be conceived? In either case it is a question of the long-range usefulness of the competing conceptions.[1]

Hullfish and Smith suggest that we test the validity of a framework of values by looking at their long-range "usefulness." This conception of the problem assumes that one can observe "social usefulness" in the same sense that one observes "trouble-free automobiles." Such is the case, however, only when men can agree on the definition of a trouble-free automobile.

A more fundamental difficulty is the pragmatist's inability to deal with extreme violations of important social values, which may be justified "rationally." Suppose, for example, that after due deliberation we find it socially useful to sterilize or deport all citizens of subnormal intelligence. The long-range social consequences, it is argued, will be to strengthen the intellectual quality of the community and lead to more responsible social living. All our evidence indicates that crime, delinquency, illegitimacy, unexcused absenteeism from work, and other kinds of irresponsibility will be markedly decreased. Would we then proceed with the action? One might very well argue that Soviet treatment of the kulaks was "rationally" conceived and led to many "beneficial" results. Is it appropriate, for example, to debate the reasons for and against Hitler's extermination of the Jews in central Europe in terms of possible consequences? While there may be justifiable homicide, is there ever justifiable genocide?

Pragmatism, we feel, is only a fragment of an ethical theory. It attempts to clarify the use of values as instrumental concepts and the experimental process by which these concepts can then be tested empirically. Its naturalistic metaphysical basis, implied by such words as *growth* and *development,* is obvious but usually not made explicit.

A more adequate pragmatic approach than simply "testing consequences" is presented by Raup, Axtelle, Benne, and Smith[2] and by Hunt and Metcalf.[3] These authors suggest that conflict between two values may be resolved by referring to a more basic third value upon which there is agreement. Suppose one man suggests that railroads should be taken over by the government because the people might then have some effective control over a basic utility. A second man suggests that this would be an invasion of the free enterprise system. Here is a value conflict of democratic control versus private property rights. Both positions might then be evaluated in terms of a third value — economic efficiency. Economic efficiency can be translated into agreed-upon "good" and "bad" consequences and the issue can be settled by transforming the third value into an empirical issue: Under which system are we likely to get the most frequent and the cheapest rail service?

This approach, while certainly more adequate than simply suggesting that political or ethical conflicts be resolved by testing consequences, also has difficulties. It deals with only one kind of political controversy, that in which a third value clearly takes precedence and has a testable referent. As Hunt and Metcalf point out, in most cases the only third value we can use as a criterion must be stated in the vague terms of the Creed, e.g., justice, freedom, equality. The situation is then thrust into the kind of definitional-value controversy already discussed. In the desegregation issue, for example, we might obtain agreement from both integrationists and segregationists that Negroes should get equal protection under the law. But the conflict persists because the segregationist defines equality in terms of "separate-but-equal" and the integrationist defines equality in terms of racially mixed schools. The question now arises: Is "separate-but-equal" equal enough to be considered equal protection? Or does race have to be eliminated altogether as a criterion of pupil assignment before we have equality?

To carry the example farther, let us assume that by all objective standards of educational quality, including the developing self-image of the student, segregated schools were demonstrably equal to integrated schools. Would all protests against racial segregation end? We suspect not. For at a certain point the literal meaning of equality in "separate-but-equal" loses its importance, and whether or not all children get equal *educational* opportunity is no longer the issue. Segregation becomes an essential defining characteristic in inequality, and the liberal would cling to his moral indignation in the face of substantial evidence of educational equality.

Resolving value conflicts by referring them to the more basic third value has the difficulty of requiring us to assume that the values involved can somehow be placed in a logical hierarchy. But the salience and importance of a value as a construct for dealing with a particular problem depend to a large degree on the specific situation to which it is applied. There is, therefore, apparently no permanent or fixed hierarchy of values in the Creed. While this leads to the uncomfortable conclusion that value conflicts can never really be resolved but are always suspended in a kind of permanent tension, it is probably useful to face up to this way of viewing the world as a fundamental condition of living within a pluralistic democratic society. In the following section we shall try to point out the difficulties in a number of theories which attempt to do precisely what we maintain cannot be done: set up a value hierarchy, or at least identify a root value, from which others can be derived.

THE RADICAL PRIORITY APPROACH

A third way of dealing with political controversy is to demonstrate or assume that one of the values in the Creed is more basic or more radical than the others, and that the others are implied by or can be derived from the first. A situation is then evaluated by determining to what extent it violates or supports the more basic value. Although this position is in some ways similar to our own, we feel that the level of specificity of the root value which one places on the highest moral plane is critical. Human dignity was selected as our root value partly because of its vagueness and its rich connotative meaning, rather than because of its specific meaning. Our own position comes to rest on the assumption that within certain controversial limits there is a common sense of human dignity which most men share, and which is often best expressed by a balance of values rather than by asserting that one or more of these values is pre-eminent. When we remove ourselves from this general moral plane and deal specifically with the values of the Creed, placing one above the other, we run into difficulties. We shall now consider a number of theories which place one of the values of the Creed above the others and point out what in our opinion are some of their shortcomings.

Democratic Procedure as the Central Principle of Political Conduct

In much educational literature democratic process (more specifically, group process) has become the central ethical principle behind the resolution of conflict. This position treads the narrow line between the individual and society by talking about both the reconstruction of the society and the reconstruction of individuals through the use of intelligence in group discussion. Procedural values, i.e., consent procedures and due process, become final values.

The theory has the doubtful virtue of avoiding the problem of defining the ends of society, at least of the good society, except in procedural terms. It does, however, have something to say about the "democratic person." He is the person who rejects force as an instrument of politics and is willing to work toward consensus in a group situation through the use of intelligent persuasion. It is an ethic in which the means of decision become the social end. The process by which one arrives at decisions rather than the decision itself is what makes the decision "good" or "right." The position is rationalized on both humanistic and utilitarian grounds. It is assumed that dignified human beings should participate in decisions which affect them. It is also assumed that when all who are affected by a decision participate in it, either directly or indirectly, the decision tends to be better, fairer, or wiser, at least in the long run.

Because the theory does not define ends, it does not have the problem of distinguishing higher ends and lower ends. Because "rights" are defined concretely by democratic process, it has little trouble with the distinction between general moral goods and individual goods. Right emanates not from a higher rational faculty which can discern universal consequences, but from the concrete use of rationality in a group of people facing a common problem.

A modern vigorous defense of the position has been made by Thomas Thorson in *The Logic of Democracy*. Thorson concludes after a long and tortuous discussion of various alternative approaches to the justification of democracy with the following recommendation:

> Out of the context of man's inability to prove the ultimate validity of political proposals springs the general recommendation that serves as the foundation of political philosophy. Language creaks and strains at the prospect of formulating this recommendation. The problem is to translate the categorical "Be rational" into language appropriate to the context of making political decisions. One hesitates to suggest a phrase, for fear that the inadequacies of the power of expression will cause it to be misinterpreted. For want of better words, I propose these: "Do not block the possibility of change with respect to social goals."
>
> This, however inadequately expressed, is the ultimate "must" of politics. Like Pierce's "Do not block the road to inquiry" *it* cannot be *proved;* but it is absolutely justified unless someone can prove that a certain state of affairs is absolutely "right" and therefore that one is justified in blocking any change.[4]

Thorson claims that "the majority principle is the only decision-making procedure which comports with the previous dictates of our recommendation." Moreover, he maintains that the "majority principle" includes a cluster of democratic principles: popular sovereignty, political equality, individual political rights, and majority rule.

Although Thorson's arguments are persuasive, they do not tell us why one man should treat another man with some minimal degree of decency and respect, nor does the government apparently *have* to concern itself with this problem. Perhaps political democracy would, in fact, protect each man's claim to dignity and respect in a simple open community. But it is precisely the complexity brought about by modern technology that has so radically changed our conception of such rights as "free speech" and "free association." It is our contention that for a complex industrial society to operate within the framework of a pluralistic tradition each citizen must not only tolerate the political rights of his fellow citizens but respect others as human beings who have to some degree the same claim on the "pursuit of happiness" as does he. Lippmann eloquently discusses this position in an article entitled "Bryan and the Dogma of Majority Rule," which deals with Bryan's position in the Dayton Trial in Tennessee in 1925:

> In exploring this dogma it will be best to begin at the very beginning with the primitive intuition from which the whole democratic view of life is derived. It is a feeling of ultimate equality and fellowship with all other creatures.
>
> There is no worldly sense in this feeling, for it is reasoned from the heart: "there you are, sir, and there is your neighbor. You are better born than he, you are richer, you are stronger, you are handsomer, nay you are better, wiser, kinder, more likeable; you have given more to our fellow men and take less than he. By any and every test of intelligence, of virtue, of usefulness, you are demonstrably a better man than he, and yet — absurd as it sounds — these differences do not matter, for the last part of him is untouchable and incomparable and unique and universal." Either you feel this or you do not; when you do not feel it, the superiorities that the world acknowledges seem like mountainous waves at sea; when you do feel it they are slight and impermanent ripples upon a vast ocean. Men were possessed by this feeling long before they had imagined the possibility of democratic government. They spoke of it in many ways, but the essential quality of feeling is the same from Buddha to St. Francis to Whitman.
>
> There is no way of proving the doctrine that all souls are precious in the eyes of God, or, as Dean Inge recently put it, that "the personality of every man and woman is sacred and inviolable." The doctrine proceeds from a mystical intuition. There is felt to be a spiritual reality behind and independent of the visible character and behavior of a man. We have no scientific evidence that this reality exists, and in the nature of things we can have none. But we know, each of us, in a way too certain for doubting, that after all the weighing and comparing and judging of us is done, there is something left over which is the heart of the matter. Hence our conviction when we ourselves are judged that mercy is more just than justice. When we know the facts as we can know only the facts about ourselves, there is something too coarse in all the concepts of the intelli-

gence and something too rough in all the standards of morality. The judgments of men fall upon behavior. They may be necessary judgments, but we do not believe they are final. There is something else which is inadmissible, perhaps, as evidence in this world, which would weigh mightily before divine justice. . . .

It is not possible for most of us, however, to consider anything very clearly or steadily in the light of eternity. The doctrine of ultimate human equality cannot be tested in human experience; it rests on a faith which transcends experience. That is why those who understood the doctrine have always been ascetic; they ignored or renounced worldly goods and worldly standards. These things belonged to Caesar. The mystical democrat did not say that they should not belong to Caesar; he said they would be of no use to Caesar ultimately, and that, therefore, they were not to be taken seriously now.

But in the reception of this subtle argument the essential reservation was soon obscured. The mystics were preaching equality only to those men who had renounced their carnal appetites; they were welcomed as preachers of equality in this world. Thus the doctrine that I am as good as you in eternity, because all standards of goodness are finite and temporary, was converted into the doctrine that I am as good as you are in this world by this world's standards. The mystics had attained a sense of equality by transcending and renouncing all the standards with which we measure inequality. The populace retained its appetites and its standards and then sought to deny the inequalities which they produced and revealed.

The mystical democrat had said, "gold and precious stones are of no account"; the literal democrat understood him to say that everybody ought to have gold and precious stones. The mystical democrat had said, "beauty is only skin deep" and the literal democrat preened himself and said, "I always suspected I was as handsome as you." Reason, intelligence, learning, wisdom, dealt for the mystic only with passing events in a temporal world and could help men little to fathom the ultimate meaning of creation; to the literal democrat this incapacity of reason was evidence that one man's notion was intrinsically as good as another's.

Thus the primitive intuition of democracy became the animus of a philosophy which denied that there could be an order of values among men. Any opinion, any taste, any action was intrinsically as good as any other. Each stands on its own bottom and guarantees itself. If I feel strongly about it, it is right, there is no other test. It is right not only as against your opinion, but against my own opinions, about which I no longer feel so strongly. There is no arbitrament by which the relative value of opinions is determined. They are all free, they are all equal, all have the same right and powers.

Since no value can be placed on an opinion, there is no way in this philosophy of deciding between opinions except to count them. Thus the mystical sense of equality was translated to mean in practice that two minds are better than one mind and two souls are better than one soul.

Your true mystic would be horrified at the notion that you can add up souls and that the greater number is superior to the lesser. To him souls are imponderable and incommensurable; that is the only sense in which they are truly equal. And yet in the name of that sense of equality which he attains by denying that the worth of a soul can be measured, the worldly democrats have made the counting of souls the final arbiter of all worth. It is a curious misunderstanding; Mr. Bryan brought it into high relief during the Tennessee case. The spiritual doctrine that all men will stand at last equal before the throne of God meant to him that all men are equally good biologists before the ballot box of Tennessee. That kind of democracy is quite evidently a gross materialization of an idea that in essence cannot be materialized. It is a confusing interchange of two worlds that are not interchangeable.[5]

Lindsay, after quoting this passage, goes on to raise the obvious question, "If 'mystical democracy' is what really matters and if it is quite distinct from literal democracy, why should we concern ourselves about democratic machinery at all?"[6] He then replies to his own question:

If democracy is to survive, it will have to employ and use every bit of skill and knowledge and leadership it can get hold of. This complicated interdependent modern world in which we are living cannot be run without knowledge and skill, foresight and leadership. Any cult of incompetence can only lead to disaster. A modern democratic state is only possible if it can combine appreciation of skill, knowledge, and expertness with reverence for the common humanity of everyday people. It is that conception of equality which its institutions will have to express.[7]

From our point of view both the "reverence for the common humanity" and the respect for "expertness" are missing components in Thorson's analysis.

There are, moreover, other difficulties in the democratic process approach which are of more than theoretical importance. For example, what does one do with those who refuse to accept reasonable standards of reason and intelligence? What do we do with a McCarthy who plays upon the irrational fears and tensions of the uninformed but does not resort to open violence? What do we do with a Hitler who has the hypnotic power to anesthetize reason on a large scale? The democratic process doctrine assumes that the majority of people exercise reason at all critical choice points, for it takes but a short period of lethargic or irrational behavior on the part of the majority to cast away the whole system of democratic process.

Nor is the problem simply one of controlling the irrational impulses of those participating in the democratic process. There is the deeper problem of identifying *who* is irrational or "unreasonable" in a particular conflict.

Let us suppose that a strong pacifist movement gains momentum in the United States, and the government finally prosecutes the movement as an immediate threat to the "national security." The pacifists assert, however, that it is the government's foreign policy that threatens the national security, not the pacifists. Are not the standards of reason equivocal? Using the same data, we can come up with markedly different interpretations of "correct" government policy. And when the community is sharply split over such different interpretations of reasonability, what decision do we make? The question, simply put, is: what do we do with an obdurate minority which "threatens" the security of the community because it honestly differs with the government or the majority on how to improve, maintain, or preserve the community? How long do we cling to peaceful persuasion as the final instrument of social control? And if we reject peaceful persuasion in favor of force, how do we justify it?

A variation of the same problem concerns how to deal with a strong minority which overtly proclaims that the democratic process is *not* the best way to handle political controversy. Nor is this an abstract problem. In 1933 the German government requested Hitler to assume control of the state while his party openly advocated the overthrow of democratic institutions. Is it legitimate to defend democratic processes by force and repression in the face of organized threats to the institutions which protect these very processes? At some point should individuals or groups be branded as "undemocratic" and locked up? This is precisely what Adenauer did to a popular Facist leader in 1953. Was he not justified in doing it? A similar crisis occurred in Czechoslovakia in 1948. The Czechs, however, did not restrict the Communist party. It was allowed political freedom; finally, through intrigue and force, the party overthrew the government and with it, democratic institutions.

The problem is basic to any democratic theory: How can a community handle a deviant minority which threatens either the safety of the community or the safety of the democratic institutions within the community? At what point do we reject the right of this kind of minority to use persuasion, and demand that it be silent, change its views, or go to jail? The "clear and present danger" doctrine, rather than providing an answer, is simply another way of stating the problem. For some the danger will never be clear enough or present enough to reject democratic process; for others the dangers are so clear and present that the community is never secure enough to entertain the use of democratic principles. The views of most of us fall somewhere in between.

Another problem of the democratic process approach is what has commonly been called the tyranny of the majority. It is the converse of the problem discussed above. In one case we ask, How can the majority be protected from an "irrational" minority which threatens the community?

Now we ask: How can an innocuous minority be protected from an irrational majority? The extreme case, of course, is the will of the majority to commit genocide in the name of progress or general welfare. Again the question is not academic. One might fairly state that essentially this was done to groups of American Indians in the United States. The advocate of democratic process commonly offers two arguments in rebuttal: First, it would be "unreasonable" and "senseless" to persecute a minority; second, the minority can be protected by requiring a high degree of consensus for critical political decisions. To the first rebuttal one may only say that for the long-range progress and welfare of the United States it was very "reasonable" to wipe out large segments of the Indian population. It was probably very "reasonable" for Stalin to wipe out the kulaks, a major source of resistance to the government's programs in Russia. One must call on values other than "reason" to justify the humane treatment of minorities. To the argument that minorities can be protected by demanding higher degrees of agreement for important political decisions one need only observe the United Nations Security Council or the rules of the United States Senate to see the problem this presents. Giving veto power to a minority is a double-edged weapon: It can prevent unreasonable and inhumane treatment of a minority group; it can also allow a greedy and shortsighted minority to continue acting in the worst interests of the community.

Individualism as an Ethical Approach to Political Controversy

The extreme individualist position is essentially subjective-relativism. It makes two important assumptions: (1) that it is possible to maintain a society of convenience in the Hobbesian sense, when the main motive is self-interest, and (2) that it is, in fact, in the best interests of the community to allow a maximum degree of individual freedom even at the cost of considerable anarchy and wide margins of human inequality. Thus government sanctions are to be used only to restrict the use of physical violence and to protect contract and property rights.[8]

While this position seems quite reasonable when stated in general terms, it tends to break down under the weight of practical consequences. Our experience indicates that when the government acts only to restrict and control overt violence and to protect propery rights, extreme inequalities occur among men; they are inherited, become rigidified, and hence persist. Thus the argument of the Social Darwinist that such a system ultimately will produce the most noble individuals and the most efficient society may be countered by the observation that weak children are kept in power by the wealth and estate of the parents, and strong children are crushed by the misfortunes of their parents before they have the opportunity to develop. When personal liberty and the power of the government to protect this liberty are extolled over all considerations of equality, freedom turns out to mean liberty only for the favored classes.

The individualist position might be defended if one could demonstrate that the people in each generation have a reasonably equal opportunity to fulfill their ambitions in the race for power and progress. But it is precisely such things as income taxes, public education, public health, inheritance taxes, and public housing measures, which help bring about the conditions of a fair race for each new generation, that are most often feared and abhorred by the rugged individualist. The problem is further compounded by the tremendous growth of capital wealth since the industrial revolution, which tends to aggrevate inequalities from one generation to another.

There are at least two major difficulties with this position, then. First, how is the innocent child to be prevented from suffering for his father's inadequacies, and, conversely, how is the privileged child to be prevented from gaining power and control when he may be incompetent? Individualism stresses the doctrine that freedom, especially economic freedom, should be the reward for competence — the competence of each individual, not the collective competence of one's relatives. The second weakness rests upon the question: What if the plight of the "weak" becomes no better than that of slaves or animals? Don't the obvious common qualities of humanity, such as sympathy and love, become perverted in the competent individualist when he can live in the midst of and tolerate extreme poverty? Do the strong not then lose some of their humanity also? (This is certainly the message in much of Dickens' work.)

The individualist position *can be* a clear and consistent guide to political action. It breaks down only if the individual defending it also values equal opportunity and universal fellowship as complementary values. And in the American society it is difficult to avoid some concern for these other values.

Enlightened Self-Interest as a Variation of Radical Self-Interest

Enlightened self-interest, as we use the term, refers to a policy whereby one acts for the highest good of the self, after reflection about the long-range consequences of one's conduct for the whole community. It is this long-range reflective component that distinguishes it from simple individualism. The position argues that each man, if taught to reflect upon the total implications of his own acts for the self, including his reciprocal relationships with his fellowmen, will quite naturally conduct himself in the interests not only of the self but also of the community. It assumes that what is good for the individual is good in most cases for the community, and vice versa.

The common strategy for attacking this position is to point to a case of heroic self-sacrifice (e.g., the soldier who sacrifices his own life to save the lives of his comrades) and ask, Was this in the individual's own self-interest? The rebuttal gives an affirmative answer. We then see that all conduct, no matter how altruistic, is based on self-interest because the individual has so internalized his duty to others that he could not live with himself if he did not act thus. The question we then must ask is: If all actions are out of self-interest, and self-interest is the standard of good, then is not all behavior good?

The distinction between the enlightened individual and the amoral psychopath or the simple hedonist becomes central. Here the argument for enlightened self-interest generally shifts from "self-interest" to "enlightened." Political action should be designed by and for those who are intelligent and reflective enough to distinguish shortsighted greed from the long-term good. While this shift gets away from the circularity pointed out above, it offers no basis for evaluating who is right when two "enlightened" minds come up with different public policies.

Suppose, for example, one person sees his enlightened self-interest in terms of immediate unilateral disarmament. Reflecting carefully over what is best for him and what is best for his community, he decides that it may be preferable — assuming atomic war is imminent — for the nation to be occupied by the Soviet Union in the hope of developing that society into a liberal democracy than to risk further suffering to and possible destruction of all humanity. His opponent sees his enlightened self-interest differently. It would be intolerable for him or for any free man to live under the restrictions imposed by a totalitarian government. He believes we are better off to risk our own destruction than to capitulate, since life would have little meaning without the freedom guaranteed each of us in a constitutional democracy. Each sees his own long-range self-interest differently; each sees the limits of a tolerable society differently. Obviously the principle of enlightened self-interest will not resolve this dispute. It simply clarifies the varying weight each person places on the values of personal freedom, avoidance of physical suffering, and the relationships between the two values. It does not indicate which value is more important. If our main concern centers on the question of which conception of self-interest will contribute more to the interests of the community as a whole, the concept of self-interest has lost its importance as an ethical principle and utilitarianism has taken over.

Although the enlightened self-interested position has difficulties, it is a useful part of the analysis of many types of problems. When there is conflict over short-run as against long-run public policies, and it can be demonstrated with some certainty that the advantages of a short-run policy tend to be more than negated by long-range consequences, this does provide a guide for practical judgment. In arguments over the conservation of timber resources, for example, if one can demonstrate that the long-range consequence of overcutting is massive soil erosion, the policy may be seen to be destructive to the long-range interests of the person doing the cutting as well as to the interests of the community. The emphasis which the proponent of enlightened self-interest places on reflection about long-range consequences is worthy of note and is an important step in the clarification of almost any political controversy.

General Welfare, or Utilitarianism, as a Central Standard from Which to Judge Polical Controversy

The extreme individualist position breaks down or becomes less meaningful if it can be shown that a healthy community is necessary for the fulfillment of personal self-interest. Once this is demonstrated, there is a shift to enlightened self-interest, where one feels a responsibility for the community because the interests of the community are tied in with one's own interests. This position has the strength of admitting that community interest and self-interest are closely related and not necessarily incompatible but offers no clear guide to political conduct when a conflict of value arises over what is, in fact, good for the community.

The principle of general welfare, or utilitarianism, does provide, at least on the surface, a standard by which to judge conflicting public policies. The standard is simple: the greatest good for the greatest number. The obvious difficulty of utilitarianism is defining and measuring the "greatest good." If the main concern is with elementary economic goods, such as food, clothing, medical care, and shelter, the problem is relatively easy. When we move from the fulfillment of the basic animal needs of man to intellectual and spiritual matters, however, we run into trouble. In modern societies, economic or aesthetic elites, generally more creative than the "common man," constantly develop new expressions of the good life, which the common man then chooses to imitate. If the common man comes to interpret the good life in the same terms as the elite, should the progress of the creative elite be halted to let the common man "catch up"? How large an economic gap should there be between the richer and the poorer groups in society?

The Communist answer to this question is a simple formula: From each according to his ability; to each according to his need. The Communist doctrine assumes further that man's motives in a true Communist society would not be economic but rather creative or aesthetic. Although this may sound good in theory, no modern society is without stratification, least of all the Soviet society, which embraces the Communist formula.

The utilitarian doctrine, rather than resolving basic ethical issues, simply poses more explicitly the question: What are the legitimate standards of good? Good must be construed in more sophisticated terms than either physical needs or hedonistic pleasure. Problems again. How does one measure the higher goods? Who in society answers this question: Experts? An elected elite? The majority? A group elected from a cross section of the community?

It is probably unfair to be overly critical of the utilitarian doctrine, for it developed and grew in a period when the economic deprivations of the vast majority of people were salient and obvious. Women and children were forced to work in factories and mines to survive, when survival meant living in the midst of poverty, malnutrition, and disease. The exploitation of the masses of poor people by a wealthy minority was not a myth. The relative affluence today of the common man in America, however, has changed the picture. Currently, for example, questions regarding the kind and quality of education children should receive get far more attention from most Americans than the question of how to meet minimum nutritional needs. And determining appropriate educational standards is inherently a far more subtle and controversial question than is determining appropriate nutritional standards. Utilitarianism in its broadest sense has the same basic objective as our own approach — the greatest dignity for all men within society. Its difficulty is that "the greatest good for the greatest number" is an historically conditioned concept the original meaning of which is less relevant to modern America than it was to eighteenth-century England. And if we leave this more specific meaning, the term leads straight to all the difficulties inherent in man's attempt to define a general good for man in all realms of experience.

A value concept similar to utilitarianism, general welfare, should be considered here. One distinction between the "greatest good" doctrine and general welfare is critical. It is a distinction between what is good for the *majority* and what is good for the *community.* One can construe the community as an organic whole and attempt to determine what a community needs to continue a healthy existence, or to be cured of a "perverse" existence. One can thus conceive of the community as governed by certain moral imperatives if it is to survive and develop. Buchanan has discussed this position within the framework of a Kantian view of natural law:

> Whatever there may be of theological overtones or presuppositions in the vision, the key phrase is "a kingdom of nature." The regulative consequence of the vision ought to appear from an examination of the constitution of the kingdom. Part of the kingdom consists of persons as rational beings whose dignity and freedom are exercised in giving to themselves universal laws in the acts of their wills. By virtue of this power of self-government they are ends-in-themselves. The constitution of nature is violated if any of the kingly persons are treated merely as means. The constitutional situation is rather that the persons act reciprocally as means and ends regarding one another, or as mutual means to their common

end, as the organs in an organism or as members of a free community. They may serve each other, but the royalty in each servant must also be respected.[9]

Buchanan then goes on to illustrate:

> . . . This and other similar lessons [of conservation] have now led to long-term planning for the allocation of resources in which the aim of the prudent saving of resources for future use is always combined with the increase and enhancement of nature. Such thinking is best epitomized in the original act that established the TVA. Its stated purpose was to serve the welfare of the valley, and the purpose was carried out by planning forests, fertilizer plants, soil analysis, and flood control as well as electric power. The welfare of the valley obviously and necessarily includes concern for natural ends, non-human as well as human.
>
> Out of this dialectical learning there has developed a new and somewhat mysterious science, ecology. As I understand it, ecology was originally an attempt to collate various lines of linear exploitative planning, such as an industrial firm might practice to make an integral pattern of the side-effects and unintended consequences of procurement, employment and production. Industrial production in a complex city would present the acute problem. The result of the attempt led to another definition and posing of the problem, namely to conceive the plant as an organism with the city as the environment. Soon it was necessary to conceive the city as an organism with its environment. And so one might go on to national economies and to the world community. This is surreptitious teleological thinking, which, made explicit, would mean that everything in the situation would be viewed reciprocally with the others as means and ends. Such a conception is the aim of Patrick Geddes and Lewis Mumford when they take the organic view of the neo-technic period in the enhancement of nature including human nature in the valley. Human beings would no longer be exploiting nature or themselves. They would be free citizens in a constitutional kingdom of nature.[10]

This conception of "general welfare" or "community welfare" as a supra-individual criterion for the determination of public policy is undoubtedly a fruitful and necessary extension of our own central value concept, human dignity. We see no contradiction or inconsistency here between the human dignity position and the "kingdom of nature." Ultimately, the definition of human dignity must take into account the natural and social context in which human dignity can best be expressed.

Equality as a Basic Standard from Which to Judge Political Controversy

There are three components in the concept of equality, and it is important to distinguish among them. The first is the idea of making rules which are then applied to everyone impartially — the idea of equal protection under the law. The second has to do with making rules to provide for equal advantage or injury. In games, for example, we make the rules which define the game. Applying the rules impartially is the first concept of equality. Seeing that opponents play only when they are evenly matched is the second concept of equality. The two are obviously related but they are to some extent independent. Rules can be made which favor one group over the other, even though they may be impartially applied — segregation laws, for instance. Both concepts merge into the idea of justice, which includes both a concern that laws be made which benefit the total community rather than a favored individual or group and a concern for equal and impartial application of the laws.

The third component of equality is the product of Hebraic-Christian thought — the idea of the universal brotherhood of man. Men are equal because they all possess an inner spiritual quality, expressed symbolically in the idea that all are children of God, more naturalistically in the idea that sympathy, charity, and selflessness are uniquely human qualities which represent the highest sense of man. Through the development of these qualities, all men can live a decent and good life. When men discover their brotherhood with other men and their common relationship to God, they will reject the use of power and coercion as a means of dealing with human conflict.

The same concept of equality is the moving force behind Marxism-Leninism. It shares the assumption with Christianity that there is no inherent conflict between the individual and society or between organized groups within society and the interests of the society as a whole. Communism, in contrast to Christianity, rejects the spiritual basis of this equality and condones the use of force and violence as means of achieving the perfect world in which all human relations are carried on in peace and harmony.

The problem of the Christian or the humanist who embraces the universal brotherhood of man as the highest value is obvious: How does one deal with those who have not yet accepted one's own point of view regarding universal brotherhood? How does one maintain a stable society in which peaceful persuasion is the instrument of conversion when some members of society reject the central concept? The essential question here is whether or not force can be considered a reasonable instrument for managing the affairs of men until the greedy and ignorant accept conversion — which may be never. Whatever the answer, it is clear that no stable complex democratic society has been produced without a political system which relied ultimately on the threat of force and violence to prevent violence and disorder.

Christian or universal love as a practical political ideology is thus burdened with the problem of demonstrating that men can be universally socialized to the point of rejecting self-interest as a criterion for judging political policies, and, more important, that men can be universally socialized to the point of rejecting force as an instrument for achieving personal goals. On the other hand, the Anglo-American system of law and parliamentary democracy demands only that most people accept the basic tenets of reason and due process as a means of resolving disputes. Force and coercion can still be used to restrict individuals and minorities who would resort to violence to gain their ends.

Equality as the unbiased application of law is usually not defended as a radical "first principle" of political theory; it is a corollary of individualism. Hyack, for example, shows the contradiction between the equal protection concept and the use of government action to effect greater social or economic equality.[11] In the latter situation the government makes laws which deliberately penalize the more affluent and benefit the poorer classes of society, e.g., the graduated income tax. Equality as social justice or equal opportunity is generally defended on utilitarian grounds: it benefits the whole community.

A major difficulty of making the concept of equality a primary principle for the solution of political controversy is the obvious fact that in terms of physical and mental capabilities men are not equal. This leads to the controversy over whether equality should be conceived in literal terms or should simply mean equal treatment under the law. To build a society in which men are given equal benefits in terms of the tangible goods of the society is anathema to most Americans, since different men work and sacrifice for the community in different degrees. But even if we accept the principle of rewarding men for their contribution to the community, the community must find some way to determine each person's relative contribution. Here again, we are forced back to a quest for standards: Should the criterion be beauty, intelligence, practical cleverness, effort, amount of wealth produced, or what? Like utilitarianism, equalitarianism is not a final standard of good; it is a standard which describes reasonable conduct once a standard of good has been decided upon. Also like utilitarianism, it is most powerful when large groups of men are denied those necessities of civilized existence about whose worth there is a high degree of consensus. To defend equalitarianism as in the statement "We hold these truths to be self-evident, that all men are created equal" is no less than a defense of our basic value, human dignity. In this sense, equality is the basis of liberty; the values of personal freedom and personal choice are guaranteed to all men because all share a common quality: humanity.

THE SOURCE OF VALUES

Before leaving a discussion of the ethical bases of political analysis and controversy we should raise at least one more question: What is the ultimate source of values? There are, of course, many answers: God, natural law, prophets and saints, man himself. Our own position, presented earlier, refused to take a stand and identify the source of our ultimate value, human dignity. It seems to us that various aspects of the Creed have developed somewhat fortuitously through historical invention (e.g., the jury trial) and are sustained partly because of their instrumental efficacy and partly through myths which give them a degree of sanctity independent of the underlying values they support. We repeat here that it seems beyond man's intellectual capacity to use reason to arrive at an ultimate commitment upon which all intelligent and educated men can agree.

The major controversy over the source of values tends to polarize into whether the source is man himself or some force beyond man. The position one takes on this question has implications for one's view of values as permanent and unchanging or as relative and flexible. For the sake of discussion, let us call the position which conceptualizes values as permanent and unchanging — because their source is beyond man himself — the natural rights position. The alternative position — values are transient and changing because they are created by man — may be called the relativistic position.

The natural law, or natural rights, position states that man is endowed with certain inalienable rights which he intuitively perceives and which are self-evident to all right-thinking men. The difficulty of the position is most succinctly and clearly presented by White:

> Finally we must ask ourselves about the man who *does* believe that there are certain self-evident principles of morality. Can he be persuaded that there are essences which, when unpacked, yield moral principles? Unfortunately he is often persuaded too easily and our success with him should not give us too much confidence. The point is, then, that all of the philosophical machinery is not so much an effective instrument of rational persuasion as a kind of self-encouragement, useful for philosophical whistling in the dark. Having persuaded himself of the truth of certain moral principles and having discovered that some people in other places and at other times have doubted it, the weak man needs support. He needs to be able to say that, even though it is not obvious to everyone, things in the realm of essence are so related as to substantiate or corroborate these principles of morality. The impulse is, of course, quite like that which leads men to say that "the facts" of the physical universe are such as to corroborate or verify their statements about *it*. But we see the otiose character of the latter view when we ask whether it has any use for a scientist in doubt or controversy. To say over and over again that the facts are such as to make your theory true is perfectly useless. It may buck *you* up, but it cannot persuade anyone who seriously doubts what you say.

· · · · · · ·

Moral, mathematical, metaphysical, chemical, biological, economic — all sorts of beliefs make up this stock . . . [of] terminal beliefs. We want them to be consistent with each other and to fit in harmoniously and simply with other less confidently held beliefs; we want this structure to mesh with experience and feeling. We also, other things being equal, prefer to have other people adopt a similar system of belief. Both individuals and societies have in fact surrendered many beliefs which they once accepted as terminal, and some of these beliefs are moral beliefs. We do this for all sorts of good reasons. What, then, is the purpose of inventing a mysterious realm of essence *of which* our terminal beliefs are supposed to be true? Having gotten to the end of the line, why do we need to inch a bit further in the direction of darkness? Wouldn't it be saner to recognize that we all have our ultimate convictions at any moment, that they are not absolutely immune to change (although we can resolve, at our own peril, to make them permanently immune), that some people adopt the same beliefs as terminal and others don't? Who are the people we get along with? Very often the people with whom we have a great deal of agreement on these fundamental beliefs. Who are the people we quarrel with? Very often those with whom we don't share these beliefs. The point is that we and those whose lines, as it were, end up at the same terminal as ours shouldn't need the kind of mutual encouragement that comes from inventing a realm of essences beneath (or above) the terminal, and those who go in different directions are the last people in the world who are likely to use essences in the same way even if they agreed that there were such things.[12]

If the natural rights position has problems, the relativistic position mires down even more quickly. For the relativist, who states that we create or develop values which are simply historically conditioned within a particular cultural context, must explain widely shared values across cultures, and the unusual appeal of particular value syndromes, e.g., those in the Western tradition. From our point of view, it seems reasonable to assume that there are certain stable elements in the nature of man which limit what man wants and what is good for man. To this extent there is something called "natural law." How far this assumption alone will lead in the direction of an explicit moral code is, however, very much of an open question.

The distinction between the relativistic and the natural rights position, we think, is more one of the explicitness with which final values are stated and the extent to which one distinguishes between instrumental and final values. There is substantial agreement upon what range of human behavior constitutes an expression of human dignity, what range is debatable, and what behavior is clearly brutal or uncivilized. But there is often sharp disagreement over the extent to which man should experiment with instrumental values implied by existing institutions in an effort to attain greater dignity.

Our own position regarding the source of values has an intuitive basis, and thus problems.[13] That is, we assume that most men will intuitively agree upon what behavior is brutish and uncivilized, what behavior is essentially human, and what behavior is within the realm of legitimate controversy. Beyond this point we can only assert that decisions must be made by rational debate. We thus have particular difficulty with means-ends arguments: To what extent should certain agreed-upon civilized values (e.g., the consent process) be sacrificed to attain other important values (e.g., economic development or domestic tranquillity)? On such questions we can give only relativistic answers: The answer depends upon what persuasion finally triumphs within the group which asks the questions. But we would add that if the members of the group who make the decision disclaim universal human dignity as the final criterion for judging their actions, the decision-making situation has become immoral. Sacrificing freedom for bread or survival, from our point of view, is moral if it is sincerely rationalized in terms of the ultimate of universal dignity; it is immoral if it is a cynical decision made in the interests of personal power, the promotion of a superrace of men, or the like. Ends do justify means. It is the only way means can be justified. And we can only say that the extent to which each of us should allow certain of our rights to be violated in an effort to promote greater long-range dignity for all men is a matter for each person to decide for himself. We believe there is a point beyond which means destroy ends, i.e., man's ability to be essentially human; and it is beyond this point that withdrawal from the community, or, more realistically, revolution, is justified.

References

1. H. Gordon Hullfish and Philip G. Smith, *Reflective Thinking: The Method of Education* (New York: Dodd, Mead & Co., 1961), pp. 98-99.

2. R. Bruce Raup *et al., The Improvement of Practical Intelligence* (New York: Harper & Row, Publishers, 1943).

3. M. P. Hunt and L. E. Metcalf, *Teaching High School Social Studies* (New York: Harper & Row, Publishers, 1955).

4. Thomas Thorson, *The Logic of Democracy* (New York: Holt, Rinehart & Winston, Inc., 1962), p. 139.

5. Quoted in A. D. Lindsay, *The Modern Democratic State* (London: Oxford University Press, 1943), pp. 253-255.

6. *Ibid.,* p. 255.

7. *Ibid.,* p. 261.

8. For a rationalized defense of this position see F. A. Hyack, *The Constitution of Liberty* (Chicago: University of Chicago Press, 1960).

9. Scott Buchanan, *Rediscovering Natural Law,* A Report of the Center for the Study of Democratic Institutions (New York: Fund for the Republic, 1962), pp. 48-49.

10. *Ibid.,* p. 57.

11. Hyack, *op. cit.*

12. Morton White, *Social Thought in America: The Revolt Against Formalism* (Boston: Beacon Press, 1957), pp. 275-277.

13. A comment by Buchanan (*op. cit.,* p. 48) is relevant: "I have always been puzzled by the tortuous reasoning by which Kant ostensibly arrives at the insight that the categorical imperative expresses; the reasoning is much less revealing and convincing than the bare insight." From our point of view, the same could be said about a number of the basic ethical and political principles which constitute our moral heritage.

PART TWO

A Conceptual Framework for

Teaching the Analysis

of Public Issues

in American Society

CHAPTER FOUR

The Ethical Commitment
of a Democratic Society

In Part One we outlined a general approach to the selection of content in the social studies. We suggested that the selection of content involves two major decisions: What topics will one choose as the basis for selecting specific materials of instruction? What intellectual framework will be used to guide the teacher and, in turn, the student in handling these materials? We presented contemporary political controversy as the major criterion for guiding the selection of topics and suggested a particular view of the pluralistic society as providing an intellectual framework within which these topics might be analyzed. Neither of these decisions is bold, unique, or startling. Such general descriptions of approaches to the social studies and outlines of content to be "covered" are common in educational literature. Guides which simply list topics and describe desirable intellectual processes in terms of "critical thinking," "appreciation of the American heritage," or "understanding of world interdependence" are, from our point of view, all but useless. Such vague terms place the burden of translation on the individual teacher, who very often must then rely upon his own implicit and unreflected frame of reference for the intellectual approach which the student is to adopt.

Part One was intended not only to describe our own position with respect to content selection but also to set the stage for a more detailed statement of the specific content which might be included in a curriculum directed toward the intelligent analysis of public controversy. Part Two is, therefore, a more specific statement of selected concepts one might employ to frame and analyze political controversy in a democratic society. This statement is in "working" form. It is not in its present condition suitable as a text for teaching these concepts, although parts of it have been used as such. It is best looked at, we feel, as a guide to the development or selection of specific materials of instruction for students of varying ages and abilities. In general, this is the way it has been used in our own experimental work.

The present chapter and Chapter Five have been written in relatively simple and direct language, for two reasons. First, we want to demonstrate that teaching such a framework to adolescents is plausible. Second, we suspect that there is a strong relationship between the degree of complexity of such a framework and the extent to which it will express much that is idiosyncratic to the authors. We assume that the teacher begins with a frame of reference similar to our own, but in some ways different. We assume also that the student begins with his own implicit but inadequate frame of reference with respect to the analysis of political issues. As teacher and student deal with complex political issues, areas of disagreement will most certainly develop between the way the teacher chooses to analyze a problem and the way the student chooses to analyze the same problem. We want our framework to provide a sufficiently simple and general approach so that both teacher and student can use it to clarify, elaborate, and communicate their own individual modes of analysis.

SOCIAL VALUES AND HUMAN DIGNITY

Community Conflict and Controversy

There appear to be three important facts about human beings and the groups in which they live. First, each person is somehow different from all other people; he is often different in what he believes, what he desires, what he thinks is good for himself, how he feels about other people and other things in the world around him. Second, regardless of their individual differences, people generally choose to live in groups and modify some of their own personal desires and beliefs in order to get along with others who live in the same groups. So, although each person is unique and different, all of us as social beings share enough in common so that we desire to live in groups and depend upon one another for safety, shelter, and companionship. Third, the fact of being different and yet living in communities which face common problems leads to controversy and disagreement about decisions affecting the community. The controversy may erupt when we place our own desires and preferences above those of other members of the community; it may be caused by different interpretations of what is in the best interests of the community. Whatever the situation, it is usually difficult to establish a clear-cut case for the rightness or wrongness of any specific proposal which is presented to resolve, or may be the basis for, public controversy.

Public and Private Decisions

We should qualify our initial statement about community conflict by noting that every controversy over right and wrong, good and bad, is not the business of the whole community. Some of our actions affect mainly our own personal welfare and are nobody's business but our own. On the other hand, many if not most of the decisions we make affect not only ourselves but many of the people around us. It is important to distinguish between these two kinds of decisions. Decisions which affect the community we shall call public decisions; those which affect only an individual or a small private group we shall call private decisions. Decisions affecting the control of communicable diseases in the community, for example, are obviously the concern of the community in general. Those about the choice of the food, clothes, music, or art one enjoys are usually private matters. Those about choice of occupation or the number of children one chooses to bear and raise are at present private personal concerns yet have an important effect upon the community.

One of the major sources of community controversy springs from this question: "Should my decision be a matter for only me to consider, or should it be discussed, regulated, or controlled to some degree by other members of the community?" The problem of determining the point at which a private decision might be a legitimate public concern can perhaps best be described by illustration. Suppose we look at the simple problem of deciding what color to paint a house. Few would deny that this is clearly a private decision. Suppose we then move over into the problem of decorating the outside of a store. Should the community be able to regulate the size and appearance of the signs which advertise the name and nature of the store? Signs are now usually regulated by zoning laws. The town fathers of an old New England community, for example, recently became very indignant because the sign displayed by a new F. W. Woolworth store clashed with the colonial decor of the town, which had both monetary (tourist) as well as aesthetic value. The store gave in to community pressure and now displays a "colonial" store front.

It is not difficult to find other instances that illustrate the difficulty of drawing the line between personal preferences and general social values. In which kinds of situations, for example, does the effort to "compete with" or "outdo" another person remain a private concern and in which kinds of situations does it violate some important general social value? The following is illustrative:

According to the complaint he filed in court, Edward C. Tuttle had for many years been a successful and popular barber in the Minnesota village where he lived. He had maintained his family comfortably and had actually saved $800 a year, which in 1909 when his case was litigated could certainly be called "a considerable sum." But somehow he incurred the enmity of Cassius B———, a rich local banker. B———, Tuttle pleaded, decided to drive him out of business and, to that end, opened up and furnished a second barber shop in the village, hired a barber to run it, and used his wealth and prominence to divert Tuttle's customers to B———'s shop. Tuttle alleged that B——— took these steps maliciously to destroy Tuttle's business, and that, far from trying to serve any business purpose of his own, B——— had started the new shop without regard to any loss it might entail. Therefore Tuttle sued for damages.

B——— contended that even if these allegations were proved, he would not be liable, because, however ill his motives might be, he had only exercised the right everyone has to enter into competition in a lawful trade.

The highest court of Minnesota decided (3-2) that, if Tuttle could prove the truth of his pleading, B——— should be held liable for damages. B———'s alleged conduct was not competition but a brutal "application of force."[1]

This situation is interesting because of certain obvious questions it raises. If B———'s anger had led him to boycott Tuttle's barber shop, this would certainly have been considered a private matter between B——— and Tuttle. If B——— had hired three thugs to stand outside the shop and discourage customers from entering, it would clearly have been a public matter. But what of the use of cutthroat competition to satisfy feelings of personal antagonism? B——— has legally purchased and established a business to compete with Tuttle. On the other hand, in no sense does Tuttle have a chance to compete with B——— on equal or fair terms. At this point it is important to note that we begin to employ the language of social values; terms such as *property rights* and *a fair or equal chance to compete*. Both parties to the dispute support or justify their positions in the language of social values.

Human Dignity and Standards of Conduct

What, then, is the purpose and function of social value concepts in public dispute? One answer to this question may be stated as follows: When we are faced with a public dispute in which it is difficult to determine who is right and who is wrong, or when it is difficult to say whether the community or individual parties in the dispute should make this decision, we often seek to resolve the situation by searching for general principles of ethical or moral conduct. We attempt to discover rules of behavior by which our lives can be guided. Moreover, we want to anticipate stable and predictable ways of resolving future conflicts with others. From these stable approaches to conflict more or less general rules of conduct are generated which allow us to evaluate or judge many different kinds of situations. In the conflict between Tuttle and B——— there are clearly two general principles involved: B———'s right to use his own money or property to start a business, and Tuttle's right to compete with others on a fair and equal basis. In this troublesome situation two general rules or values which we want to employ to make an ethical decision have come into conflict. So while the use of general rules of conduct or social values allows us to clarify or evaluate social conduct more consistently, often these values clash. In such a conflict we may appeal to a more basic standard — our intuitive sense of human dignity, which will tell us, perhaps, that a particular application of a social value is in itself a perverted use of the concept. As the court decided in the Tuttle case, property rights can be used as a "brutal application of force" rather than to protect this more basic standard.

But if there is a more important and more basic value, why do we need to think in terms of specific values, such as property rights, to evaluate social and political decisions? Why not judge all behavior by the extent to which it contributes to human dignity and respect for the individual? Some philosophers have, in fact, tried to compress all ethical principles into a single general prescription to guide behavior. We are familiar with the general recommendation: Do unto others as you would have others do unto you. This is a powerful yet simple statement telling us how to behave toward one another. It is a guide to the resolution of human controversy. But such general prescriptions, although they are simple and powerful, often create as many problems as they solve. Since men interpret how they would like to be treated in different ways, thoughtful persons have sought to construct more specific principles or guidelines to help us behave in accordance with the fundamental standard of human conduct we are calling *the dignity of man*.

What we have been saying about the use of social standards, or values, to judge situations or human conduct is summarized in the following three statements:

1. People often try to develop general principles of behavior to guide their action; the most general and basic principle in our society is a commitment to human dignity.

2. While respect for human dignity and the rights of the individual may be the essential basis of judgment in a controversial situation, it is often difficult to understand or communicate the reasonability of alternative decisions on the basis of this principle alone.

3. Throughout history, men have developed more specific values which, when followed, are believed to promote the value of human dignity. These specific values or rights may be thought of as both elements of and bridges

leading toward the more basic value. Examples of such values or principles are:

a. The right to think, to believe, to speak, to worship as one's conscience and personal experience dictate.
b. The right to be secure from physical attack or injury.
c. The right to make agreements with other men and have these agreements respected.
d. The right to have one's own personal property protected from seizure and destruction.

The more specific values give a clearer idea of what we mean by human dignity. They help us understand better how to interpret and protect our freedom. But, as noted above, the use of the more specific values leads to the problem of what to do when two such values conflict. How can people go about resolving their controversies within the limits of these basic values?

RATIONAL CONSENT

In the framework described here we assume that respect for human dignity is the basic social value in the American community. When two people disagree over public policy, each should appeal to this basic value when he defends and rationalizes his position. But how does one go about defending and rationalizing a point of view? How does a society which is committed to human dignity as a final value deal with public disputes?

Our own society has developed an elaborate set of procedures for handling public disputes which are, hopefully, consistent with the fundamental value, human dignity. The principle behind the procedures developed for settling disputes with peace and dignity we shall call *rational consent*. Before describing rational consent, however, we might consider two common alternative approaches.

One of the oldest principles of conflict resolution is "Might makes right." When there is conflict, the bigger and more powerful individual in the conflict settles it by force or threat of force. In our first example, B_____ is richer and more powerful than Tuttle, so he simply runs Tuttle out of business. Or, if there is some doubt as to who is stronger, they fight it out. The use of force or the threat of force to resolve conflicts is coercion. Coercion as a means of settling questions of belief and value so often violates our sense of justice and human dignity that it must be rejected. A commonly accepted aspect of the "civilized" man involves just this: the rejection of coercion or force as a method of resolving human conflict while more rational means are still available.

A second method of resolving conflict is thought control. An individual or group may control so many sources of information that it can shape and regulate others' beliefs and values. In this way everyone can be taught the same ideas and values. There is little room for public conflict. Thought control and coercion are often used as weapons by a dictator to maintain his own power. Both methods, however, violate one of man's most distinctive characteristics, perhaps the one thing above all else that gives him dignity: his ability to think, to reason, to use words and symbols to persuade himself and others that his beliefs are right or his actions good. Coercion rejects reason. It says, "No matter what reason dictates, the final decision is made by strength." Thought control is a method of thwarting reason by not allowing it to draw freely from many sources of information.

Let us return now to rational consent as an approach to human conflict. The word *rational* emphasizes commitment to reason and thoughtful reflection. *Consent* emphasizes the principle that each person who is involved in the conflict should have a chance to express his opinion in one way or another; each person should have his say before he can be bound by a decision affecting him.

The process of rational consent begins with free and open discussion of a controversial issue. The purpose of the discussion is to encourage individuals and groups involved in the conflict to arrive at an understanding of their respective positions and, hopefully, to agree upon a common course of action. After honestly describing the conflict as best we can, we make our decisions as consistent as possible with our basic social values. Thus we should avoid the use of trickery, deceit, or distorted information to persuade others. The fact that words have poetic or emotive power in varying degrees presents particular problems. It may well be necessary to use "strong" words and powerful metaphors to discuss a value-laden issue, but to select and use such words *only* because they are likely to sway a decision in an irrational manner may involve trickery or deceit.

The problem of distinguishing between rational persuasion and demagogy is, of course, difficult and complex. It has at least three important dimensions: the intentions, motives, and sincerity of the speaker; the truthfulness of the message uttered by the speaker; and the extent to which the message plays on irrational or uncontrollable fears and emotions of the listener. Hitler is an obvious example of the demagogic extreme. He was often insincere and dishonest in the motives and intentions he conveyed to his listeners; he lied unconscionably; and he often played on unreasonable fears and impulses of his audience, at times deliberately whipping them into a state in which reason was completely rejected. A book like *Uncle Tom's Cabin* presents a more ambiguous case. The author was sincere. The events in the book may have been fictionalized accounts of similar events that had actually occurred, but the book, *in toto,* did present a distorted picture of slavery in the South. Metaphorically, however, perhaps the book was accurate in portraying the inhumanity of the whole institution of slavery. The point is simply that the line between sincere persuasion and deceitful demagogy is extremely fine. For this reason one must be careful to discriminate when he thinks demagogy is taking place and to expose it. But one must be doubly careful not to make false accusations of demagogy, especially by accusing another of insincerity, for proof of insincerity is difficult to come by.

Two Meanings of Consent

We have, then, rejected coercion and the deliberate censorship and control of information as methods of resolving disputes, in favor of a process more consistent with the value of human dignity: rational consent. People using this process freely debate possible courses of action which may affect them. But commitment to the process of rational consent as the major procedure for settling disputes brings with it many problems. Perhaps we can best describe the most important problem in the following example.

Let us suppose a flood is threatening a community. The river is rising rapidly. Members of the community are in sharp disagreement about what action should be taken. Some want everyone to leave and avoid personal risk. Others want to evacuate only the women and children and require the men to stay and fortify the levees in an effort to protect their homes and property. If the community is committed to complete agreement as the criterion for the resolution of this conflict, three alternatives are available. Everyone can be persuaded that leaving is the best policy. Everyone can be persuaded that the men should stay and make a stand against the river. Or, failing to arrive at consensus, everyone may stay and debate the issue until the community is swept away in the flood. Clearly either of the first two alternatives is better than the third.

In many situations any one of the controversial alternatives available to a community is better than endless debate over what to do. When the need for action is desperate, it may be foolish to wait until all parties have given their consent before a decision can be translated into action. For this reason the principle of complete consent is rarely used in practice as a means of resolving disputes. Decisions are usually made when the majority of members in a dispute agree that one decision is the best. The majority may be one more than one-half, two-thirds, three-fourths, or whatever the group decides in advance will constitute "consent."

In another sense, however, we often do demand complete consent. We demand that all citizens consent to abide by the decisions made by the group, provided that the *process* by which agreement is to be reached has been faithfully carried out. Thus, for example, the members of a club may agree that the process of debate and election with the majority ruling is the proper way to resolve a disagreement over who will be president. If the process is followed, all agree in advance to honor as president the person elected to the office. If one refuses to accept the process, he is likely to lose membership in the club. Loss of membership in the political community, of course, has more serious consequences.

The idea of consent, then, can be thought of in two different ways. We can give our consent to specific decisions, like agreeing that Jones will be president, or that everyone will evacuate the town during a flood. Or we can give our consent to abide by any decision made in accordance with a specific set of consent procedures. In general, we demand only that a majority of citizens or their representatives reach agreement before a *specific* decision becomes binding. However, we insist that all citizens be bound by a decision-making process.[2]

In the kind of communities in which we live and in the kind of groups to which we belong most persons act in accordance with the process of rational consent as a means of resolving conflict. Specific debating and voting procedures in this country are generally consistent with the spirit of rational consent.

THE GOVERNMENT AND BASIC SOCIAL VALUES

Because in our daily lives each of us assumes some group responsibility, we are often to some extent embroiled in group controversy on the community level, and even in our own personal groups and families. It is important, however, to distinguish between a relationship to a group with governmental power and sanctions and a relationship to groups which depend more on voluntary action. The government has the authority to require obedience, no matter what our personal wishes may be, as long as legitimate consent procedures are followed. Other groups are likely to depend on the voluntary actions of their members to achieve their purposes. In our own society, for example, we can decide to which church we wish to belong, although factors such as our parents' church membership may mean that we never really exercise this right. And after joining a church we cannot legally be required to follow its doctrines, unless in breaking them we also break the law. But by virtue of being born in this country we are citizens (unless we explicitly reject this status), and we must obey the government's decisions or suffer the legal consequences.

The situation of the naturalized citizen is more like that of membership in a voluntary group (although alien status does not leave one free to decide which governmental laws to obey). This serves to illustrate that the differences between voluntary and governmental groups are a matter of degree. Voluntary groups often exercise powers approaching those exercised by the government, as where the threat of eternal damnation is used to enforce church membership. The picture is further complicated by the use of governmental sanction to encourage membership in voluntary groups, as in the case of labor union membership in the states where the union shop is legal.

Civil Disputes

In this same connection we should also distinguish between rules and laws. The penalties for breaking rules of non-governmental groups are generally less harsh than penalties imposed on those who break government laws. Refusal to obey the rules of a group joined voluntarily can bring denial of future membership in the group, but that is usually the most extreme penalty that can be inflicted. Disobeying a governmental law or decree can mean loss of property, liberty, and even life. Moreover, a government usually has a monopoly of power, by which it can force its citizens to obey its decisions.

Why should a government be given such a monopoly? Doesn't this power over lives and liberties threaten the whole idea of personal freedom and human dignity? Shouldn't there be only voluntary groups which one can freely join and leave? The answer to these questions is complicated. In general, an ethical government can *justify* the use of force and coercion only when it is employed to preserve or promote the dignity and freedom of the individual within the community or nation. (We might note that governments, even democratic governments, may use force unjustifiably.)

To understand better how governments can justifiably use force and coercion, let us look at an example. Suppose the great majority of people in the community are in favor of fair and public trials of those accused of crimes. A man is accused of kidnapping and murdering a small child. He is arrested. Here the government has chosen to use force to restrain temporarily a man who might further threaten the safety of the community if allowed to go free. At this point the accused cannot solve his problem by leaving the community. His membership in and responsibility to the community are more or less permanent. (At the very least, he must be a member in good standing before he can choose to leave.) To extend our example, suppose the father of the murdered child recruits a number of his friends to storm the jail and hang the man accused of the murder. Again, the government must use force to prevent such action, since it clearly violates the community's responsibility to provide the accused with a fair trial.

This illustration suggests that when the individual becomes a member of a community he gains important privileges and takes on important responsibilities. Since carrying out the responsibilities is necessary to maintain a peaceful and orderly community, the community cannot depend upon voluntary obedience to laws. If it could, one man (as the man who kidnapped and murdered the child) or a small group of men (as those led by the father who wanted to lynch the person accused of the kidnapping) could violate the rights of others without fear of any penalty other than being disliked or disapproved by members of the group. Experience has shown that community disapproval is not generally a strong enough sanction to protect the rights of citizens. Even threat of force or coercion is not enough, for we do have jails and prisoners.

Two Systems of Government

To maintain law and order and to insure that citizens will have the opportunity to use rational processes to settle their disputes, communities delegate power to a government. Governments are made up of those people within the community who are given political power — the power to force the people to obey the demands made upon them by the government. In a closed community or nation the government uses its power to restrict the formation of voluntary groups, to censor the flow of information, to destroy or restrain people who speak against the government. In an "open" society the government restrains itself as much as possible from interfering with voluntary groups and the free flow of information, so that the people may intelligently evaluate the quality of the government and, at regular intervals, change the officers who govern if they feel that the government is not acting wisely. Thus, a closed society may well be ruled by the consent of the people, because most citizens feel that the decisions made are wise ones. But in no sense are the citizens allowed to participate in the process of rational consent. They cannot speak and think freely about the wisdom of the decisions made by their government, nor can they change it when they feel unwise decisions have been made. We ordinarily feel that democratic government is a better way of exercising political power because it is more responsive to the wishes of the nation and community.[3] But even in a democracy individuals and voluntary groups can be frightened and persecuted by an intolerant majority or a clever and powerful minority.

Constitutionalism

When a society establishes and maintains a government limited by a body of laws and principles which protect the central values of a democratic society, i.e., human dignity and rational consent, we say that the nation operates within the framework of constitutional democracy. Such a government is termed constitutional because its actions are restricted by a body of fundamental laws and principles which limits and defines the authority of the government and of the people.[4]

A constitutional democracy has at least two important characteristics:

1. The government restricts the use of its power to those areas of

concern to which the people or a majority of the people have given their consent.

2. The government is responsible for protecting the rights and freedoms of individuals even when these rights are invaded by the majority of citizens. That is, even though the majority may agree to undertake certain actions, the government is obligated to restrain the majority from violating basic rights of individuals who happen to be in the minority. For example, the right to speak freely and join voluntary groups is protected under the United States Constitution.

Another way of looking at democratic constitutionalism is through the concepts of delegated and final authority. The government exercises power *delegated* to it by the people through a constitution. *Final authority,* however, rests with the people. It is further assumed that the people will exercise their final power and authority only in accordance with the rules stated in the constitution.

How does this process of delegating power first take place? How does a society get a constitutional government? Let us look at our own country as an example.[5] In 1787 the people of the thirteen states could not all meet together to write a set of rules by which the new country would be governed. They had few roads; they could not all be away from their homes for several months. Yet many of them wanted a better government than the Articles of Confederation provided. The people of the thirteen states had many interests in common, as well as the will to carry them out. But they had found no way of delegating authority to a government which could effectively promote these common interests. Furthermore, they were cautious about delegating power to a central government because they thought it might not respect the final power that rested with the people. This fear was based, of course, upon their recent experiences with the government of England, which, many thought, had violated the dignity and freedom of the people within the thirteen colonies.

The majority of citizens in the separate states delegated to elected representatives the authority to plan a government that would better serve the interests of all the people in the nation. These delegates, however, were not given the authority to adopt a new plan of government. A Constitution was written and submitted to the electorate for a vote. At this point there was much discussion, thought, and argument about the worth of the proposed Constitution. After the open discussion, representatives with authority delegated to them by the people or their representatives voted "yes" or "no" on whether each state and the people within it would consent to the new Constitution. The Constitution provided that when nine of the thirteen states gave their consent, those that had done so would be bound by its authority. This act of consent was given, and the American Constitution became an important landmark in the history of mankind, largely because of its emphasis on explicitly limiting the power of government and protecting individual rights.

The desire to obtain and use unlimited power has been a common tendency of political leaders, even those initially committed to democratic constitutional ideals. Most governments in the history of the world have not been restrained by the concept of constitutional democracy. The framers of the American Constitution recognized the necessity of placing limitations on political power, recognizing also that the government required enough authority and power to deal with the pressing problems that faced the new country. They confronted the challenge of creating a constitutional government that would reflect some reasonable balance between authority and restraint. In carrying out this task the framers of the Constitution were guided by a number of principles of governmental conduct which still guide us today. They are especially important because it is assumed that the government is one of the major institutions within society which may promote, sustain, or violate essential aspects of human dignity and rational consent.

These guiding principles of government make many assumptions about what constitutes an appropriate definition of dignity and consent. We shall describe some of the most important and their relationship to our basic values and note how they have been specifically included in the Constitution.

References

1. This example is taken from Edmond Cahn, *The Moral Decision* (Bloomington: Indiana University Press, 1956), pp. 135-136.

2. It should be pointed out that some political philosophers, e.g., Thoreau and Laski, have stated that the individual has an obligation to obey only those decisions which are consistent with his own conscience. Some Quakers' refusal to serve in the army despite a declaration of war through the legal counsent process is an example of the application of this principle. We might note that democratic societies tend to tolerate higher degrees of antisocietal or antilegal conduct when it is justified in terms of conscience rather than expediency.

3. In our discussion of the democratic society we should like to make it clear that we are not suggesting that government based on rational consent is necessarily good for all societies. The procedures for dealing with community controversy based on rational consent are certainly not appropriate under all human conditions. For a complex society to be democratic, it probably must have, at the very least, a high rate of literacy, well-educated and responsible leadership, and a stable political and economic system.

4. Although constitutions are generally written documents, their importance rests upon the willingness of people to restrain their own actions in accordance with the values the constitution seeks to protect.

5. Obviously any brief sketch of the process by which the American Constitution came to be written and ratified must be grossly oversimplified. While democratic

idealism played a major part in this process, certainly economic issues as well as petty problems of personal vanity and power were also critical. This brief description is simply meant to illustrate one instance of how an "act of consent" might be given to the total consent process. We might have selected a simpler example, such as the Mayflower Compact, with less distortion and simplification. The United States Constitution, however, provides the legal basis for many of the problems on which our curriculum centers.

CHAPTER FIVE

Principles of American Government

We have presented two values which we think are at the heart of the liberal democratic society: human dignity and rational consent. We have also discussed the problem of protecting these values from abuse. The central governmental principle protecting these values, we stated, was democratic constitutionalism. Moreover, democratic constitutionalism, as we are using the term, is more than a principle of government; it implies a set of procedures for deciding questions in a rational, intelligent, and humane way. It depends, too, upon certain assumptions about the nature of man himself. The most important are (1) that he can be trained to restrain his own impulses in the interests of others and (2) that he will inevitably strive toward some degree of personal freedom and self-expression. One of the great questions of history is whether or not these assumptions are borne out — whether man can in fact translate faith in his rational and humane qualities into specific instruments of government which can protect and promote these qualities.

In this chapter we hope to show how some specific provisions of our American constitutional system are related to general legal and political principles which derive their importance from a fundamental concern with the protection of individual human dignity. Although we dwell on the federal Constitution as providing "scripture" through which we can demonstrate how these principles are presumably applied, it is important to note that we are using the American experience as one example of the broader concept of constitutionalism. Constitutionalism in the wider sense relates to a type of polity whereby power relationships among various interests and the government are so defined as to leave broad areas of freedom, development, and change open to voluntary groups and individuals. The struggle of man to create and develop such a polity is documented in the work of pioneers like Zechariah Chafee, Jr., which lays out important constitutional crises in historical perspective, the development of technical procedures of law and politics resulting from such crises, and the overall progress of the doctrine of constitutionalism. Obviously, we cannot present such a history here, nor can we describe or document in detail presumed relationships between fundamental law, technical procedures that give the law meaning, and the maintenance of a society committed to human dignity and rational consent. What we shall offer is a very schematic statement of *some* of these relationships, using American constitutional theory for illustrative purposes. It should be clear that we are talking mainly about *principles* and *theory,* not about the realities of power politics or political process. Because of the schematic and theoretical nature of this chapter, it may well appear to be much oversimplified. We have risked oversimplification, however, because we think it is important to present the political ideals — and some notion of the conceptual instruments by which society hopes to achieve these ideals — in uncluttered skeletal form as standards the student can use to judge the strength and the shortcomings of the men who manage the affairs of the community within this political framework.

While we are unequivocally committed to a firm, though deliberately vague, conception of human dignity, we are committed to the principles of American government only to the extent that they are a part of or instrumental to the maintenance of these more basic values.[1] The United States Constitution, from our point of view, is not "sacred." The goals it explicitly attempts to achieve, however, are, we believe, permanent and enduring. It should also be understood that the principles set forth on the following pages do not exhaust the list of important principles of American constitutional government, nor are they mutually exclusive. In fact, they are closely interwoven, and often the secondary meaning of one principle is the primary meaning of another. Regardless of the obvious difficulties this presents to one who wishes to enumerate the principles, an initial effort must be made before the debate over the exclusiveness or the relevance of specific principles can begin.

SELECTED PRINCIPLES OF AMERICAN GOVERNMENTAL PROCEDURE

Rule of Law

The phrase *rule of law* refers to the proposition that the actions carried out with governmental power should be authorized by laws promulgated through established procedures instead of being dictated by personal whim or private ambition. Constitutionalism is, of course, a concept very close to rule of law and, as a matter of fact, represents one explicit form of rule of law. Insofar as there is a "contract" between the people and the government as expressed in a constitution regarding the conditions under which power can be legitimately exercised by the government, the government is pledged to remain within these limits. The United States government, with its written Constitution and officers who take it seriously, is a government under law. It is interesting to note, for example, that our Constitution spells out not only areas for positive action by the federal government, but the principle of federal limitation:

> The enumeration in the Constitution of certain rights shall not be construed to deny or disparage others retained by the people. [Amendment IX]
>
> The powers not delegated to the United States by the Constitution, nor prohibited by it to the States, are reserved to the States respectively, or to the people. [Amendment X]

In this conception of government, the idea of contract is critical; it is possible for the government, as well as the people, to violate the law. Governmental violation can take place when the government exercises power which has not been delegated to it under the Constitution, or when an official does not go through proper consent procedures before exercising power. For example, if the President of the United States sent American soldiers to war without the consent of Congress either by joint resolution or a formal declaration, this act might be termed unlawful or unconstitutional, and in violation of the precept of rule of law.

Obviously the people also violate laws made under the powers delegated to the government. There are times, however, when it is difficult to know whether the government or the people (or which of the various agencies of government) are violating the law. For example, several southern states have refused to send white and Negro children to the same public schools, even though the Supreme Court has reached the decision that under certain conditions such refusal is unlawful or unconstitutional. Many people in the South maintain that the Supreme Court violated the Constitution by exercising power not delegated to it under the Constitution. Thus, while the rule-of-law principle can be defined clearly in general terms, it is sometimes difficult to determine when a law has been broken and by whom.

A second aspect of the meaning of rule of law refers specifically to the government's obligation to make general rules which apply to all citizens equally. Once a law is made, each one is required to obey it no matter what his status or position — rich man, poor man, or government official.

The wording of a recent court decision on forced confessions clearly illustrates the principle:

> The abhorrence of society to the use of involuntary confessions does not turn alone on their inherent untrustworthiness. It also turns on the deep-rooted feeling that the police must obey the law while enforcing the law; that in the end life and liberty can be as much endangered from illegal methods used to convict those thought to be criminals as from the actual criminals themselves.[2]

While many provisions of the federal Constitution reflect application of this respect of the rule-of-law principle, e.g., setting up an explicit lawmaking body, restricting the power of the President to the administration of law, a number of specific constitutional provisions clearly illustrate the principle. Article I, section 9, paragraph 3, states that "No bill of attainder or ex post facto law shall be passed." A bill of attainder is essentially a legislative act which invades the citizen's right to a trial before the courts. An ex post facto law is a law which would allow a person to be punished for an act which, when it was committed, was legal. The ex post facto "law" violates the spirit of rule of law, since, if it were allowed, one would never know when in fact he was acting legally or illegally. Laws that are vague or sweeping violate the same principle. Rule of law includes the idea that the citizen should have a clear idea of the limits of legal activity.

Equal Protection Under the Law

Equal protection under the law is commonly understood to mean that existing laws must be administered in a fair and impartial manner to all citizens. In this sense its meaning clearly overlaps the concept of rule of law.

In another more inclusive sense, equal protection under the law means that laws should not be made which extend special privileges or inflict special penalties on specific individuals or groups. Laws may in fact operate so as to confer privileges or inflict penalties on special groups, e.g., farm subsidies, but these actions must be justified in terms of the welfare of the whole community. The Supreme Court decided in 1954, for example, that state laws requiring whites and Negroes in the same school district to attend separate schools were treating the Negro as an inferior human being and thus violated the principle of equal protection. The right to equal protection is guaranteed to citizens of all the States in the Constitution: ". . . nor shall any State . . . deny to any person within its jurisdiction the equal protection of the laws (Amendment XIV).

Consent and Representation

The principle of consent means that citizens are allowed to participate at least indirectly in the governmental decisions which affect them. As pointed out in the previous chapter, there are two levels of consent. We can give our consent or agree to specific decisions which might affect us; we can also consent to the *process* by which decisions will be made. The principle of consent applies to both situations. In our federal and state governments, with the thousands of decisions made each day, it would be impossible to poll all citizens on each decision. Yet we want the people to have some check, some say, about what decisions will be made. To resolve this problem of giving the people some say in government, yet giving the government effective power to deal with immediate problems, a consent process is provided which delegates to representatives the right to act for citizens. That is, since people cannot come together to use their final authority, they must choose, directly or indirectly, a smaller number of people to represent their wishes and interests — representatives who pass laws, officers who enforce them, and judges who interpret them and decide how they will be applied. The form of democracy using this system is often called a republic. The major rules which tell what power is delegated to the government by the people and how this power can be exercised are found in the Constitution. Each decision made by the federal government, for example, is an exercise of authority granted under or implied by the Constitution. The Constitution and the history of its use, which provides guidelines for further application and interpretation, thus constitute the major basis of the American consent process. It is this process to which the American people give their continuing "consent."

The major procedures described in the Constitution which tell how the federal government is organized, what powers have been delegated to it, and how citizens may assume the responsibility of public office and obtain consent for their actions are explained in detail in many social studies texts, including those in history, civics, and problems of American democracy. As one reads the Constitution and various interpretations of it, the structure and mechanics of government seem difficult and complicated. From our point of view, before one becomes enmeshed in the mechanics and complexities of the process, he should understand clearly the purpose behind the mechanics: to give people the right to have some say in the decisions which affect them. This includes the right to review from time to time the actions of the government to determine the extent to which it is doing a satisfactory job; the right to be represented in government by people who will look after the various interests of the community; and the right to vote for those who represent them, or the right to vote for those who will choose people to represent them. These rights and privileges of citizenship in a democratic society are summarized by the term *the consent of the governed.*

Due Process

We have discussed three important principles of American government: (1) *rule of law:* making decisions in terms of general rules rather than by the personal decrees of officials; (2) *equal protection under the law:* making and applying laws in the interests of the whole community, rather than for the benefit of privileged groups; (3) *consent:* the process by which the people can actively participate, at least indirectly, in the decisions of the government. These principles are presumably instrumental in the conduct of a government whose central concern is the protection of rational consent and the preservation of human dignity.

Another concept which runs through these three principles, but is so important that it must be stated as a precept in its own right, is due process. Due process of law refers to the prohibition of arbitrary action on the part of the government in depriving individual citizens of their life, liberty, or property. Construed broadly, it includes such matters as proper notice of impending governmental action, restrictions on methods used in obtaining confessions, hearings before land-taking for governmental use, and restrictions on the use of legislative power to take away personal rights. It is, however, most commonly used and best illustrated in its application to criminal law enforcement and court action.

When the government accuses a person of breaking a law, at least three considerations must be taken into account: (1) Is the government given the authority under the Constitution to make such a law? (2) Is the act which the government alleges was committed outlawed? (3) Did the person really perform the act which the government claims is outlawed?

Let us take an example. Suppose Congress passes a law against publishing magazines which favor Communism. Joe Jones is arrested for publishing a magazine which states that the people in the Soviet Union live happier lives than do Americans. Three questions must be answered before we know whether Joe Jones is guilty of breaking the law. (1) Does Congress have the power under the Constitution to prohibit publication of magazines which favor Communism? (2) Is the statement about the Soviet people's enjoying happier lives than Americans an example of "favoring Communism"? (3) Did Joe Jones actually publish the magazine which made this statement?

Who is to decide these questions? In our system of government the task falls largely upon the courts. The process the courts go through in deliberating and deciding such questions makes up one aspect of due process. For the courts, then, it is a process which includes weighing evidence and interpreting the relationship between action and law, both constitutional and legislative.

While due process of law has been established to protect individuals from a government which may abuse its powers, it is also a basis for rationally identifying individuals who may abuse their freedom and harm the community. As applied to criminal trials, it includes a set of procedures in which reason, deliberation, and careful weighing of evidence are to be used by men in determining whether or not the accusation that one of their fellowmen has committed a crime is correct. The specific procedures that define due process in this context, therefore, are designed to protect both the community and the individual.

In broad outline, due process for the federal government is defined mainly in Amendments II, V, and VI of the Constitution, as well as in the sections of the Constitution dealing with the privilege of habeas corpus and protection from ex post facto laws and bills of attainder.

In the simplest language, the right to due process in a criminal trial means the right to a fair trial. While the technical definition of "fair trial" is under constant re-examination by the courts, it includes the following important dimensions:

1. Evidence against the accused person must be legally obtained. The government cannot invade the privacy of a person's home to obtain evidence without a search warrant.

2. No person can be held for a crime unless a grand jury or a judge feels that there is enough evidence to justify a trial.

3. No person can be tried twice for the same crime.

4. No person can be forced to testify against himself.

5. Every person accused of a crime has the right to a speedy trial by an impartial or unbiased jury in the area where the crime was committed. This means that the government cannot hold someone in prison for an indefinite length of time before bringing him to trial.

6. The accused has a right to be informed of the specific crime of which he is accused.

7. The accused has a right to confront personally the witnesses who are accusing him.

8. The accused can require people to testify if he thinks their testimony might help him.

9. The accused has a right to a lawyer to help him defend himself.

While these provisions for a fair trial apply specifically to the federal courts, the constitutions of the several states have similar provisions — an important point since most crimes are actually tried in state courts.

Separation of Powers: Checks and Balances

The federal and state governments are, at least in theory, separated into three branches, each with its own main function. In its simplest sense this means that the legislative branch makes laws to meet the needs of the community or country; the executive branch sees that the laws are carried out; the judicial branch determines whether or not the government has the delegated authority to make a law, and sees that the law is correctly interpreted and applied by the executive branch. Separation of powers, however, is more than simply a way of dividing the work and responsibility of government. It is a method of restraining the power of the government and protecting the rights of the states and of individual citizens. It is a method of preventing the government from exercising powers that belong to the people and have not been delegated to the government. Each branch of government can check or restrain the others in certain ways. Following are illustrations of how various branches of the federal government check and balance each other:

1. The President can veto or refuse to sign a bill passed by Congress. Congress is then required to pass the same bill again by a two-thirds majority rather than by a simple majority if it wishes the bill to become law.

2. Congress can refuse to pass a bill suggested by the President; or Congress can refuse to appropriate money needed to enforce a law which the President thinks ought to be enforced.

3. The Senate can refuse to approve appointments to federal office made by the President.

4. Once a law is passed by Congress and enforced by the President, the courts can declare that the authority to make such a law was not delegated to the Congress by the Constitution. Thus, the courts can declare laws unconstitutional.

5. The President and Congress have some control over the membership of the Supreme Court as vacancies occur. The President appoints members of this Court with the consent of two-thirds of the Senate. If the Court disagrees with the other branches of government about what powers have been delegated to the government, it is possible to change the view of the Court over time by appointing men who would tend to agree with the President and Congress.

6. Aside from specific powers which are given to the Supreme Court under Article III in the Constitution, its most important powers are granted by Congress. In Article III the Constitution states that "in all cases before mentioned, the Supreme Court shall have appellate jurisdiction, both as to law and fact, with such exceptions, and under such regulations as the Congress shall make."

While there are many ways that the separation of powers tends to restrain the power of government,[3] those above describe some of the more important ones. And of these, probably the most important is the separation of the judicial process from the power to make and enforce laws. The courts guard the citizen's right to due process and have the greatest responsibility for protecting individuals from abuses of government. The legislative and executive branches tend to represent the more powerful interest groups in the community — powerful in numbers, powerful in wealth, powerful in influence. These branches of government respond to the influence of those who can exercise it, whereas the courts deal with individual people, one at a time. Due process is given to each individual whose rights or privileges are threatened by the government or other private groups. The court then weighs the rights of the individual against the responsibility of the government to other individuals and to the community. The debate over the rights of the individual usually takes place in a quiet courtroom, not in the crowded corridors of a legislative hall. The debate should be, and usually is, carried on in an atmosphere of caution and deliberation. Probably the most basic guarantee of a free society which values human dignity and rational consent is the supporting and strengthening of due process and the independence of the court system which guards this basic principle of government.

Federalism

The United States Constitution provides for two different levels of government within a single nation: the national government of the United States and the state governments which run the affairs of the individual states. A system of government in which authority is divided constitutionally between the central government and local governments is called a federal system.

The federal system was set up in the United States for many reasons. The framers of the Constitution feared that a single strong central government might threaten the rights of individuals in the same way that England had threatened the rights of the American colonists before the Revolution. The citizens of each of the American colonies had developed a strong sense of loyalty to their colony. Each colony had a considerable degree of self-government, even before the United States separated from England. The individual colonies, and later the states, jealously guarded the right to govern many of their own affairs. Yet the Americans learned by bitter experience during and after the Revolution the high cost of a weak and ineffective central government.

The federal system is based on the assumption that the people in each state know best how to deal with local problems; but some problems affecting the whole nation must be handled by a central government. Throughout the history of the United States there has been persistent controversy about what problems were local and what problems were national. The growth of national groups, such as business corporations and labor unions, has aggravated the matter of defining what problems should be handled locally.

Although the federal government has increased in importance over the last hundred years, state governments are still a major instrument of local control and local rule. Furthermore, the people's right to organize and run their own state government is guaranteed under the Constitution. It does, however, place some restrictions upon the authority state governments can exercise. Most of these restrictions are described in Article IV. For example: (1) The judicial proceedings carried on in one state are to be recognized as legal in other states. (2) The United States guarantees to every state a republican form of government. (3) The citizens of each state are entitled to the privileges of citizens of the several states. This means that each state is required to respect the privileges guaranteed to individuals by citizenship in other states.

The Constitution places other restrictions on state governments in the amendments. For example: (1) Slavery is outlawed in the states (Amendment XIII). (2) No state can deprive a citizen of life, liberty, or property without due process of law (Amendment XIV). (3) No state can deprive a citizen of equal protection under the law (Amendment XIV). (4) No state can deprive a person of the right to be a citizen or the right to vote because of race (Amendment XV). (5) No state can deprive a person of the right to vote because of sex (Amendment XIX).

It should be noted, however, that there are other democratic countries which value human dignity and rational consent fully as much as Americans do and which have preserved their way of life without a federal system of government — e.g., England. Nevertheless, for many Americans, state citizenship is prized and valued as a symbol of local independence and considered necessary to protect the individual from a federal government which is seen as anxious to take away more and more of their freedoms. For others, the federal principle, meaning the careful restriction of federal power and the preservation of states' rights, is much less important since the revolution in transportation and communication that began some 100 years ago. These people assert that telephones and television, jet planes, and modern cars and highways make us all members of one closely knit community in which one state's problems are everyone's problems. Regardless of how one looks at federalism, it is a traditional value of American government which is intended to restrain both the federal and state governments and, in so doing, protect the rights of individuals.

Substantive Goals of American Government

We have now talked about the basic values which should, in our society, govern man's relationship to his neighbor, his community, and his nation. We have called these values human dignity and rational consent: Each person is valued and respected simply because he is an individual human being, and the principle which should guide men in settling their public disagreements is rational consent.

In our description of American government we tried to illustrate how one of the main purposes of the procedural principles behind our governmental system is protection of human freedom and dignity as well as protection of rational consent as a process for dealing with conflicts and disagreements within the community. Democratic government and the principles supporting the idea of constitutionalism all have this goal. But these principles say little about how to evaluate alternative actions that a government might consider in an effort to improve the community. Thus far we have talked mainly about methods of checking the possible abuses brought about by irresponsible members of the community or by an unrestrained or tyrannical government. Now we shall look at principles by which one might judge the worth of possible consequences of governmental actions designed specifically to improve the community. One of the best statements of the positive purposes of our own government is presented in the Preamble of the Constitution: "We the people of the United States, in order to form a more perfect Union, establish justice, ensure domestic tranquillity, provide for the common defence, promote the general welfare, and secure the blessings of liberty to ourselves and our prosperity, do ordain and establish this Constitution for the United States of America." Our own conception of the most salient points included among these values is discussed briefly below.

Justice

To establish justice means to see that all of the people within the community are treated fairly. *Justice* or *fairness* is, of course, a vague term. In one sense it means much the same thing as equal protection under the law — laws should not be made which favor some groups over others. More recently the term has taken on a broader meaning and refers to equal opportunity or an equal chance in life. Wherever one draws the line, the basic idea is that each person deserves a reasonable chance to foster his talents and to develop himself as a worthy and self-respecting individual. If the government is to "establish justice," it is required to see that some men are not so downtrodden and/or exploited that they never have a chance to deal with others as dignified human beings.

Domestic Tranquillity and the Common Defense

Both of these terms are related to a more basic idea: the preservation of peace and order within the community. To insure domestic tranquillity means to prevent disorder and violence among our own citizens. To provide for the common defense means to prevent other nations or governments from injuring us or restricting our rights. The Constitution attempts to implement these objectives by giving states the right to have a militia and the federal government the authority to support an armed force.

General Welfare

The term *general welfare* refers to the progress and welfare of the whole community or the whole nation. Welfare can be defined in many ways; certainly the very least it means is that individuals in the community should not want for the necessities of life and health. This suggests that the government has some responsibility for seeing that all Americans have a decent education, decent medical care, a decent standard of living, and an opportunity to do productive work. It does not mean, of course, that the government itself must provide these things but only that the government is charged to some degree with preventing major violations of these standards.

The Blessings of Liberty

The government cannot "give" people freedom. Freedom is a condition achieved when men can make choices which are not forced upon them. It is achieved, too, when choices can be made because one is released from the burden of simply maintaining life and health. People living in the midst of poverty and suffering disease have a difficult time being "free." Insofar as the government can provide ways for men to resolve their differences through rational consent rather than coercion and prevent some men and some groups from forcing others to do their bidding simply because of power or wealth, and insofar as men can make free choices which are important to them, the blessings of liberty are secured. To secure the blessings of liberty also means that the government will restrain its own actions which might interfere with free choice, as well as that it will restrain the actions of those who would irresponsibly coerce or restrict the choices of others.

The Constitution defines the freedoms which have special importance to Americans:

Freedom of Expression. Amendment I of the Constitution places unqualified restrictions upon Congress regarding freedom of expression: "Congress shall make no law . . . abridging the freedom of speech or of the press; or the right of the people peaceably to assemble, and to petition the government for a redress of grievances."

Also included in the First Amendment is freedom of religion: "Congress shall make no law respecting an establishment of religion, or prohibiting the free exercise thereof. . . ." The courts have interpreted broadly this restriction on government. They have said that the restrictions placed on Congress under the First Amendment also apply to the states under Amendment XIV.

Private Property Rights. The right to own and control property is a very important freedom. The value of property is often the result of one's talent, ingenuity, and hard work. In this sense property rights are supported in a number of places in the Constitution. Amendment IV, for example, states that "The right of the people to be secure in their persons, houses, papers, and effects, against unreasonable searches and seizures, shall not be violated, and no warrants shall issue but upon probable cause, supported by oath or affirmation, and particularly describing the place to be searched, and the persons or things to be seized."

While property rights are often thought to be vested in land, money, or goods of some sort, they also include the right to make binding agreements or contracts with others. A man's right to sell his services to another and his right to sell his land or his house to another are contract rights secured under the law.

The rights of property and contract are specifically guaranteed in Amendments V and XIV, which state that no one can "be deprived of life, liberty, or property, without due process of law." Amendment V also states that the government cannot take away private property for public use without paying a fair price: ". . . nor shall private property be taken for public use without just compensation." And Section 10 of Article I specifies that states may not pass laws which impair contractual obligations.

Government Regulation of the "Blessings of Liberty." Personal freedoms are not unconditionally guaranteed. One cannot freely speak into a loudspeaker which blares into his neighbor's window at two o'clock in the morning. One cannot justifiably yell "Fire" in a crowded theatre unless there is a fire. One cannot legally practice a religion which advocates not paying taxes. One cannot legally operate a factory which blows poisonous fumes into private homes. Personal freedoms are obviously limited by considerations of the rights of others and the rights of the whole community. The great problem of a society committed to the value of free choice is deciding where to draw the line between personal freedom and community welfare. To restrict freedom simply to satisfy the whims of government or the majority of people is an unreasonable invasion of freedom. To guarantee a right which may threaten the health or safety of the whole community is foolish. The main purpose of our discourse here is to provide a framework within which we can handle this basic problem of defining the legitimate exercise of free choice and the legitimate exercise of government regulation.

Ethical Principles Underlying the Analysis of Controversy in a Democratic Society: A Summary

In dealing with problems of public conflict and controversy, the American nation has both inherited and developed a tradition that government and law should be the outgrowth of public debate. Important to this tradition is the value placed on the dignity and worth of each individual and, as a corollary, the value placed on the use of reason and persuasion in resolving disputes among people who define differently human dignity and the conditions that promote it. From our point of view, a major goal of the society is to develop a public awareness that these basic values should be respected and applied as standards for making public policy. One way of working toward the goal is to commit ourselves to these general values in terms of the more specific concepts in which they have traditionally been set forth. But identifying and committing oneself to values as an individual citizen is not enough to insure their being taken seriously as the working values of the community. The political institutions of the community must operate in a way that is consistent with the values.

The framers of the American Constitution and their successors tried to construct a government with procedures to a large extent defined and restricted by important principles closely related to these values. The principles have been described as rule of law, rule by consent, equal protection under the law, due process, separation of powers, and federalism or states' rights. They mean a great deal to most of us because we believe they protect the more basic values of society: personal liberty, justice, peace, and community welfare.

We assume that violation of the governmental principles which support the basic social values tends to endanger the values themselves. For example, if the government were to cast aside the restraints imposed by the notion of rule of law, the most fundamental of personal liberties, such as freedom of speech and assembly, might be endangered. We therefore assume that basic social values depend upon a government committed to certain procedural principles. Individuals might well question whether each or all of these governmental principles promote the more basic values. In our present framework, however, we have generally accepted the assumption that the violation of any of the principles is cause for concern. But we should be careful to use the more basic values in our final judgment of a controversial issue, for it is from them that the governmental principles gain their significance.

SOME QUALIFICATIONS OF THE "DEMOCRATIC CONSTITUTIONALISM" MODEL

The ethical basis of democratic constitutionalism, or what might be called the American democratic "myth" presented above, is little more than the systematic selection of Jeffersonian principles, which were clearly conditioned by the facts of life in America in the latter half of the eighteenth century. Many of those facts of life have long since passed on. We shall present briefly certain qualifications one should bear in mind as a result of the more important of these changes.

1. The early conceptualization of the American democratic system grossly underestimated the importance of national political factions and parties as an integral part of the consent process. It is dishonest, if not dangerous, to present to the student the principles outlined above as an image of the way things "turned out to be." The concepts of government previously listed that were built into the American political structure are better thought of as evaluative principles by which political controversy can more clearly be described and debated; they are by no means necessarily the most important considerations which might allow one to predict accurately what specific political decisions will in fact be made. Personal power and vanity, exigencies of time, and political expediency, among other things, undoubtedly play a major part in what individual citizens and the government actually decide to do. However, a concern for the realities of political process should not be allowed to undermine the student's effort to ground his political actions in the ideals by which both the process and the substantive decision might be judged. From our point of view, the citizen is to be encouraged to develop a reasoned position with respect to public controversy within the framework described by these principles. The extent to which factors such as power, personal friendship, private greed, and expediency influence political decisions should become apparent as he studies real issues and the real people who must make decisions.

Although it was clearly not within the scope of our study, we think it both important and useful to give considerable systematic treatment to the concepts and generalizations which describe the political process in action. The reader should not assume, therefore, that this omission in our work reflects any bias against the importance of studying political process. It means simply that, given limits of time and resources, one must establish priorities. We chose to develop a model based largely on ethical considerations and to teach students to apply this model to selected national political controversies. The student is then restricted to an evaluation of the merits of alternative solutions to specific problems within the limits set up by the model. He is not prepared to face the problem of how to implement any political decision he might make. For strategic reasons, then, we have avoided teaching about the practical problems of transforming decision into action, proposal into law.

2. The general position outlined above does not deal with the question of what framework to use in dealing with political controversy when one or more parties in the dispute operate from a different ethical base. The most critical problems today are, in fact, of this nature. The United

States as a community must work out problems with other communities which have rejected basic elements in the liberal Western political tradition, either in the form of Fascism (Spain), or in the form of state Socialism (Russia). It must deal with nascent communities which never participated in the development of the political, economic, and intellectual basis of the liberal Western democracy, e.g., Nigeria, Ghana, Congo. It must also deal with countries which are conglomerates of the Western political and ethical traditions but which have proud indigenous ethical traditions, e.g., India.

Developing a frame of reference which will place the Western political tradition within a broader and more comprehensive world structure is clearly beyond the scope of this work. Such a position would force us to make far more controversial statements than anything said thus far and hence require lengthy justification. We would obviously be inclined toward extending certain basic principles of democratic government, e.g., constitutionalism and rule of law, to the world. But how to do this in a world where hunger, oppression, fear, and suspicion prevent any progress beyond the institution of a United Nations, and where the use of force for the solution of fundamental international disagreements is unthinkable, poses an almost unanswerable question. It is, nevertheless, a question which must be faced by social studies teachers. Some ethical position consistent with the basic values of our own society must be defined and applied. Our own tentative approach to this problem would include the support of any actions which would strengthen constitutional governments within other nations and which would strengthen the rule of law as a guiding principle in international relations. This criterion is difficult to apply to specific situations because of the problem of defining the conditions which foster the development of rule of law on a national or international basis. On a national basis, for example, it may be that a nation must have a high degree of literacy, intelligent leadership, and a standard of living well above subsistence before a constitutional government is even feasible. The United States might thus choose to help non-democratic countries achieve these preconditions of a democratic society. It should be clear that we are not suggesting such a stand; we are explicating the difficulty of applying the policy.

It is quite possible, we might add, that the student's ability to deal with domestic problems in an explicit ethical and legal framework will help him deal with international issues more intelligently. First, if the student learns to distinguish essential ethical commitments from superficial custom within our own society, he may well be able to make the same judgments regarding other nations. (The fact that the Soviet Union places severe restrictions on free speech and the organization of voluntary groups is greater cause for concern than the fact that the Soviet national sport is not baseball or football.) Second, by describing the ethical basis of our own governmental system, the student is introduced to the general subject of political philosophy, a much neglected subject in the social studies. Since ultimately the international struggle is going to be decided in the minds of individual human beings, the more politically sophisticated our own citizens become, the more intelligent will be their ideological choices.

In this context a comment on the much discussed topic "teaching about Communism" is in order. Teaching an explicit doctrine of hate and suspicion is inconsistent with the essential basis of our own tradition — the concept of human dignity and rational consent. And it is this doctrine which is apparently at the bottom of much of the "teaching about Communism" movement.[4] If we must surrender our basic commitment to human dignity — and to the idea that *all men* are human — in order to survive as a nation, survival, at this cost, may not be worth the price.

3. To what extent are the political-ethical concepts presented above still appropriate in a society which has been so dramatically transformed in the years since their introduction? Lindsay frames the question as follows:

> In the early nineteenth-century democracy, i.e. the democracies of the United States and Switzerland, where society being mainly agricultural was naturally democratic, there was little need for any functions of government except the function of keeping order. A naturally democratic society had to be protected from violence from within and without. "Administrative nihilism plus the policeman" was an exaggerated but not hopelessly false description of the government required for such a society. The Industrial Revolution has entirely altered the situation. If government is to serve the community, and to help to make it more of a community, it has to take on, as it has taken on, all kinds of more positive and constructive functions. If it is true to say that the purpose of organized force is negative, to keep off forces which would disturb the free life of society, no such clear line can be drawn between the many other functions performed by a modern government and those performed by voluntary associations. Compulsion fades into the background: consultation and deliberation takes its place. With this difference in the methods by which government performs its functions may go a corresponding difference in the methods of democratic control.[5]

Lindsay's statement of the dramatic change in the role of government from watchdog to participant in the life of the community is now a fact. The problems of establishing corresponding changes in democratic control, however, still face us. Implicit in Lindsay's thesis is the notion that the relationship between the individual and the government might change, but the importance of the individual would not diminish even though the importance of the voluntary group might. This assumption is seriously questioned today. A recent statement by Arthur S. Miller, bearing on this specific point, is worth quoting at length:

1. Power (as formal authority) is divided spatially (the federal system) and functionally (separation of powers).

2. The formal allocation of power in the Constitution relates only to political decisions. The other important decisions, of which those of an economic nature are of particular significance, are dealt with in express terms.

3. The twentieth century has witnessed the growth of large semi-autonomous economic organizations, called by Peter Drucker the "industrial enterprise" and by Adolf Berle the "corporate concentrate," which are the basic units of economic federalism. The name used here for these organizations is the "factory community."

4. While orthodox theory and constitutional doctrine presupposed only two entities — the State and the individual person — it is now widely believed that the isolated individual does not exist as such and that he is significant only as a member of a group. In addition to the large corporate enterprise, which includes both the managerial class and the labor union, the new groups include farm organizations, veterans' associations, and charitable foundations, among others.

5. Assuming that real power is formal authority conjoined with effective control, it can be said that no *one* person or *one* group, however large or comprehensive — including the State — exercises real power over any area of decision. Real power is diffused, shared by a congeries of groups including the State, which is probably merely the most powerful, but not necessarily the dominant, group.

6. Given this wide dispersion of power, it is important to have an arbiter among the power-wielders. Relative priorities must be assigned to the various demands, and hierarchies among the groups must be determined. This may well be the major role that the State plays in the American system today.

7. During the nineteenth and early twentieth centuries, when the negative "watchguard" theory of governmental action prevailed, the United States Supreme Court was the principal organ of State power. Umpiring the system of formal federalism and providing "a nexus between our fundamental law and our fundamental economic institutions," it formulated final policy in matters relating to political economy. Today, the Supreme Court apparently shares control of this job with Congress and the bureaucracy.

8. The urgent problems for constitutional law and theory today are the relationship of the State and the individual to the other centers of power within the nation, and the relationship of the United States to the remainder of the world.[6]

Here we can do little more than state the problem, posed in many different contexts by modern scholars. The nation has always been conceived as a community of smaller communities. A critical question now is: What is the nature of these smaller communities and the relationship between them and the individual? Is the individual so pigeonholed and restricted in the economic structure that there is little room for meaningful decision-making in the social, cultural, and political realms? The appropriateness of our political principles and instruments, as we have stated before, depends on their ability to support a pluralistic society in which the basic values of dignity and freedom can survive, and in which rational dissent is broadly tolerated. To the extent that social scientists can demonstrate that existing political instruments allow these more basic values to erode, the instruments must be rethought and either modified or replaced by new ones.

References

1. For a detailed analysis of the need to modify our governmental institutions see M. Judd Harmon, *The Search for Consensus,* Faculty Honor Lecture (Logan, Utah: The Faculty Association, Utah State University, 1964).

2. Spano v. New York, 360 U.S. 315, 318 (1959). Quoted in Richard C. Connelly, "Police Authority and Practices," *Annals of the American Academy of Political and Social Science* (1962), 339:106.

3. It should be noted that the separation of the executive and legislative functions through a written constitution, while characteristic of the "American system," does not hold in the parliamentary model. There is, in fact, much debate about the relative effectiveness of the two models in supporting the values of the modern democratic state. Probably much less controversy exists over the importance of an "independent judiciary," at least in the Anglo-American experience. See Harmon, *op. cit.,* for a discussion of separation of powers as a hindrance to necessary action.

4. One example may illustrate our point. The book *The Profile of Communism* (New York: Anti-Defamation League of B'Nai B'rith, 1951), distributed by the Anti-Defamation League, decidedly *not* a conservative or right-wing group, begins as follows: "What is Communism? Is it an integrated, centralized, worldwide movement, motivated by the Marxist-Leninist ideology, propelled by the apparatus of the supranational Communist Party, abetted by the Party's auxiliaries, powered and directed by the ruling hierarchy of the Communist Party and dictatorial government of the Union of Soviet Socialist Republics" (p. 3). Aside from this gross oversimplification, part of the statement is highly questionable on factual grounds: For example, is the movement truly integrated and centralized? Such questionable and oversimplified statements, we feel, stem from and feed on a paronoia which is already interfering with the American's more humane and rational impulses.

5. A. D. Lindsay, *The Modern Democratic State* (London: Oxford University Press, 1943), p. 286.

6. Arthur S. Miller, *Private Governments and the Constitution,* An Occasional Paper on the Role of the Corporation in the Free Society (Santa Barbara, Calif.: Center for the Study of Democratic Institutions, 1959), p. 4.

CHAPTER SIX

Selected Analytic Concepts for the Clarification of Public Issues

Up to this point it may seem that problems involving human conflict in a democracy are easily resolved. Two people or two groups within a community have an argument over a public issue. Each takes a different position. Who is right? We find out which person is basing his argument on an important value or upon a governmental principle which supports the value. Whoever can rationalize his position in terms of a supporting principle must be right; the other person must be wrong.

There are obviously a number of difficulties with this approach:

1. As most problems which affect the welfare of the American community are discussed, different individuals or groups take different positions. Usually each position can be reasonably supported by important social values.

2. Claiming that a position is supported by an important value or that a position violates some value does not necessarily make the claim true. Such claims must be examined to see exactly how the problem situation is described, as well as the extent to which the description is accurate. Often precise descriptions are not available, so one has difficulty judging the extent to which a value has in fact been violated or is supported.

3. Even when all the facts are clear, people often use differently the words which describe or label values and value-loaded situations. Terms

such as *adequate education* and *equal protection* mean different things to different people, although all may be committed to whatever values are described by these labels.

We are likely, then, to encounter problems in analyzing political controversies in our community and nation. One problem involves clarifying which values or legal principles are in conflict and choosing between or among them. A second problem involves clarifying the facts around which the conflict has developed. A third involves clarifying the meanings or uses of words which describe the controversy. As we shall see, there are different strategies for dealing with each problem. It is important, therefore, to distinguish a value problem from a factual problem and a factual problem from a definitional problem. Dealing with political issues usually means resolving disagreements in all these areas. Perhaps we can best illustrate these points, as well as how they might be treated in the classroom, by looking at a concrete incident based on an actual case presented to the Supreme Court.

The Sidewalk Speech

On a raw, windy afternoon in March, a hot-headed, earnest young student named Barry Schwartz was making a speech to a crowd in a small shopping area. The street was in a Negro neighborhood in Poughkeepsie, New York. Schwartz stood on a large wooden box on the sidewalk and shouted at the crowd in a high-pitched voice through a loudspeaker system attached to an automobile. He waved his arms, stamped his feet, and once in a while smacked a fist in his palm. He wanted to publicize a meeting of the Young Progressives of America that was to be held that evening. Among other things, Schwartz said,

"The mayor of this city is a champagne-sipping bum; he doesn't care who crushes the Negro people."

"The President of the United States is a bum."

"The Legion of American Veterans is a Nazi Gestapo."

"The Negroes don't have equal rights; they should rise up in arms and fight for their rights."

The crowd listening to Schwartz numbered 75 or 80 people, both Negro and white. It filled the sidewalk and spread out into the street. The people were restless. There was some pushing, shoving, and milling around. Some men picked up bricks and threatened to throw them at Schwartz. Lincoln Frost, who owned a nearby store, was afraid for his plate glass windows, so he phoned the police.

Lieutenant Collins and Sergeant Davis drove up in a squad car to investigate. For a while they just sat in the car and watched. Then one of the women onlookers who thought Schwartz should get a chance came over and said, "What's the matter? You scared? Can't you cops make people behave right?" A big, muscular man nearby turned around and said, "If you cops don't get that guy off his orange crate in two minutes,

I'll shove it down his throat." Then he elbowed his way into the crowd until he was very close to Schwartz.

Lieutenant Collins pushed his way after him through the crowd and asked Schwartz to break up the crowd "to prevent it from resulting in a fight." He repeated the suggestion several times. Each time Schwartz ignored the policeman and went on talking. During all this time the crowd was pressing closer around Lieutenant Collins and Schwartz. The muscular man began urging the men near him to "Get Schwartz." Finally, Collins told Schwartz he'd have to arrest him for his own safety, and ordered him to get down from the box.

Schwartz got off the box, but as Collins took him through the crowd to the squad car, he shouted, "What's happening to free speech in this country? I've got a right to say what I think even if the big-wigs don't like it. I've got a right to talk even if some bigots standing around here want me to shut up."

Schwartz was tried and convicted of disorderly conduct and sentenced to thirty days in the county jail. Schwartz appealed the conviction because he said it took away his rights under the First and Fourteenth Amendments of the American Constitution.

In discussing "The Sidewalk Speech" we can ask a number of important questions to clarify the problem. Are any important values being violated? Barry Schwartz claims his freedom of speech is abridged. The Poughkeepsie police claim that the peace and order of the neighborhood is threatened. Clearly, there is a conflict over important values. Further questions: Is there any legal basis to support these values? Does the violation of a value in these circumstances also violate a law? And even more important: Does the government have the power under the Constitution to make the law which has allegedly been violated? In this particular case, is there any constitutional protection for freedom of speech? The answer is plain, as Barry Schwartz points out: in the First and Fourteenth Amendments. We might also ask: Does the community have the authority to make laws prohibiting disorderly conduct? Again the answer is surely "yes." We now have a conflict not only between values but also between laws which are designed to protect these values. Although we know that constitutional law is supreme, we also know that the First Amendment does not necessarily protect people from unreasonable use of free speech. Assuming that we want to protect peace and order, then, how is order to be preserved? By arresting the speaker or by restraining those who threaten the speaker with violence. Which course of action is taken depends to a large degree on how "reasonable" use of free speech is defined.

This is not only a definitional and a value problem. It is closely related to an important factual issue: What is a clear and accurate description of the problem situation? The relevant factual questions in "The Sidewalk Speech" center on how much violence actually occurred and to what extent there was an immediate threat of more violence. In this connection the following factual questions might be important:

How large was the crowd?

To what extent did the crowd obstruct traffic or pedestrians?

To what extent was there "pushing, shoving, and milling around"?

How many people actually threatened Schwartz?

How serious were their intentions?

How many policemen were available to keep order?

Analyzing a case such as "The Sidewalk Speech" is a complicated business. We must identify the different kinds of problems involved: value conflicts, legal and constitutional problems, factual problems, problems regarding the interpretation or definition of value, and problems regarding the definition of terms used in the factual description. While this process of analysis is a creative endeavor, and will be done differently by different individuals, there are, we believe, concepts which might generally be useful as guidelines.

It is important to note, however, that in teaching, the objective of analyzing such a case is not simply to impart conceptual abstractions; more particularly it is to teach the ability to shift alternately from conceptual analysis to the testing ground for the validity and adequacy of the analysis — the concrete facts in the case itself. With such a goal, the "case method" is a powerful tool. Instead of being provided with pre-analyzed material which he then applies to new situations, the student is engaged in a process that allows him latitude in testing the utility of alternative conceptual systems. Cases, then, are not simply a means of *illustrating* and *teaching* concepts; they provide the grounds by which general statements about public policy can be generated and tested. The classroom discussion that follows a case will of necessity be dialectical and controversial in the type of curriculum we suggest — no one conception of a case is necessarily the "right" one. This does not preclude the idea that there are *principles of analysis,* which the teacher should have in mind, that give such discussion focus and direction in raising appropriate questions. The following sections lay out some of these principles. Again, the fact that they are made explicit does not mean they should necessarily be taught as final principles. They do, however, provide guidelines for the testing of questions which inevitably arise in the attempt to come to general principles of public policy and public conduct.

ANALYZING THREE TYPES OF DISAGREEMENT AND STRATEGIES FOR THEIR RESOLUTION

It is important at the outset to note that although we often will discuss controversies over definition, value, and fact as though they were different and distinct types of problems, they are closely related. Our purpose in this section is to describe certain distinctions between these types of problems and various strategies for dealing with them. In Chapter Seven we will try to show the interrelationships among these problems as one attempts to deal with complex social issues.

Definitional Problems

A basic problem in discussions of public controversy involves the ambiguous or confusing use of words or symbols. It is important, therefore, that words have reasonably common meanings for those taking part in a discussion. Without such common understanding, discussions are likely to be frustrating, fruitless, or even needless.

There are two main aspects to defining or describing how words are to be used. The first is ascertaining how a word is actually being used in the discussion, i.e., what meaning it has for the participants. The second is determining what the most useful definition of a word is when it becomes clear that there is disagreement over its meaning. Also related to the problem of definition, and an important element of it, is the issue of clarification. Arguments over classification, for example, can often be settled or clarified by careful definition of the class name.

Two Types of Definition. In clarifying and resolving definitional disputes it is probably useful to distinguish between two types of definitional operation: defining by example and defining by the use of general criteria. Suppose, for instance, that a creature from another planet landed in our backyard and there were severe problems of communication. If it appeared to be an intelligent being that could speak, we might want to talk to it. As a start, we might point to ourselves and say "man" (or "woman") and then point to it and say "creature," thus quickly reaching some common understanding of what to call or label each other. With a little practice, the creature could probably look at any adult human and say "man." Communicating what is meant by a term through pointing at or enumerating examples of persons, objects, actions, or any specific referent might be called a *pointing definition* or *definition by example.*

Although it is possible to create or "invent" a word-referent relationship (scientists and advertisers do it all the time), most of us communicate with labels which are learned within a highly structured cultural framework, and which are intricately woven into a complex system of meaning. When we try to define by citing examples, therefore, we are probably relating the example to an implied system of classification. Thus the effort to define one word usually involves us in the clarification of class names, and soon becomes a question of distinguishing between two classes which overlap in meaning. In these situations general criteria by which a class can be defined are ordinarily used to clarify or resolve definitional disagreement.

To illustrate the development of such a disagreement, consider the following example. Suppose we defined "democratic country" by referring to the United States, the United Kingdom, France, and Belgium. A fellow discussant, however, asks why we include Belgium and do not include the Soviet Union. We reply that the answer is simple: Belgium is a democratic country and the Soviet Union is not. He disagrees, claiming that the Soviet Union is a democracy and Belgium is a dictatorship. At this point the pointing definition has broken down.

In order to determine more precisely how we are disagreeing over the term *democratic country,* we may list specific characteristics, or *criteria,* that distinguish those countries we consider democratic from those we consider non-democratic. For example, we say a democratic country is one which (1) has a constitution that provides certain basic rights for all the people and (2) elects directly or indirectly the major officers of government. Such an attempt to delineate the appropriate uses of a word by listing the distinguishing characteristics or criteria of its referents may be called a *criterial definition.*

The Resolution of Definitional Disagreements. The initial problem, of course, is determining whether or not a term is being used in a discussion in more than one way; the second problem is how a common meaning can be established for the participants in the discussion. This is a matter of inquiry into the *facts of meaning* for the individuals involved and usually boils down to determining what shall be the "correct" usage of a word. In definitional disagreements, it is important to remember first that the "correct" relationship between a label or term and the thing for which it stands is a matter of convention. There is no "natural" relationship between a word and its referent. Using the word *boys* to label young male humans and *girls* to label young female humans, for example, is based simply on the need for common symbolic meaning if communication is to take place. We could just as well change the convention, reverse the terms, and call a young male human a girl and a young female human a boy. (This, of course, assumes agreement plus adequate dissemination of the change so that confusion would not result. It also ignores the fact that people become emotionally attached to symbol-referent relationships, tend to see them as real, and resist usages which are "unnatural," i.e., unfamiliar.) What the example points up is that a definition can be changed whenever people can be persuaded that a different example, in the case of a pointing definition, or a different set of criteria would appropriately define the word.

Since convention is the basis for definition, one approach to definitional controversy is an appeal to popular or common usage. This may entail research designed to find out how most people use the word. Since most people have neither the time nor the resources to engage in such projects, the dictionary fills the gap as an authority on word usage. If the definition found there serves as a common ground for discussion, the purpose is fulfilled. However, one must be cautious not to assume that all people will use the word as it is defined in the dictionary. Dictionary definitions are often outdated. Moreover, dictionaries sometimes do not contain words which have been in use a relatively short period of time. Or dictionary definitions may be inadequate because they are only exemplary or pointing in character, because they are circular, or because they are not complete or specific enough to meet the needs of the particular argument.

To cope with uncertainties arising from deficiencies in dictionaries, *stipulation* is often used to resolve definitional problems. The discussants spell out, or stipulate, the meaning which the word is to have in their discussion, preferably by listing agreed-upon criteria. Here again, the danger is that the definition will be assumed to be adequate outside of the specific discussion context — which, in fact, it may be. It is also essential to keep the criteria in mind as the discussion progresses because definitions can shift very subtly and imperceptibly.

The use of stipulation may well involve the process of translation for some discussants. If, for example, it is agreed that for the purposes of discussion an essential criterion of the term *democratic society* is that there is public ownership of property, any participant who is not accustomed to using the term in this way must translate it to encompass this meaning whenever the words are used in this particular discussion. It is easy to see how a shift in the standards of translation could result, causing confusion or misunderstanding.

Perhaps the most important problem in resolving definitional disputes occurs when there is disagreement over classification. Let's look again at the case of the "democratic country." Two criteria were stated having to do with the existence of a constitution and the election of officials. We have suggested that recourse to convention or stipulation is in order if there is disagreement over the correctness of these criteria. But suppose the discussants agree on the criteria but one participant still insists that the Soviet Union is a democratic country, i.e., should be classified as a democratic country, because it has a constitution and elections. To this claim the reply might well be, "In the Soviet Union there is a constitution, but it does not *in fact* restrain the government and prevent it from trampling on important rights of the people; there are elections, but they are 'rigged' by the government and do not *in fact* allow the people to freely express their will." Obviously our criteria must have greater specificity. A democratic country is one which (1) has a constitution that guarantees important rights to all the people and that is respected and obeyed by the government and (2) has elections in which the people can express their wishes freely without fear of intimidation. Before actually getting to the problem of determining whether or not the Soviet Union conforms to these criteria, we may yet have to define key terms and phrases such as *respect for basic rights* and *free elections.* The process of definition involves specifying the criteria which define the class and determining whether or not references commonly included in the class conform to the criteria and therefore whether or not the criteria are useful and adequate. The next problem of classification, once the category definitions are agreed upon, is to determine whether the controversial referent (in our example, the Soviet Union) has the characteristics implied by the class. And this is fundamentally a matter of testing factual claims — in this case gathering evidence to determine whether or not in fact constitutional restraints and free elections are part of the Soviet Union's political system.

Ideological or Value-Laden Class Names in Political Controversy. One of the major difficulties in discussing broad public issues is the extent to which labels or terms are used which stand for broad political or ideological positions. For example, we can place the following situations in a single value class.

A strong boy fighting with a weak boy.

A teacher keeping one boy after school and not keeping another boy after school, when both boys were caught breaking the same rule.

One man being allowed to vote and a second not being allowed to vote, when both have the same qualifications.

Two men making the same amount of money but one paying half of it in taxes, the other paying a quarter of it in taxes.

All of these situations can be described as violating one value position — equal treatment. We have classed them together because they evidence one characteristic — inequality. The process of putting objects or events into broad value classes and giving them a common label goes on all the time and is apparently a necessary element of political debate. As we have pointed out, however, it is not so natural to consider carefully the criteria according to which some objects or events are included in a class and others are excluded.

The use of class names is especially dangerous in that it leads toward hasty generalizations. We may see a man giving a speech criticizing the United States and classify him as "red" or Communist. Putting him in this class means that we will make certain assumptions about many of his political views. If the speech is the only information on which the classification is based, we may jump to unwarranted conclusions. General terms such as *Communist,* which are common in political arguments, are difficult to define and are often used for their emotional appeal rather than to convey a specific message. We often hear someone referred to as conservative, reactionary, liberal, left-wing, subversive, yet we rarely hear a careful definition of these terms.

We might define a Communist, for example, as one who (1) believes in the teachings of Karl Marx, (2) goes to Communist party meetings, and (3) works for world domination by Russia, China, or any country friendly to Russia or China. If these were our criteria, a person would have to meet all three to be classified as a Communist. The fact that a person believed in the teachings of Karl Marx would not be enough; we might call him a Marxist, but not a Communist. The fact that someone had gone to Communist party meetings would not give us sufficient information to classify him as a Communist; an FBI undercover agent or a curious college student might go to meetings of the Communist party.

Liberal is another ambiguous term commonly used in politics. Some men are described as liberals because they believe that the federal government should take greater leadership and spend more money to improve the general welfare of the people in all the states: through better education, more dams for public power, public aid to people for medical care. Others are called liberals because of their strong commitment to civil liberties for minority groups: voting rights for Negroes, the right of free speech for Communists. The label thus has two quite different meanings. How do we then classify a person who believes in greater federal leadership in welfare spending but who expresses no concern about the loss of civil liberties by minority groups?

The Emotional Component of Words. One of the most widely discussed aspects of controversy analysis is the emotional impact of language. A sample of the literature on this subject is instructive. The following remarks are taken from *How Do You Talk About People?* by Irving Lee:

> A story is told about the way a Greek communist newspaper reported some remarks of Paul Porter, made at a banquet in Macedonia while on an economic mission. He said, "It is indeed a pleasure to be here tonight with you good citizens of Greece. You Greeks and we Americans have very much in common. We like to eat. We like to drink. And we like to sit around and talk." The newspaper said, "Ambassador Porter said that we are just like Americans, gluttons, drunkards, and gossips."
>
> It is one of the commonplaces of studies in semantics that a number of words may refer to the same thing though each may imply strikingly different attitudes to it. As Sam Weller said, "When a poor fellow takes a piece of goods from a shop, it is called theft, but if a wealthy lady does the same thing, it is called monomania." It has been recently observed that "the rich are alcoholics and the poor are drunks." We learn rather quickly to reserve some words for use when things are considered pleasant and

desirable and others for the contrary. If you wished to express approval of someone, would you not be likely to choose the former of the following pairs? Strength of purpose — pigheadedness, generous — spendthrift, zealot — fanatic, patriot — chauvinist, progressive — new-fangled, supporter of free enterprise — capitalist.

A language will include terms which can point to things as well as convey the speaker's attitude toward them. This is relevant to our concern with evaluation, because so many people seem prone to judge others in accordance with the attitudes which accompany the words they apply to them. They not only choose words which by custom come to reflect their positive or negative notions but they are in turn influenced to look at people or things in terms of the notions implied by the terms which are used.[1]

The point is simply that political terms have strong emotional loadings and are especially difficult to define and use. Faced with such words in a discussion, we should remember to keep our thoughts on the accuracy of the description or on the criteria which define the words, not on the feelings they may summon.

To summarize: In this section we have discussed definitional problems and the problem of communication in a political controversy. We noted first that it is essential to determine whether the same words have different meanings for participants involved in a discussion, and whether different words are actually being used to suggest the same referent. If it is suspected that a disagreement has a definitional basis, communication can be clarified either by determining how the word is commonly used, i.e., what the social conventions are, or by stipulating the meaning which is to be applied to the word for the purposes of the specific discussion.

A second and related type of problem often occurs during controversies over public policy. It involves disagreement about the proper classification of an object, action, or person. The resolution of arguments over classification may entail one or more of the following steps: (1) determining what the proper class definition shall be if there is disagreement over the appropriateness or relevance of one or more of the criteria, (2) greater specification if it is found that there is disagreement or confusion over the meanings of specific words used in the criteria, and (3) inquiry into the factual description of the particular example being classified to determine whether its characteristics meet appropriate criteria.

It was also noted that because political labels are frequently used loosely one must be alert to their ambiguity and vagueness, especially when the label carries a strong emotional loading which will affect one's attitudes toward the object being classified.

Value Problems

Since we have already talked a great deal about value problems, the statements in this section are, in part, summaries of what has gone before. The act of valuing involves classifying objects or actions as "good" or "bad," "right" or "wrong." Values are those actions or objects that are valued. When we say due process is a value, we mean that to us actions or procedures labeled *due process* are good.

Personal Preferences, Aesthetic Judgments, and Social Values. Suppose we noted the following terms: *the music of Beethoven, blue neckties, equal voting rights.* If these are considered values, the phrase *is good* or *are good* is implied after each term. Intuitively, we know there is something quite different about asserting that blue neckties are good and that equal voting rights are good. Probably the most useful way to describe the distinction is in terms of the number of people our value judgment may affect and the extent to which each person may be affected. It is difficult to imagine the community's suffering any severe injury if people do not value blue neckties. This is not the case with such values as free speech and voting rights.

Values which are *not* significant enough to become the subject of general community or governmental concern we will call personal preferences. The problem of controversy over personal preference will not be dealt with here. (This is not to suggest that liking blondes rather than brunettes is not important. It is simply that such preferences are just as well left as private matters.)

Values which involve artistic taste or judgments of beauty, i.e., aesthetics, will also not be discussed. Again, they are indeed important to individuals. Unlike personal preferences, however, they are often the subject of wide discussion and social controversy.

The values with which we are mainly concerned are those political and social values—e.g., personal freedom, equality and justice, general welfare, and peace and order — which were discussed earlier. They are appropriate for discussion in a public school because they are the major concepts used by our government and private groups to justify public policies and decisions.

Values and Decisions. A value judgment suggests not only that something has been judged good or bad but also that a person will act on the basis of this judgment. A social value judgment, moreover, suggests that all people should act on the basis of the judgment. Likewise, suggested actions or decisions imply the support of a value judgment. That is, value judgments suggest decisions; decisions imply the support of value judgments. For example:

Value Judgment		*Decision*
Equal educational opportunity is good	Suggests that	Negroes should be given just as good instruction in the public schools as whites
A peaceful community is good	Suggests that	We should have an adequate police force
Free speech is good	Suggests that	We shouldn't pass laws censoring Communist literature

Decisions or policy stands describe the actions one is likely to support or carry out. Decisions can be justified by predicting that certain consequences will occur or that other consequences will be avoided if a decision is carried out. This assumes that everyone agrees on the goodness or badness of the consequences. Decisions can also be justified by demonstrating that important social values will be violated if the decision is not made.

Disagreements which center on whether or not a predicted consequence will occur as a result of a decision can often be resolved by gathering factual information and evidence to support one's prediction. Disagreements over whether or not the consequences themselves are good or bad must first be dealt with by referring both the consequences and the decisions back to important social values. For example:

Decision	*Specific Consequence*
We should arrest people who make Communist-sounding speeches because	these people will spread Communist ideas

If the person who gives this argument is confronted with evidence that arresting people who make Communist-sounding speeches does not prevent the spread of Communist ideas it weakens his position. But if he produces evidence that such arrests do in fact halt the spread of Communist ideas, someone might say, "That is bad. We should have as many people as possible know about Communist ideas. We should have a free market place of ideas."

At this point in a value disagreement, the people disagreeing can refer back to more basic social values that each wants to preserve in the community. For example:

	Decision	*Social Value*
Mr. Smith might say:	We should jail people who talk in favor of Communism because	. . such talk threatens the safety of the community.
Mr. Jones might say:	We should let everyone speak on any subject he pleases, as long as he does not use lies to damage people's reputations, because	. . . free speech is an essential ingredient of personal freedom.

Justifying decisions by asserting that they tend to support or violate basic social values forces us into the problem of value conflict. A single decision may be defended on the grounds that it preserves one social value and at the same time denounced because it violates another. In the example above, censorship of Communist speeches was defended on the grounds that it preserved peace and order and denounced on the grounds that it abridged free speech.

Confrontation between these controversial points of view, however, depends upon the assumption that there is at least *some truth* to the implied claims of consequences behind each person's value position. For example, the person who stresses the importance of peace and order assumes that Communist speeches will lead to violence and disorder and to a general weakening of important societal values. If we found upon careful investigation that there was very little chance that Communist speeches and publications would lead to violence, disorder, and the deterioration of important values, there would be no value conflict. Censorship would be seen as simply bad. If, on the other hand, we found that in several countries where Communists were given freedom of speech there was a loss of respect for law and individual freedom resulting in riots, or even revolutions, we might seriously consider some censorship on the grounds that it would help preserve a lawful society. We can see, therefore, that value conflicts may disappear when the factual assumptions behind each value position are tested.

But suppose we test the factual assumptions behind each value position and find that for a given situation any reasonable decision will lead to the violation of at least one important value. For example:

Situation	*Alternative Decisions*
The Amish, a religious group in Pennsylvania, believe that the government should not provide citizens with old-age pensions. It is part of their religious conviction that each person should take care of his own family in sickness and in old age.	1. The government can force the Amish to pay their social security taxes, which will never benefit them, and which violate their religious convictions; *or*
	2. The government can exempt the Amish from the tax and violate equal protection under the law, i.e., everyone but the Amish will be required to pay the tax.
There is a national emergency. The North Korean Communists have invaded South Korea. President Truman wants to call up several military reserve units. Many of the men in these units served three and four years in the armed forces during World War II. Their lives were disrupted once by war, and now they will be disrupted again. But the President needs troops.	1. The President can call up the troops in the reserve units and have a better-trained defense force to protect the national security; *or*
	2. The President can draft young men who have never served their country, and give all young citizens more equal treatment.

Let us assume that in these situations (and in many like them) there is a genuine value conflict, one that does not disappear when the facts are in. No simple solution exists. One cannot resolve the conflict by saying that the answer is only a matter of opinion. Public policy is at stake, and a wrong decision may affect the future of the nation. One cannot resolve it by simply saying it is a matter of definition, using the right words to describe the situation. No matter how the situation is described, there is, in some sense, a violation of fairness or justice. One cannot solve the problem by saying "Get more evidence." The evidence indicates more and more clearly that some people's rights are going to be violated in the interests of the community.

In confronting this issue we must accept the fact that there is no "correct" or "right" solution. We must create or accept that policy which least violates our concept of human dignity and which least violates any of the social values that promote human dignity. The purpose of analyzing political problems of this type is to lead to a decision which will minimize the violation of important values, not to pretend that no conflict between these values exists.

Importance of Reflective Analysis. In general, value problems are at the center of political and social disagreements. In a community which is concerned with maintaining a balance between governmental actions that benefit the community and governmental actions that protect the freedom of each individual, every one of us has an obligation to weigh in our own minds the wisdom of proposed governmental action and make a decision in terms of its benefit to the dignity of each individual. To surrender this obligation to influence governmental actions through carefully thought-out decisions can lead to loss of the freedoms that are most important to us all.

Factual Problems

We have discussed some concepts related to both definitional problems and value problems. In this section we will take up disagreements over fact — what we will call *claims*. In political argument the center of a controversy is usually a disagreement over conflicting values: Which value is more closely associated with human dignity or rational consent? Whether or not there actually is a value conflict often depends upon the accuracy of factual information. The accuracy of factual information in an argument over public decisions is important in at least two ways:

1. While a decision itself is based on the elements in a situation which each person thinks are good and bad, right and wrong, and cannot be "proved" true or false, the decision very soon leads to certain implied factual considerations. For example, the statement "Voting rights of Negroes in the South are violated" implies certain facts. This is quite a different statement from "Negroes should have full voting rights," which does not say whether or not Negroes have these rights. Thus, it is important to establish the facts suggested by the claim that a value has been violated before assuming that a value conflict exists. After a careful investigation of the facts all may agree that there is no value conflict at all.

2. In a political controversy people make factual predictions to support a value position. For example, it is often stated that a social security program guaranteeing unemployment assistance and old-age pensions will weaken the initiative and self-reliance of workers; or that high personal income taxes weaken the initiative of business and professional people because most of what they earn will be taken in taxes by the government. Although often such arguments are put forward by people who favor private property rights over efforts of the government to provide for the general welfare, the arguments themselves depend upon the reliability of specific factual claims, not upon the validity of one's values. The dispute is not over whether property rights or taxes are good but rather over whether or not governmental action will, in fact, lead to certain undesirable consequences: a lazy and irresponsible work force.

Determining the Reliability of Factual Claims. It is important to distinguish among *conclusions* drawn from specific observations of events, the *observations* themselves, and the *events* observed. An event may be defined as a happening or a state of affairs in the world around us. All knowledge, as we define knowledge, depends upon the observation and description of these events. The raw material of an event consists of living things, objects, and actions. When we describe events we are actually describing our perception of events. We never know *for sure* what the exact nature of an event is. We know only what our senses have told our brain and what our brain has interpreted the event to mean. These general interpretations of specific observations we are here calling *conclusions*. The distinction between factual observation and conclusion is well illustrated by the following anecdote.

President Eliot of Harvard enjoyed telling the story of an experience he once had, illustrating proper caution in drawing a conclusion. When he entered a crowded New York restaurant, he handed his hat to the doorman. As he came out he was astonished to see the doorman promptly pick his hat out of the hundreds there and hand it to him. In his surprise he asked, "How did you know that was my hat?" "I didn't know that was your hat, sir," was the answer. "Why then," asked Mr. Eliot, "did you hand it to me?" Very courteously the doorman replied, "Because you handed it to me, sir."[2]

When a factual conclusion is questioned, we usually defend it in two ways. First, we try to show that specific observations tend to support the more general conclusion. Second, we try to show that other facts fit into a logical pattern if the conclusion under question is also assumed to be true.

For example, suppose we make the claim

Workers who belong to labor unions are better off than workers who have no such affiliation.

First we must settle the definitional problem of what "better off" means. Suppose we agree that "better off" is defined in such terms as wages, working conditions, vacation pay, sick leave, pension funds, and job security. The first way we might support the statement is to look at more specific claims. We might find that

1. Truck drivers in the Teamsters Union get 45 per cent higher wages than non-union truck drivers.
2. Construction workers in Georgia are paid less than construction workers in New York City. The construction workers in Georgia are largely unorganized, while the construction workers in New York City almost all belong to unions.

The greater number of specific claims we can identify which tend to support the conclusion we are trying to prove, the more reliable the conclusion becomes.

A second way to support the claim is to relate it to other general facts which are accepted as true. For example, we might cite a dramatic rise in wages paid to unskilled factory workers between the years 1935 and 1940, knowing that this was the period when many unskilled factory workers joined unions. These facts would be consistent with the conclusion that union workers are better off than non-union workers. (Note that this does *not* prove that joining unions was the cause of higher wages.) In general, then, we back our factual conclusions by giving specific information which supports the general conclusion under dispute and by showing that the conclusion is logically related to other facts.

Specific claims are descriptive statements about events occurring at a particular time in a particular place. "Franklin Roosevelt died in 1945." "The United States dropped two atomic bombs on Japan in August 1945." While the exact time or place may not be stated, these are examples of specific claims. There is, however, another kind of claim which is not tied to a particular time and place. For example:

1. Negroes are not as intelligent as whites.
2. Depressions occur when corporations refuse to increase the wages of workers to keep pace with increase in production efficiency.

These claims describe or summarize events which allegedly occur consistently and predictably. They are general claims or *generalizations*. Generalizations tend to be confirmed when we find specific examples to support them. In the generalizations listed above we would

1. Look at individual Negroes and whites, or look at groups of Negroes and whites, to find out whether or not Negroes were *generally* as intelligent as whites.
2. Compare periods in our history in which production efficiency increased rapidly and wages remained the same, and see whether such periods were followed by depressions.

Generalizations are a particular kind of conclusion arrived at by looking at a number of instances of a type of event. Note that they not only summarize a number of specific claims or facts but imply that, because particular types of events have been observed in the past, evidence gathered in the future will probably support the general conclusion already reached. In this sense, all generalizations are predictions. In checking whether or not a generalization is sound, it is important to evaluate the number and reliability of specific instances or specific facts which tend to support the generalization.

We commonly call generalizations, as well as specific claims, *facts*. As has just been pointed out, whether or not a generalization, like a specific claim, is a fact depends upon the reliability and quantity of evidence supporting it. *Evidence* is defined here as any statement that can be used to support the truth or reliability of another statement. Thus, evidence can be specific or general. It is likely, however, to be more specific than the statement it supports.

For example, the general conclusion "The United States is the richest nation in the world" can be supported by many "facts." These facts can be generalizations or general conclusions: The United States produces more cars than any other nation; the United States produces more wheat than any other nation; and so on. Each general statement can then be supported by a more specific statement. Thus we can build a general-to-specific chain of evidence:

The United States is the richest nation in the world [because]

It produces more cars per capita than any other nation [which is confirmed by the fact that]

The United States produced five million cars last year and this was more than the number produced by all other nations combined [which is confirmed by figures recently released by]

The United States Department of Commerce indicating the number of cars produced in the United States and abroad.

Each more specific statement could be considered "evidence" supporting the statement above it. When generalizations are questioned, we try to back them with more specific generalizations, statistics, or reliable sources.

Statistics. A statistic is a numerical estimate based on a count of several events that have been observed. It summarizes a number of observations. Some statistical statements are not generalizations because they refer to specific observations that have already been made and assume nothing about the nature of future observations. However, some statistical statements are generalizations because, while they may be based on a specific enumeration of events, they go on to a general inference or prediction. For example, we might look at the rate of economic growth of the Soviet Union and that of the United States in terms of specific statistics. A summary of these observations would be a descriptive statistic. If we went on to conclude that the Soviet Union has, in general, a higher rate of economic growth than the United States, this would be an inference, or generalization, based on the statistic.

Sources. When a specific claim, a generalization, or a statistic is questioned, we often try to prove its reliability by identifying where we obtained the information, i.e., its source. The following types of sources are convenient labels to begin to describe sources and test their reliability.

1. *Intuition as a source of evidence.* Intuition is often called "common sense." Someone supports a statement by saying, "It's common sense." If pressed, he may go on to explain, "Well, I just know that it is true." Many claims we believe to be true are based on intuitive evidence. Intui-

tion is, as a rule, a poor source of evidence because it offers no way of proving to other people that our claim is a fact and that their claim is false. When there is a factual disagreement, it is usually best to look beyond intuition and seek other sources of evidence.

Intuition is, however, related to two other types of evidence which we shall discuss. In the first place, intuitions are often based on experiences the person has had. So a statement that "I just have a feeling that the Chinese people will never be able to revolt against the Communists" may actually have some implicit factual basis; i.e., there may be observational data sufficient to warrant a reasonable "hunch." Or if the person said that it was just "common sense" that such a revolution would not take place now, he may actually have based this statement on some historical data with which he is familiar. In this case it would be important to move to the evaluation of those data. If one had to make a choice between relying on intuition supported by no experiences or information and intuition rooted in some concrete evidence even though not thoroughly substantiated by it, the latter would certainly provide a firmer ground for action.

It should also be recognized that some intuitions are more "respectable" than others because of specific past experiences an individual has had or because he seems to have particularly valid insights about some things. For example, we would probably give Ambassador Thompson's "hunch" about how the Russians would react to a specific treaty proposal a great deal of weight even though his judgment was based only on a "hunch." So, while in general we should apply rigorous standards of proof to intuitively based claims, we should at the same time recognize that an intuitional statement by a person with some competence in the field under consideration, even though not substantiated by concrete evidence, is probably a better basis for a decision than no evidence at all.

2. *Authority as a source of evidence.* The claim is made by a history student that "Germany was defeated in World War II." When we ask him how he knows, he says, "My history book says so." Someone makes the claim that there has been a revolution in a Latin-American country. He says he knows it is true because he read it in yesterday's *New York Times*. Often a person faced with the problem of proving a claim points to someone else who has made the claim. The "someones" are usually people, like the author of a history book or a *New York Times* reporter, who are supposed to know more than we do about a given claim. In othei words, these are people who we believe are reliable authorities.

What makes an authority reliable? The following questions can be used to gather evidence of reliability:

a. Is the authority a firsthand observer of the events about which he tells? Did the newspaper reporter, for instance, actually witness the Latin-American revolution?

b. If the authority is not a firsthand observer, does he state who told him the claims he is repeating?

Different people may present contradictory reports, even though they have read or heard the same piece of information. It is important, therefore, to know the original source from which each person got his information so that we can find out what it really said. Because we cannot check testimony unless we know where to find it, most reliable authorities indicate the source of their information.

c. Is the authority an expert on the subject about which he is writing? How much training and experience has he had in his field?

Someone may report that Brazil is becoming a Communist country. This testimony may very probably require knowledge about Communism, knowledge about the leaders of Brazil and its history and tradition. Before believing the claim that Brazil is becoming a Communist country, we must be convinced that the man who made the claim has the necessary knowledge to make accurate observations on the subject. When an authority is reporting an observation for which technical knowledge is necessary, it is important to obtain information about his technical competence.

d. Is there any information about the authority that would lead us to believe that he has a personal bias or prejudice?

If the officer of a corporation is asked whether high corporation taxes are slowing the growth of business, he will almost certainly answer "yes." If asked why, he will give a number of very good reasons. It is possible that he has given a fair view of the situation and that corporations are actually overtaxed. It is also possible, however, that he favors corporations because he runs one, and has built a set of reasons to justify his own biases.

The word *bias* indicates that a strong personal feeling about the goodness or badness of a person, action, or object may interfere with the evaluation of truth or falsity of a related claim or set of claims. People do not usually admit that they have biases or prejudices. They prefer to think that they believe certain claims because they are actually true.

A person who has no personal "interest" in a subject under discussion is often referred to as "disinterested." He does not have money, property, or his reputation at stake in the outcome of an issue. Because he has no personal interests involved, he has no obvious reason to be biased for or against the claim under question. The corporation officer would not be disinterested about taxes because his living depends on running a corporation profitably, which in turn may depend on convincing us (or the government) that corporations are being overtaxed.

An authority can, however, have a personal interest in an issue and still make reliable claims. Many reporters, like the southern Negro who makes a statement on race relations, have a personal interest in what they report. The way to evaluate the testimony of any reporter who we suspect has a personal interest in an issue is to attempt to assess whether his interest prevents him from giving accurate testimony. We can determine this by asking other questions about the authority's account.

e. Does the authority contradict himself at any point?

Does the authority give a careful, consistent argument? For example, the corporation officer may claim that corporations are being "taxed broke" and then in another setting boast about the high dividends paid to the stockholders.

f. Are the claims supported by other authorities?

The southern Negro claims there is discrimination in the South. If other authorities familiar with the South agree with him, we would tend to accept the Negro's claim.

These are only a few of the more important questions we may ask about authorities to help us judge their reliability. It should also be noted here that people sometimes look for symbols of authority which may have little to do with the question of whether or not a person is competent. Some of these questionable symbols are suggested below:

Many children and young people believe that *being an adult* makes a person an authority. We commonly assume that the older we get, the more we know. People sometimes try to prove claims by saying that an older person "told me so." Older people obviously have limited knowledge, and, in fact, often disagree with one another.

Some people believe anything they read. *A claim in print* — black print on white paper — seems to cast a magic spell of seeming truth. Yet it is almost as easy to make false or exaggerated claims on paper as it is by word of mouth. It is just a little more expensive.

Many people believe that because a man has *status* — because he is *important* in the eyes of the community — he is a reliable authority on all subjects. Businessmen, political leaders, doctors, television stars, and people with a great deal of money have high status. We often believe what they say, whether or not they are expert on the subject about which they are making claims.

3. *Personal observation as a source of evidence.* A third source of evidence is direct personal observation. While in some situations it is one of the best types of evidence, it does have important limitations, especially in the study of political controversy, where one often cannot prove things by personal observations. In evaluating historical evidence, it is impossible to set up a demonstration that enables us to see firsthand exactly what happened in some earlier period. For this reason, in issues of public policy which depend largely on historical knowledge we try to prove things more often by use of authorities than by use of personal observation and demonstration.

Another difficulty is the tendency to see what we wish to see or hear what we wish to hear, selecting and remembering those aspects of an experience which are most consonant with our previous experience and background.

4. *Proof by analogy.* Frequently the lengthy process of carefully evaluating evidence in the effort to support a claim is bypassed in favor of a much simpler method — proof by analogy. Someone claims, for example, that a constitution is necessary to run a government. Instead of gathering evidence to show that his claim is true, he simply says, "A written constitution is as necessary to a government as a rulebook is to an orderly game of football." We know that a complicated game like football would be very confusing without a rulebook. We know that government is complicated too. We are likely to accept the claim that government and football are alike in requiring a written constitution or a rulebook because they are alike in being complicated. We might then conclude that memory or informal customs can't be depended on to solve disputes in government any more than in football. A comparison is made between something simple or familiar and something more abstract or complex.

Analogies can, however, be misleading. Although two objects, acts, or situations may be analogous in certain ways, they may be different in other important ways. A football rulebook spells things out in great detail. A constitution tends to be more general. If our Constitution, written almost 200 years ago, had been very specific, it would be out of date today and perhaps have been cast aside long since. Constitutional amendments are much more difficult to make than changes in a football rulebook and have more serious consequences for the community. In these respects a constitution is very different from a football rulebook. The person comparing two similar objects or situations in an effort to prove a point, therefore, must be careful to notice the ways in which they are different as well as the ways in which they are alike.

Sampling: How Much Evidence Do We Need? We have talked about the need for distinguishing between conclusions and evidence, or specific observations which are given to support them. A further point is that the accuracy and reliability of conclusions based on specific claims depend not only on the *truth* of the specific claims upon which the conclusion is based but also upon the *number* and *type* of events actually observed. In other words, we have to be concerned not only with the *reliability* of our evidence but also with the *amount* of evidence. The process of selecting and observing facts which may support a particular generalization or conclusion is called *sampling*. There are two important considerations to keep in mind in evaluating the sample of evidence supporting a conclusion. (1) The sample must be large enough to justify the generalization or conclusion. If we assert that "the average labor union member is dissatisfied with his labor leaders," it is better to have asked 1000 members than to have asked 10. (2) The sample must be representative of the types of events about which conclusions are to be drawn. To conclude that union members are dissatisfied with their leaders, the evidence should be based on the sampling of a variety of different kinds of unions in a variety of different kinds of industries. Some labor unions, for example, are made up mainly of unskilled workers. Others are mostly for skilled workers. Still others are organized on an industry-wide basis, like those of the steel and rubber workers, and include both skilled and unskilled workers. If a classification such as "skilled" versus "unskilled" might be related to the type of leadership a union has, or to whether or not the worker might be dissatisfied with this leadership, we would want to be certain that the sample of workers included a representative number of workers who belonged to both kinds of unions.

Telling How Sure We Are That Factual Statements Are Reliable. Whether or not a claim is actually true depends upon the quality and quantity of evidence supporting it. Because evidence is always limited, we never know for sure whether a claim is absolutely correct or absolutely false. And since there is always some degree of doubt about the truth or falsity of a claim, we need some way to express the degree of certainty we feel in making a factual statement.

When there is a great deal of evidence to support a claim, it is usually called a *fact*. In our terms, a fact is a claim that can be proved beyond reasonable doubt, e.g., Abraham Lincoln was elected President in 1860. This does not mean that the statement is absolutely true; it may still be possible to cast doubt on its reliability. However, for all intents and purposes, we can treat it as true. Specific claims are more likely to be true beyond reasonable doubt than are conclusions.

In many cases there is scarcity of evidence supporting a claim, or some contradictory evidence. The history of labor unions shows, for example, that they usually have helped workers, although there is also some evidence that unions have damaged the workers' interests. When most of the evidence available indicates that a statement like "Labor unions help workers" is true, we can say that a statement is *probably true*.

When the great preponderance of evidence indicates that a statement is not true, the statement can be called *false beyond reasonable doubt*. This also is a fact, if in a negative sense.

When most of the evidence indicates that a statement is false, we might say that the statement is *probably false*.

Some statements cannot be thought of in any of these terms because the evidence is too scanty or because what evidence is available is too contradictory. When such situations arise, we can consider the statements *doubtful* or *controversial.* It is sometimes important, however, not to accept doubtful or controversial statements as they stand, but rather to deal with statements at a lower level of generality which may be susceptible of proof with additional evidence. For example, in arguments over the race problem in America, a common issue raised is whether or not there is a genetic basis for intellectual differences between Negroes and whites. The evidence on this issue is so cloudy that almost any statement one can make is, at best, controversial. It is well established, however, that in general the white performs better than the Negro on intelligence tests and measures of academic achievement. This fact may itself require clarification and qualification quite apart from the question of whether one can adequately deal with the more general question of innate intellectual differences.

While the language one uses in describing certainty of knowledge may seem trivial, this often seems to be a point on which arguments become stalemated. The simple true-false dichotomy sets a requirement that, in many cases, is unattainable. What is suggested here is a rhetoric allowing for degrees of provisional truth.

Loaded Statements: The Thin Line Between Value Judgments and Factual Claims. We have already discussed the problem of loaded definitions and labels. The general problem of affectively toned language is even more difficult to deal with when considered in the context of total statements. The fact of the matter is that value judgments and claims are seldom clearly separated in statements. More often values and preferences are woven into factual claims, which are then commonly called loaded statements.

Two questions can always be asked about any loaded statement: (1) Does the statement contain an accurate descriptive claim? and (2) Do we agree or disagree with the value or preference that the statement expresses? Let's ask these two questions of the following statement: "The President spends more time vacationing than he does taking care of public business." This can be treated as a claim and subjected to a factual test, or we can simply react to the implied value judgment. In answering the two questions about this statement, we may find that (a) we like the President even though he plays golf more than he attends to public business (we accept the accuracy of the facts but we disagree with the preference expressed); (b) or we dislike the President even though he spends most of his time attending to public business (we agree with the preference expressed but we do not accept the accuracy of the facts); (c) or we like the President and know that he spends most of his time attending to public business (we disagree with the preference and do not accept the accuracy of the facts expressed); (d) or we dislike the President because he spends more time vacationing than he does attending to public business (we accept the accuracy of the facts and agree with the preference expressed). The point is that we must be careful to analyze both the feelings and the claims expressed in a loaded statement, for, although our values may differ from those implied in the loaded statement, we may be forced to agree that the facts are correct.

Sometimes it is possible to change a few key words and thereby change the value-loading implied in the statement even though the facts expressed remain the same. For example, a person might say, "Through radical and reckless spending on socialistic schemes our state is now on the verge of bankruptcy and financial disaster." Or he might say, "In our effort to provide state funds to give a decent standard of living to the sick, the needy, and the disabled we have spent much money, and new sources of revenue are now needed to keep our state solvent." From a factual point of view, both statements may be saying pretty much the same thing. However, the feelings expressed by the two statements are quite different.

It is important that we understand clearly why we are attacking or defending a statement. Are we doing it on the basis of its factual meaning or on the basis of its value implication? Unless the basis of attack is clear, we may end up defending a factual claim simply because it "sounds good" rather than because it can be supported by evidence.

Conclusion

We have now talked about three different kinds of disagreement: disagreement over the use or meaning of words, disagreement over the relative importance of certain principles of social and political conduct, and disagreement over the accuracy or plausibility of certain events in the world around us. A controversial discussion may embrace disagreements falling into one or more types, and the relationship between them may be subtle and complex. Categorizing disagreements in this way is a useful initial step in the analysis of political discussion, since the appropriateness of one's approach to the controversy depends upon seeing the specific nature of the conflict. Intense discussions over the value of fallout shelters during the summer and fall of 1961 illustrate this point very well. The following questions were commonly raised: (1) After an atomic war, would life be worth living in the midst of what was left? (2) Would a shelter program actually decrease or increase the likelihood of war? (3) Does a man have the right to lock his neighbor out of his shelter to protect his own family?

The initial strategies for dealing with these three questions might be quite different. In the first question a great deal hinges on the definition of two terms: *worth living* and *what was left*. The second term (*what was left*) can immediately be translated into a factual issue whereas the first term (*worth living*) explicitly presents a value issue. The second question is clearly a factual one. The third, however, is again a value question. Discussions commonly raised these important questions but failed to deal with them systematically. Each antagonist tended to dwell on those issues he intuitively felt favored his side of the argument; he refused to deal with the issues which tended to operate against him. If one is aware of the fact that discussion becomes more fruitful when individuals go beyond the initial statement of issues to the question of an appropriate strategy for resolution, the process of rational consent may hopefully be carried out with greater intelligence. This chapter has sought to provide a framework with which sources of disagreement may be conceptualized as well as to suggest strategies by which different types of controversy may be clarified or resolved.

References

1. Irving Lee, *How Do You Talk About People?* (New York: Anti-Defamation League of B'nai B'rith, 1956), p. 18.
2. Walter B. Cannon, *The Way of an Investigator* (New York: W. W. Norton & Company, Inc., 1945), p. 337, quoted in Lee *op. cit.*, p. 13.

CHAPTER SEVEN

The Use of a Jurisprudential Framework in the Teaching of Public Issues

In the last three chapters we have attempted to develop some concepts that can be used in relating moral imperatives, principles of government, and standards of proof. These can be fitted together into a framework which allows the teacher — and the student — to focus on a limited number of important questions whenever issues of public policy arise. A curricular approach needs a "handle" for easy reference. We have called our model simply a "legal-ethical," or "jurisprudential," framework. It has been difficult to label because of its complexity; it combines several ingredients not commonly put together in the social studies curriculum. Beginning with a type of contemporary issue commonly mentioned in the problems of democracy course, but initially stating the issue in terms of a concrete setting most often included in "current events" discussions, it then relates the contemporary case to cases which range widely in time and space, appealing especially to historical analogies to broaden the context of discussion. The initial questions raised by this material tend to be "should"-type ethical questions, but the class is inevitably thrust into legal, factual, and definitional questions when the students' own views of the "good" solution are compared with other "legitimate" social solutions. It is this amalgamation of law-government, ethics, contemporary, and historical factual questions developed around perennial issues of public policy that we refer to as *jurisprudential teaching.*

It is important to distinguish between jurisprudential teaching and what is commonly called "critical thinking." Many of the concepts developed in Chapter Six are ordinarily associated with the latter — in both English and social studies classes. Critical thinking in this context refers to the ability to differentiate factual statements from opinion statements, the ability to identify logical fallacies, etc. While there is clearly a relationship between such a notion of "critical thinking" and the approach described here, there are major differences. Our approach emphasizes the clarification of two or more legitimately held points of view as they bear on a public policy question. In general there is much less concern with rhetorical devices or the logic of deductive reasoning than with the anatomy of legitimate communication and persuasion.

The distinction between the conventional teaching of "critical thinking" or applied logic and the approach suggested here can, perhaps, best be understood by thinking about the pedagogical strategies employed in each. The direct teaching of "critical thinking" usually involves the analysis of the persuasive message (sometimes referred to as propaganda) or the analysis of different accounts of the same events to illustrate the problem of interpreting information and drawing conclusions. In the jurisprudential framework, the teacher is likely to begin the discussion by reading a provocative message presenting a controversial situation and quickly move to a dialogue about the substance of the issue or problem described in the message. What he seeks to analyze is less the controversy-provoking message than the disputative discussion about the controversy that ensues. Our focus, then, is on the dialogue, either between teacher and student or among students.

The role of the teacher in such a dialogue is complex, requiring that he think on two levels at the same time. He must first know how to handle himself as he challenges the student's position and as his own position is challenged by the student. This is the socratic role. Second, he must be sensitive to and aware of the general processes of clarification or obscuration that take place as the dialogue unfolds. He must, that is, be able to identify and analyze complicated strategies being employed by various protagonists to persuade others that a particular stand is "reasonable" or "correct." Nor is it sufficient for the teacher simply to teach a process of questioning evidence, questioning assumptions, or pointing out "loaded words." In matters of public policy, factual issues are generally handmaids to ethical or legal stands, which cannot be sloughed off as "only matters of opinion." Clarification of evaluative and legal issues, then, becomes a central concern. At this point in the curriculum the student is not taught to believe or accept certain values but rather to clarify his evaluative commitments and to understand the relationships among the justification of a value position, the clarification of a definitional issue, and the proof process involved in a factual issue.

It should be stressed again that teaching oneself to be sensitive to strategies of justification, clarification, and proof requires the teacher to "double think" or think at two levels simultaneously. He must be aware of the substantive issues on which the controversy has focused *and* the intellectual process by which these issues might be clarified, if not resolved. Moreover, it is our contention that the intellectual processes or strategies are much more complex than have conventionally been described in "critical thinking" or "how to think" educational literature. Below we suggest a few such strategies by way of illustration. The context is obviously *not* one in which the teacher simply describes these strategies to students. The student must, in fact, engage in a controversial discussion before the definition of a strategy becomes relevant or meaningful. Such engagement may be between the teacher and the student or between students. Again we would affirm that such discussions are not *simply* to teach the student intellectual process, nor are they only to teach about the topic under discussion. There is a dual purpose requiring a dual intellectual process by the teacher, and eventually by the student: the student must learn the legal, ethical, and factual substance of the issues under discussion, the way this information relates to his own personal knowledge and values, *and* sensitivity to the general processes by which the issues might be clarified.

The second or analytic level, moreover, involves not only *identifying* definitional, evaluative, or factual problems that are embedded within broader public issues but also awareness of the more complex relationships among these different kinds of problems. In a controversial discussion there are undoubtedly an infinite number of patterns by which these problems can be usefully related. At this point we will suggest only a few such patterns which commonly arise in political controversy, and show how the three dimensions of political conflict play a part. We do *not* think it useful or desirable for students to "memorize" something called "patterns of intellectual clarification." The point is that the teacher, and in turn the students, hopefully will develop a general rhetoric for describing strategies involved in political arguments. At best, the patterns described below can only suggest that it is possible to talk about strategies of persuasion in a useful way; they do not constitute a "handbook for public debate."

Pattern 1. Establishing the Point at Which a Value is Violated: The Factual Emphasis

The problem of determining *when* a social situation violates an important social value is both definitional — does the value term apply? — and evaluative. Arguments along these lines, however, often center on a descriptive controversy over the nature of the situation under discussion, emphasizing factual disagreement.

In school segregation, for example, the argument often has focused on the issue of whether or not the separate schools provided for the Negro were in fact equal to those provided for whites in terms of objective criteria like quality of buildings, teaching load, teacher salary, and physical equipment. Both antagonists in such an argument may assume that separate-but-equal could be a legitimate answer to the problem of race relations in the schools, but they disagree on whether or not Negro schools will ever be brought up to white standards under segregated conditions. The 1954 desegregation decision of the Supreme Court was finally argued on such factual grounds. Both segregationists and integrationists agreed on the value of an equal education for the Negro. The question was: Does the situation that exists (segregation) prevent the Negro from getting an equal education?

A second point in the segregation problem which may begin with a value statement but soon reverts to a factual controversy is the "self-determination" issue: the right of each state to deal with its own race relations problems as it sees fit — the states' rights doctrine. The southerner argues this position because he believes that most southerners are violently opposed to desegregation. Some integrationists have questioned this assumption, asserting that in fact many southern moderates would prefer integration to breaking the law but are intimidated and forced to remain silent by more vocal extremists. Whether or not the majority of southerners would prefer to comply with the Supreme Court's decision of 1954 or the Civil Rights Act of 1964 is, of course, an empirical, or factual, question.

It is on the basis of factual questions such as these that political disputes can perhaps best be initiated. Unless solid evidence exists that the description of the situation by an "injured" party is to some extent accurate, there is little sound basis for extended debate.

We are not suggesting, however, that once the problem situation is accurately described the factual issues are resolved. More probably the argument will proceed through *alternating cycles* among the various issues. For example, the controversy may well begin with an "atrocity story" describing a situation in which an individual or group is allegedly being treated unjustly. Implicit but obvious is the assumption that an important value is violated. The argument may turn from emphasis on the violation of the value to the question of whether or not the atrocity story is true or representative of a larger class of situations. (Are the poor educational facilities provided for Negroes in rural Mississippi representative of all segregated Negro facilities?) The factual discussion will often reveal a wide spectrum of degrees of justice and injustice.

The alternating-cycle concept in argument analysis has direct implications for teaching. Teachers commonly comment that students must know the "facts" before they can get into issues of public policy, which inevitably involve "opinions" or values. This is a somewhat simplistic way of stating the problem. A critical pedagogical objective is teaching the student to select those factual claims (not facts) which, if their validity were known, would have an important bearing on the controversy. To teach the student the "relevant background information" before the argument begins short-circuits the opportunity for the student to evaluate the relevance of facts needed to argue policy questions intelligently. This is not to say that the student should start discussing an issue with no background whatsoever. It does contend that the student should learn to accumulate information as he sees its bearing on the central legal and ethical issues surrounding a public question.

Pattern 2. *Establishing the Point at Which a Value Is Violated: The Emphasis Upon Evaluative Clarification*

We may now look at the problem of clarifying the hypothetical point at which a value is violated, e.g., when liberty becomes license; when equal opportunity becomes enforced mediocrity. Extreme violations of American social and political values are generally obvious to the large majority of citizens. Such violations create special problems for political decision-making when they are suppressed or ignored by an uninterested majority or when they can be justified by facts indicating that other equally important values are thereby maintained, e.g., censorship in wartime. In the center of the value continuum, however, is that vague area in which the citizen may not know whether an abuse being perpetrated is sufficiently important to require governmental action or governmental coercion.

For example, to what extent would the policy of separate-but-equal, actually enforced, be a violation of "equal protection under the law"? The history of the separate-but-equal doctrine is itself a study of conflicting interpretations of the point at which justice or dignity is sufficiently violated so that the Supreme Court feels obligated to interfere with the rights of the states. This kind of conflict cannot immediately be resolved or clarified with facts. There is often agreement on the facts. One person describes segregation as a badge of slavery and therefore a violation of equal protection. The other person describes segregation as protecting the cultural integrity of two distinct racial groups and sees no violation of constitutional rights.

The Use of Analogy in the Process of Ethical Clarification. One approach to the clarification of this type of conflict is the use of comparative cases or analogies. The case in question is analyzed by comparing and contrasting it with an array of real or hypothetical situations in which are embedded the same value conflict. We then ask ourselves which of the comparative cases are violations of an important value and how similar these cases are to the one in question.

Let us again take the example of racial segregation in the public schools. Suppose we compare and contrast this with segregation by sex in the public schools in areas such as the practical arts or physical education. Boys and girls are normally given separate facilities and training for physical education. If each group has equally good instruction and equipment, is our idea of equality violated? Probably not. We might rationalize our position by saying that there are good reasons for segregating the sexes in physical education. It is commonly assumed that girls are not physically equal to boys. They have different interests. Boys and girls are somewhat self-conscious and modest in the presence of one another, especially in gym suits. But would these arguments not apply as well to racial segregation? Perhaps girls could achieve the same physical prowess as boys if they did not have a negative self-image concerning their ability to perform athletic feats.

Now let us take a second comparative situation. Would segregation by social class be a violation of equal protection? Suppose the population were divided into thirds according to income, and three separate school systems for these groups were established. Most Americans, including racial segregationists, would probably oppose this kind of segregation (although many schools in fact condone and promote it). But wouldn't the protection of the cultural integrity of various social classes apply as an argument for this kind of segregation, as well as for racial segregation? (One might even say that the lower classes provide a kind of uninhibited response to life which invigorates the culture; efforts should therefore be made to preserve its integrity.)

We thus have three situations, each violating with increasing intensity the common use of the equal protection concept. Americans in general appear to have no great stake in the inequalities brought about by sexual segregation or discrimination in physical education. Racial segregation is subject to much controversy: Is it or is it not a violation of equal protection? Undoubtedly, most Americans would be horrified if social class segregation were legalized and enforced in the public schools.

The use of analogous cases allows us to broaden the context of discussion by developing a series of points along the continuum of equality-inequality, and thus to clarify the depth of our own commitment to a particular value. It does not, however, solve the problem of how to determine which particular case provides the critical point at which equality must have priority over cultural self-determination. This point is determined by each individual, although all may agree that a common legal standard should exist.[1]

The use of analogous cases not only clarifies the range of situations we might consider as violations and non-violations of a particular value but also impels us to seek criteria which will distinguish one situation from another. For example, the person who sees sexual segregation as legitimate but racial and social class segregation as wrong may say that the basic difference is that men and women, boys and girls, are really considered social equals in the society, whereas Negroes and members of lower-class families are not. (This, of course, may be subject to question.) On the other hand, the person who sees sexual segregation and racial segregation as similar but who sees social class segregation as the violation might assert that, while many lower-class people want to be like middle-class people and live near them, girls do not want to participate in sports with boys and the great majority of Negroes do not want to live among or go to school with whites.

The Return to Factual Problems. Once we begin to categorize one group of cases as a "violation of equality" and another group as a "non-violation," we again move from our intuitive judgment of "rights" in the controversial situation to questions of fact. In this situation we might ask: Do women and girls really feel equal to men and boys, or do they envy them as social superiors? Do most Negroes really want to move from a segregated way of life to closer association with whites? The analogy thus leads us to identify characteristics in several similar situations which differentiate those that violate a value from those that apparently do not. Analogy thus becomes a powerful instrument of rational ethical clarification.

The use of analogy in *teaching* issues of public controversy deserves comment on two counts. In logical terms, teachers tend to be suspicious of the analogy as a method of "false reasoning," or at least one of questionable validity. We would point out, first, that proving a factual point by the use of analogy is quite different from presenting an array of analogous situations to clarify and rationalize decisions on public policy. Attempting to differentiate among seemingly similar cases is, in fact, a fundamental element of legal reasoning.

Second, the use of analogy is probably the most effective way to test the consistency of a student's policy stand and to show him that the major problem of justification is rationalizing inconsistency rather than learning how to be consistent. (Americans do believe in segregation under certain circumstances.) Moreover, "good" analogies, i.e., analogies which require more than a trivial rebuttal, are often difficult to come by. They may be hypothetical situations or real cases. In the planning of a controversial discussion, therefore, it is usually important to anticipate what issues will come up, what inconsistencies should be illustrated, and what analogies can serve this purpose. (See Chapter Eight for examples of unit plans with analogies.)

Pattern 3. The Clarification of Value Conflicts

In dealing with public controversy probably the most important type of issue revolves around a value conflict or political dilemma. A political dilemma occurs when we are faced with a choice in which any of the available alternatives will enhance one value at the expense or violation of another. Dilemmas are commonly handled in two ways: We either deny, distort, or repress the negative consequences which attend our actions so that the value violation remains below the level of consciousness; or we maintain that the value we are preserving is more important than the value we are violating — we assign static priorities to values. The latter strategy deserves more extensive comment.

The usual static value priority approach, which was discussed at some length in Chapter Three, asserts that the value given the higher priority is more important because it more closely approximates our conception of human freedom and dignity or the conditions necessary to preserve dignity. The school desegregation situation, for example, has been characterized by assertions from both sides that the values each upholds are more closely associated with "human freedom." The southern white generally selects two values to support his position: local control or states' rights and the individual freedom of the parent to protect his child's cultural integrity. The first argument, of course, has a constitutional basis. The northern liberal bases his argument on the value of equal opportunity, which enjoys constitutional support in the equal protection clause of the Fourteenth Amendment. Within the framework of a value priority position, it is possible to argue that the "higher" value is inviolable and then refuse to consider the "facts" of the case. The "conservative" stand on desegregation illustrates such a position: Constitutionally guaranteed states' rights and local control must be supported, although we know that the races are given unequal educational opportunity within certain states; the federal government has simply never been delegated constitutional power to deal with the problem of education, including racial inequality in the public schools. Constitutionalism must be upheld because it is the basis of freedom and justice, even to the point of tolerating temporary injustice.

While the initial statement of such a position appears irrefutable, the persuasiveness of the argument depends partly on the extent to which there is in fact a gross violation of the value which is given second priority — in this case equal educational opportunity. If one can demonstrate that the

Negroes in a particular southern state have been getting few or no educational privileges compared to white children, the states' rights argument becomes somewhat hollow. And if the dogmatic states' rights advocate maintains that extreme violation of equal educational opportunity is irrelevant to the argument, he is forced to ignore or deny a fundamental value of the Creed. As Myrdal pointed out, since most Americans have internalized the whole Creed, this becomes a difficult position to maintain.

In general, appeal to one value as "more basic" than another operates effectively in political controversy only when the "less basic" value is not under extreme violation. This is why the separate-but-equal position, assuming that it has been fairly implemented, is so persuasive. While imposing a system of race relations on the majority of people within a state is clearly an extreme violation of the concept of local control and states' rights (especially when no such powers have been expressly delegated to the federal government), separate-but-equal does not appear to be so extreme a violation of the value of equality.[2] Only when we see overwhelming factual evidence indicating that although separate-but-equal is a legal fact it is, in reality, a myth, or that it is inherently impossible because of its damaging psychological effects on young Negro children, does the integrationist's argument gain force.

So while initially simply giving one value permanent priority over another appears to be a secure political position in the face of conflicting values, the position loses force when there is a major violation of the "secondary" value. The basic values of the Creed are usually so important to people that they cannot simply be ignored.

As we have already indicated in Pattern 2, analogies are particularly useful to clarify value issues and especially to underline the fact that there is a real *conflict* over values which cannot be obscured by the rhetoric of a static value priority argument. Situations analogous to an initial problem case can be suggested from which one can abstract the same values as those in the problem case. In each of two situations — the problem case and the analogy — one value is being supported at the expense of another. Yet one situation may be judged "good" and the other "bad," although both involve the support of one value and the violation of another. The problem is to clarify the reasons and accept the inconsistency. The following example illustrates this process:

Between 1763 and 1776 the British became increasingly restrictive on the rights of self-government which American colonists had come to assume were theirs. Finally, some colonists considered the restrictions an unbearable loss of freedom. In pursuit of greater freedom they struck out at the British by holding the "Boston Tea Party" and storing arms and ammunition in Concord. Committees of Correspondence were set up to increase agitation against the British. For some the purpose of this agitation was to gain concessions from the British. For others it was to gain independence through violent revolution, if necessary.

How do most Americans feel about these efforts to gain independence? We celebrate the men who worked toward independence; we celebrate the day on which it occurred as a national holiday.

Now let us look at a similar hypothetical case or analogy:

Some states in the South have traditionally refused to give the Negroes voting privileges and equal educational and job opportunities and have excluded them from the full privileges of citizenship. Suppose Negroes were able to accumulate stores of arms and ammunition and plot a general uprising against such states as Mississippi and Alabama, as well as the United States. The Negro claims he is fighting for some territory in the South which is now largely occupied by Negroes. Should the United States put down such a revolt? Should Mississippi and Alabama put down such a revolt?

It is quite possible that many Americans would admit that the Negro might have some justification for revolting, but probably few would support the revolt. Both situations could be extended by the suggestion that Russia might give arms to the Negroes in their fight for independence just as France gave military aid to the English colonies in America.

Does it not seem as though we have contradicted our stand from the first situation to the second? More precisely, what is the nature of the contradiction? We can begin to answer this question by asking ourselves what values were being defended in the American Revolution. The interests of the American colonies were not represented in the decisions of the King and the English Parliament, the colonists felt; nor were the colonists being given the rights that Englishmen of comparable social class were accorded in England. In order to gain their rights they had to achieve independence, which finally meant fighting a revolution, violating English law, and committing acts of subversion and violence. The hypothetical Negro revolution in America has obvious similarities. The Negro is denied basic rights of citizenship: representation and equal treatment under the law. The American colonist was denied similar rights. The Negro is (in our hypothetical example) resorting to lawlessness and violence to gain his rights. This is what the American actually did in the American Revolution.

The analysis of these two cases illustrates a number of points. A political problem often begins when a specific decision violates an important social value. The problem becomes more complicated when we recognize that the social value given to support our decision in one situation may well be ignored by a second decision we make in a comparable situation. We are thus faced with inconsistent decisions.

It is possible, of course, to give some values such high priority that few value conflicts or inconsistencies are faced. Many Quakers, for example, place so much importance on the values of peace and non-violence that when situations involve the choice of violence or non-violence they usually behave consistently. Most of us, however, are not in this position. We value many of our personal freedoms so much that if we felt they were being taken away unjustly or illegally we would physically injure others to protect them. We would violate one value to protect another when in a particular situation the first value seemed more important for the protection of human dignity. For example, Negroes claim the protection of the law and also the right to ignore and violate laws that they do not approve. And the more important point is that we do *not consistently* violate one value and *consistently* protect another. We often deal with similar situations in different ways because each has its own unique characteristics which must be taken into account if we wish to protect the basic value of human dignity as each of us may define it.

While inconsistency on the general value level may well be justified in terms of the specifics of the two cases we are comparing, it is often disconcerting to the person who considers consistency an essential criterion of rationality. As the inconsistency begins to impinge upon our consciousness, we may find it easier to pretend that the salient value, the value that is obviously supported in one particular situation, surely leads to the most reasonable decision. In thinking about the American Revolution, for example, we focus our attention upon the values of political independence and self-government (and the fact that these values were violated by the English) rather than upon the value of remaining within the legal boundaries of English law to effect an orderly, peaceful settlement of disputes. One of the major difficulties in discussing a controversial political situation, then, is forcing antagonists to recognize that they share *both* of the conflicting values involved in it. (This fact is precisely what provides the basis for a controversial dialogue.) The American patriot has so often been conditioned to associate the American Revolution with "fighting for freedom," for example, that he cannot see that the phrase upholds one value but violates another important value. The analogy is an effective device by which to expose values "in the shadow of consciousness," as Myrdal puts it, and force an antagonist to admit that a dilemma does, in fact, exist. It serves the function of pointing up a latent value which the person would just as soon play down or ignore.

There is no implication here that by casting the Revolution in an unfavorable light through the use of analogy we can or should teach students to reject the total situation. The point is simply that a political decision and its consequent actions often involve conflicts in value, and by understanding this fact we are in a better position to rationalize our position and consider alternative positions that we might otherwise ignore. In most cases, however, we are forced to accept the fact that the final decision will have some negative consequences. It is better to admit this with honesty and candor and deal with it than to conceal it with euphemistic phrases or a turning of the head.

Pattern 4: *Translating a Value Conflict into an Issue of Fact*

This strategy for dealing with value conflicts is, of course, commonly associated with pragmatism. As White says, "The important point is that Dewey thinks that judgments of *desirability* are simply judgments that something is desired under conditions which have been thoroughly investigated in the way that a scientist checks his test conditions."[3] Commonly the strategy involves initially asking the question "What are the consequences of my value or policy position?" If it turns out that individuals or groups holding differing policy positions based on different values ask this question and arrive at the same consequences, or vice versa, the difference in policy position (and value) theoretically may be resolved by empirically testing whether the assumed relationship between policy and social consequence does in fact hold up. For example, the segregationist often argues that he wants to maintain the cultural integrity of the two races, because it will lead to the greatest *mutual respect* and *harmony* in race relations. The integrationist will argue that this violates the "brotherhood of man" doctrine. He believes that all races, creeds, and colors should mingle freely with each other because such interaction fosters mutual respect and harmony. One supports the value of cultural integrity and "freedom of association" by legal safeguards, if necessary; the other supports the value of sharing common experiences and closer association. Both justify their conflicting value positions on the basis of their common concern for peaceful and harmonious relations between the races.

From the pragmatic point of view, the approach to this controversy is, in the broad sense, experimental. We look at particular situations in which one or the other method has been tried and evaluate the extent to which each has contributed to racial peace within the community. Often, however, when either assumption is contradicted by substantial factual evidence, the antagonist on the "wrong" side of the issue reverses the priority of his values and places the instrumental value above the final value. If the evidence indicates that segregation produces more violence and ill will between races, for example, this consequence is justified as a necessary evil to maintain a greater good, cultural integrity. If the evidence indicates that close association between the races produces racial strife, this is looked upon as perhaps a temporary evil that must be endured for the sake of the greater good, practicing brotherhood. But when the controversy is genuinely approached as an experimental problem, it is potentially "solvable."

Obtaining firm and non-controversial data bearing on such problems is, of course, difficult. While broad sociological, historical, and journalistic studies provide the most appropriate kind of data, they are also the most sensitive to contamination by the author's personal biases. And although the behavioral sciences offer a more objective methodology, they usually lack the depth and scope for dealing with complex political issues.[4] Obviously there is no recourse but to use whatever data are available, however variable their quality and relevance. Unfortunately, many factual questions in politics begin as controversial issues and after exhaustive historical or scientific research end up being just as controversial.[5]

A GENERAL STRATEGY FOR TEACHING THE ANALYSIS OF POLITICAL CONTROVERSY

In Chapter Six we described a number of important concepts which we thought might be useful in the analysis of political controversy. We differentiated among three types of disagreement and described various lines of inquiry for clarifying if not resolving them. In this chapter we have attempted to give the reader some notion of the complex relationships which exist among these elements of disagreement. In all of this discussion our orientation has been toward the analysis of controversy and the general process of inquiry that might be applied to it. But we have specifically tried to avoid formularizing an approach to political-ethical problems. The reason is simple: We believe that the process of argumentative inquiry into such problems is too complex to be comprehended by a single approach.

From the point of view of pedagogy, however, the analytic formulation presented thus far is unwieldly, complicated, and difficult to translate into a teaching strategy. It is relatively easy, for example, to teach the analytic concepts; the difficult question is: How does one teach the student to select and focus the appropriate concepts on a particular problem? In attempting to answer this question, we have tried to steer a middle course between "a problem-solving formula" on the one hand and the general mandate "Take our analytic formulations and face the problem in any way you see fit" on the other. We have attempted (1) to *summarize* the major intellectual operations which can be made explicit in the analysis of political controversy and (2) to place the operations in some rough logical order. The following description of the intellectual operations, therefore, not only is a restatement of certain analytic concepts already described in greater detail but also implies a strategy or order of consideration.

Summary of Major Operations in the Analysis of Public Controversy

1. *Abstracting General Values from Concrete Situations.* In order to

use the patterns of analysis suggested above, the student must understand selected ethical and legal concepts and be able to construe concrete problem situations in these terms. If the problem is whether or not Congress should pass an antitrust act, for example, the student must be able to see that the decision can be construed in terms of such general values as property and contract rights, protection of equal rights for large and small businessmen alike, and protection of the interests of the community at large.

2. *Using General Value Concepts as Dimensional Constructs.* People commonly interpret general values as categorical concepts, as ideals or "goods." When we abstract two or more conflicting values from a single situation and reflect about how the situation may be changed to lessen the conflict, it is difficult to use values as all-or-none categories. In the segregation issue, the northern liberal asserts that the Negro's rights are violated; the southern conservative asserts that school integration violates his right to freedom of association. Under these circumstances the concept of compromise is simply not possible. One must give up his whole value position or none of it. Our approach to this problem is to deal with social values as dimensional constructs. For example:

Freedom of speech ———————— Censorship
Equal opportunity ———————— Caste system
Christian brotherhood ———————— Self-interest

Dealing with values as constructs allows us to conceptualize the higher value, human dignity, as a "blend" or amalgamation of values attained through compromise. In a particular value conflict we seek such a compromise, recognizing that everyone cannot be satisfied. Moreover, the resolution of a problem usually does not dissolve the value conflict; it rather adjusts a situation to the interests of the debating parties. But adjustment does not necessarily mean that the basic value of human dignity has been diluted or violated; it may, in fact, mean that we have come closer to it.

3. *Identifying Conflicts Between Value Constructs.* Once the student can abstract general values from concrete situations, and see them as dimensional constructs which can be violated to a greater or lesser degree, he must be able to see that two or more values can be abstracted from the same situation, and that often these values conflict. That is, a decision which enhances one value may work to the detriment of one or more other values.

4. *Identifying a Class of Value Conflict Situations.* In order to compare one situation in which a value conflict occurs with others similar to it,

the student has to see a particular situation as an instance of a general type of value conflict. For example, he might see that violations of state segregation laws by Negroes in the South are similar to violations of English law by the colonists before the American Revolution. The problem is one of violation of the "rights of man" by the legally constituted government versus violation of the law in the protection of these rights.

5. *Discovering or Creating Value Conflict Situations Which Are Analogous to the Problem Under Consideration.* The purpose of constructing analogies is to force an antagonist to compare a number of similar situations to which he reacts inconsistently. If the comparison is to be useful, the situations must embrace conflicting values both of which are likely to be favored. For example, while most of us support the actions of the English colonists in America during the American Revolution, probably few of us would support a comparable action by the Negroes in Mississippi, although the issue is similar. As we have indicated in our pattern analysis, the purpose of analogy is to expose the inconsistency between positions. The person is then forced to change one position or to rationalize the apparent inconsistency by seeking criteria which differentiate the two seemingly similar cases.

6. *Working Toward a General Qualified Position.* The quest for criteria by which to differentiate two situations characterized by the same conflicting values should lead to a qualified decision stating under what circumstances priority will be given to one value or the other. For example, a person who approved of the 1776 revolt of the English colonists in America but disapproved of a current revolt by Negroes in Mississippi might rationalize his position in the following way: Negroes are citizens not only of Mississippi but also of the United States. The national government is sympathetic to their cause and is in the process of ameliorating their condition. However, the colonists were citizens of one government, and it was actually responsible for the "abuses" they were suffering. He might then generalize that whenever a major governmental force is working successfully to reduce inequalities among citizens, and whenever there is a realistic chance that they will eventually be removed, it is better to stay within the legal framework of government. As Jefferson said, ". . . governments long established should not be changed for light and transient causes. . . ." When hope of reform is finally gone, however, this person may conclude that one can justifiably resort to violence and revolt.

One is thus "driven" to the process of qualification by a series of antecedent intellectual operations. The person states a general policy with respect to a given case. He then encounters a similar case in which his decision is reversed; opposite values are supported in the two cases. He then tries to find some general characteristics about one situation which make him judge it to be "good" while at the same time rejecting the other situation as "bad." Finally, he arrives at a general policy statement, including the qualification, which will anticipate future cases and how he will deal with them, e.g., "I will support a violent revolution only when and if it can be shown that all reasonable hope of governmental reform is gone."

Perhaps another example will further clarify this process. Americans of Japanese ancestry on the west coast were forcibly relocated shortly after the attack on Pearl Harbor in 1941. Let us assume that we support the relocation, seeing in the situation a value conflict between certain freedoms guaranteed to all citizens, in this case the right to due process under law, as against the security of the community or nation. We then think of an analogy which reverses our position. Suppose there are five Americans of Japanese ancestry in a community. One is seen committing a murder. The witnesses who observe the crime from a distance know only that the murderer had Oriental physical characteristics. Should all five men who have Oriental physical characteristics be locked up to protect the security of the community? Most of us would answer "no." It is the same dilemma, however; the security of the community versus denial of due process. How do we explain our inconsistency? We might say that "security" of the nation or community has two different meanings. In the Japanese relocation case, the legal framework of government which guarantees our basic rights was threatened; in the murder case, while perhaps some citizens' lives were jeopardized by allowing all suspects to go free for lack of evidence, the government itself was not threatened. We then arrive at a general position: The government can justifiably deny citizens basic rights only when that government itself, which is committed to protect those rights, is threatened with destruction; otherwise the action is wrong. This is not to say that one cannot argue convincingly the opposite position, and qualify it in another way.

7. *Testing the Factual Assumptions Behind a Qualified Value Position.*
Stating a qualified value position will, to some extent, "explain" our inconsistency or clarify our reasoning in a controversy, but it does not necessarily resolve the differences with someone who takes an opposite position, even though both of us have similar ethical commitments. Our position depends not only upon the weight we give conflicting values in two situations but also upon a number of factual assumptions. In the Negro revolt in Mississippi, we are assuming that the Negro's position will be ameliorated by the federal government. There may be little evidence to support the assumption. In the Japanese relocation situation, we assume that there was an immediate danger to the security of the American government which could be partially removed by relocating citizens of "doubtful" allegiance. Today this assumption is generally rejected as false.

As stated before, the analogy exposes inconsistency, the inconsistency forces one to state the factual differences between the situations about which he makes inconsistent judgments, and the argument can then shift from a controversy over the priority or relative importance of values to a test of the factual differences which each antagonist claims support his qualified position. The concepts describing the appropriate strategy for attacking factual disagreements are given in Chapter Six. They include the identification of conflicting claims; the search for evidence bearing upon the claims; the evaluation of types of evidence; the evaluation of the quality of evidence, especially that coming from authorities with various kinds of qualifications and biases; and the evaluation of the quantity of evidence (e.g., a consideration of how many sources are sampled, the basis of each source, and the extent to which the sources are representative).

8. *Testing the Relevance of Statements.* The various patterns of analysis and intellectual operations described above presumably apply to a wide variety of controversial political situations. A valid pattern of analysis, however, is not necessarily useful in the context of a *particular* discussion. The pattern must not only be valid but relevant to the issue. In an argument over segregation in housing, for example, the southerner will often charge that there is more segregation in New York City than in southern cities. One is prone to ask, "So what if this is true?" The claim has no bearing on whether segregated housing is good or bad. It would be relevant only if one defended segregation in one place and not in the other, or if one were trying to demonstrate that there is some "natural" or "normal" tendency toward segregation.

Relevance is difficult to define and teach. It has both a *specific factor,* which applies to the particular points being made in a discussion, and a *general factor,* which applies to the total issue under consideration. That is, a statement can be relevant to the general discussion but irrelevant at a particular point in a discussion. It is important that both types of relevance be kept in mind in evaluating statements or strategies. Fruitful argumentative progression is often sidetracked by issues relevant to the total issue but not to the point under discussion.

Conclusion

We have now described some major concepts and analytic processes we would select as a basis for a social studies curriculum whose major topical focus is political controversy. The justification for selecting these analytic concepts depends upon a number of assumptions, some of the more important of which are:

1. It is useful to distinguish facts from values.

2. It is useful to describe political controversy in terms of general values rather than simply in terms of specific controversial cases.

3. It is useful to differentiate the general values of the Creed from the ultimate concern of a democratic society, the dignity of man.

4. The process of using comparative cases or analogies has the value of clarifying one's value position and leading one toward an empirical statement of a political disagreement.

5. The methods of history, journalism, and the social sciences are appropriate ways of dealing with empirical disagreements.

It is difficult to justify any particular selection of analytical processes by which one might approach political controversy because so little is known about how to release man's creative problem-solving energies, especially in the direction of clarifying and resolving political and ethical disagreement. The basic reason for choosing these particular concepts and operations, aside from their presence in the literature on logic and ethics, is simply that they have proved useful to us in discussing ethical issues; they appear to help clarify and resolve political disagreement. What else can one say? Nor can we describe or finally justify the intellectual operations we went through ourselves in arriving at these patterns and processes of analysis.

A second question, of course, is whether or not a student should be taught directly or indirectly any explicit analytical framework. Our own position on this issue is clear. It is necessary to have *some* framework from which to approach political conflict in order to feel any sense of adequacy or competence in handling it. The framework we have described, however skeletal and inadequate, gives the student an orientation from which to begin analysis. This is especially important from a pedagogical standpoint. Without a framework the student is likely to view social controversy as a maze of facts, opinions, and conflicting claims. When his own opinions are challenged, he approaches the controversy by simply embracing unreflected judgments. And because he cannot distinguish different kinds of conflict, different kinds of disagreements, he strikes in several directions at once in an effort to regain a comfortable equilibrium of contradictory beliefs and values. Myrdal has described one aspect of this tortuous process:

> We have already hinted at the fact that valuations are seldom overtly expressed except when they emerge in the course of a person's attempts to formulate his beliefs concerning the facts and their implication in relation to some section of social reality. Beliefs concerning the facts are the very building stones for the logical hierarchies of valuations into which a person tries to shape his opinions. When the valuations are conflicting, as they normally are, beliefs serve the rationalization function of bridging illogicalities. The beliefs are thus not only determined by available scientific knowledge in society and the efficacy of the means of its

communication to various population groups but are regularly "biased," by which we mean that they are systematically twisted in the one direction which fits them best for purposes of rationalization.[6]

One cannot hope adequately to understand and control either his natural or social universe unless he has some analytic elements in his frame of reference, no matter how crude and inadequate they may be. Without such a framework he is a creature of impulse, wasting his energies by rationalizing his failures rather than focusing his reason upon the challenges to his existence.

It is crucial, however, that the student be taught at some point to question the framework we have presented, to identify shortcomings in it, and to reject it if, from his point of view, it fails to deal with important issues adequately. (The framework herein presented is obviously not the first version of our own analytic construction of political controversy.) Many of the concepts presented above should certainly be changed, discarded, or forgotten, depending upon how useful they turn out to be. This is as it should be. The most useful tools of analysis for each of us are often the ones we invent ourselves. Good arguments are complex, subtle, and intricate. They defy explicit rules of analysis. They are the creation of an original mind. So our hope is not just that people can be taught to use *our* analytic scheme. It is that concepts such as these will be useful enough to make each person recognize their shortcomings and inadequacies, and that, as necessary, each person can discard them in favor of more appropriate ones.

PATTERN ANALYSIS AND THE TEACHING OF THE SOCIAL STUDIES

The implications of pattern analysis for teaching the social studies should be quite clear. First, the patterns illustrate the inadequacy of the simple dichotomy made between "facts" and "opinions." The social studies teacher who assumes that his job is to teach the "facts" and then let the student form his own "opinions" is simply ignoring the complex problem of teaching the student *to relate* fact to "opinion" or value. Second, to assume that it is efficient pedagogically to teach a "fund" or "storehouse" of facts or abstract skills which will, at some later time, be used by the student is to ignore the very obvious point that the facts surrounding a political controversy are both useless and meaningless unless they are related in the student's mind to broader questions of public policy. Third, the process of teaching suggested here means that a central objective is to relate the way social problems are framed *publicly* to the way the student construes them in his own mind. This inevitably means that students must take "personal" positions and attempt to justify them. It is the only way complex patterns of justification can, in fact, be made manifest in the classroom.

Allowing (and in fact encouraging) the student to take an active role in judging the rightness of public decisions, moreover, is likely to affect not only the intellectual climate of the classroom but the student's attitude toward the responsibility and role of the teacher as well. If the teacher is well informed on public issues and intellectually facile, there is little problem. If, on the other hand, the teacher depends on the symbols of adult authority to maintain the respect of the student, obviously the student will reveal personal attitudes which may contradict those of the teacher. For "truth" and "goodness" now become open classroom issues to be determined by a process of public intellectual justification. They are no longer in the hands of the teacher. Static facts or generalizations that happen to appear on a printed page or are uttered by an authority figure are no longer adequate.

Finally, a word should be said about the relationship between jurisprudential teaching and self-instruction. When a student "joins an issue" or engages in controversy, he is often relating fundamental components of his own personality (e.g., beliefs, attitudes) to a public decision-making situation. It is, therefore, more than likely that different students will construe a controversy in very different terms. Different questions become important to individual students. Part of the process of teaching involves defining these questions so that they have some common meaning and relevance for all students. Probably just as important, however, is teaching the student the research skills to deal with his own individual questions.

Obviously there is nothing new in teaching high school students the process of social or historical research. What might be stressed is the source of questions researched. Students are perennially asked to write themes on such questions as "Did FDR abuse Presidential power?" or "Was the American 'Revolution' really a revolution?" The questions usually are either found at the end of the chapter or invented by the teacher. More important, they are as a rule the questions of the "academic mind" rather than those of the politician. It is our experience that students are more likely to ask specific factual questions that bear on general legal or value questions, e.g.: What were the living conditions like, in personal terms, for an unemployed worker in 1933? In a jurisprudential approach to the teaching of public issues, individual student research becomes a much more substantial part of the curriculum, and, more important, this research evolves from the *student's efforts* to define and grapple with issues.

References

1. While the use of analogous cases may not resolve the issue, it is sometimes an effective device in causing people to change their position which, in fact, does

resolve the issue. For example, although a person may have first been against racial segregation, through the use of our analogy he may come to see it as no different from sexual segregation, with which he finds nothing wrong. Or initially he may have seen nothing wrong with racial segregation, but after seeing its similarity to social class segregation he may change his mind and be firmly against both.

2. Such segregation on religious grounds exists, for example, in Montreal with little apparent sense of "atrocity" by either party.

3. Morton White, *Social Thought in America: The Revolt Against Formalism* (Boston: Beacon Press, 1957), p. 213.

4. Some exceptions to this statement might be noted: the work of Myrdal on the American Negro, the work of Allport on prejudice, the work of Riesman on mass culture, and the general work of Lewin, which has influenced many social psychologists, as evidenced, for example, by Ralph White and Ronald Lippitt, *Autocracy and Democracy* (New York: Harper & Row, Publishers, 1960).

5. See e.g., Alfred Kelly's address to the American Historical Association, 1961, parts of which are reprinted in *U.S. News and World Report,* February 5, 1962. Kelly makes the point that the litigants of the segregation cases of 1953 were commissioned by the Supreme Court to determine whether or not the framers of the Fourteenth Amendment intended it to apply to such areas as public education. The Court reached the conclusion after hearing exhaustive testimony on both sides that a clear conclusion could not be arrived at, and finally made its decision on sociological rather than historical grounds. The incident well illustrates our point. One must make political decisions, which in some cases should be based on empirical considerations, using whatever data seem relevant and appropriate, although they may be clearly inadequate.

6. Gunnar Myrdal, *An American Dilemma* (New York: Harper & Row, Publishers, 1944), p. 1030.

PART THREE

Application of the Jurisprudential Framework to the Teaching of Public Issues

period

CHAPTER EIGHT

Selecting and Organizing Problem Units

In developing a rationale for the selection of content, we made the distinction between topical content, i.e., categories or models by which to organize facts in the social or natural world, and the analytic concepts which provide criteria for judging the relevance, truth, or goodness of topical content. Part Two presented a set of related concepts to serve as an analytic framework for dealing with political controversy. This represents the first step in our effort to implement the appproach to content selection suggested in Part One. Now we shall describe and illustrate materials of instruction by which the student might learn about the substance of political issues and through which he might also learn and apply the analytic concepts.

A major difficulty in using any "problems approach" as a criterion for the selection of content is determining what "problems" should or should not be included in the curriculum. How does the person concerned with the teaching of contemporary issues decide which of the multitude of issues are of sufficient importance to be presented systematically to the student? We would argue that, in general, it is not hard to find agreement among professional social scientists, people in government, journalists, and other professional observers of the contemporary scene regarding what are the most pressing issues threatening the stability and freedom of the society. We would suggest, moreover, that there is a great deal more disagreement over methods of organizing and teaching these issues than over whether the issues are sufficiently important to be taught.

At least six pedagogical approaches are commonly used to organize materials for the teaching of contemporary issues. These might be briefly stated as follows: (1) the injection of contemporary issues into regular history and government courses whenever they appear relevant; (2) the treatment of the "daily news" as the main substance of the course, often through programs provided by daily or weekly newspapers or newsmagazines; (3) the treatment of "current events" periodically (usually once a week) as a regularly scheduled activity; (4) the thematic approach to history wherein a topic such as "Church and State" or "The Democratization of American Society" is injected into the regular historical content; (5) the historical crisis approach, in which particularly critical historical episodes or eras are identified and analyzed in the search for useful generalizations which might help one analyze or explain contemporary problems; (6) the problem-topic approach, which gives priority to particular topics, and then seeks to develop them from some point in the past to the contemporary definition of the problem.

While there may be strengths and weaknesses in all of these approaches, the first three have a fundamental shortcoming; they make little systematic effort to integrate the historical background of an issue with its contemporary form. Injecting current events into a discussion of history is usually done to demonstrate that some history has relevance to the modern world, or vice versa. The obvious question is: Why shouldn't all the history actually taught have such relevance? And if it does, why is it not taught this way? The "newspaper approach" is essentially a course in random contemporary issues. Although it may teach intelligent reading habits, there is no evidence that it teaches the student to approach policy questions inherent in contemporary events with greater historical perspective or analytic clarity. The "once a week" approach has essentially the same weakness as the "daily news" approach.

We would suggest that the latter three approaches have much in common and all deserve serious consideration. We have used both the historical crisis approach and the problem-topic approach.

The Historical Crisis Approach

One begins by looking at historical periods which are analogous to or may be contrasted with contemporary history, and which may help explain contemporary problems. Once the historical period to be investigated has been identified, the teacher must consider each of the variety of problems that converge at this point in history. In the American Revolution, for example, a number of important issues converge: the social class upheaval; the ideological revolution embodied in the words of the Declaration of Independence; the legitimacy of resorting to violence as a means of resolving political and economic questions; the formation of a new government. The New Deal likewise contains a number of interrelated problems and issues which reach crisis proportions simultaneously: the imbalance between agriculture and industry; the flood-drought problems in agriculture; the stock market crash and the consequent economic depression; the ideological assaults on free enterprise and existing political institutions; the absence of adequate political instruments to handle growing problems in labor-management relations; and internal labor disagreements caused by the rise of industrial labor unions. All of these issues have contemporary analogues.

In general, the historical crisis approach to the organization of content gives initial priority to a specific historical setting and then seeks to analyze the complex interplay of problems within that setting. The study of specific historical settings clearly has two kinds of relevance to contemporary issues: (1) It allows the identification of direct or indirect causal relationships between historical antecedents and a contemporary fact or state of affairs. For example, current southern attitudes toward northern "interference" in the race problems of the South are partly conditioned by the way these problems were handled during the Civil War and Reconstruction Periods. (2) It may lead toward the development of general principles of political or social behavior from analogous historical situations, i.e., what might be called "lessons of history." For example, since it is commonly believed that the appeasement of Hitler in his early days of conquest was a great mistake in the foreign policy of the Western democracies, we now operate under the assumption that future appeasement will lead to war rather than peace. The principle evolved that if force is actually used in the critical phase of a dictator's attempt to consolidate power, the dictator may be overthrown and the community of nations saved from the ravages of an outlaw state. Thus, in one sense, the French and English attacked Nasser's Egypt in 1956 "for historical reasons."

THE PROBLEM-TOPIC APPROACH

The problem-topic approach begins with the selection of a contemporary issue which is deemed important and persistent. The issue or topic then determines what data are relevant and should be presented to the student. These data may be mainly historical (which they usually are), or journalistic, sociological, etc. The approach is clearly causal or explanatory. Only those historical or social scientific facts and generalizations are sought which help clarify or explain the nature of the contemporary problem.

From our point of view there is little purpose in debating the relative merits of the thematic, historical crisis, or problem-topic approach in the development of teaching units. There is no reason to think that one approach is invariably better than another, or to think that one approach cannot be used to complement another. Certain historical periods are crisis ridden because several problems in an aggravated form converge at that point in history. One cannot understand the full impact of these problems, or their interrelationships, without studying the crisis as a whole. The problem-topic approach, however, does provide the student with a clearer interpretation of the historical development of a problem, as well as making it easier to use contemporary social science information in its analysis. For example, in studying racial desegregation as a historical topic, sociology, psychology, anthropology, and law, as well as history, can all play a major role.

Before we discuss the problem-topic approach in more detail, a note of caution should be sounded regarding the use of an explicit analytic framework to select and organize materials of instruction. However one goes about selecting and organizing specific materials for the teaching of contemporary political controversy, he should realize that once a problem is classified and described, even in a tentative way, the student is already predisposed to deal with it as the writer or teacher has seen and presented it. This is unavoidable. Even when we decide to deal with content as "controversial," and therefore seek to present and justify various sides of an issue, we are not necessarily immune from bias or distortion. The problem of the instability of central Europe, for example, which has plagued the Western world for the past 1500 years would be framed and taught quite differently by a Russian, a German, or a Pole, although all would probably agree that it was controversial and that there was a problem. Social and political problems begin with the emotional reactions in the minds of people, not within an analytical framework. Only after these visceral reactions make their presence known are intellectual structures built by which to understand and resolve them. The description of a problem should flow initially from this fundamental source of controversy.

It is only by keeping, to some extent, the analytical frame separate from the original intuitive conception of the problem that we can discover when the frame is inadequate. To demonstrate that this is not an academic question, one might look, for example, at the difficulty Communists often have discovering the inadequacy of their ideology, because they refuse to see or deal with those aspects of a problem which the ideology cannot handle. For example, African nationalism and anticolonialism may both play important parts in the belief system of modern Africans, but because Marxism-Leninism can more easily handle the issue of anticolonialism, the problems of modern Africa tend to be distorted and construed only within the anticolonialism frame.

We are thus faced with something of a paradox in building a curriculum. A framework is necessary to "make sense" out of problematic data and deal with them systematically. But the framework tends to predispose us to include some aspects of the problem and to exclude others. Obviously, although we hope to teach the student our particular frame of reference, it is necessary to be alert to the fact that each student will modify it to meet the idiosyncracies of his own personal history. This, of course, is the basic corrective in any social or political theory designed for instruction in the area of public controversy: It can be communicated or taught only imperfectly, thus allowing for growth and change in the theory itself as each new mind struggles to comprehend it and apply it to the facts of the day.

In our approach we see conflicts between social values — both within the individual and between individuals and groups — as the basis of important problems. And although we have tried to guard against distorting reality in order that societal problems can be understood and more easily handled within this framework, our identification and analysis of problems will inevitably reflect our way of looking at political controversy.

Specific Problem-Topics

With these words of warning, we shall proceed to describe a set of problem areas and some specific units or topics implied by each area, admitting from the outset that our treatment is neither systematic (in the sense that it evolves from some overall theory of social conflict) nor exhaustive. The scheme is based on a problem-topic approach; the student studies the history of a single topic or problem from its first acute symptoms to its contemporary manifestations.

Table 1 presents an outline of problem areas, topics, and the value conflicts in each. An obvious point brought out by the table is the abundance of problem-units that could conceivably be treated in a regular high school social studies program. Our own experience indicates that it takes from three to six weeks, at a minimum, to provide a "one-shot" treatment for such a unit. There must, therefore, be even more selection than is suggested by the outline. The student cannot be taught the historical background of all the problems he must face as a citizen, let alone all of "history" in general.

In selecting specific problem units from among such a list, a number of useful criteria come to mind: (1) The teacher might select topics that seem most critical on the contemporary scene. (2) The teacher might select topics which are *least* understood because of the geographical area or the type of student body he teaches. (3) The teacher might select topics which he is personally most competent to handle. (4) The teacher might first select topics which are less complex and work toward greater complexity, insofar as this can be determined. Since many such criteria can be identified, these four are meant only to be suggestive.

TABLE 1

Identification of General Problem Areas

Problem Areas	Sample Unit Topics	Conflicting Values[a]
Racial and Ethnic Conflict	School Desegregation Civil Rights for Non-Whites and Ethnic Minorities Housing for Non-Whites and Ethnic Minorities Job Opportunities for Non-Whites and Ethnic Minorities Immigration Policy	Equal Protection Due Process Brotherhood of Man v. Peace and Order Property and Contract Rights Personal Privacy and Association
Religious and Ideological Conflict	Rights of the Communist Party in America Religion and Public Education Control of "Dangerous" or "Immoral" Literature Religion and National Security: 　Oaths 　Conscientious Objectors Taxation of Religious Property	Freedom of Speech and Conscience v. Equal Protection Safety and Security of Democratic Institutions
Security of the Individual	Crime and Delinquency	Standards of Freedom Due Process v. Peace and Order Community Welfare
Conflict Among Economic Groups	Organized Labor Business Competition and Monopoly "Overproduction" of Farm Goods Conservation of Natural Resources	Equal or Fair Bargaining Power and Competition General Welfare and Progress of the Community v. Property and Contract Rights
Health, Education, and Welfare	Adequate Medical Care: 　for the Aged 　for the Poor Adequate Educational Opportunity Old-Age Security Job and Income Security	Equal Opportunity Brotherhood of Man v. Property and Contract Rights

Security of the Nation	Federal Loyalty-Security Programs [Foreign Policy][b]	Freedom of Speech, Conscience, and Association Due Process Personal Privacy v. Safety and Security of Democratic Institutions

[a] The "vs." in the listing of values suggests that the top values conflict with the bottom values. While this is generally true, there are, of course, many exceptions. One can argue, for example, that a minimum wage law was a violation of property and contract rights and that it also was against the general welfare.

[b] This topic obviously should be the center of a new curriculum, extending our analysis of domestic problems. It might consist of a wide variety of subtopics, such as disarmament, the uncommitted nations, the stabilization of central Europe, the underdeveloped countries, etc. Such a curriculum would have to deal with a totally new problem: the relationship between power and law in the international scene. This problem is handled in our curriculum by the concept of constitutionalism and its subsidiary legal concepts. There is, however, no general constitutional framework within which world problems can now be worked out. Current work at Harvard does include not only an exploration of the problem of developing a legal-ethical frame for international problems but also development of teaching materials and strategies to implement this framework.

Selecting Specific Materials of Instruction

There is a great leap from the point of selecting a general course of instruction, or selecting specific units of instruction, to the point of selecting actual documents, films, or other sources which will be presented to the student. It is important to make the distinction between *materials of instruction* and the *dialogue* between the student and the teacher based on them. The student-teacher dialogue will be discussed systematically in Chapters Nine and Section Four of the Appendix. Here we are concerned with the kinds of materials that might be presented to and observed by the student as they relate to the more general objective of teaching about a specific social issue.

To discover types of instructional materials necessary to lay the foundation for a critical political judgment, we first asked ourselves what information and commitments the student is likely to bring to a discussion, what information we must give him before a dialogue can begin, and what additional information he is likely to need or seek as he gets deeper into a problem. Certain distinctions in types of materials became apparent as we discovered that simply "presenting" the issue was an extremely difficult task which could not be handled by a single type of document. (Our first impulse had been simply to use "cases.") We found it difficult, for example, to meet the competing demands of *complexity* and *saliency*. An issue must be presented as personal, relevant, and salient to the student if he is to become sufficiently concerned to want to handle it or structure it in his own mind. Yet we want him to see the problem in broader, more complex terms than those which will appear relevant or important at first encounter. To meet these competing demands, several different types of materials were developed.

Materials to Effect Empathy and Emotional Impact. Political and social problems begin in personal emotional reactions to concrete situations, and it is then that people begin to reflect about and rationalize reactions. It is therefore not enough to "tell" the student how others conceptualize the problem or have reacted to problem situations. He must see the controversial situation in a "raw" concrete setting; and he must experience, at least vicariously, the emotional reactions of the antagonists in the problem situation.

We have found that materials most appropriate for this purpose tend to be in art form, including both fiction and history. The main requirement of empathic materials is that they be highly personal so that the student can identify with individuals who are actually involved in the problem situation. Labor-management relations, for example, which are discussed in such terms as *labor union, union security, strike, unemployment, union intimidation,* and the like must have as referents concrete situations as well as abstract definitions. Moreover, it is this type of material that helps to bridge the gap between the artificial culture of the school and the real problems of the society. For an empathic case to have appeal it must have personal relevance and a ring of authenticity for the student.

Materials for Historical and Conceptual Clarification. Before a student can intelligently develop a position in a controversy, he must certainly become familiar with its broad historical, sociological, economic, and political background, as well as with the technical language in which this background may be presented. In discussing race problems in America, for example, he should know the distinction between race and culture, the differences between the Negro and the white which are attributable to each, and sufficient psychological and sociological conceptual background to evaluate controversies over which characteristics may be attributable to race and which may be attributable to culture. Furthermore, the student obviously should know why and under what circumstances the Negro came to America, and something of the bitter sectional rivalry culminating in the Civil War and Reconstruction Period around which revolved the Negro's destiny on this continent.

It is likely, however, that much of the background of a problem *cannot* be presented *before* the student is allowed to discuss an issue in a controversial context. A *cyclical model* is probably more appropriate. The student is provided with historical-conceptual information on some facet of a general problem. He is then challenged to adopt and defend a position with respect to the issue, after which he realizes that his position must be supported with further information, so he embarks on the search of it. Thus the student's position should become more qualified and sophisticated as he seeks out new data to support an initial position. The corrective for the student who seeks only that information which supports his own biases is the teacher and students who have different biases. This is, of course, the basic function of the classroom as a "free marketplace of ideas."

Cases to Provide Situational Referents for Abstract Social and Political Procedures. The purpose of conceptual case material is to provide specific referents for general ethical, legal, or social science concepts. The term *collective bargaining,* for example, describes a complex set of procedures and is often related to such concepts as *strike, strike settlement,* and *union contract.* While the general abstract characteristics implied by these terms can be described, it is doubtful that the concepts can really be understood before the student has actually seen one or more examples in operation.

Conceptual case materials can, of course, be either simple and brief or elaborate and complex. Conventional textbooks are sprinkled with short examples illustrating general conceptual information. Characteristically, however, the examples are not sufficiently detailed to handle the complexity of many of the concepts which must be understood in order to cope with social and political problems.

The Controversial Case. The controversial case describes a specific situation about which there are controversial ethical, legal, factual, or definitional interpretations. It may be a classic historical or legal situation, like Plessy v. Ferguson in race relations, or the Wagner Act or Kohler strike in labor relations. Or it may be a short story or fictionalized account of a situation which expresses the essential nature of societal controversy, e.g., Orwell's *Animal Farm.* These cases are designed to provide a focus for controversial dialogue between teacher and student or among students.

A controversial case, in its actual write-up, may contain elements of historical information as well as emotional impact. We have found, however, that when it is heavily loaded with value imagery the student may become so emotionally moved that he is in no position to discuss anything. Likewise, when a great deal of factual information is placed in the case, it may become so dull, cumbersome, and complicated that the student loses sight of the specific issues which make the facts significant and relevant.

To illustrate how the controversial case is selected and analyzed as a basis for teaching, an example is given in Appendix A and Appendix B at the end of this chapter, along with a lesson plan describing discussion strategy. The case, called "Little Rock I," describes the first major incident in the South's attempt to implement the Supreme Court's desegregation ruling.

Takeoff Materials. The general teaching model within which we have operated gives the dialogue a central position. Although initially the student is given information that makes it easy for him to empathize with antagonists who differ over a political or social issue or that will allow him to understand the background and circumstances surrounding the issue, "teaching" takes place when the teacher begins a dialogue with the student. We assume that the ultimate purpose of teaching, however, is to make the student independent of the teacher. Specifically the student should learn to carry on a dialogue or argument and counterargument with himself and his peers. He should learn to question his own statements as well as those made by others outside the classroom. The implications of this position for instructional materials are obvious: The student must learn to seek out newspapers, including both news accounts and editorials, magazines, journals, books, and TV and radio accounts presenting positions which lend themselves to critical evaluation. When he does this spontaneously, without prodding from the formal sanctions of school, we may say that he has arrived at "takeoff."

General Comments on Materials. While we have found it useful to identify various functions for different types of materials, it is plainly only a crude first step. Other questions immediately present themselves:

1. Through what media can different types of materials best be presented?

2. Is it possible to present social science conceptual materials through programed instruction, and is this the most efficient way to do it?

3. Although film and TV undoubtedly present case material more realistically, are there special problems of distorted emphasis because of the emotive power these media possess?

At our present level of pedagogical knowledge, answers to such questions are simply not available, and decisions must be made on the basis of intuitive clinical knowledge.

There is, however, a more serious question than that associated with the selection and organization of a battery of materials designed to fit the specifications of a particular problem framework: Is the structure of the dialogue to be in the teacher's mind or in the materials designed for the student? This question arises from the possible inability of the teacher to comprehend the relationship between teaching materials and the use of these materials as the basis of a controversial dialogue. Unfortunately, our experience indicates that teachers are generally predisposed to use the *information* and *conceptual structure present in the materials themselves* as the basis of student discussion rather than *to think through and operate from a broader framework.* It is common, for example, for teachers to use controversial cases in the same way as emotional impact cases — as simple motivational devices. Such cases are rarely followed up by finding out where the student stands in the controversy, what kind of analytic skills he uses to defend and justify his position, and what additional information he needs to strengthen his position. The notion that a "good curriculum" can be defined as a sequence of materials of instruction embedded in carefully worked out unit outlines which will somehow lead to "good teaching" is, we think, naïvely optimistic. The model of teaching we are presenting here comes to life only when the student reacts to a challenge — when he encounters the teacher or other students in a critical dialogue.

The Order of Units in a Course and the Order of Controversial Cases in a Unit

Several obvious standards can be used to order a series of specific units. Units can be taught when a particular issue is "in the news." If a labor unit were taught during a local labor dispute or a protracted national strike, the teacher could capitalize on local resources or current newscasting. (We know, however, of an instance in which a labor unit was *not* taught because of the bitter feelings in the community over a local strike.) In our own work we have placed the units within a broad historical setting and allowed chronology to dictate roughly the order of the units. In this scheme the general problem of cultural and political revolution is treated within the context of the American Revolution; school desegregation is treated as an extension of pre-Civil War tensions, the Civil War, and Reconstruction; labor-management relations, fair standards of business competition, farm problems, immigration, the "final solution" to the Indian problem are all treated as elements in the history of the rapid industrialization of the country in the latter part of the nineteenth century. The twenties, the Great Depression, and the New Deal are treated separately as an historical crisis unit. The problem of the internal Communist threat and the indirect pressure it places on civil liberties is treated only as a modern problem. The topic-problem and historical crisis organization of content can thus easily be fitted into a "conventional" history course. The rationale for our decision was partly convenience: It was more in line with the expectations of children and parents. But it also stemmed from the conviction that a broad chronological framework does give the course additional structure and meaning.

The order in which one presents specific documents, especially controversial cases, within a single unit is another matter. Again we have relied mainly upon a chronological organization. In school desegregation, for example, there are four major phases in the development of the unit: the events leading up to legalized segregation; the separate-but-equal doctrine, its implementation, and the evolution of the meaning of that legal concept; the Supreme Court decision of 1954; and efforts to implement that decision.

Qualifications Regarding the Problem-Topic Unit Organization

It seems to be commonly assumed that the teaching of a topic should result in the students' "mastery" of information and issues surrounding the topic. And "teaching a topic," at least for the individual teacher, means a single run through a topic during one academic year. Two points should be made: (1) It is impossible to make the student a sophisticated and competent observer of a complex issue in the first instructional run through such an issue. This means that (2) we must assume that a single topic will be touched upon several times in a single curriculum and/or skills and interests will be developed so that the student will continue to educate himself outside of school. Obviously these limitations apply to both topical and chronological material. We are, in fact, lucky if we can sketch the broad outlines of a major issue in one run. Moreover, because we use a great deal of specific case material, the possibility of inadvertently misinforming the student through misplaced emphasis or omission of important facets of a problem is a real danger. In short, one makes a calculated guess that it is better to risk distorting certain issues in order to present them in a realistic, vivid setting so that they will have personal meaning for the student than to present the issues in an objective, analytic way and never make contact with the student's own frame of reference. We have to work, moreover, within a second limitation: After studying an issue from four to six weeks, the student becomes saturated with the problem and rapidly loses interest. The first three weeks of a unit are, therefore, critical, and the amount of material selected for teaching ordinarily cannot exceed these boundaries. Ideally, in a curriculum of the type we have suggested here, topics would be treated several times over the course of several years, each time with greater depth, complexity, and comprehensiveness. And through all the units would run the more powerful concepts of the social sciences as well as classic situations for historical, political, and ethical analysis.

A second qualification relates to the criteria used for evaluating topical units. We would emphasize the fact that a unit should be evaluated in the light of two criteria: (1) It should convey a reasonably accurate and balanced impression of the nature of the problem; and (2) the materials should provide a useful vehicle for teaching the conceptual and analytic skills by which the student can more intelligently handle similar problems. The first criterion of adequacy must be handled by historians, social scientists, and experienced observers of the contemporary scene. The second criterion must be handled by research into the process of instruction and, in the absence of such research, by the best insights of a sensitive, intelligent teacher. This requirement points up the increased responsibility placed on the teacher who uses this approach. The teacher is responsible not simply for teaching a catalogue of factual material but for teaching a complex analytic process. To meet the challenge he may be given a variety of "documents," including films, short stories, pamphlets, magazines, and texts. The length of time he spends on a document, the organization of the documents for teaching, the choice of which documents to omit and which to stress — these decisions depend upon the nature of the student and the nature of the instructional situation, e.g., the number and type of students in the class, the amount of time he has with the class, etc. In summary, the selection and the organization of the materials of instruction are more or less arbitrary intuitive attempts to give meaning to a general approach for teaching the analysis of political controversy. The validity of the approach and the adequacy of the materials should be treated as two different questions, as should the validity of the materials and their pedagogical appropriateness.

A third qualification is the relative importance of the various kinds of materials described above. One should certainly not conclude that the approach consists mainly in teaching different types of content written with different styles. Like any so-called case method, our approach includes much more. It includes a set of ethical-legal concepts which must be taught through the materials. It includes a type of dialectical interchange between student and teacher and among students. It includes a particular emphasis upon the evaluation of oral interaction as a process of assessing student progress. In a very general way the approach is well described by Myrdal: "By this democratic process of open discussion there is started a tendency which constantly forces a larger and larger part of the valuation sphere into conscious attention. More is made conscious than any single person or group would on his own initiative find it advantageous to bring forward at the particular moment."[1]

With this goal in mind, it should be stated emphatically that the "content" (or the materials of instruction which specify the content) is only one component of the approach suggested here. Our concern is *not* for issues or problems in the abstract; it is for issues as they exist and may be clarified in the minds of individual citizens. We do *not* teach the *problem;* we do *not* teach the issue; we do *not* teach *points of view* about the issue; we do *not* simply teach the *background* of the issue. Our purpose is to encourage the student to explore a controversial area, to find out himself where *he* stands in the controversy and how he might best defend his position in terms of the values of his culture and society, taking into account the realities of the situation that confront him. It is therefore impossible to bring the teaching of this material to life in the form of a unit outline of abstract issues or even with concrete materials of instruction. The approach comes to life only when the student *reacts* to a challenging confrontation. In a real sense, then, instruction begins, not when the student begins to *read* about the problem, but when he becomes personally involved in dialogue about it. Some sense of this interaction process, which is at the heart of the approach, may be seen in the following annotated excerpts from a student-teacher dialogue.

Excerpt of a Discussion That Has Focused on the Question of Full Voting Rights for Negroes

Dialogue	Annotation
Teacher: What do you think, Steve?	
Steve: I think that the police power of local government can go only so far, that the constitutional rights of voting — maybe the Negroes should have them.	
Teacher: Negroes should have the right to vote, even though there may be all kinds of violence and resistance. We should send troops into the South and protect every individual's right to vote?	The teacher suggests that providing voting rights may threaten a second important value: the safety of the community; and this in turn may threaten local control by the states, if federal intervention is required to keep order.
Steve: I'm not saying that. I don't think that we would have to send down troops.	Questions factual assumption of teacher. The teacher can, at this point, choose to debate the factual assumption or treat the assumption hypothetically and clarify the value commitment of the student.
Teacher: But what if it did go that far?	
Steve: Probably; yes.	The teacher chooses the latter course.
Teacher: Suppose people called Negroes on the phone who intended to vote and said, "If you vote tomorrow, something might very well happen to your kids." Do you think we should send the FBI down there to investigate these intimidations?	The teacher modifies the hypothetical situation to determine the point at which the student's position will change in favor of local control and against federal intervention. He is shifting the meaning of "violence" to do this.

Dialogue	*Annotation*
Steve: No.	The student reverses his position with the shift in the situation.
Teacher: Why not?	
Steve: If the threat is carried out; then I would send down troops or the FBI.	The student is aware of the reversal of his position and explains the essential criterion determining the reversal: overt use of force to prevent the Negro from voting. The student has qualified his position.
Teacher: After something has happened to the courageous Negro's family, then you would send someone down to stop it.	Emphasizes the negative consequences of the student's position.
You don't go along with the notion that if there is an atmosphere of fear and intimidation we should do something to change the atmosphere so that people will be free to vote. We shouldn't do anything until there is actual violence?	The teacher now raises the definitional question: Do we have to commit an act of physical violence against a person before we have violated his rights? Is threat of violence, to some degree, also "violence"?
Steve: In the case of Negroes, yes.	
Teacher: Why?	
Steve: Because I don't want to give them the complete power to vote. This is taking a little of it away.	
Teacher: You want to deny some Negroes the right to vote, a right you are willing to give whites?	
Steve: Yes.	
Teacher: Why?	The student is operating with two categories of citizenship. The teacher is here asking him to justify classification on the basis of race.
Steve: Because I feel that Negroes are inferior to whites.	Children are classified as different from adults and denied full rights of citizenship. In a sense, it is because they are "inferior." This response does have a rational component which the teacher feels obligated to explore.
Teacher: In what respect?	
Steve: In intelligence; in health, in crime rates.	The student states the criteria on which his classification is based.

Dialogue	*Annotation*
Teacher: You are suggesting that if a person is tubercular or sick, you should deny him the right to vote.	The teacher is here challenging the relevance of a criterion on the basis of which the student is making his classification.
Steve: No.	
Teacher: But if a Negro is sick we don't let him vote?	
Steve: Let him vote, sure. It is just that I think they are inferior for these reasons. I'm not saying because of these reasons I'm not going to let him vote.	
Teacher: Then for what reasons aren't you going to let them vote?	
Steve: Because I think they are inferior because of these reasons. (Student then laughs self-consciously, aware of his inconsistency.)	At this point the student has contradicted an earlier position.

A dialogue such as this embodies some of the major elements in our previous analysis and illustrates the secondary function served by materials of instruction. The focus of the curriculum is upon the way the student looks at political problems, which explains why the dialogue is in the center of our thinking. The dialogue, that is, serves two functions: It reveals the implicit framework of the student, and it allows the teacher to intervene in the functioning of this framework to add elements and clarify inadequacies in it. Materials of instruction may also serve these functions, but only to the extent that the student can learn to approach them in the same critical fashion by which he appoaches the teacher's challenge. It is this dynamic conception of materials of instruction that we hope to communicate to the reader.

Reference

1. Gunnar Myrdal, *An American Dilemma* (New York: Harper & Row, Publishers, 1944), p. 1029.

Appendix A. Unit Outline and Descriptions of Teaching Materials

On the following pages the outline of a topic-problem is analyzed for teaching purposes. The issue considered, segregation, is a contemporary one. But even issues that are to a considerable degree "settled," such as whether or not collective bargaining can be required under the law, can be treated in the classroom as if they were current problems. The historical perspective for modern issues must be rediscovered in each new generation, and the student should recapitulate the options that society has had over the last 100 years. Nor do such issues seem phony or passe to the student, who in fact is often shocked at the extent to which government regulation has become a part of our daily lives. He usually "wants" employers to behave in a fair and charitable manner and is somewhat upset when there is evidence to the contrary. But he finds himself in inner conflict when he must choose between government coercion and abuse of private power.

A major difficulty of *not* recapitulating the choices of the society in the classroom is that the student assumes that prior choices were ordained and correct, and that only the current choices present any real conflict. Obviously, this attitude drastically restricts the ethical and legal framework within which a contemporary political choice is made. The student must not only see that laws are made and changed, Supreme Court decisions made and reversed, but also feel a sense of personal involvement and ethical inclusion regarding these changes and the ethical and legal inconsistencies in them.

The major purpose of the description of materials is to show the reader the variety of documents required to present the issues in the unit outlines. While some of these materials are commercially available, most are experimental documents written, selected, and adapted specifically for our own program. The materials are at present being revised within a much broader framework and will be commercially available.

Descriptive Guide to Materials Used to Teach School Desegregation

Title	*Type of Material*	*Specific Function*
The Negro in America, 1600 to 1865	Historical background	A general historical account describing how the Negro came to America, the purpose for which he was brought, and the conditions under which he lived. Because this unit is ordinarily taught within the broader context of a course in American history, the document does not include the events leading up to the Civil War, the war itself, and the bitter Reconstruction Period

Title	Type of Material	Specific Function
		that followed. This material is contained in history textbooks and is readily available.
School Desegregation (a film) Clinton and the Law (a film) The First Day of School	Emotional impact	"School Desegregation" vividly portrays a KKK meeting. "Clinton and the Law" is a case study in the southerner's mixed feelings over acceptance of desegregation and obedience to the law. "The First Day of School" presents a parent's mixed feelings about her responsibility to principles of equality when these are challenged by a concern for the welfare of her own child. The functions of these documents are threefold: to help a northern student empathize with the way the white southerner feels about the problem, to portray how the Negro in the South is treated, and to bring to a level of consciousness the student's own mixed feelings about equality for the Negro.
Plessy v. Ferguson Separate-but-Equal	Controversial cases	The Plessy case is used to present the basic conflict between association and equal rights. "Separate-but-Equal" is the follow-up on the actual implementation of Plessy. The focus here is on the problems of implementation: Does one risk revolution to secure the rights of a minority of people?
Judicial History of School Integration	Historical and legal background	This is a second historical document concentrating on the legal status of segregation, bringing it up to the Brown

Title	Type of Material	Specific Function
		case. Its main job is to present key changes in the concept of separate-but-equal.
The Quiet One (a film)	Emotional impact	This is a case study of a preadolescent Negro boy raised in a New York slum. It presents in very personal terms a reasonable explanation for the style of life adopted by many Negroes: broken homes, delinquency, lack of a sense of moral responsibility.
Racial and Cultural Differences Between Negroes and Whites	Sociological and psychological background	A systematic presentation of racial and cultural similarities and differences between Negroes and whites.
The May 17th Decision	Controversial case	This presents some of the essential facts in the 1954 desegregation decision.
Implementing the Supreme Court Decision on Desegregation	Historical and legal background	A systematic presentation of the 1955 Supreme Court decision on implementation.
Baltimore St. Louis Arlington, Va. Front Royal, Va.	Illustrative cases	These four cases present some of the possibilities and problems in implementing the Supreme Court decision.
Washington, D.C. Little Rock, Part I Summerton, S.C.	Controversial cases	These three cases present three quite different reactions to the desegregation decision in three different communities. The cases allow the teacher to explore the full range of legal, political, and moral questions involved.

Outline of a Unit on School Desegregation

I. The Central Issue: Does the white segregationist have the right to control which races his children will associate with in the public schools, or should the right of the Negro to attend racially mixed schools be assured so that he can obtain equal educational opportunities?

A. The Value Conflict: freedom of association v. equal education opportunity
The Legal Conflict: states' rights v. equal protection under the law

B. Important Factual Questions Behind the Conflict
   1. Do most southern whites actually feel that going to school with Negroes seriously infringes upon their freedom of association? Would most whites feel a personal injury if they were forced to attend school with Negroes?
   2. Will Negroes get an inferior education unless the southern schools are desegregated?
   Are segregated schools "inherently inferior" for the Negro?

C. Definitional Problems
   1. What does "equal treatment" mean? Does it mean that each person should be treated exactly the same? Why isn't separate-but-equal actually equal treatment?
   2. What does the word "associate" mean in freedom of association? Does one have to associate with the Negro when one goes to school with him? Do you associate with a person living in the same community with him, or by walking down the same street he does?

D. Analogies to Make the Value Conflict More Salient
   1. Analogies emphasizing association rights
      a. If a group of Indians moved into your town and it was known that there was a very high rate of TB among Indians, would you want them to have a special school?
      b. Is the principal justified in segregating boys and girls on the playground?
      c. What if you and your friends enjoy playing football in one corner of the playground every afternoon? Several boys, who can't play very well and who are always starting fights, want to play with you. Do you have the right to exclude these boys from your game simply because you and your friends don't like them? What if this exclusion makes them feel inferior?
   2. Anologies emphasizing equality rights
      a. Suppose a doctor just doesn't like to associate with people who have dark kinky hair. Does he have the right to refuse to treat such a man who is brought to him for emergency treatment? Does he have a right to refuse him treatment for any kind of medical problem?
      b. Suppose the majority of people in a community decide they do not want to associate in social or school activities with anyone named Smith. Smiths are not allowed to attend the large, well-established local high school; they are, however, given an "equal" education by being sent to a small rural school some 20 miles out of town. Is this equal treatment?

II. The Implementation Issue: Should a whole section of the country be forced to go through a period of increased tension, violence, and civil strife in order to give the Negro equal educational rights, or should the South be allowed to work out the problem itself, perhaps very gradually, so that there will be less threat of violence and less disruption to the normal activities of the community?

A. The Value Conflict: peace and order v. equal educational opportunity
B. Important Factual Questions Behind the Value Conflict
  1. Will there actually be violence and civil strife if we try to desegregate the schools?
  2. Is the violence caused by desegregation itself, or by radical and unstable people within the community who simply use desegregation as an opportunity to vent their pent-up hostilities?
  3. Can the more subtle forms of violence (economic reprisal, intimidation by anonymous phone calls, etc.) be controlled by law enforcement agencies?
  4. Will both Negro and white suffer more through attempts at desegregation than if everyone accepted separate-but-equal?
C. Definitional Problems
  What do we really mean by violence? Are tensions and threats violence? Are boycotts, economic sanctions, or threats of being fired violence? Is mass picketing and jeering violence?
D. Analogies to Make the Value Conflict More Salient
  1. Analogies emphasizing the importance of basic rights and justifying violence
    a. The American Revolution.
    b. World War II.
    c. A man is giving a lecture. Several people start shouting him down and heckling him. Do the police have a right to remove these men from the hall?
    d. You and your friends enter a public playground. Several boys threaten to prevent you from using the baseball field. Should you go ahead and use the field, even though there may be a fight?
  2. Analogies emphasizing peace and order
    a. The Hungarian Revolution of 1956. Should we have risked atomic war to free the Hungarian people?
    b. The seizure of Tibet by Communist China.
    c. A store manager is enraged at a clerk for knocking over a box of cans. You know the clerk did not do it. Should you get into the argument too, especially when you know that the manager is likely to become very angry at you?

III. The Issue of Government, Law, and Higher Morality: Do people have the right to break a law or ruling when they think it goes against a higher moral principle? Can the people of the South justifiably ignore or evade the Supreme Court decision on desegregation, by open or subtle means, because they sincerely believe that it is morally wrong?

A. The Value Conflict: rule of law v. freedom to obey one's conscience
B. Important Factual Questions Behind the Value Conflict
   1. Under what conditions does the federal government consider that a law has actually been broken when a southern school fails to desegregate?
   2. How many southern whites actually feel that it is morally higher to maintain segregation than to obey a federal court order? How many southern whites feel that segregation has a deep moral basis?
C. Definitional Problems
   1. What is the distinction between morality and law? Can a law be immoral? Are some immoral acts lawful?
   2. What is the distinction between state law and constitutional law? Which applies here?
D. Analogies to Make the Value Conflict More Salient
   1. Analogies emphasizing higher morality over law
      a. In the American Revolution, colonists broke English law to defend the rights of man.
      b. Before the Civil War many New Englanders helped slaves escape to Canada. This was a direct violation of the Fugitive Slave Act.
   2. Analogies emphasizing rule of law
      a. Suppose there is an American religious group which requires human sacrifice. Should we let members of this group obey their religious conscience and practice their religion?
      b. Suppose a religious group does not believe in war or killing under any circumstances. Should they be penalized for refusing to serve in the armed forces?
      c. Suppose a religious group believes in polygamy. Should they be allowed to practice this aspect of their religion?

IV. The Federalism Issue: To what extent should people be allowed to run their own affairs within their own community or state, and to what extent should a more distant, and perhaps a more impartial, central government tell the local community what it can and cannot do? Does the federal government have the right under the Constitution to regulate a public school system to implement its own interpretation of equal protection for Negroes?
A. The Value Conflict: states' rights v. equal protection under the law
B. Important Factual Questions Behind the Value Conflict
   1. Are Negroes actually being denied their constitutional rights? Is there anything in the Constitution which states or implies that Negroes have a right to go to integrated schools?
   2. What is the constitutional basis for the southern claim to states' rights?
C. Definitional Problems
     Interpretation of the equal protection clause of the Fourteenth Amendment and the states' rights clause of the Tenth Amendment

D. Analogies to Make the Value Conflict More Salient
1. Analogies emphasizing equal protection over states' rights
   a. Suppose Massachusetts passed a law requiring that everyone whose name begins with *S* go to a separate school. Should the federal government be able to insure equal treatment?
   b. Suppose Massachusetts fined anyone caught speeding $50, unless he came from Boston, in which case he was only warned not to do it again. Should the federal government be able to insure equal treatment?
   c. Equal representation: Should one town or community have proportionately more representatives than another town?
2. Analogies emphasizing states' rights over equal protection
   a. Suppose the state decides to send delinquent and mentally defective children to separate schools. The federal government then steps in and demands that all be sent to the same schools, so that they will be given equal protection under the law.
   b. Suppose the federal government decided that boys and girls should participate in the same sports for physical education and interscholastic athletics in order to get an equal education. Should the right to make this decision be taken away from the local community?

V. The Majority Rule Issue: Which "majority" can make decisions that are best for the community — the majority within a state or the majority within the nation?
A. The Value Conflict: rule of a community by the people within the community v. rule of a community both by the people within the community and by the people who constitute the larger community.
B. Important Factual Questions Behind the Value Conflict
   1. Do the majority of people within the southern states want integrated schools?
   2. Do the majority of people within the nation want integrated schools?
   3. Do the Negroes themselves want integrated schools?
   4. Do the state legislatures in the South fairly represent the will of all the people within these states?
C. Definitional Problems
   When we say that the country should be ruled by the will of the majority, whom do we mean by the "majority"?
   The majority of people on the Supreme Court?
   The majority as "power" possessed by the federal government?
   The majority of those people who have the power to pass an amendment to the Constitution?
   The majority of voters in the whole country?
D. Analogies
   See analogies under "The Federalism Issue."

Appendix B.   Little Rock I

Little Rock is the capital and largest city of Arkansas. Its population is about 120,000, one-quarter of which is Negro. In many ways it is like a typical Southern city. Negroes and whites have separate hotels, restaurants, theaters, swimming pools, and golf courses. In the last twenty years, however, there has been less and less segregation. In 1956, segregation on buses ended. The Arkansas public colleges and medical school admit Negroes. City hospitals let in people of both races.

The people in Little Rock boast that "they are the friendliest people on earth." Many visitors agree. Most people there are against integration but think it will come, sooner or later. The people in Little Rock are almost all against the use of violence. They say it goes against the Bible.

In 1955 the Little Rock School Board decided on a plan for gradual integration of the schools. The white high schools would accept a few Negroes in 1957. The junior high schools would be integrated in 1960, and the elementary schools in 1963. The NAACP went to court saying that the plan was too slow. In April, 1956, the Federal Court decided that the plan met the requirements of "all deliberate speed," and approved the plan. This meant that integration would start when school opened on September 3.

On August 29 a group of white citizens went to the local state court. They asked the court to prevent school integration. One of the witnesses was the Governor of Arkansas, Orval Faubus. He testified that there would be riots and bloodshed if the schools let in Negroes. The judge agreed and ordered the city *not* to integrate.

On August 30, the Little Rock School Board went to the Federal Court. They disagreed with Governor Faubus and asked the court to overrule the state court decision. The judge, Ronald N. Davies, did just that. He ordered the citizens of Little Rock not to interfere with integration. The stage was now set for the dramatic events of the next three weeks.

On Monday evening, September 2, most of the people in Little Rock tuned in their television sets to hear their governor make a speech. Governor Faubus spoke slowly, quietly, and seriously. He said that if the schools integrated on Tuesday there would be serious trouble. To prevent trouble, he had called out the Arkansas National Guard. He said that he was doing this not to prevent integration but to keep law and order. He read the telegram he had sent to Major General Sherman T. Clinger, Commanding Officer of the Arkansas National Guard. The order read: "You are directed to place off limits to white students those schools for colored students and to place off limits to colored students those schools heretofore operated and recently set up for white students. This order will remain in effect until the demobilization of the Guard or until further orders."

The members of the school board were stunned by the news. They called a special meeting right after the telecast. At the meeting they decided to ask the Negro children not to try to attend Central High School in the morning.

Tuesday morning, September 3, was hot. When the 1900 students of Central

High returned to school they saw a strange sight. Surrounding the school were 270 soldiers in full uniform. They wore shiny helmets and carried bayonetted rifles, clubs, and gas masks. No Negro students showed up and there was no trouble.

Later that day, there was a hearing in Judge Davies' federal courtroom. He ordered the school board to forget the soldiers and let the Negroes enter the school.

On Wednesday morning, September 4, nine Negro students decided to try to attend Central High School. There was a crowd of about 400 people in front of the school building. As the Negroes approached the school someone yelled, "A nigger! They're coming! Here they come."

The crowd surged forward. There was yelling and screaming. People cursed and spat. The Negro students continued their quiet and serious walk. Fifteen-year-old Elizabeth Eckford was the first Negro to reach the school entrance. A soldier brought his rifle up and barred the way. Elizabeth was trembling with fear and close to tears. She turned and started to walk away from the school. As she walked back to the bus-stop, the crowd yelled and jeered at her. Some people looked as if they were going to hit her. She finally reached the bus-stop bench and sat down. She burst into tears.

The other Negro students were also forbidden to enter the school. The soldiers kept order and the Negroes left without any fights. When the Negroes were gone, the crowd gradually melted away.

The F.B.I. began an immediate investigation on instructions from Judge Davies. This made Governor Faubus angry. He sent a long telegram to President Eisenhower. In this telegram, the Governor protested this "interference." He said that it was his duty to keep law and order. He asked the President for cooperation and understanding. The Governor also charged that his telephone was being tapped.

On Thursday the President, who was on vacation in Newport, Rhode Island, replied to Governor Faubus' telegram. Mr. Eisenhower denied that the F.B.I. was tapping the Governor's phone. He also said, "The Constitution will be upheld by me by every legal means at my command."

On the same day the school board went back to Judge Davies' court. They asked the Judge to postpone integration temporarily because of all the excitement. The Judge refused to do this. He ordered the school board to integrate Central High School. He pointed out that the Mayor of Little Rock, Woodrow Wilson Mann, had said that the local police could take care of any trouble.

During the next week, the National Guard remained on duty outside Central High School. None of the Negroes tried to enter. Governor Faubus said that he had evidence that there would be serious riots if the National Guard were removed. President Eisenhower kept in close touch with events. The F.B.I. continued its investigations. There were rumors that federal troops would be sent in to force integration in Central High. On September 11 Governor Faubus sent a telegram to the President asking for a conference on the matter. Eisenhower agreed and a meeting was set for September 14.

On September 14, Faubus flew to Newport to see the President. After their meeting, both men seemed happy. They said that the court decision would be respected but gave no details on any agreement.

The people who thought this meant the National Guard would be taken away were disappointed. The soldiers remained on duty and no Negroes tried to enter the high school. The Governor gave no hint as to when he might remove the soldiers.

On September 20 Judge Davies called in the lawyers of the state of Arkansas. He ordered the Governor and the National Guard commanders to stop preventing Negros from entering Central High School.

That night Governor Faubus went on the radio. He criticized Judge Davies' decision but said he would obey it. He ordered the National Guard withdrawn. The Governor asked the people to remain calm and avoid violence.

Although the National Guard had left, the high school was still guarded on Monday, September 23. This time it was guarded by a strong detail of city and state police. In addition, there was a crowd of about 500 people when the nine Negro students arrived at the school.

The crowd was a hysterical and shrieking mob. The police could not hold the crowd back. The mass of people swarmed all over the building, yelling and cursing. "We'll lynch them all!" some yelled. "Where are those niggers?" others screamed. "We'll never let them get in!"

At 8:45 four of five Negro newspapermen started walking toward the front door of the school. The crowd, mistaking them for the students, gave out a yell. They pounced on the four men, punching and pushing them. One reporter was jumped upon and beaten. While this was going on, the nine Negro students calmly slipped into a side door and entered school.

This enraged the crowd, which had now grown to 1,000 persons. They became hysterical. People were howling and crying. Some people shook with rage. The police were now completely powerless.

Soon white students began leaving the school. There were rumors of severe fighting going on inside the building. The crowd got larger and nastier. One policeman took off his badge and joined the crowd. There were attempts to start a mass rush into the school.

Finally, at noon, the Mayor gave in. He decided to remove the Negro students because of the danger of even worse trouble. The Negroes were taken out by the back door and driven away unharmed. The chief of police announced to the crowd that the Negroes had left. The mob refused to believe him. A few people went inside and thoroughly searched the building. They came back and told the crowd they had found no Negroes. Only then did the crowd start to leave.

That evening, at 6:23 Eastern Daylight Time, President Eisenhower made a formal proclamation. He ordered the people of Little Rock to stop preventing integration. He said he would use any force that was necessary to carry out the orders of the Federal Court.

No Negroes showed up for school on September 24. There was a big crowd on hand, though this time it was much quieter. At 10:22 A.M., Little Rock time, the President ordered United States soldiers into the city to enforce integration. Five hours later, members of the famous battle-hardened 101st Airborne Division began to arrive in Little Rock. They moved quickly and efficiently to set up positions around the school. The city was quiet and grim.

In the morning the federal soldiers took firm command of the situation. Heavily armed troops were stationed at all important points. The soldiers wore helmets, carried clubs, and rifles with bayonets. The soldiers were instructed to break up any trouble immediately.

Somebody yelled, "The South has been occupied."

Another yelled, "Put down that rifle and I'll take you on!"

A woman screamed, "They're trying to cram this thing down our throats."

A larger crowd started to form at one point. A lieutenant shouted orders. Immediately a platoon of soldiers arrived in double-time. They pushed the crowd back. One man refused to move. A tight-lipped soldier jabbed his bayonet into the man, C. E. Blake, a railroad worker. Blake still refused to move. He grabbed at the rifle and tried to push the soldier away. Suddenly, a rifle butt came crashing down on his head. Blake went down with a blood-stained forehead. The soldiers moved on.

A hundred yards away from the school another small group refused to move away. Lieutenant William Ness looked at the crowd for a moment. Then he said, "Either you move or we'll move you." The crowd moved.

At 9:22 A.M. the air was filled with screaming sirens. Racing down the street was a huge Army limousine escorted by jeeps loaded with armed soldiers. The vehicles stopped in front of the school. Nine Negro students guarded by heavily armed United States soldiers entered the school. A squad of soldiers also went in to prevent trouble inside the school.

There was no serious trouble outside the school. Whenever anyone started anything he was quickly moved out or arrested. The Army was firm and tough. There were stories that there was some trouble inside the school. Some said the Negroes were cursed at, tripped, and shoved around. The Negro students denied all this.

There was no further serious violence during school year '57-'58. A few white students were expelled for starting fights with Negroes. But outside the school the Army kept tight control. The number of soldiers on duty there was gradually cut. However, most people agree that Central High School has Negro students only because there were heavily armed U.S. troops stationed there. Many people believed that if they had been removed, there would have been more riots and fighting.

References

"Another Tragic Era?" *U.S. News and World Report,* October 4, 1957, pp. 33-69.

"Little Rock Arkansas," in "The News of the Week in Review," *New York Times,* Sunday, September 8, 1957, p. 1.

"Mixed-School Issue Comes to a Head," *U.S. News and World Report,* September 13, 1957, pp. 27-30.

New York Times, September 24, 1957, pp. 1, 18.

Illustrative Lesson Plan

LITTLE ROCK I

I. Background Questions: Orientation to Case
   1. In what year did the school crisis take place?
   2. Compare the percentage of Negroes in Little Rock to those in some of the other cities about which we have studied.
   3. What are some of the segregation practices in the city?
   4. What reason did Governor Faubus give for not wanting to integrate the schools?
   5. Over what court did Judge Davies preside?
   6. Why were U.S. soldiers sent into Little Rock?

II. Values: This case illustrates several important government principles.
   1. Can you name some of the principles involved?
   2. We shall focus on the dilemma of peace and order vs. equality. Which principle is Governor Faubus upholding? Which principle are the Negroes upholding?

III. Challenging the Student's Position with Analogies
   1. Analogies emphasizing fair treatment at the risk of violence.
      a. Should we have fought the American Revolution? After all, that meant resorting to violence, e.g., the Boston Tea Party.
      b. Should this country have gone to war in 1941 against Germany? Is it worth fighting a war simply to guarantee freedom to somebody? What about Cuba or Hungary?
      c. Some nasty kids keep interfering with your ball game. You tell them to leave you alone in a nice way. If they refuse, do you have a right to fight with them in order to protect your right to play the game?
   2. Analogies emphasizing the importance of peace and order at the expense of human rights.
      a. You are all dressed up going to church. You see a big boy picking on a smaller boy. You know if you start a fight you might lose and will get all dirtied up. Would you start a fight with the big boy to protect the smaller boy?
      b. Communist China is interfering with the rights of the peaceful Tibetans. This is a small country thousands of miles away. Should we start a war with China and risk hydrogen warfare over Tibet?

IV. Important Factual Assumptions Behind Conflict
   1. Will there actually be violence and civil strife if desegregation of the schools is attempted?
   2. Will the violence be caused by the fact of desegregation rather than by radical or extremist groups who might be only a small minority? Was the violence in Little Rock caused by Faubus or by the original court order?

V. Definitional Problem

Governor Faubus claimed that if integration took place there would be violence. What is "violence"? Is the intimidation of the Negro violence? Is the increase in racial tension violence? Are large and noisy meetings of extremist groups violence?

VI. A Problem of Prediction

Governor Faubus made the claim that if integration took place there would be violence. How would you go about testing this claim in advance of the actual integration?

CHAPTER NINE

Analysis of the Teaching Dialogue

Although automated teaching devices, audio-visual media, and large-group instruction may supplant the inefficient methods by which much information is now "taught" to students, the classroom dialogue will undoubtedly remain the major vehicle through which complex learning outcomes are achieved. This is certainly the case for the approach to social studies instruction presented in this book, since our central objective is to teach the student to carry on an intelligent dialogue bearing on important public issues.

RESEARCH ON CLASSROOM INTERACTION

During the last fifty years educators have approached the analysis of classroom discourse in a variety of ways. Dewey, for example, suggested that the anatomy of problem-solving be described and the findings applied in the classroom. Other investigators have attempted to determine the effect of classroom interaction on learning through systematic empirical research. While this research is not specifically related to the teaching of public issues, it does have implications for the teacher or researcher who is dealing with the type of social studies program described in earlier chapters. How one conceptualizes the act of teaching has much to do with the kinds of statements he sees as relevant and available in the classroom dialogue. One teacher, for example, might be mostly concerned with the quality of personal feelings and interpersonal attitudes exhibited in the classroom; a second might focus on the accuracy of the information presented by text or teacher and repeated by the student; a third might deal mainly with the problem of eliciting and clarifying student description of a particular issue or problem. Obviously each of these teachers is sensitive to and seeks to evoke quite a different range of behavior.

Although at present there is little definitive research by which to judge the effectiveness of various types of teaching, a substantial body of research literature is based on the theoretical premise that interpersonal and affective components play a major role in determining an effective classroom dialogue. This, of course, is in sharp contrast to the conceptual framework presented so far in this book. Our main emphasis has been on the intellectual qualities of the dialogue as they move a problematic situation toward clarification and/or resolution. It should be clear that the two types of framework are not mutually exclusive or contradictory. They do, however, emphasize quite different elements in the interaction process, as can perhaps best be explicated by briefly reviewing three selected studies which illustrate the "interpersonal approach" and then giving a detailed presentation of our own analysis of the teaching dialogue.

The central theoretical proposition out of which the interpersonal approach operates is summarized by R. C. Anderson:

> In most teaching methods textbooks you will find reference to two basic teaching styles which can be called teacher-centered and learner-centered. (See, for example, Brandwein, Watson and Blackwood, 1958; Burnett, 1957; Burton, 1952; Cronbach, 1954; Grambs, Iverson, and Patterson, 1958). . . . Leadership is universally defined in terms of a hypothetical authoritian-democratic dimension. Many labels have been applied to this dimension — perhaps it should be called a dichotomy, for such it has been in practice: dominative-integrative, employer-centered — employee-centered, teacher-centered — learner-centered, therapist-centered — client-centered, supervisory-participatory, directive — nondirective; but the idea is basically the same.[1]

Pioneer research along these lines was carried out by H. H. Anderson,[2] who developed the theoretical construct "domination-integration." He defined dominative behavior as a mode of response to others characterized by resistance to change, the use of threat or force, or unwillingness to entertain or use the ideas of others. Integrative behavior involves willingness to change, the use of voluntary controls, and willingness to use the ideas of others. With these definitions as a basis, Anderson devised a system of thirty-five major categories to be used in classifying student and teacher behavior. Flanders summarizes the findings that have accumulated within this theoretical framework:

First, the dominative and integrative contacts of the teacher set a pattern of behavior that spreads throughout the classroom; the behavior of the teacher, more than any other individual, sets the climate of the classroom. The rule is that when either type of contact predominates, domination incites further domination, and integration stimulates further integration. It is the teacher's tendency that spreads among pupils and is continued even when the teacher is no longer in the room. Furthermore, the pattern a teacher develops in one year is likely to persist in his classroom the following year with different pupils. Second, when a teacher has a higher proportion of integrative contacts, pupils show more spontaneity and initiative, voluntary social contributions and acts of problem solving. Third, when a teacher has a higher proportion of dominative contacts, the pupils are more easily distracted from school work, and show greater compliance to as well as rejection of teacher domination.[3]

While H. H. Anderson was primarily concerned with the relationships among gross classroom behaviors, e.g., "spontaneous activity," Flanders has stressed the student-teacher dialogue itself.[4] He suggests that the important underlying quality of the interpersonal relationship is the method by which the teacher seeks to influence the student's behavior: Does the teacher attempt to use *direct* influence on the student by arbitrarily focusing his attention on the teacher's statements and commands? Or does the teacher use *indirect* influence by encouraging the student to reflect upon his own behavior as the central focus of the classroom? In the latter case, presumably the student has greater freedom because there is the opportunity to construe the content of the dialogue as well as procedures in the classroom in a way that will make sense to him.

To quantify differences in the teacher's classroom behavior, Flanders developed an observational scheme containing ten categories: (1) clarify feeling constructively; (2) praise or encourage; (3) clarify, develop, or make use of ideas suggested by students; (4) ask questions; (5) lecture; (6) give directions; (7) criticize or justify authority; (8) student talk — initiated by the teacher; (9) student-initiated talk; (10) silence or confusion. Categories 8 and 9 are used for classifying student talk. Categories 1 through 4 are considered by Flanders to characterize *indirect* influence, while categories 5, 6, and 7 are considered indicators of *direct* influence. An index of the quality of influence is the ratio of indirect to direct categorizations for each teacher (the I/D Ratio).

Flanders investigated the effect of teacher behavior characterized as having high and low I/D ratios on learning using objective tests of information in mathematics and social studies. The results indicated that high I/D teachers were significantly more effective than low I/D teachers, although only the extremes showed striking differences. This finding is especially interesting, since studies in which quantitative criteria of teaching style have been significantly related to independent measures of learning are somewhat unusual.

Although not designed to investigate the relationship between teaching style and student learning, a study carried out by Marie Hughes[5] should be mentioned here, since it illustrates some of the difficulties in the basic constructs utilized by H. H. Anderson and Flanders. Hughes was concerned with the identification of general criteria for classifying "good" and "bad" teaching. Relying largely on the work of H. H. Anderson, she developed an observational system based on the "socially integrative" and "dominative" construct. Observers classified descriptions of raw classroom behavior in seven categories, according to the "function" performed in the discussion:

1. *Controlling Functions:* Teacher activities designating the thing to which children are to give their attention, and the individual or group that is to do it; stating or asking for a recall of the proper and accepted way of doing things; judging who is right when there is a conflict of interest or dispute.
2. *Imposition of the Teacher:* Teacher projecting herself into a child's activity without being asked; doing routine clerical work for children (handing out paper, etc.); helping a child when he doesn't ask for it; giving information to the child which is not centrally relevant to the conversation, but which the teacher feels is "necessary."
3. *Facilitating Functions:* Neutral functions which facilitate the movement of content or activity underway. These activities include checking for information or clarifying a procedure.
4. *Functions that Develop Content:* This function involves such behaviors as repeating what the child has said, stating it in different words, and elaborating on what has been said; also asking the child for a personal opinion.
5. *Functions of Personal Response:* This function is a response to a personal problem expressed by the child. The problem may be asking for a piece of paper, asking for the teacher's attention, responding to a personal experience as it is recited by a child. Also included in this category is acknowledgement of a teacher mistake.
6. *Functions of Positive Affectivity:* This includes support, encouragement, solicitousness.
7. *Functions of Negative Affectivity:* This includes such subcategories as admonish, reprimand, accuse, threaten, ignore.

Behaviors falling into categories 4, 5, and 6 are considered integrative, while categories 1, 2, and 7 are dominative categories. A quantitative definition of the "model teacher" was derived from specimens of teaching from a sample of 129 classroom sessions. Although the process of deriving the "model teacher" is not made clear, the final conceptualization is explicitly related to the integrative-dominative model. It is clear that integrative teaching is assumed to produce the flexible, inquiring student who will be a more useful, reflective, autonomous citizen. The actual impact of dominative or integrative behavior on learning outcomes, however, is not systematically investigated. Hughes does make some interesting observations about the large proportion of teacher statements which serve "controlling" or "imposition" functions and the relatively small number of statements which serve the function of "developing content."

In the work of both Flanders and Hughes the undifferentiated nature of their "logical" or intellectual categories is evident. Flanders, for example, has a category for statements that "clarify a student's idea," while Hughes has one for statements that function to "develop content." Both apparently refer to the extent to which the teacher is responsive to information as it is construed and presented by the *student*. From our point of view this is only a precondition to judging the quality of the teacher's behavior. It is necessary to ask further questions. For example, what relevance does the teacher's response have to the intellectual content of the child's statement? Hughes' model teacher might well score high on "content development functions" by reinforcing "loose" thinking — that is, overgeneralization and egocentric construction of social issues. Without a more careful definition of the processes involved in the "development of content," how does one know how to evaluate behavior in this category?

Although some valuable research has come out of the work of H. H. Anderson, Flanders, and Hughes, adherents of the interpersonal approach to classroom interaction have generally not found the objective evidence to support their position. R. C. Anderson, for example, after an exhaustive critical review of research bearing on the learning outcomes or productivity of groups or individuals in groups conducted in a "learner-centered" versus a "teacher-centered" way, concludes,

> To summarize the educational research reviewed in this article, eleven studies have reported greater learning for learner-centered groups, thirteen have shown no difference, and eight have found teacher-centered methods superior to learner-centered. It should be noted that while some investigations have reported a *statistically* significant difference favoring one method or other, it is doubtful if any of these differences are of *practical* or *social* significance.[6]

It is likely that the oversimplified categorization of information exchanged in the teacher-pupil dialogue, and the attendant failure to get at the processes by which such information is challenged and justified, is a major reason that these studies have failed to make a definitive impact on our knowledge of the effects of classroom interaction on learning. Smith, in reporting one of the first systematic efforts to describe in detail the intellectual processes carried on in the classroom, has made similar criticisms of educational research carried on with a psychosocial, or interpersonal, model.[7] He notes, for instance, that the development of empirical methods in psychology led to the reduction of mental processes to sensations, images, and associative mechanisms. And while Dewey looked at teaching as guiding the learner through the process of discovery and verification according to his model of logical thinking, Kilpatrick and others who followed Dewey generally ignored the logical aspects of Dewey's thinking and emphasized the psychological and social needs of the learner. As a result, Smith maintains, distinctions between valid and invalid thinking have been discarded as unnecessary to a psychological analysis of the act of teaching, and the logic by which we judge the rigor of any inquiry has been ignored as a basis of inquiry into classroom discourse.

Smith has developed a category system to describe the "logically relevant tasks" of teaching, as distinguished from "directive tasks" and "admonitory acts." Following are the major categories: (1) defining (four types), (2) describing, (3) designating (five types), (4) stating, (5) reporting, (6) substituting, (7) valuating, (8) opining, (9) classifying, (10) comparing and contrasting, (11) conditional inferring, (12) explaining (six types), and (13) directing and managing classroom. Using these categories to quantify classroom discourse, Smith has found systematic differences among teachers in a single content field, and different patterns of logical operations in different content fields.

In an effort to bring the logical elements of classroom discourse back into the center of research in teaching, Smith and his associates have emphasized the need to discover ways not only of encouraging the child to reflect and inquire but also of teaching the child to reflect and inquire in a disciplined and intelligent way. Although we are in substantial agreement with this position, two reservations are in order. First, Smith apparently begins with a conception of "logic" which is presumed to be generally useful for analyzing a wide spectrum of "problems" in various curriculum areas. Perhaps one might better begin with the species of problem with which a particular type of student-teacher dialogue is intended to deal and inquire into the intellectual framework required to clarify or resolve this type of problem. The number and specificity of distinctions in the category scheme could then be limited to those which seem necessary to pick up such clarification. In Parts One and Two of this book, for example, we identified a type of problem and a framework within which such problems might be construed. It is from this basis that our own analysis of the "logic" of classroom interaction began.

Second, in ignoring the role of interpersonal affect and the problems of classroom procedure and control, Smith dismisses the possibility that effective classroom teaching may be based on affective and procedural as well as logical factors. It may well be that the interrelationships among a number of such dimensions will best predict successful teaching. In our analysis of the pupil-teacher dialogue — although our emphasis is clearly on the intellectual requirements of the dialogue — we have taken into account other major dimensions.

A MULTIDIMENSIONAL ANALYSIS OF THE ACT OF TEACHING

In attempting to conceptualize a more adequate theoretical framework within which to look at the teacher-student dialogue, we started with the distinction, set forth by Bales in *Interaction Process Analysis*,[8] between social-emotional and task responses. We then made a further breakdown in the task area between those responses which attempt to structure the task in the immediate interpersonal situation and those responses which deal with the political problem under discussion. We called the former *procedural* responses and the latter *cognitive* task responses. These distinctions have substantial support from systematic investigation, as suggested by R. C. Anderson:

> There are probably many variables of leadership and group life. Hemphill (1949), after analysis of some five hundred existing groups, arrived at sixteen descriptive variables. Factor analysis of Hemphill's variables (Gekoski, 1952), as well as factor analyses by Carter and Couch (1953), yield three dimensions which the present author likes to interpret as follows:
>
> 1. *The Affective area.* Includes degree of interpersonal warmth or coolness, tension or relaxation; degree of antagonism or solidarity. Opposes friendly pleasant exchange to hostility and constraint.
> 2. *The Procedural area.* Includes statement and control of agenda, control of communication, division of labor. Refers to amount of structure and degree of organization as opposed to degree of disorganization or looseness of structure.
> 3. *The Task area.* Includes quantity and quality of work done, units produced, ideas presented, solutions considered. Opposes solution reached, problem solved, high performance maintained to no solution, problem unsolved, poor performance. Productivity versus sterility.[9]

We then analyzed the affective-procedural-task trichotomy into a number of more specific dimensions, which are summarized below.

A Set of Dimensions for Describing the Teaching Dialogue

Cognitive or Task Dimensions.
1. *Statement posture.*[10] Statement posture refers to whether the teacher

or student is making a positive assertion, asking a question, questioning or challenging a statement made by another individual, or expressing self-doubt, by questioning either his own statement or his own competence to make a statement. Statement posture was a major discriminating factor in Flanders' work and has obvious implications for describing important distinctions in teacher style.

2. *Discussion posture.* We have been concerned with two aspects of the teacher's approach to the *content* of a discussion. The first has to do with whether issues in a discussion are viewed as problematic. If the content is seen as problematic with no definite "right" answers to be conveyed to the students, we would call the discussion, or that part of a discussion, *dialectical.* If the teacher discusses the content, through either statements or questions, with the assumption that he is dealing with definitive truth — that is, certain knowledge which is either present or available — we would call the dialogue (or monologue, if in lecture form) *descriptive.* To state it another way, while both descriptive and dialectical teaching *may* assume a problem or question before the class, the dialectical posture necessarily does assume it. In the latter case, it is also assumed that the student has some degree of autonomy in the way he deals with the question or problem. In the pure sense of the dialectic, it is assumed that the outcome of the discussion will not be the sum of the teacher's contributions but a result of teacher and student contributions.[11]

A second dimension of discussion posture, which may be applied in either a dialectical or a descriptive situation, is the extent to which the discussion is centered around the *substantive issue* described by a commonly agreed-upon set of categories, as opposed to an *analytic approach* to the problem. In the latter an effort is made to explore new ways of looking at or structuring the nature and scope of the problem so that its substance can be more adequately handled. For example, a group might discuss whether the United States should support or withdraw from the United Nations. The argument might focus on whether or not UN actions are a beneficial extension of the United States' foreign policy of collective security. At this point, collective security might constitute the substantive issue under discussion. One member of the group might then suggest that the evaluation of the UN could be discussed in several contexts: (a) as a primitive instrument of world law which supersedes the concept of "foreign policy"; (b) as a propaganda safety valve which allows various governments to gauge world opinion; (c) as a tool of foreign policy for individual nations. Although a statement such as this might broaden the context of discussion and suggest a more complex framework within which to deal with the issue, it makes no judgment itself concerning whether or not the UN is a worthwhile institution. We call such statements analytic rather than substantive, since they focus not on a suggested solution to the point under controversy but rather on the conceptual context within which the point under controversy is to be handled.

In summary, then, we are suggesting two dimensions of discussion posture: descriptive v. dialectical, and substantive v. analytic.

3. *Statement types.* Another level of cognitive analysis concerns the content of statements used in classroom discussion. Does the teacher give or ask for a large number of value judgments or is he basically concerned with either giving or asking for factual claims about reality? Does he spend a great deal of time repeating and summarizing what has gone before in the discussion? If he asks his students to make value judgments, are the requests aimed at eliciting general societal commitments or the evaluation of specific acts not put in the broader context? In our systematic analysis of classroom discussion we have, for example, differentiated the following statement types: general values, specific values, general legal claims, specific legal claims, factual generalizations, specific factual statements, sources of evidence, statements of clarification, statements of repetition, definitions, and analogies or "cases."

4. *Logical or intellectual operations.* A fourth level of analysis deals with the logical or intellectual operations performed by the teacher or student as each attempts to break down or develop a policy decision. In general terms, some of these operations are: problem differentiation and focus (determining whether the problem is mainly ethical, factual, or definitional); relevance testing (Is a statement relevant to the discussion and to the particular problem being considered?); dialectical strategy (the use of specific instances to contradict more general statements, and the use of qualifying statements to cover the inconsistencies). It should be noted that some "statement types," e.g., factual generalizations, imply logical or intellectual operations. The two dimensions are not mutually exclusive. Also the complexity of a cognitive episode should be kept in mind. An argument or "brief" might consist of two vaguely related statements (e.g., The United States should continue nuclear testing because you can't trust the Russians), or it might consist of a complex series of explicitly interrelated propositions.

Defining teacher style in terms of statement types and intellectual operations is of critical importance in the area of political controversy analysis, where both the efficiency of the teaching situation and the learning outcomes of students may be defined with the same intellectual or logical concepts. The extent to which the teacher tends to be consistently concerned with the relevance of statements made in discussions; the extent to which he gives and demands evidence for claims; the extent to which he chooses to treat problems of word usage as arbitrary matters of convention by a rather free and easy use of stipulative definitions, or feels constrained to handle definitional problems within the network of existing meaning of words — these kinds of decisions on the part of the teacher may well be reflected in the way the *student* comes to handle similar problems, and thus may be important predictors of student learning. Both statement types and logical operations are, in fact, the basis of an assessment procedure described in Chapter Eleven.

Social-Emotional Dimensions. Another important dimension of classroom behavior is *interpersonal affect,* i.e., the positive or negative feelings communicated in the interaction process. The dimension is so obvious as to require little explanation. We should point out, however, that it is possible to discriminate at least two different types of affective expression: support v. antagonism, and tension v. tension release.

The behavioral cues for the first dimension are self-explanatory. The most obvious example of behavior indicating tension release is laughter. Evidence of tension is more difficult to infer from observable classroom behavior. It can, however, be operationally defined by such actions as pencil-tapping, pacing the floor, and nervous laughter. Of course, it is assumed that tension underlies, and is the cause of, the more boisterous laughter which is taken to be indicative of tension release.

Procedural Dimensions. Procedure refers to direct efforts to control the behavior of group members: giving directions for the conduct of a discussion, giving assignments, handling discipline problems, etc. In our own work we distinguish between task-oriented procedural acts and those mainly concerned with deviance control. For example, asking students to take out their books at the beginning of the period would be task oriented; telling the student to stop talking to his neighbor would be deviance control.

Even with the gross distinctions suggested above, the systematic analysis of the teacher-student dialogue becomes a very complex business. Operationally, we can ask the following questions as we observe each statement in a discussion.

1. Is the act (or interact) a statement, a question, the questioning of another statement, or an expression of self-doubt?
2. Is the act cognitive or procedural? If it is cognitive, we can ask a number of more specific questions:
   a. Is the act descriptive or dialectical?
   b. Is the act substantive or analytic with respect to the problem under consideration?
   c. What type of statement is being made: value judgment, factual claim, definitional statement, clarification, etc.?
   d. What intellectual operations are in evidence: discriminating among statements with different degrees of relevance, generalizing from specific cases, specifying the meaning of a general statement, quali-

fying a general statement to take into account inconsistency, etc.?
3. If the statement is procedural, is it simply to facilitate the completion of the task, or is it an attempt to control deviant behavior on the part of group members?
4. Are there observable affective overtones to the cognitive or procedural message? If so, are these overtones antagonistic or supportive? Is tension or tension release present?

A Broader View of Discussion Style

Although the dialogue can be dissected into any number of appropriate dimensions, and teaching behavior identified along these dimensions, we recognize that, at least intuitively, consistent clusterings of certain types of statements, or *general* styles of teaching, seem to be observable. In dealing with the problem of describing general styles an important question arises: Which of the various dimensions set forth should be considered central and which should be considered secondary in the definitions? In describing a general style of teaching in order to investigate its effect on learning, for example, is it more important that teachers be alike in the posture used, in the intellectual operations performed, in the amount and direction of affectivity shown, or in all three areas? Experimentally, there are at least two strategies one might use in answering this question. One might obtain a large sample of teachers, give them the same materials to teach, ask them to direct the class's attention toward the analysis and clarification of controversial political issues, and then observe the range and profiles of behavior that follow and relate these to learning outcomes. Or one might define two or more particular styles of teaching along those dimensions of behavior that seemed critical, train teachers to use the styles, observe to what extent the dimensions of teaching not included in the definition were also affected by the different styles, and again determine the relationship of behavioral dimensions to student learning. In the long run, we are saying that with both strategies our ability to identify and differentiate teaching styles is justified by the kinds of predictions we can make about learning outcomes. No matter how different two teaching styles may appear to an observer, they are "significantly different" from an educational standpoint only if they lead to different learning outcomes.

In our own work we have chosen to define styles of discourse according to certain conceptual dimensions, train teachers in these styles, and then observe what differences occur, if any, in teacher behavior. This approach can best be illustrated by describing two style models we have investigated experimentally — "recitation" and "socratic" teaching.

Recitation Teaching. Probably the basic characteristic of recitation teaching is the teacher's attitude toward and control of knowledge.

Through reading assignments — usually a text — and through his role in class discussions he provides the correct information which the students are to know. The student is expected to respond when called upon to fill in the sequence of information which the teacher wishes to develop in class. This involves mainly relating personal experiences or repeating or paraphrasing what the teacher or a text has said, although it may require the use of some independent thought, such as reorganizing previously read material or applying it to a new situation. In essence, then, evidence of learning is contingent upon the extent to which the student can respond to questions regarding information given him by the teacher, either in class or through texts and other media.

Socratic Teaching. Socratic teaching, as we have conceived it, is clearly adversarial. When the center of discussion is a controversial political topic — as in our work — socratic teaching requires that the student do more than describe the controversy in the terms in which the teacher (or assigned materials) has presented it. Rather, the teacher requires the student to take a position on the issue, state that position, and defend it. Here the emphasis is not only on knowledge provided by the teacher as background for the discussion but on the process by which the student arrives at a decision about the topic under consideration, on the careful consideration of alternative decisions, and on the utilization of analytic concepts and strategies, regardless of the position which is finally reached.

Describing General Styles Dimensionally. While these brief descriptions of the two styles suggest that we "know" what are, in fact, the differences between socratic and recitation teaching, when one begins to work in the classroom situation, the general descriptions very quickly prove inadequate to interpret subtle differences between the two teaching situations. It is this fact that has led us to systematic dimensional analysis. Clearly, however, such analysis does not replace general style description. Theoretically, it will simply provide a more precise and reliable way of defining what may well be general or "natural" teaching styles.

To illustrate how systematic analysis contributes to the description of teaching style, we shall define some of the similarities and differences between socratic and recitation teaching in terms of the dimensions set forth above. This description might well be viewed as a set of hypotheses about the behavior to be observed when teachers use the two styles of discourse in the classroom.

Statement posture. Recitation teaching is characterized by a high frequency of "stating" and "question-asking," with less emphasis on "questioning" or "expressions of self-doubt." With its adversarial nature, socratic teaching shows a much higher frequency in "questioning" responses.

Discussion posture. Recitation teaching tends to be descriptive; it is assumed that the truth of the situation is available and that one has only to present and clarify information or an analytic structure by which information can be organized. The attempt to push the student toward a personal decision in which values are at stake is inappropriate for this style. The socratic style is clearly dialectical. It assumes that the problem can be clarified only in an adversarial context, in which various points of view are presented and defended.

Both recitation and socratic teaching may emphasize either substantive or analytic responses. The recitation teacher, however, will be concerned with the substance of the issue only insofar as he is interested in clarifying and presenting the correct position. In the process of clarifying, he may well be analytic, asking that his students explain, for example, "What are the possible ways one might look at this problem?" The concepts which the students apply to the analysis will be those given them by the teacher as correct. The recitation teacher will often avoid giving an answer to the substantive issue. In using the socratic style, on the other hand, the teacher focuses directly on the substantive issue and possible answers to it. From time to time, however, the socratic teacher may depart from the dialectical posture and treat the problem analytically in order to facilitate conceptualization of the problem. The structure used for such an analysis may have been taught in a descriptive manner or, if the teacher maintains a "pure" style throughout, will probably have evolved from a dialectical discussion of the proper framework for viewing controversial political issues.

Statement types. Recitation teaching involves mainly factual claims. The teacher tends to deal with descriptions of reality, rather than with what reality should be like. The recitation teacher in maintaining the sequence of his lesson — to the extent that it is successfully programed — tends to proceed by gradual, well-related steps, using a great many summarizing, repeating, and focusing statements. The socratic teacher, on the other hand, in dealing with political controversy, tends to ask for value judgments or decisions and to challenge them. Factual claims will function mainly as background to the issue and as support for value statements. There is also a sequential factor involved in socratic teaching. It is likely to involve an emphasis on factual statements and questions as the discussion gets under way with the emphasis on value issues coming later. Recitation teaching is not likely to reflect any such clear-cut sequential pattern.

Intellectual operations. Since the socratic teacher is engaged in an adversarial role, he may well use a higher frequency of logical operations.

It is also likely that, because the teacher and students are engaging in controversy rather than talking about it, the intellectual episodes will be longer and more complex than in recitation teaching.

The procedural dimension. Procedurally, we have considered the teacher as the focus of a dialogue between himself and the students, regardless of which of the two styles he is using. Within this context, there is no reason to expect systematic differences between recitation and socratic teachers on this dimension.

The affective dimension. Both the socratic and the recitation teacher need to be supportive of the students. On the other hand, because the open controversy on the cognitive level "spills" over into the affective domain, the socratic discussion will tend to be highly charged with negative affect.

Utility of a Dimensional Analysis of Classroom Discourse

A dimensional analysis of classroom discourse can be useful in a number of ways. First, it allows — as well as requires — the researcher to describe classroom behavior precisely. Instead of beginning with polar constructs such as student-centered, teacher-centered, or democratic-autocratic, for example, and developing categories to differentiate the poles, we have defined a number of dimensions of teaching and proceeded to identify the characteristics of a teacher whom one would judge to be, say, "student-centered," "democratic," "truth-seeking," or "socratic." Thus we are less constrained by a conceptualization of teacher behavior that works with only some types of teaching.

Second, the dimensional approach allows the description of variations in teaching styles which may or may not significantly affect learning outcomes. Instead of setting up styles in terms of single dichotomies and defining these operationally with "good" and "bad" categories, we can attempt to identify commonly observed styles of teaching and determine which elements in the style, when varied, will or will not affect learning outcomes. Thus we can develop an empirical approach to the evaluation of classroom discourse. In the socratic style, for example, we can ask whether the affective overflow which occurs when the student feels a personal threat to his ideas is a necessary part of the style, or whether a low-affect socratic style is possible and just as effective. In other words, is it the logical performance of the teacher that makes the learning more or less effective (if it is), or is it the logical performance plus the affective charge injected into the discourse?

From a research point of view this approach allows us to investigate a number of interesting problems:

1. Is it possible for individual teachers to manipulate their behavior and use more than one style, or must we identify teachers who have natural styles we wish to investigate and compare?

2. If it is possible for a teacher to manipulate his style, and employ more than one style, what variations occur within a single style, and are there overlapping areas in which one style cannot be differentiated from another?

3. If students are subjected to two quite different teaching styles on a systematic basis over a sustained period of time, what will be the differential effects on learning?

4. What is the relative importance of the style of discourse and the intellectual or other personal characteristics of students, and of the individual teacher, as these interact with style and variations in style in effecting learning outcomes?

5. Is it possible to develop an observational instrument to describe the general style characteristics of the teacher that will also be of sufficient complexity in the statement type and intellectual operations dimensions to be used to assess student learning?

6. How difficult is it to train teachers to operate consistently from a particular teaching style, and are there personality factors which make certain teachers incapable of learning some styles of teaching?

A quantitative methodology by which these questions can be experimentally investigated as well as data bearing on them are the subject of Section Four of the Appendix.

References

1. Richard C. Anderson, "Learning in Discussions: A Résumé of the Authoritarian-Democratic Studies," *Harvard Educational Review* (1959), 29:201.

2. See, e.g., H. H. Anderson, "The Measurement of Domination and of Socially Integrative Behavior in Teachers' Contacts with children," *Child Development* (1939), 10:73-89; H. H. Anderson, "The Variability of Teachers' Behavior Toward Kindergarten Children," in H. H. Anderson and H. M. Brewer, "Studies of Teachers' Classroom Personalities, I: Dominative and Socially Integrative Behavior of Kindergarten Teachers," *Applied Psychological Monographs*, No. 6, chap. 2, pp. 43-108; H. H. Anderson, "A Revised Method for Recording Teachers' Dominative and Socially Integrative Behavior in the Schoolroom," in H. H. Anderson and H. M. Brewer, "Studies of Teachers' Classroom Personalities, II: Effects of Teacher Dominative and Integrative Contacts on Children's Behavior," *Applied Psychological Monographs*, No. 8, chap. 1, pp. 15-32; H. H. Anderson, "Dominative and Socially Integrative Behavior at the Fourth and Sixth Grade Levels," *Applied Psychological Monographs*, No. 8, chap. 3, pp. 88-122.

3. Ned A. Flanders, "Teacher Influence, Pupil Attitudes, and Achievement," prepared at the University of Minnesota, Minneapolis, under Cooperative Research Project No. 397 of the U.S. Office of Education, 1960 (mimeographed), pp. 7-8.

4. *Ibid.*

5. Marie M. Hughes and others, *A Research Report: Development of the Means for the Assessment of the Quality of Teaching in Elementary Schools* (Salt Lake City: University of Utah, 1959).

6. Richard C. Anderson, *op. cit.,* p. 209.

7. B. Othanel Smith and others, "A Study of the Logic of Teaching: The Logical Structure of Teaching and the Development of Critical Thinking, a Report on the First Phase of a Five Year Project," prepared at the University of Illinois, Urbana, under Cooperative Research Project No. 258 (7257) of the U.S. Office of Education, 1959 (mimeographed).

8. Robert B. Bales, *Interaction Process Analysis* (Reading, Mass.: Addison-Wesley Publishing Company, Inc., 1951).

9. Richard C. Anderson, *op. cit.,* pp. 209-210.

10. The reader should understand that these are arbitrary stipulative definitions of the terms used to denote these dimensions.

11. We would emphasize again that this analysis is meant to handle only the general domain of political controversy; it has not been developed for the analysis of teaching in mathematics, science, literature, and so on. It might, however, be appropriate in those subjects as well.

CHAPTER TEN

Assessing Student Competence: Overview and Paper-and-Pencil Tests

The measures used for evaluating curricula constitute one of the most serious problems in educational research today.[1] Too often researchers use a measure because it is available, regardless of whether it bears any close logical relationship to the objectives of instruction of an experimental program. Evaluation instruments should be as carefully derived from the objectives as the materials and methods used by the teacher.[2] In this chapter and the next we shall review a number of measures for assessing competence in the analysis of public controversy, as well as suggest some guidelines for more valid measurements in this area.

Several available measures are relevant to the goals of a curriculum suggested by our theoretical model. The Watson-Glaser Critical Thinking Appraisal,[3] a frequently used test, is one. Several measures developed by the Eight Year Study of the Progressive Education Association[4] were directed at aspects of "critical thinking" such as "logical reasoning," "the interpretation of data," "the nature of proof," "the application of value principles or democratic tenets to social problems," and "the application of facts and explanatory generalizations to social problems."[5] The Cooperative Study of Evaluation in General Education, sponsored by the American Council on Education, also developed measures of "critical thinking" in its attempt to evaluate the general education programs in twenty colleges and universities.[6] A Test of Critical Thinking in Social Science[7] and a Test of Critical Thinking[8] were developed by two of the Cooperative Study's evaluation committees. The Iowa Test of Educational Development No. 5, "Interpretation — Social Studies," is another commercially available test related to "critical thinking."[9] Other relevant non-standardized tests include the Test of Critical Thinking of the Illinois Critical Thinking Project[10] and the Cornell Critical Thinkng Test.[11]

These measures, however, have a number of shortcomings, all of them related to the concept of validity.[12] The first difficulty concerns the adequacy and validity of the conceptual model of "critical thinking" that served as a basis for construction of the tests. While in each case the authors of the Watson-Glaser Critical Thinking Appraisal, the Eight Year Study measures, and the tests for the American Council on Education's study were concerned with critical thinking as an element in good citizenship, there was little consideration of the components of the total decision-making process in public controversy. The earlier portions of this book are an attempt to develop a framework within which to handle public controversy in the context of Western political values. Included are not only the statement of important analytic processes and operations but also an effort to relate the operations to the societal context in which issues are debated, and to indicate how they are to be used in a "real-life" situation. This kind of model-building is not available for the tests mentioned above.

To the extent that any intellectual framework served as the basis for test construction, it was that of "scientific method." We do not intend here to try to define scientific method or to assess the extent to which "critical thinking" tests measure its essential characteristics. However, our own analysis of decision-making in American democracy emphasizes the central position of values and conflicts between values in the analysis of public policy issues. If our stress on the importance of values is a correct one, then a model of decision-making must involve some strategy for dealing with the problem of conflicting values. Is scientific method adequate to this requirement? Beard, writing specifically about the social sciences, but in a context relevant to all science, answers the question directly:

> Now we come to the second question raised by tensions and changes in society: What choices should be made in contingencies? Here the social sciences, working as descriptive sciences wth existing and becoming reality, face, unequivocally, ideas of value and choice — argumentative systems of social philosophy based upon conceptions of desirable changes in the social order. At this occurrence empiricism breaks down absolutely. It is impossible to discover by the fact-finding operation whether this or that change is desirable. Empiricism may disclose, within limits, whether a proposed change is possible, or to what extent it is possible and the realities which condition its eventuation, but, given possibility or a degree

of possibility, empiricism has no way of evaluating value without positing value or setting up a frame of value.[13]

Beard does not stand alone in this assessment. C. I. Stevenson, John Hospers, E. C. Ewing, and Bertrand Russell,[14] although disagreeing over the specific process that one should follow to arrive at ethical decisions, do generally maintain that while scientific method is in some measure useful in the process of ethical judgment (a position with which Beard agrees) it is not alone sufficient.

Second, important questions of validity must be raised because of the testing situation in which critical thinking skills are measured. As a rule, highly structured test items are used to assess fragments of the "scientific process." The predominant instrument of examination is the short-item multiple-choice test, organized into subtests each measuring a separate analytic operation. For example, in order to determine whether the student can recognize underlying assumptions, the test might present him with a paragraph and then ask him to select possible assumptions from a list provided. In actual discussions of societal problems, of course, the various aspects of critical thinking are interrelated. The discussants do not deal with assumptions for a time and then move on, for example, to problems of valid inference. Nor will anyone ordinarily tell the student when it is appropriate to question assumptions. By the same token, the structured nature of the multiple-choice test is also unrealistic. In an argument, or in silent reflection, one does not simply choose from a number of responses; each person must structure his own responses.

Critical thinking tests commonly violate other aspects of the situation in which teachers hope their students will apply the skills of political analysis. All are paper-and-pencil tests. In "real life" outside the classroom we rarely sit at a desk checking or writing responses about political controversy but are more often engaged, as part of the political process, in spoken dialogue with others. Furthermore, the subject matter of the items is often concerned with trivia, such as advertisements for storm windows or selecting paint for a room, rather than with significant public policy questions.

In short, the tests tend to be unlike the context in which students are likely to apply the conceptual framework required to clarify and judge public issues. The objections may be made more clear by reading an excerpt from a transcript of an actual discussion held by a group of eighth-grade students on the problem of school desegregation:

Doris: I'd like to tell the people who say the Supreme Court does not have a right to tell us to integrate the schools: it is a fact that you're not giving the Negroes their constitutional rights. That's why they're telling you to integrate. It's not that they're trying to interfere with your school system, but the Negroes don't get their constitutional rights, their natural rights. The Supreme Court can rule on this.

Jean: The Supreme Court has no right to tell us what to do; it's a state right; and I believe the schools are run right.

Doris: But what about the constitutional rights, their natural rights? They're not getting an equal schooling.

Jean: They have the same schools; they have good schools.

Doris: They do not have good schools.

Bill: Right here it says segregation harms the Negroes by making them feel inferior. It doesn't matter whether the schools are equal or not. Segregation always makes the children feel inferior —

Jean: I don't think the Supreme Court has any right to make any such decision or any such generalization. Our schools for the Negroes are better than the schools for the whites. You could reverse that and say that Negroes feel superior to the whites because they have better schools. . . .

Note that the third time Doris speaks she has an opportunity to question the evidence for the prior assertion, yet does not do so. She may know *how* to question evidence, but not *when*. Note also how Bill, in effect, claims that the issue of how good the Negro schools are is irrelevant, but Jean misses Bill's meaning. It may be that she has the ability to "identify the problem" but does not recognize that she has missed an opportunity to do so here.

Our point is twofold: (1) While some instruments attempt to assess various fragments of a critical thinking process, none of them assesses the student's ability to follow a sequence of operations within a dialectical framework — e.g., the sequence that two individuals might go through of stating a generalization, questioning a generalization by providing a contradictory example, qualifying a generalization to take into account the contradictory example, and supporting it with authoritative evidence, including the credentials of the authority. (2) It is possible that a student might perform important operations on a paper-and-pencil test, yet be totally inept at performing the same operations in a "real" setting, e.g., in a street-corner argument. This validity problem is compounded by the tendency of some tests to use test instructions to teach the students how to perform the operations called for on the test.[15] And to further complicate the problem, little evidence is available on the usefulness of the tests in predicting performance outside of the testing situation.

One final comment on validity: A factor analytic study carried out by Velma Rust and her associates[16] indicates that at least two critical thinking tests[17] — and almost all such tests are quite similar — are highly loaded on a general reasoning factor that may well be as stable as general intelligence. The research results reported in the Appendix tend to confirm this finding. These tests might be better thought of as an indication of the student's potential ability to learn a process of conceptual analysis, rather than as achievement tests.

The foregoing criticisms are to a large extent a reiteration of common complaints by teachers and researchers about the validity of achievement tests. In trying to develop more valid measures of student achievement in the analysis of public controversy, we evolved a number of guidelines for improved test construction. These guidelines are presented below:

GUIDELINES FOR IMPROVED CRITICAL THINKING TESTS

A. *The nature of the problem to be analyzed by the student has to be more narrowly construed than has thus far ordinarily been the case.* It is too ambitious to try to develop a general model of "critical thinking" as the basis for analyzing a wide variety of problems. As a minimum, the important distinctions between problems which are essentially ethical, scientific, or aesthetic should be taken into account. Our work focused on the analysis of ethical decision-making in political controversy, in contrast, for example, to a focus on the empirical analysis of political process.

B. *The context for measuring analytic skills should be described more carefully and the testing situation broadened beyond the simple multiple-choice paper-and-pencil test.* A number of elements should be considered in describing the test situation: (1) the form of the message with which the student is asked to deal; (2) the content of the message which is subjected to analysis; (3) the extent to which the student is asked only to analyze an existing message in terms of analytic concepts as contrasted to being required to use the analytic concepts to evaluate or construct counterarguments; (4) the extent to which choices are prestructured for the student as against requiring the student to structure his own answer; and (5) the interpersonal context, i.e., the extent to which oral interaction is an element in the evaluative situation. These five considerations suggest the following kinds of choices, which obviously do not exhaust the alternatives that might have to be considered:

1. Form of message:
    one-sided persuasive communication v. two-sided dialogue
2. Content of message:
    scientific decisions v. public policy decisions v. aesthetic decisions
3. Level of analytic abstraction:
    test responses consisting of abstract analysis of controversial dialogue   v. responses consisting of appropriate rebuttal statements
4. Level of structure:
    test responses prestructured and simply chosen by student   v. responses created by student

5. Interpersonal context:

student dealing with a controversy only as a non-participant or observer	v. student operating within a live interaction situation (e.g., an oral examination)

This analysis allows for a more rational choice of test-making alternatives. In our own test development efforts we made the following decisions: (1) The dialogue was the basic form of message. (2) The content of the message dealt with public policy decisions. (3) Measures were developed that required the student to choose or develop appropriate rebuttal statements on his own initiative, as well as to perform an abstract analysis of the controversial dialogue. (4) Both prestructured and open-ended, unstructured tests were developed. (5) Some measurement situations were constructed in which the student participated in the give-and-take of an argument; in others he analyzed the arguments of other people.

C. *The analytic operations to be assessed must be described systematically, and the student must be required to identify not only when an operation has been carried out successfully but also when the operation is appropriate or relevant in a problem context.* Systematic efforts to describe components of "critical thinking" have been attempted by several investigators, including Smith, Ennis, Dressel and Mayhew, and the authors of the Eight Year Study.[18] The major problem with these efforts, especially the latter two, is the uncertain relationship between the specific analytic operations and the total problem being considered: How does each analytic fragment fit into a general conceptual model?

Because we started with a conceptual model, our own approach is somewhat more "wholistic" and interrelated than the work referred to above. From the total framework for the clarification of public controversy discussed in Part Two, for the purpose of constructing tests we concentrated on five areas of analysis. These are:

1. *Problem identification and differentiation.* The ability to differentiate among various classes of problems within a controversial setting is a crucial preliminary step in analysis. Our approach to public controversy differentiated among *empirical* or *factual* controversy, *value* controversy, and *definitional* controversy. Evidence of the student's ability to make these discriminations can be obtained by observing at least two types of behavior: (a) The student correctly labels or describes the nature of the problem, or (b) he uses a correct strategy for dealing with the controversy. For example, the student might say that a particular statement presents a problem over the meaning of a word, or it presents a problem concerning which of two conflicting factual claims is true Or the student might say that we deal with this kind of problem by finding out how the word is commonly used in this context, while we deal with that kind of problem by

looking for consistencies and inconsistencies in the reports of the event, investigating the credentials of the observers, and so on.

The use of an incorrect strategy can be illustrated by the following example:

> Two men are arguing over whether the absence of fire escapes from two-story buildings constitutes a menace to public health. One says it is a menace; the other says it is not. The statistics regarding deaths caused by the absence of such fire escapes are available but are not brought into the debate.

In this kind of situation students commonly state that the way to settle the argument is to go out and observe buildings without fire escapes or look up the statistics and see whether or not such buildings constitute a menace. From our point of view, one must not only observe the statistics and the buildings but also ascertain how the word *menace* is being used.

2. *Making explicit important cross-problem assumptions.* The categorization of a particular problem as definitional, factual, or ethical is only the initial step in a complex process. For every problem that is identified, one must make countless assumptions that there is agreement (or question whether or not there is agreement) regarding related problems inherent in the same issue. Suppose a person says, "The Federal Trade Commission is needlessly censoring television advertising." His antagonist says, "No!" If an argument ensues, it can take the form of a definitional disagreement (perhaps over the word *censorship*), a factual disagreement (over whether such censorship actually takes place), or a value disagreement (over whether the government should interfere with the free flow of information over the airways). Each disagreement tends, however, to make assumptions about agreement in other areas, which may, in fact, be questioned. The value disagreement in this case might assume that censorship is a real possibility or that it has actually taken place — i.e., it assumes a fact. The factual disagreement generally assumes that the disputants share common values, both with respect to the free flow of information and to government regulation in the interests of the welfare of the community; otherwise the fact would not be worth arguing. The definitional argument may also assume that censorship is imminent or is taking place, and that censorship *can* be bad.

Analyzing important empirical and definitional cross-problem assumptions is especially important in the process of argumentation, since one of the subtlest ways to press one's value commitments with respect to a given controversial situation is to distort or exaggerate the information describing the situation, or to choose vague but loaded words to describe it.

3. *Identifying and using appropriate strategies for dealing with different types of problems.* The analytic processes discussed above both involve

problem identification and differentiation. In observing many discussions, we have noticed that discussants often avoid dealing with the various aspects of an argument systematically and tend rather to argue "in circles." The following illustrates a common pattern of reasoning:

Southern schools shouldn't be segregated because
segregation of the races is bad; moreover,
the Negroes in the South are given poor treatment under
segregated conditions;
therefore, southern schools shouldn't be segregated.

Analytically, the line of reasoning can be described as follows:

A policy decision is supported by a specific value judgment (which really adds little new information).

Both of these statements are followed by an unsupported and controversial generalization.

The case is then terminated with a restatement of the initial policy decision.

This pattern of thinking is usually an inefficient way to approach an issue. Disagreement over a decision, for instance, may be better clarified by construing the decision in terms of the general values of the culture; discovering analogous situations in which the same values are in conflict so that the individual can see the problem in a broader context; identifying differences among the analogous situations which cause one to change his decision from one situation to another; and testing whether these presumed differences do, in fact, hold up under careful scrutiny. If the differences do not hold up, the individual can change his decision or simply accept his own inconsistency. Disagreements over fact can be approached by constructing testable hypotheses and looking for evidence. Definitional disagreements can be approached by empirically determining how the word is commonly used; by pragmatically testing whether a particular use of the word will avoid ambiguity and confusion; by seeking stipulative agreement on the use of the word in the particular context; or, when the problem involves whether a term should be applied to an object, event, or person, by a process of categorical reasoning, i.e., determining whether the object, event, or person fits the criteria considered essential to a definition of the term and should, therefore, be placed in that category.

The strategies suggested here are not meant to be exhaustive. The point is that some strategies are appropriate for some kinds of problems but not others. And, more important, making strategies of problem resolution explicit tends to lead the discussant to greater focus and more systematic analysis than if he simply makes casual and perhaps unrelated statements in an attempt to justify a decision.

4. *Identifying and using common dialectical operations.* In the process

of analyzing political controversy, we have identified a pattern of thought common to the strategies for handling the three major types of disagreement. The essential operations in the pattern may be described as follows: (a) *generalizing:* going from specific instances of what seems good, true, or useful to a general statement of what is good, true, or useful; (b) *specifying:* supporting, contradicting, or elaborating a general statement by pointing to specific instances in which the general statement holds or does not hold — specifying includes, then, pointing out the consistency or inconsistency of a specific statement with a more general statement; and (c) *qualifying:* taking into account in a generalization exceptional instances in which the general statement appears to be inconsistent with relevant facts, values, or definitions. The following example will illustrate:

> *Statement A:* "Desegregation will improve education for the Negroes in the South." (The individual making the statement is assumed to know of specific instances which make him think this generalization will hold, or to have heard the statement from some authoritative source, and to believe, therefore, that it is generally true. This is an example of a general statement, although only implicitly does it illustrate the process of generalizing.)
>
> *Statement B:* "Sure, just like education for the Negro improved the first year when Little Rock's Central High School was integrated." (This statement provides a specific example of a situation in which the initial generalization is presumed *not* to hold. It illustrates the process: specification — inconsistency.)
>
> *Statement C:* "When a careful plan of community education has been carried out, and the community is ready for it, integrated schools provide a better education for the Negro and white alike." (This is a reworking of statement A, with a qualification added which presumably takes into account the inconsistent example specified in statement B.)

The process of going from specific to general (generalizing), then returning to specific test examples of the general statement (specifying), then restating the general statement to take into account inconsistencies and exceptional cases applies to all three types of problems: value problems, factual problems, and definitional problems. These concepts provide, then, a model of dialectical strategy which cuts across problem types. The process of arriving at a qualified generalization is an important aspect of our definition of reflective thinking.

5. *Identifying relevance problems.* The problem of relevance can be looked at from two points of view: What statements are relevant to the argument as a whole? And what statements are relevant at a particular point in the discussion? Each discussion has a context, set mainly by the topic. Some statements are clearly not relevant because, while they may be within the appropriate political-ethical frame, they are on the wrong topic.

Within the discussion itself some statements may be relevant to the discussion in general but unrelated to a prior statement. For example, the central problem of a discussion might at one point turn on what behavioral differences there are in fact between whites and Negroes. Before this issue is in any sense settled, someone may move to the question of whether or not differences are culturally conditioned or genetically determined. While this issue may be relevant to the total discussion, it may be inappropriate at this particular point in the discussion, since it short-circuits the analysis of the issue immediately at hand.

EXPERIMENTAL MEASURES

In an effort to assess competence in the analysis of political controversy, we developed four experimental measures, each of which would evaluate the same type of competence but stress different elements in the testing situation. The four tests were all labeled Social Issues Analysis Tests and were numbered in the order of their complexity. SIAT No. 1 and SIAT No. 2 are paper-and-pencil tests, and will be discussed in this chapter. SIAT No. 3 and SIAT No. 4 involve analysis of the content of oral discussions and will be discussed in Chapter Eleven.

SIAT No. 1: ARGUMENT ANALYSIS TEST

SIAT No. 1 is a group paper-and-pencil test with prestructured multiple-choice responses. Its purpose is to assess how well students can identify selected intellectual operations occurring in an argumentative dialogue. Sample tests are given in Table 2, illustrating the form and nature of the test. It was originally pretested on groups of Master of Arts in Teaching candidates in social studies education at Harvard to determine whether the conceptual framework upon which it was based was so narrow or was expressed in such technical language that intelligent, well-educated lay people could not be expected to understand it. Table 3 summarizes a

TABLE 2

Sample Items from SIAT No. 1

A Discussion About Labor Unions
Joe: Labor unions were O.K. when they first began. Now they are corrupt and dishonest. I say unions should be outlawed.
Mike: What makes you think they are corrupt and dishonest?
(i) Joe: Look what has happened to the Teamsters Union. A couple of years ago two of their biggest leaders were convicted of stealing union money.

NOW ANSWER QUESTION (9) BELOW.

Sample Items from SIAT No. 1 (continued)

(j) Mike: Every now and then bankers are caught embezzling money from the bank. But no one suggests that banks be outlawed to get rid of dishonest bankers.

NOW ANSWER QUESTION (10) BELOW.

Joe: That's different. Banks perform a necessary service. We couldn't get along without banks.

(k) Mike: Many workers feel that labor unions are necessary to protect their welfare, to see that they are not overworked and underpaid by irresponsible business leaders.

NOW ANSWER QUESTION (11) BELOW.

(l) Joe: But once you let the labor union organize a factory, it tries to dictate how to run the whole factory: how much to pay the workers, when to give them holidays, how many hours they can work, who is first to be laid off when work is slack. Labor unions go against the whole idea of free enterprise and the right to make any kind of contract you please with your workers.

NOW ANSWER QUESTION (12) BELOW.

Answer the following questions on the basis of the discussion above.

9. What does Joe's statement (i) do in the discussion? [a]

———— a. Gives examples to support a fact or claim.
———— b. Gives examples to suggest that a definition is not adequate.
———— c. Suggests that Mike's position in the argument needs qualifying.
———— d. Gives examples to support or illustrate a definition.
———— e. Clarifies a word or phrase in the argument.

10. What does Mike's statement (j) do in the discussion?

———— a. Uses a value to support his position.
———— b. Qualifies or limits his position in the discussion.
———— c. Suggests that Joe's position in the argument needs qualifying or limiting.
———— d. Suggests that a source is unreliable or untrustworthy.
———— e. Suggests that Joe needs more proof for his last statement.

11. What does Mike's statement (k) do in the discussion?

———— a. Suggests that Joe's claim requires evidence and should be tested.
———— b. Shows that Joe's statement is not true.
———— c. Suggests that a qualification already given is not adequate.
———— d. Qualifies or limits a fact or claim.
———— e. Takes a more general position in the discussion.

12. What does Joe's statement (l) do in the discussion?

———— a. States that an important value is being violated.
———— b. Clarifies a word or phrase in the argument.
———— c. Gives a source to support the reliability of a fact or claim.
———— d. Suggests that Mike holds two contradictory values.
———— e. Clarifies his position in the argument.

---

[a] Correct answers: 9, a; 10, c; 11, c; 12, a.

TABLE 3

Responses of Harvest First-Year Graduate Students in Social Studies Education on Pretest of Experimental SIAT No. 1

Topic of Argument	\ 1.		2.		3.		4.	
Space Race	a.		a.		*a.	13	a.	
	b.		*b.	23	b.		b.	4
	c.		c.		c.	2	c.	1
	*d.	24	d.		d.	2	*d.	17
	e.		e.	2	e.	6	e.	2
Labor	*a.	23	a.		a.	5	*a.	21
	b.		b.		b.	5	b.	
	c.		*c.	17	*c.	14	c.	1
	d.	1	d.	1	d.		d.	1
	e.		e.	6	e.		e.	1
Communists in America	a.	2	a.		a.	3	a.	
	b.	2	b.		b.	1	b.	
	*c.	20	c.	1	c.		c.	2
	d.		*d.	23	d.		*d.	22
	e.		e.		*e.	20	e.	
Government Regulation of Drugs	a.	2	a.	1	a.	1	*a	24
	b.		*b.	14	*b.	20	b.	
	c.		c.	5	c.	3	c.	
	d.	1	d.	1	d.		d.	
	*e.	21	e.	3	e.		e.	
The Algerian Rebels	a.	1	*a.	20	a.		a.	
	*b.	23	b.		b.		b.	1
	c.		c.		c.		*c.	21
	d.		d.		d.		d.	2
	e.		e.	4	*e.	24	e.	

*Answers considered correct by authors.

typical first trial run. It seemed fairly clear to us that the language was not overtechnical and the conceptual framework was not idiosyncratic. The source of ambiguity in poor items was easily identified and corrected. It was possible with one or two revisions of specific items to get almost complete agreement among adult judges.

The reliability estimate for SIAT No. 1 with a sample of 109 eighth-grade students was .81. This is a split-half estimate corrected by the

Spearman-Brown formula. It should be noted that the test was administered after the students had been subjected to the experimental curriculum described in the Appendix. The test contained only twenty items because of the amount of reading required. Nevertheless, it would be practical to increase the number of items substantially and thereby bring the reliability up to a point where individual scores could be meaningfully interpreted.

SIAT No. 2: Argument Description and Rebuttal Test

SIAT No. 2 is also a group pencil-and-paper test with prestructured multiple-choice responses. Its purpose is to assess both how well the student can identify the substance of an argumentative dialogue (in contrast to the intellectual operations occurring in it) and the student's ability to select the best rebuttals which might be used to counter statements made in the dialogue. The subtest on labor (Table 4) illustrates the general form of the test. Part A requires the student to pick the statement which best summarizes the argument. The purpose is to see to what extent he

TABLE 4

SIAT No. 2 — Labor L

Read the following conversation carefully. You will be asked several questions based on what you read. While answering the questions you may look back as often as necessary.

John and Dick Discuss Labor

John: Have you read what's happening to the working man these days? He's being taken in by labor unions to the tune of millions of dollars, and all he gets out of it is headaches and strikes.

Dick: So you're an enemy of the working man. Just because the unions have found a way to give the working man a fair break, fellows like you are down on them.

John: I'm no enemy of the working man. I know labor has had a long hard road to travel. And once the unions really tried to help him. But that was years ago. Now the unions are led by a group of sharp gangsters who are only after the worker's pocketbook.

Dick: Any labor expert will tell you that if the unions get weak, businessmen will grind the working man right down into the dust.

John: Let's face it. The working man is better off than he has ever been. He doesn't need a union leader to stand over his old enemy with a loaded gun when the enemy has been dead for twenty-five years. What the worker needs today is a law to take the gun away from the gangsters and union leaders who are robbing him.

SIAT No. 2 — Labor L (continued)

Dick: Now the truth is out. You want to have Congress outlaw any kind of union that can deal effectively with business. That's just like you, always turning to the government when you want something. We all know that the working man is a long way from getting a fair break, and the union is the only way he can get it.

John: You're a fine one to talk about asking the government for help. You weren't against passing laws to give the worker higher wages and shorter hours and an old age income twenty years ago. I say when unions are packed with gangsters and thugs, it's about time Congress stepped in and put an end to them.

Dick: Maybe what you say is true of a few unions, but can you name any really important unions you think should be outlawed?

John: Sure. The Teamsters, the Longshoremen, and the Steelworkers, to name only a few. You can read all about these rotten unions in any big city newspaper.

Dick: I knew you would get around to the Teamsters sooner or later. You've had it in for them ever since you had an argument with that truck driver last year. What about all the honest unions, that everyone knows are honest?

John: Finding an honest union is like trying to find the corners on a baseball.

Dick: What about the Rubber Workers and the Auto Workers and lots and lots of others?

John: Some unions are just able to cover up their dishonesty better than others. We've put up with these blackmailing gangs long enough. The sooner laws are passed to put crooked union leaders out of business, the better off we'll all be.

Dick: There you go again, off the deep end as usual. You want to throw the baby out with the bath water. Just because a few labor leaders have not always been completely honest doesn't mean we should take away the rights of millions of workers to organize and belong to unions.

John: The only ones really who want to "organize," as you call it, are a few selfish union leaders who don't want to give up a good thing. You say I want to take away the worker's rights. That's where you're wrong, Dick. I really want to give millions of workers back their rights, not take them away.

Dick: Yah! You want to give them back their rights by outlawing the unions they have freely joined and supported.

Part A. Argument Summary

On your answer sheet check the question below which best describes what the argument is about.

1. a. Are modern labor unions useful to business, industry, and the public?
   b. Are modern labor unions with their high costs and corrupt leaders really harmful to the worker?
   c. Do workers have a good reason to be against unions and their leaders?
   d. Can dishonest labor leaders be removed from the labor movement without destroying the unions themselves?
   *e. Have modern labor unions harmed workers to the point where the government should step in and protect the workers?

SIAT No. 2 — Labor L (continued)

Part B. *Ideas of Right and Wrong*

John and Dick disagree about some important ideas of right and wrong. On your answer sheet check the statement below which best describes their disagreement over what is right and wrong.

2. *a. Should the government interfere and control unions in the interest of the workers or allow unions to have freedom with the risk of dishonest unions?

  b. Should we allow a little violence and dishonesty in the unions and have a union that can get things for its workers, or have a democratic union that does little for the worker?

  c. Is it better to leave unions alone even though they aren't doing all they can for their members than to attempt to change them and risk the possibility of their being destroyed?

  d. Is it better for dishonest union leaders to get some benefits for their members now than it is for them to "go straight" and hope for a good deal in the future?

  e. Should unions be strong and dictatorial to get high wages for their members or be honest in order not to risk government interference and control?

Part C. *Who Said What?*

Items 3 through 7 below describe in different words something John said in the argument, something Dick said in the argument, or something that neither or both might have said in the argument. On your answer sheet, check *D* if you think Dick made the statement, check *J* if you think John made the statement. If you think neither or both might have made the statement, check *Can't tell*.

3. **The worker gets more problems than benefits by belonging to a labor union. (J)

4. Without the union the worker risks getting poorer wages and working conditions. (D)

5. The purpose of the union from the very beginning was to get as much as it could from both the workers and the businessmen. (J)

6. The government should help the working man. (Can't tell)

7. Labor unions should be more severely controlled. (J)

Part D. *Supporting Statements*

Items 8 through 12 are statements of fact which you can assume are true. If these statements had been made at any time during the argument, do you think they would have supported Dick's position, John's position, or the position of neither or both? On your answer sheet, check *D* if you think the statement supports Dick's position, check *J* if you think the statement supports John's position. If you think the statement supports neither or both positions, check *Can't tell*.

SIAT No. 2 — Labor L (continued)

8. Workers who belong to powerful unions are generally paid better than workers who belong to no union at all. (D)
9. Under the leadership of Senator McClellan, the Senate Rackets Committee discovered in 1958-1959 that several large unions had a number of ex-convicts employed as high union officers. (J)
10. Many steelworkers feel that the gains which come from union bargaining with the steel companies are more than lost by having strikes every two or three years. (J)
11. Many textile companies in New England moved to the South because they didn't want to hire union labor. (J)
12. In 1947 Congress passed the Taft-Hartley Act, which gives the President the right to halt a strike for eighty days if it threatens the health and security of the nation. (Can't tell)

Part E. *Argument Reply*

Items 13 through 17 contain statements made by Dick or John in the argument. In this part of the test you are to check the *two best replies* which you might have made to each statement if you had been in the argument. The best replies are those which may clarify the disagreement or move the argument forward toward some agreement. Remember, for items 13 through 17 check the two best ways to answer each statement.

13. Now the unions are led by a group of sharp gangsters who are after the worker's pocketbook.
   *a. Do you think all unions are led by dishonest leaders or do you have some particular unions in mind?
    b. You're defining gangster as anyone who wants to give the underdog a fair chance.
    c. Would you clarify exactly what you mean by the worker's pocketbook?
    d. What evidence do you have that the worker's pocketbook is at all affected by how much money the companies make?
   *e. Do you mean that union leaders are actually breaking laws?
14. Any labor expert will tell you that if the unions get weak, businessmen will grind the working man right down into the dust.
    a. That depends on what ideas you have in mind when you talk about labor unions.
    b. Let's set up a test and find out whether the workers belong to weak or strong unions.
    c. The evidence shows that businessmen are too reasonable to grind anyone down into the dust.
   *d. Let's set up a test and find out whether the workers in weak unions get lower wages and poorer working conditions than workers in strong unions.
   *e. Who are these labor experts?
15. He [the worker] doesn't need a union leader to stand over his old enemy with a loaded gun when the enemy has been dead for twenty-five years.
    a. The unions don't have any weapon as powerful as a loaded gun.

SIAT No. 2 — Labor L (continued)

  *b. The owners and managers of companies may be "enemies," to use your expression, but in what way are they "dead"?

   c. Union leaders had to use guns because they were treated like criminals, and in many places they still are.

   d. You're making an unfair comparison when you say the union leader is like the man with a loaded gun.

  *e. Calling union leaders names isn't going to get us anywhere.

16. You can read all about these rotten unions in any big city newspaper.

   a. I guess I read the wrong newspaper.

  *b. Let's look up some of these statements made in these newspapers.

   c. Isn't there evidence that these big newspapers are just trying to sell the papers and that's the reason they make these charges against unions?

  *d. What do these newspaper reports say?

   e. Let's define clearly the difference between a big city newspaper and other good newspapers.

17. Just because a few labor leaders haven't always been completely honest doesn't mean we should take away the rights of millions of workers to organize and belong to unions.

   a. I don't know what other conclusion we could come to considering all the facts we have about modern labor unions.

  *b. You and I have a different understanding of the word "few."

   c. If workers no longer can protect their own rights, then the government must step in and protect the workers.

   d. When you say that union leaders haven't always been completely honest, you're practically admitting that unions have to be subject to control.

  *e. You're going to have to show me that having the government step in means that workers will lose their rights.

---

*Indicates correct answer for items 1, 2, 13, 14, 15, 16, and 17.
**Correct answers are in parentheses following items 3 through 12.

can focus on the major issue under discussion. Part B requires the student to evaluate summaries of the argument presented in dilemma form. In these statements the argument is raised to a general value level, with two values opposing each other. Again the student is asked to judge which values are most relevant to the argument and so can most appropriately be used to construe the argument. Part C is intended to measure the student's ability to comprehend the substance of the argument at a very specific level. Part D is similar to Part C except that the student must make a judgment regarding whether new information is relevant to one side or the other or to both sides in the argument.

Part E is the most important section and accounts for about one-half of the total test. To explain this part more fully, let us look at item 13. In evaluating the various responses, the student can analyze the argument by asking himself two questions: "On what type of problem is the argument focused at just this point in the discussion?" and "What strategy is most appropriate to clarify or resolve this point of disagreement?" The analysis might proceed as follows: Statement *a* asks for specific evidence to support a generalization, and possibly a qualification of what is probably an overgeneralization. From our point of view, the statement is relevant because the generalization being questioned is an important factor in the argument. Statement *b* accuses the antagonist of a position he has not taken. Moreover, the position which John is accused of taking is stated in vague and loaded language. Statement *c* is an important intellectual operation in argumentation, but inappropriate at this point in the argument. There is apparently no controversy over the definition of *pocketbook*. Statement *d* is also an important intellectual operation but, like *c,* irrelevant at this point in the discussion. No one is arguing over the extent to which the worker's pocketbook is affected by company earnings. Statement *e* asks for a clarification or definition of the term *gangster,* which Dick suggests is being used loosely in the argument. It asks an important question and it is relevant at this point in the argument. Thus the most reasonable answers are *a* and *e.*

The comprehensive nature of SIAT No. 2 tends to make its interpretation difficult, since it yields but a single score. Seven items are based mainly on reading comprehension; five are based on the student's ability to identify the relevance of various factual statements to the two positions in the argument; and ten points (five items with two points each) are of the type illustrated in the previous paragraph, which presumably get at the student's ability to analyze the argument explicitly or intuitively and determine whether rebuttal statements have immediate relevance to the disagreement at hand. It was our assumption that the three types of abilities required to do the whole test are in ascending level of complexity and difficulty, and that a high score could be achieved only if the student were competent at all three levels. Our present judgment is that it is probably sounder practice to develop "sharper" assessment instruments yielding either total scores or subscores based on specific abilities. SIAT No. 1, for example, has a much sharper focus than does SIAT No. 2.

Four forms of SIAT No. 2 were developed, each based on a different topic: "labor leaders" (L), "racial integration" (I), "atomic fallout" (F), and "education" (E). As with SIAT No. 1, this measure was pretested on Harvard M.A.T. candidates in the social studies. Then, as part of the research effort reported in the Appendix, the four forms were administered in the fall of 1959 to 109 seventh-grade students before they were exposed to the experimental curriculum, and again in the spring of 1961, after the two-year experimental treatment. Correlations between scores obtained on the various forms were computed for each date of administration, as were correlations between scores obtained on the same forms at the different dates of administration. Correlation coefficients were also computed for composite scores of two or more forms.

Table 5 presents these correlations. In general, the coefficients are relatively low as reliability estimates. The L (labor) Form administered in the fall of 1959, for example, correlates only .26, .35, and .44 with the

TABLE 5

*Correlations Between Forms of SIAT No. 2
Administered in November 1959 and June 1961
to 109 Junior High School Students*

Form[a]	Date[b]	1	2	3	4	5	6	7	8	9	10	11	12	13
1. L	N. '59													
2. I	N. '59	.26												
3. L & I	N. '59	.75	.78											
4. L	J. '61	.52	.23	.43										
5. I	J. '61	.43	.14	.28	.47									
6. L & I	J. '61	.52	.21	.39	.85	.79								
7. F	N. '59	.35	.32	.36	.49	.34	.44							
8. E	N. '59	.44	.33	.47	.47	.35	.41	.52						
9. F & E	N. '59	.45	.41	.53	.53	.39	.47	.88	.83					
10. F	J. '61	.47	.24	.41	.48	.49	.50	.43	.44	.45				
11. E	J. '61	.23	.07	.16	.37	.25	.33	.27	.23	.25	.35			
12. F & E	J. '61	.44	.20	.35	.53	.47	.52	.44	.42	.43	.86	.78		
13. All forms	N. '59	.71	.59	.83	.53	.39	.48	.67	.73	.82	.57	.28	.53	
14. All forms	J. '61	.58	.25	.45	.78	.73	.85	.51	.48	.53	.78	.63	.87	.60

[a] Topics of forms: L = Labor; I = Racial integration; F = Atomic fallout; and E = Quality of American education.
[b] N. = November; J. = June.

other three forms administered during the same month. Even if these coefficients were corrected with the Spearman-Brown Formula, as would be appropriate if scores for combined pairs of the forms were to be used as experimental variables, they would leave something to be desired. Increasing the length of the tests does substantially increase the reliability estimates. The composite Form L & I administered in the fall of 1959 correlates .53 with the composite Form F & E administered at the same time and .52 for the spring 1961 administration. If the two composite forms were combined to yield one experimental variable this would be essentially a split-half estimate of reliability. Corrected by the Spearman-Brown Formula, these estimates increase to .69 and .68, respectively, a level of reliability approaching adequacy for research purposes. As a matter of fact, when all four forms are combined to yield a single score and the correlation between the 1959 and the 1961 administrations computed, a coefficient of .60 is obtained. Considering that almost two years elapsed between the two administrations, the relationship is quite high.

CONCLUSION

In terms of our own criticism of critical thinking tests, SIAT No. 1 and SIAT No. 2 represent a marked improvement over the tests reviewed briefly at the beginning of this chapter. They are based on a carefully reasoned and explicated model of reflective thinking delineated in terms of the analysis of political controversy, rather than on a model of "general" reasoning supposedly appropriate to all problems. Both tests include items concerned with competence in dealing with values, as well as with factual and definitional disputes. Both are set within a context of dialogues about matters of public policy, and the student is asked to select appropriate rebuttal statements and to perform abstract analyses of the controversial dialogue. Moreover, in neither test are the intellectual operations isolated (e.g., as when a series of items is labeled "inferences" and deals only with this concept); the student is required to consider several operations at the same time. SIAT No. 2, by presenting only the substantive argument and the rebuttal statements, has the additional advantage of not telling the student the concepts upon which a successful analysis of the dialogue might be based.

Both measures, however, utilize prestructured responses, and with both the student is only indirectly involved in the controversial dialogue. In attempting to meet these problems, we turned to open-ended conversation as a test situation, using systematic content analysis to quantify student responses. The next chapter is a discussion of our exploration of this somewhat novel type of assessment.

References

1. See W. J. McKeachie, "Problems and Perils in Controlled Research in Teaching," in Erwin T. Steinberg (ed.), *Needed Research in the Teaching of English,* Cooperative Research Monograph No. 11, U.S. Department of Health, Education and Welfare, 1962, pp. 66-67.

2. See, for example, the problems encountered in the studies reported in Byron G. Massialas (ed.), *The Indiana Experiments in Inquiry: Social Studies* (Bloomington: Bulletin of the School of Education, Indiana University, 1963), vol. 39, No. 3.

3. Used in a classic experiment by Edward M. Glaser as reported in *An Experiment in the Development of Critical Thinking* (New York: Teachers College, Columbia University, 1941; test published by World Book Company).

4. Eugene R. Smith and Ralph W. Tyler, *Appraising and Recording Student Progress,* Vol. III, *Adventure in American Education* (New York: Harper & Row, Publishers, 1942), p. 19.

5. The Logical Reasoning Test and the Interpretation of Data Test were published by the Educational Testing Service, Princeton, N.J., Cooperative Test Division, 1950.

6. P. L. Dressel and L. B. Mayhew, *General Education: Explorations in Evaluation* (Washington: American Council on Education, 1954).

7. American Council on Education, Cooperative Study of Evaluation in General Education, *A Test of Critical Thinking in Social Sciences* (Washington: American Council on Education, 1951).

8. American Council on Education, Cooperative Study of Evaluation in General Education, *A Test of Critical Thinking, Form G* (Washington: American Council on Education, 1952).

9. Chicago: Science Research Associates.

10. B. O. Smith and others, *Teaching Critical Thinking.* Urbana: University of Illinois Press, in press.

11. R. H. Ennis and J. Millman, "Cornell Critical Thinking Test" (mimeographed).

12. The major work of this review was carried out by Harold Berlak, and much of the discussion of the tests which follows is based on his evaluations. For a more complete review of the measures see D. W. Oliver and J. P. Shaver, *The Analysis of Public Controversy,* chap. 10.

13. Charles A. Beard, *The Nature of the Social Sciences* (New York: Charles Scribner's Sons, 1934), pp. 171-172.

14. E. C. Ewing, "Subjectivism and Naturalism in Ethics," in W. E. Sellers and John Hospers (eds.), *Readings in Ethical Theory* (New York: Appleton-Century-Crofts, Inc., 1952), p. 120; John Hospers, *An Introduction to Philosophical Analysis* (New York: Prentice-Hall, Inc., 1953), p. 494; Bertrand Russell, "The Elements of Ethics," in W. E. Sellers and John Hospers (eds.), *Readings in Ethical Theory* (New York: Appleton-Century-Crofts, Inc., 1952), p. 8; Charles L. Stevenson, *Ethics and Language* (New Haven, Conn.: Yale University Press, 1944), pp. 113-114.

15. The Watson-Glaser Critical Thinking Appraisal in particular does this.

16. Velma I. Rust, R. Stewart Jones, and Henry F. Kaiser, "A Factor-Analytic Study of Critical Thinking," *Journal of Educational Research* (1962), 55:258.

17. The Watson-Glaser Critical Thinking Appraisal and the American Council on Education's Test of Critical Thinking, Form G.

18. B. O. Smith and others, *op. cit.;* Robert H. Ennis, "A Concept of Critical Thinking," *Harvard Educational Review* (1962), 32:81-111; Dressel and Mayhew, *op. cit.;* Smith and Tyler, *op. cit.*

CHAPTER ELEVEN

Assessing Student Competence: Content Analysis of Discussions

The two measures described in the previous chapter begin at a common point: the student is asked to read and analyze an argument. SIAT No. 1 presents specific statements in dialogue form and then asks that he choose, from among the alternatives provided, the analytic operation illustrated by a particular statement, or the operation which the response might require the antagonist to perform. In the major portion of SIAT No. 2, the student is required to evaluate alternative responses that might be made in rebuttal to statements in the argumentative dialogue. While somewhat different from each other, both measures share a number of difficulties with standard tests of "critical thinking": (1) The student responds to a fragmented argument which is likely to appear contrived and artificial. (2) The sequence of the dialogue is broken into units for the student, and his attention is directed to particular statements which are to be analyzed. (3) Not only are significant statements lifted for analysis so that no initial judgment of relevance is required of the student, but he is given an array of responses from which to choose, immediately defining for him the limits within which acceptable answers can be made.

The format of the objective paper-and-pencil tests, in short, seems to provide the student with a set and structure for approaching problems in a reflective, systematic way. Such tests, therefore, are likely to determine only whether the student knows the analytic operation appropriate to deal with an already identified problem; they are not likely to indicate whether he will use the operation, when relevant, in a less structured situation. The two paper-and-pencil SIAT's discussed in Chapter Ten do require the student to function in a situation more realistic in many of its elements than that of the usual standardized test. The fact remains, however, that making selections from a number of prestructured choices based on a one-page written dialogue is quite different from analyzing an argument in oral discourse or participating in an argument for which the only analytical structure is that provided by the participants.

In an effort, then, to meet the problems of the prestructured paper-and-pencil test, it was decided to attempt assessment in less structured settings, relying on systematic content analysis as a method of quantifying student responses. A choice had to be made between written and oral responses as the behavior to be analyzed. The latter was selected for two reasons: (1) The experimental curriculum (to be discussed in the Appendix) was directed primarily at affecting responses in oral discourse, and (2) the act of writing itself, as a means of expression, probably inhibits student spontaneity and increases the problem of communication. There are, of course, aspects of face-to-face spoken communication that might also inhibit expression, but this, at least, is a "first order" skill, practiced since shortly after infancy.

SIAT No. 3: Analysis of Written Dialogue

Our effort to "de-structure" the testing situation resulted in the development of SIAT No. 3 and SIAT No. 4. The former, like SIAT No. 1, requires the student to differentiate and identify various types of disagreements, as well as suggest how the disagreements might best be clarified or resolved through different analytic strategies. SIAT No. 3 is administered to students individually by interview. Actual administration takes the following course. The interviewer first reads the directions to the student:

> We are going to read an imaginary conversation between two men [Bob and Don]. Then I am going to ask you to describe the main points of disagreement between the two men, and I am going to ask you how you would go about settling or clarifying these points of disagreement. In analyzing these main points of disagreement try and use any critical thinking skills or knowledge you may have learned about the analysis of controversial issues.

The interviewer next reads aloud a dialogue, while the student follows along on his own copy. Throughout the interview, the student is allowed to refer to the written dialogue whenever he wishes. Table 6 presents the dialogue for one version of the test as used in our research program. The written dialogues were constructed to include the three major types of problems in our model of political controversy: definitional, factual, and evaluative. Statements (3) and (4) of the dialogue in Table 6 involve a definitional dispute over the use of the term *collective bargaining*. State-

TABLE 6

Dialogue for SIAT No. 3

Working for Mr. Spindle

(1) Don:	The trouble with Mr. Spindle, the manager of our plant, is that he just won't sit down and talk about wages and working conditions with the workers; he doesn't believe in collective bargaining.
(2) Bob:	Of course he does. Every Thursday afternoon he calls a few of the workers together and talks over conditions in the plant.
(3) Don:	That's not collective bargaining. Collective bargaining is when the boss sits down and talks to the official representatives of all the workers, not just a few men.
(4) Bob:	I say collective bargaining is when the boss talks to a group of men about their working conditions. It's as simple as that.
(5) Don:	Well, I don't care about what you call collective bargaining anyway. The fact of the matter is that old man Spindle doesn't bother to meet with any of the men on a regular basis.
(6) Bob:	He met with the men last Thursday.
(7) Don:	I think that's the first time he has met with the men for the last month.
(8) Bob:	Nonsense. I know he meets with the men every week regularly.
(9) Don:	I don't see how you can say that. I talked to four men on Friday, and they told me that the Thursday meeting was the first of its kind for a month or more.
(10) Bob:	What difference does it make, anyway, whether or not Mr. Spindle meets with the men on a regular basis? He is the boss of the plant. He shouldn't have to discuss all his plans with the men who work for him. If they don't like the way the plant is run, they can quit.
(11) Don:	What chance does one man have trying to convince old man Spindle that his working conditions are dangerous or his pay is too low? The men certainly should have some say about working conditions that affect them.

ments (5) through (9) present a factual disagreement over how often Mr. Spindle met with his men on a regular basis. The controversy in these statements might also be construed as a disagreement over the use of the word *regularly*. Statements (10) and (11) involve a value conflict over the right of workers to representation in determining their wages and working conditions, as against Mr. Spindle's right as owner to control these decisions.

The interview schedule for "Working for Mr. Spindle" is reproduced in Table 7. After reading the dialogue to the student, the interviewer asks him two sets of questions. The first set is general and open-ended. The student is asked to analyze the dialogue without specific prompts as to problem types or appropriate strategies for solution. The second set focuses on those parts of the dialogue in which, as described above, specific types of disagreement are illustrated. With this structuring the student is

TABLE 7

Interview Schedule for SIAT No. 3

Part One

I. *General*
    A. What are the main points of disagreement between B and D and how would you go about settling these points of disagreement?
    B. Are there any other main points of disagreement between B and D or anything else you would like to say about settling these points of disagreement?
        (Repeat question B above until the student says he has nothing else to add.)
    C. Now we are going to discuss some specific points in the argument more fully.
        You may have to repeat some of the things you have already told me to answer questions on these specific points. Don't hesitate to repeat or restate anything you have already said if you think it is the right answer to one of the questions I ask.

Part Two

II. *Definition Problem*
    A. What do you think is the main point of disagreement in statements 3 and 4?
        (If *succeeds* [says they are disagreeing over the definition or meaning of the word *collective bargaining*] go on to B.)
        (If says disagreement is over the meaning of a word, ask student —)
    What word are they disagreeing over?
        (If says disagreeing over collective bargaining, or disagreeing over whether or not there really was collective bargaining, ask student —)
    In what way are they disagreeing over *collective bargaining?*
        (If *succeeds*, go on to B. If *fails*, say —)
    Is there any other way you would describe the disagreement in these statements?
        (If *succeeds*, go on to B. If *partial success*, repeat appropriate steps above. If *fails*, say —)
    One other kind of disagreement B and D are having in these statements is over the definition or meaning of a word. What is the word?
        (If *succeeds*, go on to B. If *fails*, say —)
    The word is *collective bargaining.*

Interview Schedule for SIAT No. 3 (continued)

B. (If included in answer to A, omit.)
    In the disagreement over the meaning of the word *collective bargaining,* what is B's definition of the word and what is D's definition of the word?
    (If only gives either B's definition or D's definition, say —)
    Yes, that is B's definition; now what is D's definition (or vice versa)?

C. Yes. Bob thinks that collective bargaining means that the boss or owner talks with his men about wages and working conditions in small or large groups whether these groups of men represent the workers officially or not. And Don thinks that collective bargaining occurs only when the boss talks to the official representatives of all the workers.
    In this disagreement over the meaning or definition of the word *collective bargaining,* how would you go about settling the disagreement?

III. *Factual Problem*

A. What do you think is the main point of disagreement in statements 5 through 9?
    (If student *succeeds,* go on to B. If in doubt, say —)
    I'm not quite sure what you mean.
    (If student *fails,* say —)
    The disagreement seems to be over a fact. What is each man claiming to be true, and how do they disagree?
    (The men are disagreeing over whether Mr. Spindle talked regularly with even a small group of men at this plant. One says they met every Thursday. The other says they meet only every once in a while.)
    (If student *succeeds,* go on to B. If student *fails,* say —)
    The men are disagreeing over whether or not Mr. Spindle really met regularly with a group of his employees. Bob claims that they did meet regularly with Mr. Spindle. Don claims that they met only every once in a while. They are disagreeing over what claim is true.

B. Now that we know we have a factual disagreement in this part of the argument, how would you go about settling such a disagreement? That is, what would you do in this particular case to settle the disagreement?

C. Any other information you would like to have to settle this argument?

D. How might you go about making sure that the information you got was true or reliable?

E. What are some of the (other) things you would take into account in determining whether you had *enough* reliable information?

F. Can you think of any (other) special problems you might run into in gathering evidence you need?

IV. *Value Problem*

A. What do you think is the main point of disagreement in statements 10 and 11?
    1. If *specific statement* of value disagreement given, ask —
    Are there some values or rights (that is, ideas of good or right) suggested in this disagreement which B or D might give to support his position?

Interview Schedule for SIAT No. 3 (continued)

    2. If a *general statement* of value disagreement given, ask —
How were you able to figure out what principle was involved? And
in what way is (state second value, if given) involved in this disagreement?

B. (Whether or not the student succeeds in Part A, summarize the correct answer.)

    Yes. We see that there is a value question at this point in the
argument. The question is, Should Mr. Spindle bargain collectively
with his workers, and give them equal bargaining power, when in
fact he owns and runs his own factory? Two important values involved here might be the right to control the property you own and
use it as you see fit, since Mr. Spindle does own the factory; and the
right of the workers to have an equal say in determining their wages
and working conditions, since they are dependent on their jobs for
a living.

    Now, what are some of the things we might do to settle this dis-
agreement over values?

C. Are there any other things we might do?

---

asked what type of disagreement is involved in each phase of the dialogue
and how he would go about clarifying or resolving such a controversy. If the
student is unable to identify the type of controversy involved in the cluster
of statements, he is given the answer and then asked again for the appropriate way to deal with it. Additional information is given when necessary to
provide prompts for the student.

Scoring

SIAT No. 3 was scored by listening to tape-recorded interviews and
analyzing the content of student responses. Three different types of
responses served as the basis for scoring:

(1) *Identification of the Various Types of Disagreements Illustrated by
the Dialogue.* In assigning credit to a student's response, the degree of explicitness with which he identified a disagreement was taken into account.
If the student said, for example, that statements 3 and 4 constitute a definitional argument over the meaning of the term *collective bargaining,* he was
given full credit. If he said the argument was over what collective bargaining is, he was given part credit, as we considered *is* to be less explicit
than *meaning of* or *definition of.* If the student described the dispute only
in terms of the specific situation — e.g., if he said that in statements 5
through 9 there was a controversy over whether or not Mr. Spindle held
regular meetings with his men — he was given less credit. In identifying a
value disagreement, as in statements 10 and 11, the student was given

additional credit if he indicated not only the type of disagreement but also the values involved. The values suggested as the basis of the controversy had to be plausible; that is, credit was not given for values that appeared irrelevant to the conflict, unless the student gave some reasonable explanation of their relevance.

(2) *Strategies for Dealing with the Controversies.* The student's ability to deal with each controversy in a constructive fashion was assessed quantitatively by counting the number of "reasonable" strategies he presented. While most student responses were anticipated in advance, we found it necessary to add *post hoc* categories during the scoring when students came up with unanticipated reasonable alternatives.

(3) *Analytic Concepts.* A number of analytic concepts were selected as especially important for dealing with controversy. If the student used these concepts explicitly or implicitly, he was given additional credit. The concepts included, for example, *hypothesis, evidence,* and *assumption.* The complete list is given on page 1 of the interview scoring sheet, shown in Table 8.

In addition to these three bases for scoring, a valued response by a student was given more credit the earlier it occurred in the interview sequence; that is, a response received more credit if it was stated after the first open-ended question than if it was given after the dialogue had been structured into its three major parts. Moreover, in the second part of the interview, the student was given less credit as more prompts were needed to elicit a valued response. In that part of the interview dealing with the factual

TABLE 8

Scoring Sheet for SIAT No. 3

Name _____		School _____	
OPEN END	**GENERAL CONCEPT**		
Main Points of Disagreement	*Explicit*	*Implicit*	*Specific Situation*
Definition: *Collective bargaining or regularly*	_____	_____	_____
Factual: Did Mr. S. meet men regularly?	_____	_____	_____
Value: Should Mr. S. meet men regularly?	_____	_____	_____

Identifies values: e.g., general welfare _____ equality _____ property/contract _____
other (specify) _____

Scoring Sheet for SIAT No. 3 (continued)

Strategies
Definition

—— find out what collective
    bargaining means
—— identify points of disagree-
    ment
—— have each elaborate his
    definition
—— see how others use word
—— get authority
—— dictionary
—— contract
—— law
—— "expert"
—— look at other plants
—— get men to agree on one
    meaning
—— definition a matter of opinion
—— poll men or vote on meaning
—— sees problems in own position
—— procedural

Factual
—— refer to evidence in case
—— ask men
—— ask Spindle
—— question evidence in case
—— suggest get more evidence
—— check records
—— just find out
—— procedural

Value
—— prove one value's validity
—— test factual assumptions
—— work toward compromise
—— decide which is more
    important value
—— load or exaggerate a value
—— test consequences of each
    value
—— define values more specifically
    in terms of policy decisions
—— procedural

Concepts——
Definition (only if not evidence
    of above)

—— criteria or criterial definition
—— labeling or pointing definition
—— loaded definition
—— classification

Factual
—— claim
—— specific claim
—— general claim
—— generalization
—— tentativity of claims: levels
    of probability
—— hypothesis
—— assumption
—— testing a claim
—— sampling
—— representative sampling
—— contradiction or consistency
—— explanation
—— evidence
—— intuition
—— authority
—— observation

Value
—— value judgment
—— value labels:
    general welfare ——
    property/contract ——
    equality ——
    other (specify) ——
—— analogy
—— dilemma

(Note: list other responses which seem reasonable.)

problem, for example, the interviewer was to ask an initial question and then give four prompts, if needed. More credit was given if the valued response occurred after the first prompt than after the second one, and so on.

The scorer filled out the scoring booklet as he listened to the tape recording of the interview, replaying portions as needed. The first page (Table 8) was filled out for the first general open-ended question. Subsequent pages in the booklet tell how to adjust scores according to the number of prompts required to elicit a correct answer.

Reliability

Little trouble was encountered in obtaining scorer reliability for SIAT No. 3. Pairs of scorers were readily trained to reach 85 per cent agreement on the total points scored for each individual.

Obtaining behavior reliability, i.e., the consistency with which the student will respond to various parts of the interview, or the extent to which the student will perform similarly on another interview, presented more serious problems. The only reliability estimate of this sort available for SIAT No. 3 is the correlation between a pilot version of the instrument, administered in the fall of 1960, and the revised test, administered in the spring of 1961. The coefficient was a low .35. However, the experimental pretest was given to test the feasibility of using such a measure, and one of the difficulties we discovered was a lack of standardization in administration. The hypothesis that the low correlation is due largely to the unreliability of the pilot test rather than the unreliability of the final form is supported by the correlations between SIAT No. 1, the pilot version of SIAT No. 3, and the final version of SIAT No. 3. These coefficients are presented in Table 9. The correlation between SIAT No. 1 and the final version of SIAT No. 3 is .60, in comparison with .25 between SIAT No. 1 and the experimental

TABLE 9

Correlations Between Three Forms of SIAT

Form	1	2
1. SIAT No. 1 (pencil-and-paper)		
2. SIAT No. 3 (interview)	.60	
3. Experimental pretest of SIAT No. 3 (interview)	.25	.35

pretest. Consistently low correlations were also obtained between the pilot version and other measures requiring general reasoning ability, while the final version consistently correlated with them in the .50's. There are grounds, therefore, for believing that SIAT No. 3, while admittedly a somewhat crude measure in its present form, has the potential of more satisfactory reliability.

One other point might be noted in regard to the coefficients in Table 9. A criticism leveled in Chapter Ten at available standardized tests of "critical thinking" is that they provide no validity data to indicate that those who score high on the tests can apply the same intellectual operations in other, less structured situations. The correlation of .60 between SIAT No. 1 and SIAT No. 3 can be considered a coefficient of concurrent validity with SIAT No. 3 as the criterion measure.

SIAT No. 4: A System for Analyzing "Free" Discussion

Although it contains less structure and fewer built-in training procedures than available paper-and-pencil measures, SIAT No. 3 still has an essential limitation: It requires the student to deal with an issue only at an analytic level. He is not asked to take a position himself, to defend his position, and to rebut statements attacking his position or supporting other positions. Perhaps the most appropriate setting for evaluating the skills and competences used in "real-life" controversy is one involving spoken argumentation in a live discussion unstructured by the prompts of a teacher or interviewer. Argumentation in this type of setting can be evaluated by general ratings of the student's performance or assessed by systematic content analysis of the interaction process.

General ratings are fraught with methodological problems: the difficulty of making explicit the elements of performance taken into account in arriving at a final rating; and the difficulty, even when these elements are spelled out either by or for the raters, of determining what external factors have entered into the rating, i.e., rater bias.

Systematic content analysis tends to force greater specificity upon the researcher, since he must define rather precise categories of behavior in order to obtain reliability among his observers. It also yields quantitative component scores. As the behavior to be categorized becomes more complex, however, systematic content analysis encounters some of the problems of subjective ratings, such as rater bias in making subtle distinctions between categories. Moreover, the sum of quantitative scores is often not a satisfactory index of overall competence. Despite these difficulties, the desirability of obtaining quantitative estimates of various components contributing to overall competence led us to explore systematic content analysis of "free" discussion as a technique likely to lead to fruitful results in our attempt to assess competence in political discussion and analysis.

Discussion Settings

In the first "free discussion" setting with which we experimented, approximately twelve students were seated in a circle or semicircle.

Each student was given a copy of a controversial case, the case was read aloud by the teacher or an experimenter, and the students were told that their task was to come to a unanimous decision on a policy to handle the problem in the case. The "problem" was not identified. A time limit of twenty-five minutes was set, and the teacher or experimenter left the room and returned at the end of this time to hear the group's decision.

Two points about this particular testing situation should be noted. First, requiring that the students reach unanimity on a decision is an important element of the task, adopted from Robert F. Bales' work with five-man groups. Without this requirement the students would usually "solve" the issue quickly by taking a vote and letting the majority rule. Requiring concensus forces a debate of the issues. Second, since only the students witness the discussion, the problem of avoiding unintended cues by an adult observer is obviated. Whether or not the students direct themselves to the task without supervision in such a setting indicates to some extent how important the task appears to them.

The student-led discussion group, however, has certain difficulties: (1) Groups have varying degrees of interest in the task and may experience procedural problems of varying degrees of intensity, with obvious effects on the performance levels of group members. (2) If the group is treated as the unit of analysis, information is not available as to who or how many of the group facilitated or interfered with the clarification or resolution of the problem under discussion. (3) If the responses of the individuals in the group are to be analyzed, problems of equating the responses of high and low participants, or even of insuring that all students will participate in the discussion, must be faced.

These difficulties can be overcome to a large extent by using a setting in which a single adult discusses a controversial case with an individual student. This is essentially a two-man group in which the level of sophistication of the person who is *not* being evaluated is controlled. As we have used this situation, the "interviewer" reads a case to the student, asks for his opinion, and then is free to pursue whatever issues are raised by the student. Each interviewer is, however, provided with a "brief" setting forth the major issues likely to be raised in the discussion, along with arguments and analogies with which to confront the student as each issue is discussed.

A System of Content Analysis to Evaluate Political Discussion

We have used SIAT No. 4 to assess reflective competence in both student-led group discussions and interview settings. In the analysis of discussion obtained in both situations the scorer, or observer, must identify discrete units in the interaction. These he then classifies according to a number of categories based on the major analytic operations or concepts discussed in earlier chapters. In developing an interaction analysis system, three important considerations are (1) the size of the units into which the total train of interaction is broken, (2) the frame of reference of the person who carries out the unitization and categorization, and, (3) the nature of the categories into which the units are classified. The following review of our decisions about these considerations for SIAT No. 4 indicates a number of assumptions underlying the use of the instrument, as well as the many technical considerations that must be taken into account in building such a system.

The unit. Theoretically, the units into which a discussion may be broken can range in size from an entire meeting or discussion[1] to the smallest segment of it. If the unit is a segment of the discussion, it may be defined in terms of time,[2] a completed verbal interchange,[3] a "single" participation by an individual,[4] or it may be based on an arbitrary linguistic convention.[5] This last type was used for SIAT No. 4 and is similar to that described by Bales:

> The unit to be scored is the smallest discriminable segment of verbal behavior to which the observer, using the present set of categories after appropriate training, can assign a classification under conditions of continuous serial scoring. This unit may be called an act, or more properly, a single interaction, since all acts in the present scheme are regarded as interactions. The unit as defined here has also been called the single item of thought. . . . Often the unit will be a single sentence expressing or conveying a complete simple thought.[6]

SIAT No. 4, then, calls for the classification of the "single item of thought." Examples of complete units would be:
"I am sure that the southerners would not accept immediate integration."
"They are the ones who should do something about the situation."
In general, compound sentences are scored as two units, complex sentences as one. In some instances, several sentences may constitute one unit of thought, as in the presentation of a single case situation or analogy.

Frame of Reference. Scorer reliability and, to some extent, the validity of the instrument itself depend upon a careful definition of the frame of reference from which the observer, or scorer, is to view the discussion. Several questions must be posed and answered in terms of the researcher's purpose, which, for us, is the assessment of reflective competence in a discussion setting. For example, what will be *the observer's point of view* toward the group he is observing? The observer might be asked to

. . . think of himself as a generalized group member, or, insofar as he can, as the specific other to whom the actor is talking, or toward whom the actor's behavior is directed, or by whom the actor's behavior is perceived. The observer then endeavors to classify the act of the actor according to its instrumental or expressive significance to the other group member.[7]

Another point of view that the observer might adopt is one described by Steinzor: The observer is to determine the intent of the actor, so he must try to put himself in the actor's place.[8] Or the observer may be instructed to remain aloof from the process of the group and not concerned with the intent behind behavior nor its effects upon the group or its individual members. In the observational scheme used by Heyns, for example, "the observer is outside the process and views each contribution in terms of its theoretical properties as a problem solving function."[9] Carter and his associates also use a scheme in which the observer is to be concerned, not with intent or effect, but with the functional significance of an act for the discussion situation as viewed by an outsider.[10]

For SIAT No. 4, the scorer is to look for cues which indicate whether the actor is using particular categories of thought. The observer's point of view, therefore, is much like that demanded by Heyns' scheme in that he serves as an expert in applying external definitional criteria to the actor's statements. He is "outside the process," except as an understanding of the immediate discussion context is necessary to apply the criteria. For example, in deciding whether or not a student has stated a value judgment or raised a question of relevance, the observer refers to the content of the statement, not to the manner in which other students might interpret it. It should be noted, however, that our experiences confirm Bales' report that for scoring most acts the point of view of the observer is of small importance in obtaining interobserver reliability.

A second aspect of frame of reference to be considered in devising an observational instrument is *the extent to which the observer is to take into account any prior knowledge* he has *of the group or of individuals within the group.* For SIAT No. 4, we instruct the observer to try to forget all prior experiences with participants. If a statement made by a participant arouses a prejudgment in the observer when scoring subsequent statements, he is to control it. The question becomes "How would I score that act if I had not heard this person's prior statement?"

A third consideration in defining a frame of reference for the observer concerns the *context* within which particular statements are to be categorized: How much of the context of a particular discussion should the observer take into account in classifying a particular act? Should the statement be scored as an isolated act, in relation only to the previous act, within the context of the total discussion, etc.? For example, the statement

"I would agree with John" might be scored "disagreement" if scored in reference to a statement by John's antagonist in the discussion who had just spoken, but "agreement" if scored as an isolated act or in the context of the total discussion.

Categories. Since SIAT No. 4 uses two scoring systems superimposed on each other (i.e., an act may be scored in a category in each system), the observer must use two contexts: one for what we term *static categories,* the other for *dynamic categories.* The dynamic system (see Table 10) is designed to get at intellectual operations requiring the comparison and synthesis of statements. Therefore it consists of categories which explicitly require the scorer to think in the context of the relationship of one statement to another. This context may include one or several prior statements. The static categories (see Table 11) theoretically can be scored without taking into account any context beyond the scorable unit. Every unit of behavior is scored in a static category, whereas dynamic operations are scored only when they occur and are identified. Thus, when a dynamic operation is scored, we have a double categorization of the unit.[11]

TABLE 10

Dynamic Categories

---

1. *Consistency-Inconsistency:* Statements that indicate explicitly or implicity that the speaker is aware of a real or possible consistency or inconsistency within his own or another speaker's position. The inconsistency may be between two values, two facts, or two definitions.

2. *Specification and Generalization:* Specification occurs when the speaker gives a specific statement to illustrate or support a more general statement. Generalization occurs when the speaker draws a more general conclusion from one or more specific statements already given.
   Example of specification: "Desegregation is not going well. Only 7% of the Negro children in the South are now going to integrated schools after seven years of illegal segregation." The second sentence would be scored as the static operation "specific claim" and the dynamic operation "specification."
   Example of generalization: "After World War II, Russia 'captured' the countries of eastern Europe, helped China to become a Communist nation, and tried its best to take over Greece and Turkey. Russia is the greatest imperialist nation the world has ever known." The second statement would be scored as static operation "general claim" and as dynamic operation "generalization."

3. *Qualifying:* A statement which deals with an implicit or explicit inconsistency by pointing out under what general circumstances an exception to a general principle is allowable or possible we score as a qualifying act.

Dynamic Categories (continued)

Example: Mr. A: Our civil liberties are our most precious asset. To try and restrict them for any citizen is un-American.

Mr. B: If you had been in Germany in the early 1930's, would you have restricted some of the civil liberties granted Hitler when he was conducting mass hate meetings?

Mr. A: I very well might have. I would say that civil liberties should be restricted, however, only when the government which is pledged to protect them is in real danger from an undemocratic and brutal force which would destroy all civil liberties.

Mr. A's modified position would be scored as static operation "general value judgment" and dynamic operation "qualification."

TABLE 11

Static Categories

General Value Judgments: Statements in which the speaker expresses a preference for a person, object, or position in the argument in terms of a general social or legal value, such as: personal privacy, property, contract, speech, religion, general welfare of the group, equality, justice, brotherhood, due process, consent and representation, etc. "Mr. Kohler certainly should have the right to use his property as he sees fit and to make contracts with his workers without union interference."

Specific Value Judgments: Statements in which the speaker expresses a preference for a person, object, or position in the argument in terms of the specific case under discussion. "I think Mr. Kohler should have met the demands of the United Auto Workers."

General Legal Claims: Statements in which the speaker asserts that someone has a legal right to do something, expressed in terms of a general legal principle, such as: rule of law, due process, equal protection under the law, constitutional restraints, etc. "He has a right to a fair trial under the United States Constitution."

Specific Legal Claims: Statements in which the speaker asserts that someone has a legal right to do something, but does not give a legal principle as a basis for the right. "Mr. Kohler has a right to fire any worker he wants."

General Factual Claims: Causal, descriptive, or predictive generalizations. "Negroes are just as intelligent as whites."

Specific Factual Claims: Statements describing specific events delineated in time and space. "The first attempt at integration in Little Rock was on September 4, 1957."

Source: A statement or part of a statement describing the source on which a claim, definition, or value judgment is based. "Emergency is defined this way in Webster's *New International Dictionary*."

Static Categories (continued)

Definitional Claim: A statement about how a word or phrase is defined or should be defined. It is also a statement of analysis by which several meanings of a single word or statement might be distinguished. "An emergency occurs when one or more people are in danger of being injured or losing their lives and property."

Repetition: A statement in which the speaker repeats himself or communicates something already stated in order to focus the discussion.

Case: A set of statements which describes specific, real, or hypothetical situations analogous to the one under discussion. Its main purpose is to elaborate the range of situations to which one might apply a value judgment. "Suppose Negroes and whites were given schools of equal quality, teachers of equal quality, books and educational facilities of equal quality: Would Negro schools still be inferior to white schools?"

Relevance: A statement which explicitly deals with the way a statement or group of statements is related to the total argument or to the specific point under discussion. "I don't see what that statement has to do with the discussion."

Debate Strategy: *Ad hominem* or other remarks which explicitly discuss the tactics being used by a discussant. "You're just trying to confuse me."

Task — Procedural: A statement directed at controlling the immediate interpersonal situation; it assumes that everyone in the discussion is trying to do a conscientious job. "Let's take a vote." "Let's give everyone a chance to talk."

Deviance Control — Procedural: A statement directed at controlling the immediate interpersonal situation; it assumes that one or more people are violating group norms. "Get back in your seat and sit down." "You don't have to shout."

An exception to the distinction between static and dynamic categories occurs in the category "relevance." Although basically a dynamic category, it is scored as a static act because the assertion or questioning of relevance usually contains an obvious cue within the statement itself, and because there is often no static category which can be appropriately scored with it.

The system can, perhaps, be understood better by observing the sample scoring sheet provided in Table 12. Static categories are scored by marking in a square opposite the categories listed on the left margin of the sheet. Every unit is scored in a static category, and the scorer moves from left to right across the scoring sheet as the discussion progresses, scoring only one act in each vertical column. On this particular sample sheet, fifteen units of interaction would be scored from left to right. In actual scoring, the observer goes from one sheet to the next with the sheets numbered in sequence before scoring begins. If the scorer determines that an act should be scored in a dynamic category he marks the appropriate

TABLE 12

Sample Scoring Sheet, SIAT No. 4

1. GVJ											
2. SVJ											
3. GLC											
4. SLC											
5. GFC											
6. SFC											
7. Source											
8. Def.											
9. Repeat, etc.											
10. Clarif.											
11. Case											
12. Relevance											

letter within the square for the static category scored (*c* for consistency-inconsistency, *g* for generalization and specification, and *q* for qualification).

Full instructions for scoring behavior with the SIAT No. 4 require a detailed manual, but it might be well to note two other types of discriminations made in the system as we have used it. First, the observer is asked to make a judgment about whether a unit of behavior makes a statement, asks a question, questions, or expresses doubt about a prior statement (often in either the declarative or interrogative form, but with an overtone of argumentative intent), or expresses self-doubt or uncertainty about the validity of a claim that has been or is going to be made by the speaker. We have called this a judgment of the "posture" of the speaker. Posture is scored with a numerical symbol within the square for the appropriate static category.

Second, a dichotomous distinction is made concerning whether a speaker is trying to persuade other group members that his substantive position in the argument is correct, or whether he is attempting to "stay outside" the argument and analyze how the group might best construe the issues in the case. For example: "That person in the case should not have been allowed to speak because avoiding a riot is more important than his right to speak" would be scored as a persuasive statement; "The problem here is that the principles of freedom of speech and of peace and order are both involved, and we must decide which value should be given greater weight in this instance" would be scored as an analytic statement. If the observer judges a statement to be analytic, he marks *a* in the square of the appropriate static category. Otherwise, the statement is assumed to be persuasive.

Validity

Initially, of course, using the system to categorize statements in a discussion results in an abstract cognitive description of the discussion. This description must be translated into a quantitative score by determining which categories seem most valuable from the point of view of our objectives, then counting the frequency with which units are scored in these categories. The selection of *valued acts* is essentially a matter of content validity. For the purpose of the research to be reported in the Appendix, the following categories have been assigned value for a discussion involving political controversy.

Static Categories. The following static categories are valued: (1) *General value judgments* and *general legal claims* are valued because they indicate the student is dealing with the controversial case at a more abstract and general level. (2) *Specific factual claims* and *sources* are valued because they are appropriate ways of supporting more general claims. They are an important part of the empirical proof process. (3) *Definitional claims* are valued because they tend to demand or give greater precision to the various positions in the argument. *Repetition* is *not* valued, since it involves mainly statements which repeat something already said. When the student clarifies by drawing finer distinctions between positions or terms in the agreement, his statement is scored as a *definitional claim*. (4) *Case* is valued because, by definition, it is an attempt to expose the point at which an individual will reverse his position, given an array of similar situations to judge. It is essentially a defining operation. (5) *Relevance* is valued because it indicates that the student is attempting to deal with the relationship between a particular statement and some larger facet of the total argument.

Dynamic Categories. For obvious reasons, all three dynamic operations are valued. They have been selected for scoring precisely because we think they are important.

Orientation to Discussion. An *analytic orientation* to the discussion is valued because it indicates that the student is attempting to stand back from the immediate persuasive aspects of the argument and provide a more impartial framework by which to deal with the controversy. *The questioning posture* — i.e., questioning or expressing doubt about a prior statement — is valued especially in unsophisticated groups because it tends to require discussants to clarify or support a position.

It should be noted that the choice of valued acts is not simply the result of a priori guessing. In arriving at this selection, we listened to many discussions and did a good deal of "cutting and fitting" to make the quantitative scoring procedures consistent with intuitive judgments about what behavior actually seemed important for clarifying a controversial situation.

Other Estimates of Validity. The description of analytic competence in controversial political discussions presented in earlier chapters served as the basis for objectives of instruction for a curriculum research effort to be reported in the Appendix. Since SIAT No. 4 is based on the same conceptual framework, scores obtained on this measure should discriminate between the control groups and the experimental group if the instruction is at all effective and the test valid. Since SIAT No. 4 does, in fact, make such discriminations (see the Appendix), it can be considered to have construct validity.[12]

One criticism made of the standardized paper-and-pencil tests reviewed in Chapter Nine was the lack of validity data to indicate how scores on the tests related to other types of criterion behavior or judgments. In an attempt to determine further the validity of SIAT No. 4, Berlak carried out a two-pronged research study.[13] He used twenty-six two-man groups made up of college students. Each pair of students was selected to represent opposing views in a fifteen-minute discussion on the topic: Should government funds be used to support parochial schools? These discussions were tape-recorded for later playback and scored with SIAT No. 4. The data obtained were subjected to factor analysis, and, in addition, scores were compared to ratings of ten of the twenty-six discussions by two professors of philosophy and four professors of law. The results were not entirely clear-cut, but in general do support the validity of the instrument. The factor analysis was carried out to determine whether scores on the various SIAT No. 4 categories clustered in patterns which would relate to the conceptual model from which it was developed. Commenting on the factor analysis, Berlak concludes, "Overall, considering the size of the sample, the rotations provide strong support for aspects of the model [of critical thinking in political controversy]. Several of the most basic distinctions do emerge clearly."[14] However, he also notes that "The presence of several uninterpretable categories on several factors, and the absence of most of the Dynamic categories on the factors raise questions that must be answered with further work."[15]

In making comparisons with the ratings of the discussions, Berlak used what he labeled "the Valued Category Score (VCS) . . . a sum of the unweighted valued category frequencies. . . ."[16] In the findings to be reported later this was the score derived from valued units in SIAT No. 4, so a comparison of this total score is of crucial importance for estimating validity. Berlak was able to conclude, "The comparisons of rater scores with the theoretically important Valued Category Score show strong positive relationships. The intercorrelations and the multiple r of the rating scales with the VCS criterion are generally consistently high and significant."[17] And SIAT No. 4 ". . . in its present form *using only the VCS appears to be valid for use in obtaining a quantitative estimate of competence in critical thinking as it relates to political controversy.*"[18]

Further validity studies for SIAT No. 4 are being carried out, but Berlak's study is a significant step, and one rarely made for other measures of reflective thinking. Coupled with the relationship of the measure to the framework of analytic competence discussed in earlier chapters, and the discriminations obtained on SIAT No. 4 between experimental and control groups, this validity study provides us with some confidence in the measure.

Reliability

Reliability, as noted earlier in this chapter, has two meanings in content analysis or systematic observation. It can refer to the consistency of *behavior* under observation or to the consistency with which that behavior is *observed* and scored. It is the latter type of reliability, i.e., observer agreement, with which we are concerned at this point.

Initially, four graduate students in education were trained to use SIAT No. 4. Discussions were scored from tape-recorded interviews between a student and an adult interviewer in which, as noted above, the student was challenged to take and defend a position on a controversial case (the "socratic interview"). During the initial stages of training, the observers' attention was directed to the individual categories to sharpen scoring perceptions, and inter-observer agreement was checked by a graphic method, binomial probability paper,[19] that provides the observers with quick, visual feedback. Once a high level of agreement was reached on use of the individual categories, reliability was estimated for the total number of valued acts categorized for each student (Berlak's VCS) using the product-moment correlation. For this check of reliability, each scorer was paired with every one of the other three scorers. The number of discussions scored by each combination of scorers ranged from ten to eighteen. The resulting coefficients are shown in Table 13. There is no widely accepted criterion for the acceptance of such coefficients as satisfactory; as Heyns and Zander point out, whether one demands a correlation of .70 or .90 is contingent upon the uses to which the observational scores are to be put.[20] Since

TABLE 13

Reliability Estimates for Four Observers
Using SIAT No. 4

	A	B	C	D
A				
B	.55			
C	.82	.93		
D	.87	.69	.68	

SIAT No. 4 is being reported within a specific research program, it seems sufficient to point out that with the exception of one coefficient all approach at least .70, with two greater than .80, and one greater than .90. On the average, there is a relatively high level of agreement.

A second reliability study, based on frequencies assigned to individual valued categories, was carried out on a larger sample of discussions. In this case the scoring was done by two observers, one an undergraduate and the other a graduate student in education. Neither scorer knew the purpose of the scoring system or the distinction between valued and non-valued acts. The discussions scored were tape-recorded "free," student-led discussions of controversial cases. The correlation coefficients are presented in Table 14. Although one coefficient is only .42 and another .51, in general the results are quite acceptable.

TABLE 14

*Reliability Coefficients for Two SIAT No. 4 Observers
for 32 Student-Led Discussions*

Valued Acts r	Correlation (r)
General Value Judgment	.76
General Legal Claim	.79
Specific Claim	.71
Source	.77
General Definition	.86
Specific Definition	.86
Case or Analogy	.73
Relevance	.51
Questioning Posture	.60
Analysis	.42
Total valued acts	.89

The three dynamic categories are not included in Table 14 because of the low frequency of interacts scored in these categories. Between one-third and two-thirds of the discussions scored contained a frequency of less than three in each of the dynamic categories. The reliability of the dynamic categories was checked for individual discussions with binomial probability paper. For thirty-two discussions, observer scores fell outside the acceptable limits of agreement eight of a possible ninety-six times. It should also be noted here that the scoring upon which these reliability estimates are based took place shortly after the initial training period. Probably because of the abstract nature of the categories, agreement among the scorers tended to deteriorate after a relatively short period of independent scoring.

The reliability with which observers can apply the SIAT No. 4 category system has been treated above. The other aspect of reliability, i.e., whether, within the limitations of observer reliability, the instrument produces an estimation of behavior which is consistent over time, should also be considered. A factor here, of course, is whether the sample of behavior categorized is large enough to serve as a basis for prediction of future behavior, either of an individual or of a group. With paper-and-pencil measures this reliability is commonly estimated by correlating individuals' scores derived from administration of two forms of the test, from odd versus even items on the test, or from a readministration of the test at a later date. An estimate of the internal reliability of SIAT No. 4 similar to the odd-even comparison was obtained for students in the socratic interview situation.

Each scoring sheet, containing spaces for fifteen acts, was numbered in serial order and then used in that order in scoring the interviews. The scores on valued categories on the odd scoring sheets were totaled for each individual and correlated with the sums obtained from the even sheets. The resulting correlation obtained with slightly over 100 students was .67, corrected by the Spearman-Brown Formula.

CONCLUSIONS

Our efforts to develop more adequate assessment instruments for the evaluation of social studies curricula have led us to several major conclusions. In the first place, the criterion of competence in political analysis must be established in a less structured and more realistic setting than that allowed by the multiple-choice paper-and-pencil test. Evidence obtained during the curriculum research efforts to be reported later indicates that there may be little or no relationship between competence to defend one's point of view in public and competence to do well on available "critical thinking" tests. When, for example, correlations were computed between a test made up of items from the Watson-Glaser Critical Thinking Appraisal and the Michigan State Test of Problem Solving, the Iowa Test of Educational Development, No. 5, Interpretation — Social Studies, and scores obtained in socratic interviews scored with SIAT No. 4, the coefficients ranged from .11 to .23. While some of these approach statistical significance with a sample of just over 100 students, they hardly approach educational significance.

Second, the translation of a political or ethical-legal model into specific learning outcomes that can be measured with a system of content analysis such as that described in this chapter presents, we think, a particularly fruitful approach to curricular evaluation. Learning outcomes can be measured in a discussion setting which, in comparison to paper-and-pencil tests, more closely approximates the circumstances in which the desired concepts and intellectual operations are to be applied later. The reliability data presented for SIAT No. 4 suggest the feasibility of this approach to assessment both in experimentation and to a limited extent, in classroom teaching.

There is, however, no denying the impracticability of careful, complex content analysis for the day-to-day measurement needs of the average classroom. Teachers in general have neither the research competence nor the time to learn or use such a complex system. Nevertheless, just as a teacher might during any period of time teach for only one or a few of the concepts included in SIAT No. 4's category set, so might the set be modified to include fewer categories in order to simplify scoring. Moreover, complex instruments, such as SIAT No. 4, might be used to establish the validity of simpler category systems, or even of paper-and-pencil tests.[21]

Finally, the curriculum evaluator must keep in mind that the content analysis of discussions, although perhaps providing a more valid profile of the discussion process, will not tell him what types of statements or sequences of statements should be valued. This sort of appraisal must be accomplished through philosophical consideration of the nature of rational justification in a democratic society.

References

1. See, for example, N. Fouriezos, M. Hutt, and H. Quetzkow, "Measurement of Self-Oriented Needs in Discussion Groups," *Journal of Abnormal and Social Psychology* (1950), 45:685-690; and A. F. Zander, "The AP Club: An Objective Study of a Group," *Human Relations* (1948), 1:321-332.

2. See W. C. Olson and E. M. Cunningham, "Time-Sampling Techniques," *Child Development* (1934), 5:41-58.

3. See B. Othanel Smith and others, "A Study of the Logic of Teaching: The Logical Structure of Teaching and the Development of Critical Thinking, a Report on the First Phase of a Five Year Project," prepared at the University of Illinois, Urbana, under Cooperative Research Project No. 258 (7257) of the U.S. Office of Education, 1959 (mimeographed).

4. See B. Steinzor, "The Development and Evaluation of a Measure of Social Interaction," *Human Relations* (1949), 2:103-122.

5. See Robert F. Bales, *Interaction Process Analysis* (Reading, Mass.: Addison-Wesley Publishing Company, Inc., 1951).

6. *Ibid.*, p. 37. Our orientation toward the content analysis of verbal discussions has in general been markedly influenced by Bales' work.

7. *Ibid.*, p. 39.

8. Steinzor, *op. cit.*

9. R. W. Heyns and R. Lippitt, *Systematic Observation Techniques*, Vol. I of *Handbook of Social Psychology*, edited by Lindsay Gardner (Reading, Mass.: Addison-Wesley Publishing Company, Inc., 1954).

10. L. F. Carter, W. Haythorn, B. Meirowitz, and J. Lanzetta, "The Behavior of Leaders and Other Group Members," *Journal of Abnormal and Social Psychology* (1951), 46:589-595.

11. At this point it should be noted that scoring each act in at least two systems simultaneously, as is the case with both the interaction systems being discussed here and the one we used to describe teaching styles, differs markedly from the procedures used by Bales and other researchers. Multiple scoring is possible largely because we score from tapes, so that the rate of scoring can be controlled. It would be much more difficult to ue a system requiring multiple scoring in a live situation. For purposes of statistical analysis, it is important to use an observer scoring sheet which allows the researcher to determine what particular acts have been multiple-scored, so that he can distinguish the total units of behavior from the number of categorizations made.

12. See *Technical Recommendations for Achievement Tests* (Washington: American Educational Research Association, 1955), pp. 166-19.

13. Harold Berlak, "The Construct Validity of a Content Analysis System for the Evaluation of Critical Thinking in Political Competence," unpublished doctoral thesis, Harvard Graduate School of Education, 1964.

14. Harold Berlak, "The Construct Validity of a Content Analysis System for the Evaluation of Critical Thinking in Political Controversy," paper read at the annual meeting of the American Educational Research Association, Chicago, February 1964, p. 16 of a mimeographed copy.

15. *Ibid.*

16. *Ibid.*

17. *Ibid.*, pp. 18-19.

18. *Ibid.*, p. 19.

19. Frederick Mosteller and J. W. Tuckey, "The Uses and Usefulness of Binomial Probability Paper," *American Statistical Association Journal,* (1949), 44:174-212. For a statement of its application to systematic observation, see Bales, *op. cit.,* pp. 111-112.

20. R. W. Heyns and A. F. Zander, "Observation of Group Behavior," in L. Festenger and D. Katz (eds.), *Research Methods in the Behavioral Sciences* (New York: Dryden Press, 1953), p. 411.

21. See the Appendix for correlation with our own paper-and-pencil tests, SIAT's No. 1 and 2.

CHAPTER TWELVE

Jurisprudential Teaching and Prospects for the Social Studies

Throughout this book our major effort has been to develop and clarify a position which would relate a number of important aspects of social studies teaching. We have considered the pluralistic nature of the American democratic community and framed curricular objectives in that context; we have presented the basic outlines of specific types of content for a curriculum based on this formulation, the nature of the dialogue, and methods of measurement; and finally, in the Appendix, we shall report the results of an experimental trial for such a curriculum. In this chapter, we shall attempt to do three things: deal with the challenge of the social science disciplines both to the conventional history-oriented curriculum and to the jurisprudential approach; discuss three common criticisms leveled against the latter; and briefly discuss the future of jurisprudential teaching.

THE CHALLENGE OF THE SOCIAL SCIENCE DISCIPLINES

For many years the most salient characteristic of a "conventional" social studies program has been its domination by history, especially European and American history. During the post-Sputnik years the conventional curriculum has been challenged by a new approach presumably based on the "structure" of the social science disciplines. This shift toward the social sciences has undoubtedly been stimulated in large part by heavily financed and widely publicized curriculum innovations in physics, mathematics, biology, and elementary science. In these areas, university scholars and selected school teachers have jointly prepared materials and procedures designed to communicate what the scholars considered the crucial generalizations, categories, and methodology of their field — what has come to be called the "structure of the discipline." The basic assumption undergirding the notion of structure as developed by Bruner[1] is quite simple: If the basic "concepts" of a field of study are carefully identified and their sequential relationships analyzed, this will provide the most effective basis for designing and constructing a curriculum — effective in the sense that the student will more quickly understand and more easily grasp the "subject." For the clarity of "concept flow" is alleged to make the relationship of the conceptual system to the problems with which the discipline seeks to deal more evident to the student so that an unfolding of meaning will take place as the teacher moves from one concept to the next in the system. Moreover, the process of carefully revealing the elements of structure which give meaning to the problems of the discipline is presumed to have a powerful motivational effect on the student. (The evidence for this is undoubtedly a projection of the scholar's own excitement at initial discovery.) Bruner's discussion of "structure" and his speculations on related issues in learning theory, e.g., readiness, motivation, and conditions of transfer, thus suggest that curriculum development includes at least two initial steps: (1) the definition and description of the basic structure of a discipline by scholars in the field and (2) the formulation of tasks for the student which will lead him to discover (perhaps rediscover is a better term) and use this structure.[2]

It would be difficult to overestimate the current impact of the notion of structure on social studies educators,[3] although there has been little observable change in the behavior of the teacher on the firing line. It is likely that the continued chasm between the practices advocated by curriculum development programs and the practitioner in the classroom is to some degree a result of the ambiguous place of history in the galaxy of the social sciences. Is history a social science? Does history have a "structure" in the same sense as, for example, classical economics?

History cannot be written off by the social sciences, since it contains the stuff from which the other, more structured disciplines are built and by which they are tested. It is clear, however, that both social scientists and historians are uncertain regarding the scholarly and teaching function of the historian. Is the objective of the historian's work to develop a combination of fact, myth, and legend to represent the more cherished values and practices of the culture? An example would be the perpetuation of the accounts of Paul Revere's ride and the Battle of Lexington because such events illustrate a spirit of courage and independence, although it is known that to a considerable degree both stories are Homeric prose.

History can also be intended as *a specific dramatic narrative,* a reasonably accurate accounting of an event or series of events, even admitting the problems of obtaining evidence and organizing it in line with the historian's own selective biases. This type of narration has a long and distinguished record from Thucydides to Catton[4] and Shirer.[5] Or is history a *schematic narrative* of the major developments or "eras" which characterize a society or civilization over long periods of time? Most textbooks fall into this category, but so does the work of such distinguished historians as Morison,[6] Toynbee,[7] and McNeill.[8]

Some see history as a *social science,* a kind of two-dimensional behavioral science with its major purpose the explicit development of conceptual systems by which events can be ordered and related, or, to put it another way, by which hypotheses can be developed and tested systematically.[9] This last view of history is clearly necessary before we can talk about the "structure" of history in the same sense as we do the "structure" of sociology or economics.

The place accorded history in a curriculum based on the structure of the social sciences obviously depends on which view of history one adopts. And, it is questionable whether the proponents of the "structure of the disciplines" approach can convince social studies teachers, who usually lack the social science view of history, that they have found the proper purpose and place for the teaching of history. In fact, there is little evidence that this issue has been given much attention.

The current emphasis on the social sciences as a basis of curriculum development has not only created an "identity problem" for the historian and the teacher of history but has posed some serious questions about "citizenship education." The extent to which the citizen can transform the concepts of social science scholars and find them useful in the dialogue revolving around public controversy is open to question. Certainly the terminology of the economist, for example, is becoming an important part of public discourse. Yet it seems that the social scientist's perception of public issues is, perhaps, as often blocked as facilitated by the rigor of his own conceptual schemes.

To the extent that proponents of "structure" assume that the major ends of education are inquiry and the quest for knowledge within the highly specialized frameworks found in the work of those formally engaged in scholarship, the approach has questionable value for general education in the social studies. Furthermore, such a stance reflects a somewhat narrow-minded view by assuming that youth — and their teachers — should ask and answer questions according to the norms and styles preferred by scholars. It is not at all certain that the social science scholar has made such a compelling contribution to clarifying or resolving major societal issues that his mode of thought is *the* model to be followed and taught. The somewhat parochial nature of the average academician's orientation[10] as indicated by much scholarly work leads us to two major reservations about this basis for the social studies curriculum. First, there are models of reflection and action which obviously are relevant to social studies objectives but are all but ignored by the social scientists in their academic work. And, second, the social scientist seems especially prone to generalize from the fact that *his* structures make the social world meaningful and exciting to him to the proposition that the same structures will appear meaningful and exciting to all comers and especially to restless children and adolescents.

Alternative Models

Four important models which fall outside the social sciences, and which would appear to be important for the social studies, are the historian as poet and wise man (e.g., Morison); the broad-ranging socratic or prophetic philosopher (e.g., Tillich); the political activist or lawyer-statesman (e.g., Martin Luther King); and the journalist (e.g., Lippmann).

The poet-historian constructs "knowledge" in such a way that it will contribute new meaning and insight to the culture. His works allow the young to translate raw tribal impulses into civilized heroics. Milestones of our civilization — the Judeo-Christian ethic, the Anglo-American constitutional tradition, the commitment to reason over force — are given rich meaning in the dramatic and poetic writing shaped and reshaped by the great historians of each succeeding generation. Surely this is an important aspect of the education of the citizen.

The philosopher constantly raises basic questions related to the establishment of intellectual truth and probes into established standards of goodness and rightness often assumed or maintained by the scholarly world as well as by the society at large. It is precisely because the prophetic philosopher often seeks to break old structures and see society in a new light that we value his contribution. Moreover, although the scientist's role, including that of the social scientist, does include philosophical elements as he attempts the systematic ordering of knowledge, rarely does he attempt to organize formally the philosophical aspects of his work (except as they impinge on "methodology"). Nor is he likely to become involved as a scholar in axiological questions.

What of the activist, the lawyer-statesman involved in the immediate issues facing society? His role may be that of the angry young volunteer seeking to eradicate injustice, or that of a formal officer in the government. Assuming that we need activists, how do we train them? Should a social studies program deliberately plant seeds of dissent in the socratic tradition? Should it seek to temporize extreme dissent by reason and reflection? Such questions are handled only implicitly, if at all, when the social scientist talks about teaching the "structure" of the discipline.

Finally, what of the intelligent journalist who has disciplined himself to report events in objective fashion and constantly seeks as well to place these events in historical and ethical perspective? Does he present a model useful to the social studies, and is there a structure of knowledge in his *modus operandi* that can be made explicit?

It is clear that attitudinal and temperamental, as well as intellectual, dimensions run through the objectives of any social studies program — dimensions such as commitment, willingness to become engaged in society's political processes, detachment and perspective, and the inclination to use one's conceptual power and new knowledge to modify old concepts. When one views a potential social studies program with such objectives in mind, focus on the academic scholar as the model of intelligent citizenry seems inadequate.

The Student and Structure

Any social studies program must face the fact that the student comes to class with a "social theory" already in mind, one which allows him to function quite well. He brings to the instructional setting a fairly stable set of interrelated personal constructs which affect how he reacts, both emotionally and intellectually, to political and social events.[11] Instruction must be seen, therefore, as a more challenging task than simply providing the intellectual tools of the academic; rather it is one of shaping, changing, and developing intellectual and emotional orientations already present. In this respect, the social sciences undoubtedly differ from mathematics and the physical sciences; the student is less likely to have highly developed constructs in the latter fields because their domain of study is less a part of common public discourse. However, the distinction is by no means clear-cut; the American experience with the teaching of evolution, as well as Galileo's earlier problem in attempting to reorient thinking about the physical universe, illustrate the fact that even when biological or astronomical interpretations contradict the conventional wisdom of the community, teaching involves more than the discovery of structure. What makes social science theory or knowledge especially exciting, in fact, is its potential for feeding, expanding, or contradicting the student's already existing personal theories of social reality.

The curriculum developer can deal with this situation in a number of ways: he can try to exploit and relate his material to the student's existing "social theories" by framing problems or presenting information in such a way that it appears relevant to the student; he can deliberately choose material that is as abstract and unrelated as possible so that the student's learning will not be "contaminated" by his personal construction of the world; or he can simply ignore the possible intersections of the two realities. The second alternative seems obviously invalid. The third has little more appeal, yet seems to be the alternative selected by the social scientist curriculum builder as he analyzes his discipline with little reference to the students.[12] The inadequacies of this alternative are evidenced by the poor record of so many college introductory courses in the various social sciences.

The points of particular relevance and meaning to the student are usually those which have clear implications for personal or community problems or social action. Social scientists in their role as scientists may or may not choose to be concerned with the relevance of their discipline to societal issues, but as social studies educators they must deal with such considerations. To the extent that the academician honestly seeks to act as educator, he must explicate and justify the various standards of societal justice and individual virtue that underly his curricular decisions. This necessitates adopting a perspective that transcends his own discipline. More than interdisciplinary broadmindedness is called for. The social scientist must seriously consider the possible contributions of the historian from his vantage point; the historian must give reciprocal consideration to the contributions of the social scientist to the understanding and predicting of the behavior of men and communities. The legal-constitutional basis of the modern democratic state must be considered, as must the logical-rhetorical element in public discourse, usually referred to as the skill of reflective thinking. Also, societal problems must be seen as more than academic historical or social science problems; they must be seen as problems involving ethical-legal dilemmas for individuals. Each of these elements of a broad perspective emphasizes a different but vital aspect of participation in a democratic community.

This raises the more general question of critical importance to curriculum development and teaching in the social studies: Can we find or create a structure with a broader base than any of the particular university disciplines — a structure, perhaps, which allows us to put together the various elements suggested above in the context of the analysis of public controversy? Part Two of this book presents a first attempt to integrate elements of several of the conventional disciplines around the broad concept denoted "democratic constitutionalism." The development of such "metastructures" requires the collaborative efforts of unconventional scholars who can focus on the preparation of citizens to participate in a democratic community, rather than the creation of library or laboratory scholars in the university, as the goal of education.

How Much Historical "Background"?

No matter how different the source and basis of structure in the social science disciplines from those of jurisprudential teaching, the two approaches share a fundamental similarity: Both emphasize the *process* of using or discovering analytic concepts to give meaning to data and the reciprocal process of seeking data to clarify and test analytic structures. Both reject the notion that instruction should involve "pouring" knowledge into the student, to be accumulated and, presumably, "poured back" for use at a later date.

In their mutual emphasis on the more parsimonious and careful selection of content as it relates to the discovery, clarification, and testing of structure, both approaches require a radical change in the status quo of the social studies curriculum. For the history-oriented teacher operating in a history-oriented curriculum often sees knowledge of historical facts as an end in itself, or at the very least as leading to some vague intellectual faculty such as "historical perspective," or "an appreciation for the significance of the past." In the words of the Committee of Seven,

> . . . no conscious advance, no worthy reform, can be secured without both a knowledge of the present and an appreciation of how forces have worked in the social and political organization of former times. If this be so, need we seriously argue that the boys and girls in the classroom should be introduced to the past which has created the present — that historical mindedness should be in some slight measure bred within them, and that they should be given the habit, or the beginnings of a habit, of considering what has been, when they discuss what is or should be?[13]

The general thesis is that the boad view of history is essential to an adequate perspective on the present. Without this broad view, usually interpreted to mean broad course coverage, one is likely to get a distorted picture of contemporary social reality.

We have already dealt extensively with the question of the disposition of history in a jurisprudentially based curriculum. A contemporary problem must be viewed in its historical setting to be understood adequately. But the historical background of a problem can undoubtedly be introduced using either the topical or the "historical crisis" approach. There is nothing in the jurisprudential position that dictates or excludes any particular basis for organizing historical information. It is imperative, however, that the curriculum make clear to the student the relationships between the information and the uses to which it can be put in the analysis of societal issues.

Brief comment should also be made about the inadequacies of the thesis that studying history gives one a broad perspective. The study of history can, of course, give a person a narrow, slanted view of the past and pre-dispose him to look at the present in the same biased way. (Many United States history courses, in fact, have this result.) It depends on the point of view of the history studied, including the *variety* of points of view encompassed. (The same is true of the various "structures" in the social sciences.) Volumes have been written about the factors affecting the historian's perceptions and interpretations of the past.[14] Suffice it to say that a work of history cannot represent the totality of the past. Rather, it represents conceptions based on a limited number of traces of the past. Furthermore, the historian, by generally refusing to rely on quantitative data and techniques for compiling and analyzing such data,[15] has so re-stricted himself in the number of traces he can bring to bear on his analysis that questions must be raised about the validity of any one historian's picture of the past. These remarks are particularly relevant to the history textbook with its coverage of vast historical scope in a limited number of pages.

Finally, in weighing the pedagogical value of history, it is important to define carefully what is meant by "studying history." In the type of curriculum we are proposing, the student spends a great deal of time "studying history." But he does so with a specific purpose: to gain knowledge for analyzing persistent controversial issues in order to arrive at an intelligent policy stand. The historian's commitment to the value of history is un-doubtedly based on the fact that he writes it. The writing of history might have very desirable effects upon the student, for he would have to adopt an analytic framework, at least implicitly, in the effort to order his facts. Few teachers, however, teach students either to use the past to analyze the present or to write history. Generally the students memorize historical writings.[16]

CRITICISMS OF JURISPRUDENTIAL TEACHING

Is a Jurisprudential Curriculum "Safe"?

One thing can be said for sticking to "historical facts" in a social studies program: it is safe. There is little in such a curriculum that is likely to arouse strong feelings — except perhaps of boredom — on the part of students or to get them embroiled in heated discussions of controversial matters. One criticism leveled at the type of curriculum proposed in this book stems from the relative immaturity of students in Grades 7 through 12 and their consequent ability or readiness to deal with complex public issues. Students of this age are often characterized as too young to deal with national issues. It is alleged that they not only lack sufficient experience to "understand" the great problems facing society but are so immature as to suffer permanent emotional or psychological damage from being exposed to such problems at too early an age.

In contemplating the "deficient experience" criticism, one might ask: When does the individual have the most critical "real-life" experiences over which he has some control? Probably at the end of his program of formal education, when he begins to make career and family choices on his own. Of course, by that time the foundation of a general education program has presumably been laid. Despite the resurgence of adult education, it is obvious that the type of program we are proposing could not be handled there. The small percentage of people enrolled, the number of years required, and the likelihood that the individual's cognitive patterns are too well set by the end of his second decade all argue against delaying the exposure of students to public issues until the "experience deficiency" has been made up. In any event, the assumption that adults have significant experiences of *direct* relevance to broad societal issues is suspect. Age alone is probably a less important factor in assuring requisite experience than the extent to which the child's analogous experiences (for example, with government in the home or school) can be made relevant to the societal issues and other experiences can be made available vicariously through good teaching materials, such as films, television, and vivid case studies.

The criticism that secondary school students are too immature to deal with public issues is especially impersuasive. Youth in other societies facing difficult survival problems assume adult roles at an early age. With our society now facing its own survival problems, the assumption of adult concern for the society should and undoubtedly could be brought about at a much earlier age. Maturity in the understanding and practice of social graces and heterosexual behavior has been pushed back from college to junior high school. Why not give intellectual maturity the same push? In fact, we give adolescents few rewards when they do show responsible concern for national and community issues. They are likely to be punished by an attack on their "obvious" immaturity or lack of responsibility if they show active interest in such issues — especially if they oppose an adult's position. Is there any reason why young people cannot be given the considerations of intellectual integrity at puberty and dealt with accordingly? At present, the tendency is to shelter them from the intellectual responsibilities involved in analyzing the difficult problems of our society until they are eighteen or twenty, the age at which the critical personal problems of vocation, marriage, and financial independence crowd in upon them. Is it any wonder, for example, that voter turnout is so small? Why not use the years of secondary school to instill a more permanent interest in public affairs?

Admittedly, further research is needed before firm answers can be given to questions about the age at which students should be confronted with the basic problems of our society. Despite occasional warnings that our curriculum would "pull the rug" from under "children," however, it has been our experience that exposure to a jurisprudential approach is not disconcerting to the student. If anything, the opposite tends to be true. The student gets an awakened sense of his own intellectual power. He also finds the approach stimulating and satisfying as he enters into the debate of problems meaningful to the society rather than rehashing historical facts or discussing the abstract problems of the social scientists. It was not an uncommon experience after the conclusion of the Harvard Project to have students revisit the social studies teacher in the junior high school to attest to the interest provoked by the experimental curriculum, especially in contrast with the traditional history program to which they were subsequently exposed. On motivational grounds alone, a social studies curriculum that involves the students in discussion and analysis of public issues has much to commend it.

There is a third aspect of the "too dangerous" criticism that merits attention: the apparently inherent negativism in the jurisprudential approach. The danger noted is that perhaps too much emphasis is placed upon the disintegrative forces within the society and upon the violation of basic American values or the conflicts between them. It is suggested that this may undermine the student's faith in democratic society.

The first response to this criticism must be that the experimental curriculum put forth in the Appendix places much more emphasis upon and pays more explicit attention to the positive values of American society and the governmental institutions by which we hope to protect and promote these values than does the conventional social studies curriculum. It cannot be denied that a curriculum based on persistent human problems must set out explicitly to describe in depth the basic value conflicts within the society, and to make the point that these can never be resolved in any ultimate sense. This is done, however, in the hope that by making such confrontations of values salient to the student as part of his analytic framework, major disruptions of the institutions that protect a heritage of pluralism may be avoided. Appreciating the role of these institutions in mediating and mitigating conflicts arising from varying interpretations of and demands for applications of ideals is an essential part of comprehending and respecting our governmental system. And it is perhaps better to recognize that diametrically opposed positions can be supported within the American framework of values than to assume, as so many adults do, that those in opposition are necessarily narrow and bigoted. This realization provides a broadened and more empathic context for discussion and debate.

There is, of course, another serious criticism related to the concern for negativism, objecting to our central assumption that public controversy is the inevitable legacy of a free society. A critic might ask: What right do we have to build an educational program that assumes from the beginning that a culture governed by love for others, self-sacrifice, and universal brotherhood cannot be achieved through the conscious and conscientious efforts of seers and educators? The reply must be that one cannot teach men love and sacrifice without telling them what to love and for what or whom to sacrifice. The value upon which it seems possible to find universal agreement in our society — perhaps in Western civilization — is human dignity and self-realization, and this, as emphasized earlier, has different meanings for different subgroups and individuals in the society.

We cannot deny the possibility that the Christian vision of universal brotherhood — or the Communist version, for that matter — will eventually materialize on earth, allowing all men to see truth and goodness in a common way and allowing the political institutions of the society to wither away. The question then boils down to whether the public schools are responsible for teaching such a vision. We think not. Rather, it is the responsibility of general education in the social studies to present the student with the variety of political and ethical traditions that have made major contributions to the thinking of Western man. We are indebted for part of that heritage to the tough-minded jurists of Rome and England who participated in the invention of viable institutions for dealing with political and ideological controversy. Part of the tradition stems from the Christians, who identified a community of man that transcends class, race, and nation. The teaching of any of these ethical positions to the exclusion of others would be a presumption on the part of the social studies teacher overstepping his personal authority and his responsibility to a diverse society.[17]

When Is the Structure for the Analysis of Public Controversy Obsolete?

Another major criticism of our curricular approach stems from the dynamic nature of American society. Obviously, although we have called the basic social theory underpinning our experimental curriculum "democratic constitutionalism," it is primarily a systematic selection of Jeffersonian principles and is clearly conditioned by the facts of life existing in the latter half of the eighteenth century. The "facts" of life have changed. Areas of significant change include the development of semi-permanent, organized interests and factions (i.e., political parties, pressure groups, corporate organizations) with important political and, often, legal status; the emergence of several interdependent world communities, at least in the ideological, military, and economic sense; and the shift of governmental responsibility from referee of the conflicts among interest groups to full, and even intensive, participation in the creation of the "great society." The effect of these factors on the Jeffersonian model has already been dealt with in Chapter Five. We will note here only that the curriculum developer using such a model must carefully distinguish between ideals of the society and the facts of the society. That the society has changed does not necessarily mean that the ideals are no longer applicable; it does mean that care must be taken to couch interpretations and applications in the modern context. Continued attention to changes in sociey and the implications for the perspective from which one must view political-ethical issues is imperative.

THE FUTURE OF JURISPRUDENTIAL TEACHING

The basic approach to the social studies presented in this book focuses on the analysis of public issues which have at their core legal-ethical dilemmas. This approach suggests that the social studies curriculum emphasize rather than avoid the inner conflicts of the American liberal tradition as well as the conflicts among groups and factions within the society. This type of approach to education is not radical; it is as old as classical Greece. But the implementation of the approach on any large scale is so far removed from present curricular patterns as to require a major rethinking of the purposes and programs of the social studies in American secondary education. A number of points are relevant to the possibility of such rethinking.

First, the availability of case studies, the type of material best suited to the classroom discourse of the jurisprudential approach, should increase dramatically in the near future as audio-visual media and the publishing industry press forward the revolution of inexpensive communication. This will happen, however, only if curriculum developers in universities and schools provide models and set the pace for the commercial industry, and if public schools evidence a demand for such materials.

Second, while appropriate materials will be of assistance to the teacher wishing to use this approach, the essence of jurisprudential teaching is the nature of the discourse the teacher chooses to have with his students, not the nature of the materials upon which discussion is based. The teacher with a jurisprudential bent can emphasize this type of teaching within the context of the scope and sequence of practically any social studies program, regardless of the instructional media available. In Weber County, Utah, for example, a group of social studies teachers in the Wahlquist Junior High School has been operating from this basic approach, using some of the Harvard Project materials in a U.S. history, world geography, world problems sequence.

The point is that it is necessary to distinguish between a commitment to the jurisprudential approach and to specific curricular patterns and materials. Undoubtedly, programs other than the specific one used in the

Harvard Project must be developed to fit particular circumstances. Each can be an implementation of the general approach with many possible program alternatives available if the teacher really wants to teach students to recognize and think reflectively about public issues. Moreover, our research indicates that the emphasis on controversy and analysis in implementing the general approach is not likely to have a negative effect on the learning of traditional subject matter.

Third, as suggested above, much of the success of any program based on our rationale will depend on the teacher. This is not a curricular pattern to be dictated from the central office. It requires a certain type of teacher, open to the exploration of ideas, to the examination of the legal and ethical principles underlying policy decisions, able to think in other than categorical terms and to tolerate the conflict of ideas and ideals. Attitudes toward both students and subject matter are involved. For example, the teacher must himself be able to recognize the values embedded in controversies; he must be able to construe these values as continua and determine the points and nature of conflict. He must have a tentative-probabilistic view of knowledge. He must be aware of symbol-referent relationships and be able not only to distinguish the emotive from the cognitive connotations of words but to deal with words as representations of concepts rather than manifestations of reality. The need for an intelligent, open, inquiring, and imaginative mind is obvious. And, of course, the teacher must also have a good general background in history and the social sciences if he is to deal with public issues adequately in the classroom and be able to direct students to the proper sources of information.

Just as important as his characteristics in regard to the subject matter of the curriculum are the teacher's attitudes toward his students. He must perceive his students as rational human beings with a right to be involved in decision-making. In attempting to shape the students' constructions of reality the teacher must start from a basic position that values positively their ways of interpreting reality and approaching the solution of problems. The teacher must be willing to interact freely with his students in the interchange of ideas, accepting their contributions as valuable and worthwhile to build upon. In this manner, the student's conception of the legitimacy and honesty of the teacher's mode of inquiry will be enhanced.

How many teachers can adopt or fit into such a model of knowledge, attitude, and behavior? Undoubtedly, the answer will depend to some extent upon personality characteristics brought to the classroom. To what extent can the prerequisite attitudes and discussional skills be developed during the teacher education program or in an in-service training program? [18] Or to what extent can carefully developed curricular materials offset lack of background or disposition? These are open research questions — as are, for example, questions on the specific kinds of teacher behavior to be used with particular types of students to develop most effectively the attitudes and tools of inquiry. Further work along these lines is being pursued, as is the development of curricular materials and strategies.

The approach to social studies presented in this book provides a basis for radical changes which might bring the conventional curriculum more in line with the needs and commitments of a democratic, pluralistic society. The future of the approach cannot depend on the personnel of one or two university-based curriculum projects developing materials and investigating relevant research questions. It rests heavily on the willingness of public school personnel to adopt new conceptualizations of the curriculum and to experiment with new curricular structures even though long-established patterns may be altered.

References

1. Jerome S. Bruner, *The Process of Education* (Cambridge, Mass.: Harvard University Press, 1961).

2. Fred M. Newmann discusses structure and the curriculum task in his paper, "The Analysis of Public Controversy: New Focus for the Social Studies," presented at the Social Studies Curriculum Conference, Kingswood School, Cranbrook, Bloomfield Hills, Michigan, February 27, 1965.

3. See Edwin Fenton and John M. Good, "Project Social Studies: A Progress Report," *Social Education* (1965), 29:206-208.

4. For example, Bruce Catton's trilogy, *The Army of the Potomac* (Garden City, N.Y.: Doubleday & Company, Inc., 1951).

5. William L. Shirer, *The Rise and Fall of the Third Reich* (New York: Simon and Schuster, Inc., 1960).

6. Samuel E. Morison, *The Oxford History of the American People* (New York: Oxford University Press, 1965).

7. Arnold J. Toynbee, *A Study of History,* abridgment by D. C. Somervell (New York: Oxford University Press, 1947-57).

8. William H. McNeill, *The Rise of the West* (Chicago: University of Chicago Press, 1963).

9. See, e.g., W. W. Rostow, *The Stages of Economic Growth* (Cambridge, England: Cambridge University Press, 1960).

10. Here is an interesting comment by Henry Adams on the academic mind in the midst of political and social conflict: "The lecture room was futile enough, but the faculty-room was worse. American society feared total wreck in the maelstrom of political and corporate administration, but it could not look for help to college dons. Adams knew, in that capacity, both Congressmen and professors, and he preferred Congressmen." Henry Adams, *The Education of Henry Adams* (Boston: Houghton Mifflin Company, 1918), p. 307.

11. See Gloria Cammarota, "Children, Politics, and Elementary Social Studies," *Social Education* (1963), 27:205-207, 211. See also Fred I. Greenstein, *Children and Politics* (New Haven, Conn.: Yale University Press, 1965). See also

R. D. Hess and D. Easton, "The Role of the Elementary School in Political Socialization," *School Review* (1962), 70:257-265.

12. It should be noted that the Sociological Resources for Secondary Schools Projects and the Anthropology Curriculum Study Project seem less concerned with structure per se than with the manner in which concepts from their respective disciplines can help the student to construe his social environment. It should also be noted that as experienced teachers become involved in developing instructional materials and settings, intersections between the social science concepts and the student's conception of the world become of concern as a matter of pedagogical strategy.

13. Committee of Seven, *The Study of History in the Schools: Report to the American Historical Association* (New York: The Macmillan Co., 1899), p. 20.

14. See, e.g., Hans Myerhoff, ed.), *The Philosophy of History in Our Time* (Garden City, N.Y.: Doubleday & Company, Inc., 1959); and Fritz Stern (ed.), *The Varieties of History* (New York: World Book Co., 1956).

15. There are some notable exceptions to the unwillingness to use quantitative data. See, e.g., Lee Benson, *The Concept of Jacksonian Democracy* (Princeton, N.J.: Princeton University Press, 1961); Whitney Cross, *The Burned-Over District* (Ithaca, N.Y.: Cornell University Press, 1950); and Merle Curti, *The Making of an American Community* (Stanford, Calif.: Stanford University Press, 1959).

16. For a good treatment of the shortcomings of historical writings as presented in secondary school textbooks see H.. J. Noah, C. E. Prince, and C. R. Riggs, History in High School Textbooks," *School Review* (1962), 70:415-436.

17. Herein undoubtedly lies a good share of the opposition to public support in any form for sectarian schools. The use of the school to teach *one* set of religious beliefs at the same time that the student is insulated against exposure to other beliefs, as in the public school, may well work against a recognition of and respect for the pluralistic basis of our society.

18. For a somewhat skeptical view of the prospects of altering personality patterns through teacher education programs see Donald W. Oliver and James P. Shaver, "A Critique of 'Practice in Teaching,'" *Harvard Educational Review* (1961), 31:437-448.

An Experimental Curriculum Project Carried Out Within the Jurisprudential Framework

Design and Setting
of the Project

The basic goals of citizenship education described in the body of this text are commonly recognized as vital to the maintenance of a democratic society. The educational literature is replete with grave pronouncements about the importance of reflective, or critical, thinking as a goal of citizenship education.[1] Obviously, these statements do not presume that all other aspects of the student's educational development or training in the social studies should be neglected or ignored. They do suggest that social studies teachers and curriculum builders should show a deep concern for teaching those analytic skills which are essential to a society committed to rational consent as the means by which human dignity is to be redefined by each generation. If these analytic skills are of such central importance to the society, and consequently to the social studies, one might expect to find a great deal of curriculum development and research in this area. Unfortunately, not only "new ideas and practices,"[2] but also research reports on this phase of citizenship education are sparse.[3]

Glaser carried out a classic study with twelfth-grade English students that was probably the first significant piece of educational research dealing with instruction for critical thinking.[4] Hyram investigated the teaching of rules of logic to "upper level" elementary school students.[5] Miller and Weston reported an attempt to use a tenth-grade geography course to improve the critical thought of low-intelligence students.[6] The well-known Stanford Social Education Investigation had critical thinking as one of its concerns.[7] The relative effectiveness of the "doing" and "telling" methods of teaching critical thinking was investigated by Anderson, Marcham, and Dunn.[8] Henderson and his colleagues developed and evaluated materials for instruction in critical thinking in English, geometry, science, and the social studes in Grades 9 through 12.[9] The Eight Year Study of the Progressive Education Association was concerned with critical thinking,[10] but systematic assessment procedures were not carried out to evaluate the new curricula. Teaching critical thinking through Amercan history was investigated by Rothstein.[11] Some studies carried out on the college level are relevant to our own work. For example, the Co-operative Study of Evaluation in General Education, under the auspices of the American Council on Education, was concerned with critical thinking as a basic skill of citizenship.[12] And Lyle reported a study involving the use of different course procedures in a general psychology course in a study "designed to throw some light on the question of classroom methods as related to changes in critical thinking abilities in students."[13]

While these research reports have been reviewed elsewhere,[14] a general conclusion that might be drawn from available studies is that if critical thinking and reflective analysis are objectives of social studies instruction, they are not likely to be accomplished indirectly through the study of conventional social studies content. *Materials and procedures must be designed to teach the specific concepts making up critical thinking competence.* Moreover, little of a conclusive nature can now be said about the relative effectiveness of different types of materials or procedures for presenting these concepts to students. The lack of conclusive results can be attributed to several factors, among them the failure of some studies to make any but the traditional experiment-control group comparisons rather than comparing different experimental methods of instruction, the failure to match students or use statistical techniques to control for differences, the failure to describe adequately the independent variable of teacher behavior, and the failure to investigate the characteristics of students as these might be related to learning. Another major deficit in available studies is the failure to deal with the problem of teaching students to handle the ethical-legal component of political and social issues. The studies that have been reported concentrate instead upon relatively simple models of "scientific thinking," "propaganda analysis," or "logic."

The use of limited models, inadequacies in research design, and the variety of populations sampled have resulted in fragmented and, to a large extent, non-cumulative findings. The investigation designated here as the Harvard Social Studies Project (or the Project) and reported in the following sections is an attempt to deal with a number of research problems in a comprehensive way. However, with the paucity of research on the ethical-legal dimension of reflective thinking, the study to be reported must be viewed as an initial thrust. The results should be looked at not only for their immediate application to teaching but also for their implications for further curriculum development and research.

THE SCHOOL AND THE STUDENTS

The school within which the Project operated for four years is a two-year fully departmentalized junior high school in a residential suburb of Greater Boston. There is no compelling reason why the Project chose to work at the junior high school level, other than the fact that the school principal and social studies staff were eager to cooperate and highly sympathetic to the general goals of the approach. (As a point of fact, the Project is now continuing and extending its work in Grades 10, 11, and 12, and we now feel that the approach is viable in the grade range from Grades 8 through Grade 12.)

Students were regularly grouped on the basis of reading ability and prior academic achievement into an "honor" group, "average and above average students," and "average and below average students." There was considerable overlap in ability among the three groups.

Of the four years the Project was located in this junior high school, the first two years were spent developing and pretesting teaching materials and measures, while the latter two constituted a systematic effort to evaluate an experimental curriculum explicitly based on the theoretical model discussed previously in this book. The experimental curriculum was first presented to five sections of students at the beginning of the seventh grade and continued through the eighth grade. The general characteristics of the community in which the Project operated give some indication of the type of students who were in the program. Although their backgrounds were varied, the majority of students were from "middle-class" homes. With some exceptions, students were generally interested in doing well in school because their families valued formal education. The average I.Q. was approximately 113.

THE CURRICULUM

The general problem of selecting and organizing materials for a curriculum oriented around the analysis of public controversy was the focus of Chapter Eight. However, the experimental program reported here required more than dealing with general problems; it required a specific program. Table 15 presents brief descriptions of the materials developed for the experimental program and indicates how these materials were fitted into the chronological sequence of the United States history course normally taught in the junior high school. The social studies program included American history to the Civil War, plus some placement geography, in the seventh grade; American history to contemporary times, as well as a unit on vocational choice, in the eighth grade.

TABLE 15
A Summary of the Experimental Curriculum

UNIT ONE: CRITICAL THINKING   (First exposure, approximately 8 weeks)

Document	Type	Description of Content

'Learning to Think Critically"	Text	I. Describing the World Around Us
		  A. Definitions: pointing and criterial definitions
		  B. Classes and classification
		    1. Danger of classifying an object on the basis of limited information
		    2. Danger of using classes which refer to averages
		  C. Definitions and terms with value loadings

A Summary of the Experimental Curriculum (continued)

II. Testable Statement: Claims
   A. Statements that describe events in the world around us
      1. Specific claims
      2. Summarizing statements
         Generalizations
         Statistics
      3. Explanations
   B. Telling how sure we are
      1. Statements which are true beyond a reasonable doubt
      2. Statements which are probably true
      3. Statements which are false beyond a reasonable doubt
      4. Statements which are probably false
      5. Statements which are doubtful
      6. Statements which are controversial

III. Proof Process
   A. Framing hypotheses
   B. Assumptions or hidden claims implied by a hypothesis
   C. Sampling: Stating how much evidence supports a claim
   D. Testing complex explanations
   E. Sources of evidence
      1. Intuition
      2. Authority
      3. Personal observation
      4. Proof by analogy

IV. Value Judgments
   A. Value judgments and decisions
   B. Statements of preference
   C. Dilemmas
   D. Loaded statements

V. Argumentation
   A. Where an argument begins
   B. Two levels of argumentation: belief and attitude

UNIT TWO: BIRTH OF THE AMERICAN REPUBLIC   (two weeks)

Document	Type	Description of Content
Chapters 7-9 in regular textbook *This Is America's Story*, by Wilder, Ludlum, and Brown (Houghton Mifflin)[a]	Text	Background of American Revolution and early incidents

[a] Henceforth referred to as text: WLB.

A Summary of the Experimental Curriculum (continued)

Document	Type	Description of Content
Excerpts from *Oliver Wiswell*, by K. Roberts (Doubleday), Chapters 4 and 5	Emotional impact case	Dramatic account of the persecution of a loyalist family which did not believe in breaking English law
"Boston Tea Party"	Controversial case	Dramatic account of the Boston Tea Party
"George Watkins"	Controversial case	Fictionalized dramatic account of a speech by Sam Adams and a meeting of American radicals; protagonist is portrayed as a "man on the fence"

UNIT THREE: AN INTRODUCTION TO THE STRUCTURE AND PRINCIPLES OF AMERICAN GOVERNMENT   (five weeks)

A. Basic Concepts of Government

Excerpts from "Strength of the Strong," by Jack London	Conceptual background	Fictional description of development of government among Stone Age man; illustrates *power* of group versus individuals; danger of being *exploited* by leaders of group, once a group gets an organized government
Excerpts from *Two Years Before the Mast*, by Richard H. Dana, Jr.	Conceptual background	Illustrates excesses of *autocratic government* which are not checked by other agencies of government
"The Storm"	Conceptual background	Illustrates disaster which overcomes a wagon train when members refuse to accept expert *leadership* of qualified men, and substitute government by "common man"
Synopsis of *Animal Farm*, by George Orwell	Conceptual background	Illustrates governmental cycle: *autocracy — revolution — democracy — autocracy;* also importance of *propaganda* and distortion of language in maintaining political control
"Sailwell"	Conceptual background	A Robinson Crusoe story, showing how a group of shipwrecked people develop *governmental procedures* similar to American system as a response to specific problems facing an island community

B. Principles of American Government: Their Constitutional Basis and Implementation

Federal Textbook on Citizenship, by John G. Hervey, U.S. Department of Justice, Washington, 1955	Conceptual background	Basic values of American society: *Personal freedom* *Equality and justice* *Peace and order* *General welfare* *Brotherhood*

A Summary of the Experimental Curriculum (continued)

Document	Type	Description of Content
U.S. history textbook: *The Story of American Democracy*, by Casner and Gabriel (Harcourt, Brace), Chapter 7 [For a written version of essentially what was taught, see Part Two]		Governmental principles *Rule of law* *Rule by consent of governed* *Equal protection under law* *Due process of law* *Separation of powers* *Checks and balances* Constitutional basis of values and principles Mechanics of the consent system: selected provisions of the Constitution

---

UNIT FOUR: APPLICATION OF ANALYTIC AND POLITICAL CONCEPTS USING SPECIFIC CONTROVERSIAL CASES

		[Most of these cases are based on Supreme Court decisions]
"Lunch Counter"	Controversial case	Fictitious case of a Negro sit-in demonstration
"Sidewalk Speech"	Controversial case	Incident involving free speech, based on a constitutional case: Feiner v. New York, 340 U.S. 315 (1951)
"Davis Lumber"	Controversial case	Incident in which a lumber dealer challenges the constitutionality of Fair Labor Standards Act, based on a constitutional case: United States v. Darby, 312 U.S. 100 (1941)
"The House"	Controversial case	Story about housing discrimination against an American citizen of Chinese ancestry
"Flag Salute"	Controversial case	Incident in which a Jehovah's Witness refuses to allow his child to salute the flag in public school, based on two constitutional cases: Minersville School District v. Gobitis, 310 U.S. 586 (1940), and West Virginia State Board of Education v. Barnette, 319 U.S. 624 (1943)
"The Job"	Controversial case	Incident in which California prosecutes a man for helping his unemployed brother-in-law enter the state, based on a constitutional case: Edwards v. California, 314 U.S. 160 (1941)
"Radios and Buses"	Controversial case	Incident in which two men contest the right of a bus company to install radios on public buses
"Smittites"	Controversial case	Story of a religious sect which obtains special tax privileges because of a broadened definition of "religious property"

A Summary of the Experimental Curriculum (continued)

Document	Type	Description of Content
"Rabin Case"	Controversial case	Incident in which a counterfeiter's desk is searched when he is arrested (Does this constitute unreasonable search and seizure?); based on a constitutional case: United States v. Rabinowitz, 339 U.S. 56 (1950)
"Out of Bounds"	Controversial case	Story about housing discrimination against a Negro doctor
"Ota Case"	Controversial case	Fictional account of a Japanese family relocated from the west coast at the beginning of World War II, based on a constitutional case: Korematsu v. United States, 323 U.S. 214 (1944)
"Loudspeaker and the Union"	Controversial case	Incident in which a city restricts the right of a labor organization to use a loudspeaker to take its case to the public, based on a constitutional case: Kovacs v. Cooper, 336 U.S. 77 (1949)
"Hours"	Controversial case	Incident in which the government restricts a woman's right to work or to be hired for as many hours as she wants, based on a constitutional case: Adkins v. Children's Hospital, 261 U.S. 525 (1923)
"The Voyage"	Controversial case	Story of a long-time non-citizen resident of the United States who is refused readmission to the United States after visiting his native country behind the iron curtain, based on a constitutional case: Shaughnessy v. United States, *ex. rel.* Mezei, 345 U.S. 206 (1953)

[All of the above cases were used both to teach and to illustrate concepts and principles of American government as well as to teach the thought process patterns described in Part Two.]

Problem Units

UNIT FIVE: SCHOOL DESEGREGATION   (six weeks)
          [See Chapter Eight, Appendix A]

UNIT SIX: THE AMERICAN INDIAN   (one week)

Text: WLB, Chapter 21	Historical background	
"Trail of Tears"	Controversial case	Story of the forced migration of the Creek Indians
"Hopi Indian"	Historical background	Brief description of the Hopi Indian
Excerpt from "The Sun Chief," *The Autobiography of a Hopi Indian,* edited by Leo W. Simmons (Yale University Press)	Controversial case	Story of compulsory education for some Hopi Indians

A Summary of the Experimental Curriculum (continued)

Document	Type	Description of Content
A. Rise of Big Business in America		
"Economic Revolution"; text: WLB, Chapters 22 and 23	Historical background	A text to provide the student with some insight into the rapid industrial changes occurring between the Civil War and 1900
"Freight Rates — The Long Haul and the Short Haul," excerpt from the *Octopus*, by Frank Norris	Controversial case	A case showing how an arbitrary shipping policy of the railroad works an injury on the farmer
"Rise in Freight Rates," excerpt from the *Octopus*, by Frank Norris	Controversial case	A cases showing how a farmer is ruined by an arbitrary rise in freight rates
"Andrew Carnegie"	Historical and conceptual background	Case study of Carnegie to illustrate how an industrialist might gain great power; also illustrates a number of important economic concepts, e.g., vertical and horizontal integration of industry
"Some Notes on Mr. Carnegie's Business Practices"	Controversial case	Shows some of Carnegie's business practices which were legal but ethically suspect
"South Improvement Company"	Controversial case	Shows how Rockefeller gained monopoly of the refineries in Cleveland through methods of doubtful legality
"Standard Oil Again"	Controversial case	Shows how Rockefeller finally gained control of the oil industry with methods of doubtful legality and morality
"Standard Oil Aftermath"	Historical background	A brief text to bring some closure to the Standard Oil material
B. Some Government Efforts to Legislate Fair Competition in Business		
"A Brief History of Government Efforts to Promote Fair Competition"	Historical background	A text tracing history of government regulation of business from ICC through the Sherman Act, Clayton Act, and Federal Trade Commission Act
"The Federal Trade Commission and the Supreme Court"	Controversial case	Four practices branded as "unfair competition" by the Federal Trade Commission which were later appealed to the Supreme Court; student is asked whether or not he agrees with the FTC rulings
"Supreme Court Decisions on the Four Federal Trade Commission Cases"	Controversial case	Shows how the Supreme Court reversed the FTC in two cases and upheld it in two cases, partly because of its effort to maintain its own jurisdiction over such matters

A Summary of the Experimental Curriculum (continued)

Document	Type	Description of Content
C. Case Study of Contemporary Business		Practices in the Retail Sale of Gasoline
"The Gasoline Station"	Historical background	General discussion of business organization and control in the oil industry, and the various pressures placed upon the retail gasoline dealer
"Gasoline Dealers Complain to Congress"	Emotional impact	Summary of an article published in the *New Republic* showing arbitrary treatment of retail dealers by large gasoline companies (June 13, 1955, pp. 8-10)
"Gas War"	Controversial case	Presents problem of cut-rate station and efforts of company-owned and -leased stations to deal with it within the framework of free competition

UNIT EIGHT: AMERICAN IMMIGRATION POLICY (one week)

"Immigration — An American Problem" Text: WLB, Chapter 25	Historical and conceptual background	Description of major waves of immigration into the United States, reactions and discrimination against immigrants, and major legislation affecting immigrants
"Immigration — 1961"	Emotional impact	Describes a man of English-Burmese descent, who cannot enter the United States because he comes under the Burmese quota
Edward R. Murrow film on immigration	Conceptual background	Gives opinions of many national leaders on immigration, including Walters, Archbishop Cushing, etc.
"Cuban Refugees"	Controversial case	Describes problem of Cuban refugees in Miami; asks what U.S. policy should be

UNIT NINE: PROBLEMS OF AMERICAN LABOR — AN INTRODUCTION (four weeks)

UNIT TEN: THE NEW DEAL (three weeks)

"The New Deal"	Historical and conceptual background	Describes economic and social conditions of the 1920's leading up to the crash, conditions after the depression has begun, and the election of 1932
"Depression"	Emotional impact	Describes a series of specific cases of discouraged and needy people during the depression
"Happiest Man On 'Earth,'" by Albert Maltz	Emotional impact	A short story describing the complete demoralization of an unemployed worker and his exhilaration when he finds employment driving a nitroglycerin truck
"Agricultural Adjustment Act"	Controversial case	Case first describes several incidents in which farmers resort to violence to keep their farms, then discusses AAA and some problems that result from the government program

A Summary of the Experimental Curriculum (continued)

Document	Type	Description of Content
"The Blue Eagle"	Controver-sial case	Description of how the NIRA attempted to meet the problems of the depression, and some of the criticisms of the government program
"WPA"	Controver-sial case	Description of the problem that led Roosevelt to consider packing the Court, as well as other alternatives available
"Court Packing and the Public"	Controver-sial case	A dramatic presentation on tape of many of the actual statements made by political leaders as well as by the man on the street

Tables 16 and 17 present an estimate of the overall timetable for the two-year experimental period. While the materials developed for the experimental curriculum were taught over the two-year period, the teaching time required was actually only a little over one school year. Approximately one-third of the class time was occupied with a rather traditional approach to American

TABLE 16

Timetable Describing Social Studies Program for Students Engaged in Two-Year Experimental Curriculum, Grade 7

Topic	Project Activities	Non-Project Activities
Europe Discovers and Explores the New World to the West		3[a]
European Nations Develop Colonies in the New World		3
Pretest Achievement Battery	2[b]	
Critical Thinking Skills with Short Illustrative Cases	8	
Birth of the American Republic	1	1
An Introduction to the Structure and Principles of American Government	5	
Application of Model for Handling Political Controversy Using Analytic and Political Concepts	3	
Establishment of the New Nation		3
Economic Changes in the New Nation and the Rise of Sectionalism		3
First Posttest Achievement Battery	1[b]	
Total weeks, Grade 7	17	13

[a] Numbers indicate weeks.
[b] Not included in total.

TABLE 17

*Timetable Describing Social Studies Program for
Students Engaged in Two-Year Experimental Curriculum, Grade 8*

Topic	Project Activities	Non-Project Activities
Second Posttest Achievement Battery	2[a]	
American Civil War and Reconstruction		3
School Desegregation	6	
Settling the West		1
The American Indian	1	
Introduction to the Industrialization of America		1
The Problem of Fair Competition and Monopoly	4	
Vocational Guidance		1
American Immigration Policy	1	
Problems of American Labor	4	
Personality Test Battery	2[a]	
United States History: 1900-1925		2
The New Deal	3	
United States History: 1940-1960		2
Review	1	
Third Post-Test Achievement Battery	2[a]	
Total weeks, Grade 8	20	10
Total weeks, Grades 7 and 8	37	23

[a] Not included in total.

history, involving reading and discussion based on the texts normally used in the school.[15] The remainder of the time, some thirteen weeks, was occupied with place geography, current events, vocational guidance, the administration of standardized tests for the school records, and testing connected with the Project.

Table 15 reflects the fact that the experimental curriculum was initially organized around three distinct ideas: (1) the conceptual framework for dealing with public issues, (2) the background, principles, and structure of American constitutionalism, and (3) substantive problem units to which the concepts contained in (1) and (2) were to be applied. After teaching parts one and two during much of the seventh grade, it became evident that the two sets of concepts were necessarily related, and that the analysis of values described in the critical thinking materials required the use of values and principles associated with American constitutionalism. At this point it was decided to provide the students with experience in handling an analytic model, very much like that suggested in Part Two, which required them to apply both constitutional principles and critical thinking concepts to controversial cases. The teaching of the model was begun in the last unit of the seventh grade. The second year of the experimental curriculum was implemented very much as planned: Instruction was aimed at teaching the students to apply the analytic model to a series of controversial cases embedded in broader societal issues, organized largely on a topical basis. It is important to note that the documents in the curriculum listed in Table 15 were supplemented by practice exercises and brief illustrative cases developed on a day-by-day basis.

TEACHING STRATEGIES

If curriculum is defined in terms of the experiences provided the students, there are obviously two major elements to consider in setting up an experimental program: the materials to be presented to or read by the students, and the use to which the materials are to be put in the classroom dialogue. Since there were several types of materials, a number of different teaching strategies were used by the teacher. (See Chapter Eight for a description of types of materials.)

Historical and conceptual background material was handled in a straightforward, descriptive, didactic manner; the teacher amplified and explained the material, answered questions asked by the students, and asked questions of the students to test their understanding of the concepts and generalizations presented in the materials. Emotional impact or empathy-producing materials required very little "teaching," the materials carrying the weight of their own message. After reading such a document, the teacher simply phrased in more general terms the problem raised by the case: How, for example, does the problem of unemployment, which affects the worker and his family, also affect the whole community? "Takeoff" materials, i.e., materials used mainly for independent study by the students, required individual guidance by the teacher. With these specific types of materials the teachers were directed to take the same approach with each group of students taught.

In the use of controversial cases, however, students were explicitly taught to apply the political analysis model described in Part Two. It was with these documents that two different teaching styles were tried and compared. (The styles are described in detail in Appendix, Section Four.) The two styles, called "recitation-analytic" and "socratic-analytic" focused primarily on the teacher-student dialogue. In using the recitation style, the teacher first questioned the students to assure himself that they had the facts of the case clearly in mind. He then asked students to construe the case in terms of the analytic model, to suggest how differing positions with respect to the problem presented by the case might be justified within the framework of the model, and to propose critical questions that might be asked to clarify possible positions and determine which was more reasonable. In socratic discussions, on the other hand, the teacher spent less time on the factual background of the case. Instead, he encouraged the student to take a personal stand on an issue in the case, then challenged the position, particularly pointing up inconsistencies through the use of analogies. He then used, or encouraged the student to use, the analytic model to suggest, first, how the student's position might be handled more intelligently, and second, what questions the student might ask of himself to strengthen his understanding of his own and other positions. The socratic-analytic discussion was designed to alternate between a process of argumentation between the teacher and the student (with the student's position in question) and attempts by the teacher to clarify the nature of the argument within the framework of constitutional principles and critical thinking concepts. In the latter phase the teacher's behavior was similar to that of the recitation-analytic teacher.

In summary, students in the experimental program were all exposed to the same materials, and, *except for systematic differences in styles to be used with controversial cases,* the students were presented the materials in essentially the same manner.

The actual implementation of the experimental curriculum was carried out by four teachers, all of whom helped formulate it. All four had research appointments at Harvard as well as teaching appointments in the district in which the experimental school was located. Their primary responsibility in both places was to the Project, and during the two-year period of systematic experimentation, they taught only experimental classes.

RESEARCH DESIGN

The major hypothesis of the study was quite simple:

It is possible to teach adolescent students to use an abstract conceptual model for analyzing and clarifying public controversy.

In order to test this hypothesis a standard control group design was set up. Control groups in three other schools were used as a baseline against which to compare the gains of the experimental group. Some general information about these groups is presented in Table 18, and a summary of the curricula in the control schools is presented in Table 19. The West and Wheat control schools were located in suburban communities. The control school designated Big was located in an urban setting and served a wide range of students.

TABLE 18
General Characteristics of Experimental and Control Groups

School	Location	Approxi- mate School Size	Number in Control Group[a]	Grade Levels in School	I.Q.[b] Mean	S.D.
Experimental	Suburban Boston	400		7-8	113.3	12.3
West	Suburban Boston	400	140	7-8	118.7	14.6
Big	Urban Boston	1000	140	7-9	109.8	10.7
Wheat	Suburban Long Island (New York)	1200	196	7-12	116.7	10.9

[a] The number of students reported in this table will not necessarily agree exactly with the numbers used in the statistical analyses reported in the following sections. Students were absent on testing days, etc., but the attrition was slight.

[b] The means reported here are based on a number of different I.Q. measures because the tests ordinarily administered by the schools were used. This use assumes comparability of I.Q. measures, which may not be too unreasonable if one takes into account the level of reliability commonly obtained from the readministration of a single measure.

TABLE 19

Brief Description of Curricula in Control Schools

School	Curriculum	
	Grade 7	Grade 8

West	World geography
	  Latin America 18 weeks
	  Asia 12 weeks
	  Africa 6 weeks
		United States history; Structure of course is based on *This Is America's Story,* by Wilder, Ludlum, and Brown (Houghton-Mifflin)

Big	United States history from the discovery of America through the American Revolution	United States history from the forming of the new government through the Spanish-American War
	Major texts used in this two-year sequence: *This Is America's Story,* by Wilder, Ludlum, and Brown (Houghton Mifflin), and *History of a Free People,* by Bragdon and McCutchen (Macmillan)	
Wheat	Two-year sequence in United States History	

	Special features in Grade 7
	  Unit on geographic concepts
	  Unit on economic concepts
	  Anthropological unit on the
	    American Indian
		Special features in Grade 8:
		  Units on state and local history

	General comments: Emphasis on cultural history relying on biography; no single text used	

The Project's overall research design actually included an experiment within an experiment. Not only were the learning gains of the experimental students compared with those of control students, but a number of questions were investigated using only the experimental students. In particular these questions probed the relative effectiveness of the recitation and the socratic styles mentioned earlier, and the relationship between student personality and learning. The designs for these further studies will be presented in later sections, but some points should be cleared up now. In the first place, students in the experimental program knew they were being treated in a special way. They were subjected to special testing, their discussions were often recorded, they were aware that four teachers, all of them directly affiliated with Harvard, were spending a great deal of time developing their curriculum. In other words, the Hawthorne effect must certainly have been operating, providing a systematic advantage for the experimental group. On the other hand, having the Project in the school for four years undoubtedly helped to reduce this effect. Also, the teachers who participated in the Project were selected because of their interest in its objectives. Although their educational experience and training probably did not differ markedly from that of average teachers in suburban school systems, their general competence and their interest in contemporary affairs and educational innovation undoubtedly did. Judgments of competence in teaching were among the major criteria used in selecting them.

Another important qualification of the results is that for approximately half of the experimental program, regular-size classes of about twenty-five students were split for discussions in order to compare the effects of the recitation versus socratic teaching approaches; i.e., about half of the experimental teaching was done with student groups of approximately twelve, an arrangement that is not common in public schools.

Some additional qualifications should be stressed in the interpretation of the results. We would emphasize that the model of research that shaped our thinking was one of "hothouse" experimentation.[16] The intent was to establish optimum conditions for teaching in the experimental situation and then to study variations in learning. For this reason, the best possible teachers were selected. The splitting of groups for instructional purposes was based primarily on research design requirements but also was acceptable because it optimized group size for instruction. There was, moreover, little doubt that the students in the new program would show greater gains than control students on the measures directly related to the Project's instructional objectives. The work of Glaser, as well as the other corroborating research mentioned briefly at the beginning of this section, had already provided a basis for this prediction. The broad study comparing the experimental and control students was largely focused, therefore, on the question of what particular kinds of measures might best reflect learning gains from the special experiences provided the students by the experimental curriculum. This part of the research was as much an effort to test the sensitivity of measures of doubtful validity as it was a test of the experimental curriculum.

SUMMARY

The basic purpose of the Project's research was to develop and evaluate a trial curriculum consistent with the objectives suggested by our model for the analysis of public controversy. Could younger high school students learn to understand and use such a conceptual framework through a two-year treatment of systematic instruction? For this purpose, a traditional experimental-control group design was used. A "design within a design" experiment was built into the study to compare the effects of two teaching styles used with the experimental students, as well as for the analysis of the effect of student personality upon learning. The school setting, the teachers, the curricular materials, and the way they were fitted into a standard social studies curriculum have been discussed. The question now becomes: What were the results?

References

1. See, for example, H. R. Anderson, F. C. Marcham, and S. B. Dunn, "An Experiment in Teaching Certain Skills of Critical Thinking," *Journal of Educational Research* (1944) 38:241; Prudence Bostwick and others, "The Nature of Critical Thinking and Its Use in Problem Solving," *Skills in Social Studies,* 24th Yearbook of the National Council for the Social Studies, edited by Helen McCracken Carpenter (Washington: National Council for the Social Studies, 1953), p. 48; P. L. Dressel and L. B. Mayhew, *General Education: Explorations*

in Evaluation (Washington: American Council on Education, 1954), p. 35; E. F. Pfieger, "Needed Research in Education for Citizenship," *Phi Delta Kappan* (1951), Vol. 33; S. A. Rippa, "Toward a Definition of Citizenship Education," *Social Education* (1959), Vol. 23; Eugene R. Smith and Ralph W. Tyler, *Appraising and Recording Student Progress*, Vol. III of *Adventure in American Education* (New York: Harper & Row, Publishers, 1942), p. 35; G. P. Taylor, "Teaching the Art of Decision-Making," *Journal of General Education* (1955), 8:255.

2. K. B. Henderson, "The Teaching of Critical Thinking," *Phi Delta Kappan* (1958), 39:282.

3. A. F. Joyal, "Research in Citizenship Education," *Phi Delta Kappa* (1947), 29:185; and James P. Shaver, "Educational Research and Instruction for Critical Thinking," *Social Education* (1962), 26:13-16.

4. Edward M. Glaser, *An Experiment in the Development of Critical Thinking* (New York: Teachers College, Columbia University, 1941).

5. G. A. Hyram, "Experiment in Developing Critical Thinking in Children," *Journal of Experimental Education* (1957), Vol. 26.

6. J. Miller and G. L. Weston, "Slow Learners Improve in Critical Thinking," *Social Education* (1958), 22:315-316.

7. J. I. Quillen and L. A. Hanna, *Education for Social Competence* (Chicago: Scott, Foresman & Company, 1948), p. 141.

8. Anderson, Marcham, and Dunn, *op. cit.*, pp. 241-251.

9. Henderson, *op. cit.*, pp. 280-282.

10. Smith and Tyler, *op. cit.*, chap. 11.

11. Arnold Rothstein, "An Experiment in Developing Critical Thinking Through the Teaching of American History," *Dissertation Abstracts* (1960), Vol. 21.

12. Dressel and Mayhew, *op. cit.*, pp. 56, 64-67.

13. Edwin Lyle, "An Exploration in the Teaching of Critical Thinking in General Psychology," *Journal of Educational Research* (1958), 52:129.

14. Donald W. Oliver and James P. Shaver, *The Analysis of Public Controversy: A Study in Citizenship Education*, chap. 11; and Shaver, *op. cit.*

15. The basic text used was H. B. Wilder, R. P. Ludlum, and H. M. Brown, *This Is America's Story* (Boston: Houghton Mifflin Company, 1966).

16. Of course, "hothouse" experimentation is vulnerable to the criticism that findings cannot be interpreted adequately if the design does not take into account systematic (but theoretically unimportant) differences between the experimental and control groups. The major objective of this study was, except for differences in student ability, to maximize the possibility of differences between control and experimental groups while maintaining experimental rigor between the two experimental groups. The extent to which experimental gains were due to the enthusiasm or competence of the teachers or the advantages of small-group teaching was not of great concern. It was assumed that these might be necessary conditions for experimental gains, but that inclusion of the curriculum itself would also be a major necessary condition. A biological analogy was clearly in mind: People with appendicitis may do slightly better by having enthusiastic and intelligent doctors and nurses tend them, by being in private rooms rather than large wards, etc., but there is more basic treatment — an appendectomy — which makes the critical difference. One would not feel the obligation to demonstrate the effectiveness of this particular medical operation in a dirty operating room with mediocre surgeons. McKeachie, who has had much experience in classroom experimentation, makes a similar point.

"Generally I would not worry too much about the presence of uncontrolled variables which may account for positive results if there are variables in teaching. Thus you need not be too concerned at this preliminary stage over the possibility that faulty sampling or biases in test scoring are responsible for positive results. In your experiments go ahead and use teachers who are enthusiastic about the new methods you want to use. Go ahead and sell your students on the great advantages of being in an experimental group. Your most probable outcome is "No significant difference." If you come out with a significant difference, you at least have shown that your measures are sensitive enough to show differences and that under ideal circumstances you can improve on what was done in your control group. With this as a basis, you are in a much better position to go on to pin down specific variables than if your original results had been negative. The only good effect of negative results is to squelch some of the wildest claims of the enthusiasts for the latest fad." W. J. McKeachie, "Problems and Perils in Controlled Research in Teaching," *Needed Research in the Teaching of English,* Proceedings of a Conference held at Carnegie Institute of Technology, prepared by Erwin R. Steinberg, 1962, p. 70.

Effect of the Experimental Curriculum on Analytic Competence

In an attempt to provide a broad basis for evaluation of the experimental program four types of measures were used: standardized tests of "critical thinking," the Social Issues Analysis Tests developed by the Project staff, measures of factual content, and a measure of interest in public issues. The effectiveness of the program as measured by the first two types of measures is the subject of this section.

STANDARDIZED TESTS OF CRITICAL THINKING

Two critical thinking tests were administered to the experimental and control students: the Wagmis Test; and the Iowa Test of Educational Development No. 5, Interpretation, Social Studies. The Wagmis Test was composed of subtests one, two, and four from the Watson-Glaser Critical Thinking Appraisal, Form Am, and parts six and seven of the Michigan State Test of Problem Solving, Form A.[1]

The Wagmis Test and the ITED No. 5 were administered to the experimental group and the West and Wheat control groups four times over the two-year experimental period. The administrations took place in the fall and spring of two consecutive academic years. Because of administrative difficulties, the tests were not given to the Big control group during the fall of the next year. The results presented below, however, are based only on the initial and final administrations.

262

Results

The Wagmis Test. The results of the statistical analysis of data obtained in the Wagmis Test are presented in Tables 20 and 21. It is clear in both tables that the analysis of covariance[2] reveals significant differences among the posttest means of the schools. These differences are due, however, not to

TABLE 20

Comparison of Experimental Group with Control-Schools on Wagmis Test with Means Adjusted for Pretest Score (Fall, 1959) and Intelligence

| School | N | Pretest | | I.Q. | | Posttest | | Adjusted |
		Mean	S.D.	Mean	S.D.	Mean	S.D.	Mean
Experimental	109	36.50	7.96	113.51	12.31	44.94	9.56	46.36
West	126	36.70	7.29	118.47	14.48	43.34	7.82	43.28
Wheat	112	40.56	7.07	117.44	11.09	46.74	7.90	45.17

Test of Differences Between Means

	Degrees of Freedom	F-Ratio	Probability Level
Total	2/342	7.61	P < .001
Experimental v. Wheat	1/216	2.25	P > .05

TABLE 21

Comparison of Experimental Group with Control Schools on Wagmis Test with Means Adjusted for Pretest Score (Spring, 1960) and Intelligence

| School | N | Pretest | | I.Q. | | Posttest | | Adjusted |
		Mean	S.D.	Mean	S.D.	Mean	S.D.	Mean
Experimental	108	39.67	9.84	113.56	12.36	44.88	9.58	45.61
West	128	40.18	7.82	118.55	14.61	43.55	7.94	42.72
Wheat	177	41.90	8.21	116.37	11.12	46.47	7.94	45.39
Big	122	39.52	7.58	109.72	10.83	43.74	9.19	45.55

Test of Differences Between Means

Degrees of Freedom	F-Ratio	Probability Level
3/530	6.97	P < .001

higher mean scores for the experimental students, but to the lower mean scores for the West control group. Excluding West, the adjusted means for the other groups are quite similar. Although Table 20 indicates a somewhat higher adjusted mean for the experimental group as compared to the Wheat group, this difference is not significant at the .05 level.

It should be noted that the same pattern runs throughout the data. That is, the West control group consistently has the lowest adjusted mean, while the

Wheat group scores highest on the pretest. This finding is particularly significant in light of the common use in educational research of control group designs containing only one control group. Obviously, the results and interpretation would have been markedly different for this study had only the West group been used for control purposes.

The most reasonable conclusion is that the experimental curriculum did not have a significant effect on the experimental students' performance on the Wagmis Test. This is not a surprising finding, for the experimental curriculum did not emphasize the specific types of intellectual operations required to do well on the Wagmis Test. Moreover, a factor analytic study[3] that included the Watson-Glaser Critical Thinking Appraisal and a form of the Michigan State Test of Problem Solving indicates that the parts of these tests included in the Wagmis Test are heavily loaded on general reasoning. The Project's data generally indicate that the experimental curriculum did not affect any such general reasoning component.

This interpretation does contradict Glaser's finding, *viz.*, that a relatively brief period of treatment did have a significant effect on students' scores on an early form of the Watson-Glaser test.[4] The important difference between Glaser's study and the one reported here, however, is that the Project curriculum probably did not provide for the direct coaching of specific skills required to do well on the Watson-Glaser Appraisal to the extent that Glaser's curriculum did. Smith's work[5] bears out our conclusion that, when one teaches the skills of problem analysis as they bear on a specialized type of problem, e.g., ethical-legal issues, rather than on critical thinking problems in general, scores on tests such as the Watson-Glaser Appraisal and the Michigan State Test of Problem Solving are not likely to reflect the learning increments that result. In short, these tests of critical thinking probably are sensitive to two kinds of curricular treatment: (1) those that might affect general reasoning ability and (2) those that might coach the student to handle the specific types of reasoning exercises contained in the tests. The research results obtained by the Harvard Project on the Wagmis Test indicate that the experimental curriculum did not affect general reasoning, nor was it geared to the specific exercises in the tests so as to have a significant effect on the scores of the experimental group.

ITED No. 5. The results of the statistical comparisons of the experimental and the control groups on ITED No. 5, presented in Tables 22 and 23, are similar to those obtained with the Wagmis Test, if somewhat more ambiguous. There seems to be a rather consistent order of performance with Wheat at the top and West at the bottom. While the difference between the experimental group and Wheat reported in Table 22 is not significant at the .05 level, that between the experimental group and West is. However, given the trend noted in the discussion of the results with the Wagmis Test, plus the relative position of Wheat, it is more reasonable to conclude that there is something deficient in West than that the experimental curriculum had a significant effect. The results of testing in the West school are quite puzzling, since it is

TABLE 22

Comparison of Experimental Group with Control Schools on ITED No. 5
with Means Adjusted for Pretest Score (Fall, 1959) and Intelligence

| School | N | Pretest | | I.Q. | | Posttest | | Adjusted |
		Mean	S.D.	Mean	S.D.	Mean	S.D.	Mean
Experimental	107	22.56	7.15	113.85	11.73	32.38	10.28	33.98
West	129	20.50	7.17	118.53	14.69	31.20	9.73	31.53
Wheat	184	24.33	8.03	116.87	10.80	36.10	9.29	35.20

Test of Differences Between Means

	Degrees of Freedom	F-Ratio	Probability Level
Total	2/415	11.99	P < .001
Experimental v. Wheat	1/286	2.09	P > .05
Experimental v. West	1/231	5.11	P < .05 > .01

TABLE 23

Comparison of Experimental Group with Control Schools on ITED No. 5
with Means Adjusted for Pretest Score (Spring, 1960) and Intelligence

| School | N | Pretest | | I.Q. | | Posttest | | Adjusted |
		Mean	S.D.	Mean	S.D.	Mean	S.D.	Mean
Experimental	107	26.52	9.78	113.34	12.36	32.75	10.50	32.79
West	134	24.95	10.44	118.69	14.58	31.24	9.75	30.53
Wheat	192	28.02	10.15	116.69	10.88	35.90	9.39	34.11
Big	126	22.30	7.79	109.80	10.66	28.54	10.95	31.97

Test of Difference Between Means

Degrees of Freedom	F-Ratio	Probability Level
3/554	8.72	P < .001

located in an upper-middle-class suburban community that is proud of its schools. There was no evidence readily available while selecting control groups of any factor that would be expected to have such a systematically negative effect on the performance of West students.

PROJECT TESTS OF ANALYTIC ABILITY

Four measures more directly related to the Project's instructional objectives were discussed in Chapters Ten and Eleven: (1) SIAT No. 1: Argument Analysis Test — a group-administered paper-and-pencil test with multiple-choice responses, the purpose of which is to assess the student's ability to identify the intellectual operations in a written argumentative dialogue; (2)

SIAT No. 2: Argument Description and Rebuttal Test — a group-administered paper-and-pencil test with multiple-choice responses, the purpose of which is to assess the student's ability to describe the substance of a written argumentative dialogue and select the best statements to rebut points made in written dialogue; (3) SIAT No. 3: Oral Argument Analysis Test — similar to SIAT No. 1 except administered through interview with oral prompts rather than prestructured choices; (4) SIAT No. 4: Analytic Category System (ANCAS) — demonstrating use of content analysis to describe types of statements made and strategies used in oral argumentation.

Results

SIAT No. 1. Because SIAT No. 1 was developed late in the experimental period, it could be administered to only a limited sample from one control group (Wheat), and no pretest data are available. The available data were analyzed using analysis of covariance, controlling for I.Q. The results are presented in Table 24. The difference between the means is significant at the .001 level. The difference in the standard deviations of the two groups is also striking. The variance ratio is not significant but approaches significance at the .05 level.

TABLE 24

Comparison of Experimental Group with a Control School on SIAT No. 1 with Means Adjusted for Intelligence

School	N	I.Q. Mean	I.Q. S.D.	Posttest Mean	Posttest S.D.	Adjusted Mean
Experimental	109	113.51	12.31	12.38	4.40	12.79
Wheat	33	121.76	6.48	10.73	2.83	9.37

Test of Differences Between Means

Degrees of Freedom	F-Ratio	Probability Level
1/138	24.52	P < .001

It seems clear that the test scores of the experimental group reflect the impact of the experimental curriculum, especially when one takes into account the tendency of the Wheat group toward higher mean scores on the Wagmis Test and the ITED No. 5. SIAT No. 1 is probably the most direct measure of the student's ability to understand the Project's conceptual model for analyzing public controversy. A high score on this test, however, does not necessarily mean that the student can relate the conceptual system to an argument in which he is personally engaged.

SIAT No. 2. As discussed in Chapter Ten, four forms of SIAT No. 2 were developed, designated Labor (L), Integration (I), Fallout (F), and Education (E).

These particular topics were selected for two reasons. First, all were regarded as sufficiently permanent controversial issues so that the tests would not become dated over the two years of the experimental program. Second, two topics, labor and integration, were chosen because they were included in the experimental curriculum, and two topics, atomic fallout and education, were chosen because they would be excluded from consideration in the experimental curriculum. In this way we hoped to test whether performance on the subtests would be affected by the specific topics included in the experimental curriculum, or whether the students were learning a general set of analytic skills that could be applied generally to political issues similar to those studied. The results, presented in Table 25, suggest that the latter is the case. A statistical compari-

TABLE 25

Means of Experimental Students for Subtests of SIAT No. 2

		Pretest Means (Fall, 1959)		Posttest Means (Spring, 1961)	
N		*L & I*[a]	*F & E*	*L & I*[a]	*F & E*
107		19.67	19.07	23.21	23.64

[a] Indicates subtests in which topics were included in experimental curriculum.

son of the posttest means of the two sets of subtests (the value of *t* is only 1.26) confirmed what seemed obvious from inspection — no special benefit in performance occurred from having studied as part of the experimental curriculum the topic that was the basis for the subtest.

The more important question, of course, is whether the gains made by the experimental group on the subtests of SIAT No. 2 are greater than would be expected through maturation and the study of a conventional history and/or geography curriculum. The results in Table 26 make it fairly clear that SIAT No. 2 is sensitive to the effect of the experimental curriculum; i.e., the mean gain of the experimental group was significantly greater than that of the control students. This finding is more important than the difference between experimental and control groups on SIAT No. 1, for on SIAT No. 2 the student not only is required to conceptualize the argument in more general terms but must relate abstract analyses of the argument to specific rebuttal statements made to meet the challenge of a prior statement. In other words, the student is required to evaluate new substantive statements made in response to statements in an initial dialogue. Moreover, he is given no cues concerning which analytic concepts are most useful in carrying out the evaluation. To do well on the test, he must have either an intuitive sense of rational political analysis or an explicit conceptual framework such as provided in the experimental curriculum.

Again, the Wheat students' average level of performance is substantially above that of the West students, although significantly below that of the experimental group. This indicates that factors such as the extent to which casual training occurs in the school or the home may affect the competence of students not explicitly trained in political analysis, since the curriculum of neither con-

TABLE 26

*Comparison of Experimental Group with Control Schools on SIAT No. 2[a]
with Means Adjusted for Pretest Score and Intelligence*

| School | N | Pretest | | I.Q. | | Posttest | | Adjusted |
		Mean	S.D.	Mean	S.D.	Mean	S.D.	Mean
Experimental	109	18.79	5.05	113.51	12.31	23.68	5.08	24.28
West	115	19.61	4.01	117.50	14.82	20.74	4.36	20.36
Wheat	173	20.20	4.61	116.61	10.88	22.28	4.32	22.15

| | Test of Differences Between Means | | |
	Degrees of Freedom	F-Ratio	Probability Level
Total	2/392	26.70	P < .001
Experimental v. Wheat	1/277	19.64	P < .001

*Combined forms Labor and Integration.

trol school provided such systematic training. What is more important, however, is that apparently the kinds of competence measured by SIAT No. 2 can be taught to students at this level of maturity.

SIAT No. 3: Oral Argument Analysis Test. The resources of the Project did not permit the administration of SIAT No. 3 in more than one control school. This is regrettable because, as already noted, the students from the school in which the test was administered — West — performed consistently lower on other tests than did the experimental students or the Wheat control students. The difference between the experimental and the West control group indicated in Table 27 is so great, however (P less than .001), that it is highly

TABLE 27

*Comparison of Experimental Group with a Control School on SIAT No. 3
with Means Adjusted for Pretest Score and Intelligence*

| School | N | Pretest[a] | | I.Q. | | Posttest | | Adjusted |
		Mean	S.D.	Mean	S.D.	Mean	S.D.	Mean
Experimental	106	18.02	7.03	113.43	12.14	30.76	10.81	31.15
West	59	17.08	6.37	120.66	14.86	19.19	6.68	18.49

| | Test of Differences Between Means | |
	Degrees of Freedom	F-Ratio	Probability Level
	1/160	73.39	P < .001

[a] A somewhat different scoring system was used on the pretest from that used on the posttest, but presumably both were measuring the same attribute. These numbers, however, cannot be considered precisely comparable to the posttest numbers. Covariance, of course, does not make the assumption of precise comparability.

probable that the experimental group's mean score would also have been significantly higher than that of the Wheat group had data been available.

SIAT No. 4: Interview Situation. Like SIAT No. 3, this test was administered in only the West control school. The results, presented in Table 28, indicate that the measure is sensitive to what is apparently a relatively small but systematic difference between the control and the experimental group favoring the latter. It should be noted, however, that the pretest and posttest scores are not based on comparable forms, since the content analysis system was revised after the first administration; the pretest was shorter and scoring conventions were changed somewhat before scoring the posttest. The difference between pretest and posttest means therefore cannot be considered "mean gain."

TABLE 28

Comparison of Experimental Group with a Control School on SIAT No. 4, Interview Situation, with Means Adjusted for Pretest Score and Intelligence

School	N	Pretest		I.Q.		Posttest		Adjusted Mean
		Mean	S.D.	Mean	S.D.	Mean	S.D.	
Experimental	103	10.26	3.81	113.71	12.19	19.53	10.11	19.39
West	59	8.64	4.23	120.66	14.86	15.45	10.54	15.72

Test of Differences Between Means

Degrees of Freedom	F-Ratio	Probability Level
1/157	4.28	$P < .05 > .01$

One other point should be stressed. Although the experimental teaching began in the fall of 1959, the SIAT No. 4 pretest was not developed and administered until the fall of 1960. Consequently, the experimental students had undergone some fairly intensive treatment before the administration of the pretest. This probably accounts for the substantial difference between the experimental and West pretest means (1.62 in favor of the experimental group). The late administration of the pretest undoubtedly acted to "absorb" some of the initial learning increment of the experimental students, making it less likely that the difference between their mean score on the posttest and that of the control group would be highly significant. This conclusion is supported by the results obtained when SIAT No. 4 was applied to behavior in student-led discussions.

SIAT No. 4: Student-Led Discussions. The setting for student-led discussions was as follows: Approximately twelve students were seated in a semicircle and given a controversial case. The case was read aloud to the group by one of the research staff while each student followed on his own copy. The group was then asked to reach unanimous agreement on a policy to handle the problem posed in the case. (The problem was *not* identified for the students.) A time limit of twenty-five minutes was set, and the adult felt the room, returning at the end of that time to find out the group's decision. All of these discussions were tape-recorded for later scoring. The presence of microphones and other recording equipment probably gave the students added incentive to perform well.

As Bales[7] and others working with small groups have pointed out, this unstructured group situation imposes three very different kinds of problems on the group members: procedural, socio-emotional, and task. The initial and primary procedural problems for the student-led group are to decide who is going to be leader (or chairman, as the students usually designate him) and how the discussion is to be channeled in an orderly fashion. The assumption is usually made that comments will be directed through the chairman, who must recognize speakers before they address the group, but sometimes this is spelled out or reiterated during the discussion. Occasionally groups are not able to "solve" the procedural problem and the discussion is disorganized and chaotic. However, most of the groups used in the Project's assessment program quickly selected chairmen and got down to the business of dealing with the case. Only after the initial frustrations of attempting to deal with a highly controversial case do socio-emotional problems begin to erupt (although the process of selecting a chairman does at times engender some antagonism), usually in the form of deliberate attempts at tension release (e.g., jokes or wisecracks) or status rivlary (e.g., challenges to the nominal leader's authority). In general, however, junior high school students handle this type of discussion situation surprisingly well, possibly because they are operating within the implied constraints provided by the school setting.

In the course of the two-year experiment, student-led discussions were recorded six different times at approximately three-month intervals. Only two sets of discussions could be secured in the West control school, approximately a year apart. Obviously, this meant that the experimental students obtained a great deal more experience with the testing situation before the final discussions than did the control students, and practice effects could be expected to be a factor in the scores. The most interesting and meaningful findings, therefore, are the changes in behavior of the experimental group over the two-year period. These data are summarized in Table 29. Data for only some of the administrations are presented, because of methodological problems encountered during the experiment.[8]

TABLE 29

Performance of Experimental and West Student-Led Groups Scored by Modified SIAT No. 4 Content Analysis System

Date of Trial	West		Experimental			
	N^a	Mean	N^a	Total Mean	High Ability	Low Ability
February 1960			10	31.90	34.50	28.00
May 1960			10	71.70	74.00	68.25
September 1960	12	31.08	19	50.11	59.00	40.57
June 1961	12	25.08	17	59.82	74.22	43.62

[a] Total number of discussions equals number of groups times number of individual discussions.

The results in Table 29 suggest the following conclusions: (1) The gains in mean scores by the experimental groups, as compared to the stability of the scores obtained by the groups of control students, seem to reflect clearly the effects of specialized treatment. (2) SIAT No. 4 as used in this discussion setting is probably sensitive to brief, intensive teaching of the analytic model for handling public controversy. Ten short cases, based upon Supreme Court decisions, were used during a ten-day period of intensive treatment prior to the May 1960 testing. These cases were used specifically to illustrate the process of legal-ethical clarification through the generalization of value statements and the use of analogies to challenge general value positions. The dramatic increase in mean scores between February and May probably reflects this intensive teaching as much as any long-range accumulation of learning. (3) The "wash-out" effect during the three-month summer layoff was much more pronounced for low- or average-ability groups than for high-ability groups. (4) While there was a substantial increase in mean scores for the high-ability groups during the second year, they did not surpass the achievement registered at the end of the first year of the experimental program. (5) The groups composed of students with low and average ability did not regress to their initial mean score, nor did they gain in any significant way during the second year.

These findings are particularly enlightening if related to the sequence of the experimental curriculum. As stated earlier, the first year of the program was concerned mainly with the teaching of analytic skills, but *not* within the context of any *complex societal problems*. The teaching unit was a single controversial case, and most cases were relatively brief, serving primarily as a basis for illustrating the concepts being taught. The climax of the first year came with a two-week intensive effort to relate a number of the more important analytic concepts to one another in the context of issues involved in some Supreme Court cases. It was immediately after this point that the May discussions with their high scores were recorded.

During the second year an attempt was made to teach the students to place a controversial case within a broader historical context. This presented a more difficult intellectual task because the analytic and substantive structure of an argument could no longer be so simply schematized; it must now encompass a great deal of complex information. Thus the student's inability to grapple with the additional complexity and at the same time maintain some conception of the total analytic structure of the argument may account for the finding that growth, as measured by SIAT No. 4 in student-led discussions, did not reach a higher point during the second year than that reached at the end of the first year.

There is another plausible interpretation of these data. Possibly SIAT No. 4 was not sensitive to an intellectual process by which a student could operate within the general framework of the analytic model and at the same time handle information at a more sophisticated level. Although a great deal of effort was expended during the development of SIAT No. 4 to meet this contingency through differentiating factual and conceptual sophistication within the categories "general claim" and "specific claim," no satisfactory solution was ever achieved.

Actually, our hunch is that although students in the more able groups were performing at a substantially higher level in June of 1961 than they were in May of 1960, our category system simply did not pick this advance up. However, the data do, in fact, bear out our impression that students in the slower groups made considerable gains in their ability to handle the analytic model during the first year, whereas the second year yielded as much confusion as increased competence. Upon reflection, this is not surprising. Providing the student with historical background and substantive concepts, as the curriculum did the second year, adds a great deal of "noise" that may well interfere with the direct application of the ethical-legal model to the controversial case under consideration. The most fundamental understanding of how to approach a problem or issue, from the point of view of this study, would find the student proceeding from the substance or concrete facts describing the issue to the analytic concepts in a manner that would allow the placement of the issue in a class of similar historical or contemporary cases and issues. At the end of the first year, the students were capable of doing this with a limited number of relatively simple cases. In the second year, however, they were not only required to do this but asked to relate the analytic concepts to a broader body of conceptual and historical information contained in a three- to six-week substantive unit. It was this double task that seemed to overwhelm students in the slower groups.

These findings relate to a question of fundamental importance in citizenship education: How intelligent must a student be to learn to deal analytically with public controversy? Our experience suggests that a schematic model can be taught to average and slightly below average students using a small number of short cases, but that these students find it difficult to integrate the analytic model into their normal mode of thinking with more complex material. We would certainly recommend that any attempt to replicate this study or carry out a similar one should provide for a more gradual increase in the complexity of issues and the amount of background information with which slow or average students are faced. The experimental curriculum apparently jumped too quickly from simple cases to complex units, and only the abler groups had the capacity to rebound from the shock.

SUMMARY

The research discussion in this section has been concerned with one question: Would teaching junior high school students a curriculum such as that of the Harvard Social Studies Project have a significant effect on their ability to analyze societal issues, especially in the setting of an actual argument? With the variety of measures used to evaluate the impact of the curriculum on analytic behavior, a series of conclusions is in order.

In the first place, the standard tests of "critical thinking" used by the project — the Wagmis Test and the ITED No. 5. — were not sensitive to the specific intellectual training provided the experimental group. This was not a surprising result, since the experimental curriculum provided training neither in general reasoning skills nor in the particular types of intellectual operations required by the tests.

Data from the Project's paper-and-pencil tests — SIAT's No. 1 and No. 2 — indicate that students of junior high school age can be taught to think in those abstract conceptual terms set forth in Part Two of this book. The results obtained with SIAT No. 3, the oral equivalent of the SIAT No. 1, also support this conclusion.

Data from SIAT No. 4, which was used to assess behavior in oral argumentation, did not provide such clear-cut results. While there seemed to be a significant increase in dialectical skills in the interviews, the student-led discussions are somewhat more difficult to interpret. The major question is: Why did the experimental students fail to improve their average performance in student-led discussions during the second year of the program? Our own interpretation is that while they had learned the analytic model and could apply it to relatively simple cases, they had difficulty applying the model to a more complex array of information.

References

1. This is a form of the American Council on Education's Test of Critical Thinking, discussed in Chapter Ten.

2. Note that these tables contain a column headed *Adjusted Mean,* as will later tables. Analysis of covariance is a synthesis of the methods of analysis of variance *and* regression. Using the regression elements in the covariance analysis, one can estimate what the mean values on the experimental variable would have been had the groups been comparable on the control variables; i.e., the means on the experimental variable are adjusted for the sources of variation represented by the control variable or variables.

3. Discussed in Chapter Ten. Velma I. Rust, R. Stewart Jones, and Henry F. Kaiser, "A Factor-Analytic Study of Critical Thinking," *Journal of Educational Research* (1962), 55:253-259.

4. Edward M. Glaser, *An Experiment in the Development of Critical Thinking* (New York: Teachers College, Columbia University, 1941).

5. B. Othanel Smith and others, "A Study of the Logic of Teaching: The Logical Structure of Teaching and the Development of Critical Thinking, a Report on the First Phase of a Five Year Project," prepared at the University of Illinois, Urbana, under Cooperative Research Project No. 258 (7257) of the U.S. Office of Education, 1959 (mimeographed).

6. One methodological note should be made here. Four people did the interviewing in both the experimental and control schools. Three of the interviewers were also experimental teachers for the Project. In no case, however, did a teacher interview his own students. Nevertheless, all of the teachers were known by the experimental students to be associated with the Project, while the fourth interviewer was not familiar to the students or known to be connected with the Project in any direct way. A comparison of the scores of students interviewed by the "non-Project" interviewer with those of the other interviewees indicated no systematic differences. In fact, none of the interviewers had any discernible systematic effect on the responses of students he interviewed. At the same time, the interviewers knew when they were interviewing experimental or control students (information those who scored the interviews did not have, it will be remembered). Although this might have had a biasing effect on the data, the interviewers were careful to control their responses, if anything leaning backwards to give any advantage to the control students. Also, all of the interviewers were experienced teachers, and none reported any difficulties in establishing rapport with the students in either the experimental or control groups.

7. Robert F. Bales, *Interaction Process Analysis* (Reading, Mass.: Addison-Wesley Publishing Company, Inc., 1951).

8. In the first place, after the tapes were initially scored with the SIAT No. 4 content analysis instrument, reliability on the dynamic categories was seen to have deteriorated rapidly. This was not discovered until it was too late to rescore the discussions. Consequently, these categories were eliminated from the list of "valued acts" used to compute a group's score. Second, it was found that groups often made astonishingly high scores simply by talking about the case. This occurred because of a convention carried over from Bales' work: Any statement paraphrasing information from the case was categorized as a "specific claim" and any mention of the case was categorized as a "source," and both were being counted as valued acts. In retrospect, this carry-over seemed an unwise decision, and the two categories were, therefore, eliminated from the list of valued acts. Both decisions were made only after the data seemed so erratic as to make little sense.

Statistical tests of the significance of differences between means presented in Table 29 are not reported for several reasons: (1) The group means, while an indication of the relative performance of experimental and control students and of the experimental students at various points, were highly susceptible to influence by the performance of one or a few students. (2) The total number of discussions recorded at each testing date was not large because of the time and expense involved. Combining these, as in the *N's* for Table 29, presents problems of independence of data. (3) Coupled with these considerations and the methodological problems noted in the previous paragraph, the differences between the means of the experimental and control groups, and between interesting experimental group means, seemed so great as to make any statistical test an empty exercise.

Effect of the Experimental Curriculum on Knowledge of Subject Matter and Interest in Public Problems

Any experimental curriculum that replaces or condenses portions of the usual social studies content will undoubtedly draw criticism from those committed to the present curriculum. The criticism can be met in at least two ways. First, one can argue that the proposed curricular changes will better meet the needs of the individual and the community. Included in this defense is the straightforward logical argument that the experimental curriculum is more directly derived from common teaching objectives than is that part of the traditional curriculum being replaced. Such a defense is presented in the first chapters of this book. Or one can raise questions about the relative effectiveness of the proposed curriculum in achieving standard curricular objectives, such as knowledge of basic historical information, knowledge about government, and so forth. Unfortunately, arguments about questions of relative effectiveness are often carried on at an intuitive level without recourse to the systematic assessment of learning.

STANDARDIZED TESTS OF SUBJECT MATTER

To shed light on what is basically an empirical question, three tests that measure the type of information often given priority in standard curricula were included in the Project's measurement program.

1. The Iowa Test of Educational Development No. 1, Understanding Basic Social Concepts (ITED No. 1) was given as a comprehensive social studies test to assess concept attainment and information in the areas of history, geography, economics, and government. Items are of the standard multiple-choice type; for example:

What is a trial jury?
1. A court decision
2. A crime for which a man is tried
3. A promise to tell the truth and the truth only
4. A body of people who hear evidence and are expected to bring a verdict

2. The Principles of American Citizenship Test, Form A, developed by the Columbia University Citizenship Education Project, was also used. It deals with the principles and structure of American government, as well as governmental process. The following item is illustrative of those in the test:

Senator Smith has been talking on the Senate floor for several hours without rest. He is against a bill before the Senate and he is trying to delay or prevent its passage by the method of
M. Filibustering
N. Picketing
O. Logrolling
P. Pork barreling

3. The third test used was the California Test in Social and Related Sciences, Parts I and II. (The title of the test is misleading. It is actually an intensive United States history test with Part One covering the pre-Civil War period and Part Two, United States history after the Civil War.) It will be referred to hereafter as the California American History Test.

The ITED No. 1 and the Principles of American Citizenship Test were administered to the experimental group and the West and Wheat control groups at the beginning and end of the two-year experimental program. The California American History Test was administered twice — at the end of the experimental program and one year after the program had been completed. The control group for this test was made up of students in the same school where the Project was located who had *not* been included in the experimental program. Three groups of students were tested in the first administration: those who had just completed the seventh- and eighth-grade sequence with the *experimental curriculum;* those who had just completed the seventh- and eighth-grade sequence with a *conventional curriculum* (Group A in Tables 32 and 35); and students finishing the ninth grade who had *not* been exposed to the experimental curriculum while in junior high school (Group B in Tables 32 and 35). One year after the completion of the experimental program the test was again administered to the first two groups, i.e., experimental and control students who had gone through the seventh and eighth grades at the same time and who were then finishing the ninth grade. This design provided data bearing on the question of retention of historical information by experimental and control students.

Results

ITED No. 1. The comparison of the experimental group's posttest mean on ITED No. 1 with the means of the control groups is presented in Table 30. The difference among the means is significant beyond the .01 level, but the

TABLE 30

*Comparison of Experimental Group with Control Schools on ITED No. 1
with Means Adjusted for Pretest Score and Intelligence*

School	N	Pretest Mean	S.D.	I.Q. Mean	S.D.	Posttest Mean	S.D.	Adjusted Mean
Experimental	108	24.05	7.10	113.46	12.35	35.71	10.02	37.18
West	127	23.51	6.74	119.04	14.41	32.58	9.12	32.94
Wheat	180	26.91	7.28	116.57	10.50	38.43	9.06	37.30

Test of Differences Between Means

Degrees of Freedom	F-Ratio	Probability Level
2/410	17.53	$P < .001$

adjusted means indicate that it is due to the poorer performance of the West control group. This is, of course, consistent with findings reported earlier. It seems likely that either the educational program or the general educational climate in the West community is of lower quality than that for the other two schools, although the academic aptitude of the students, as indicated by mean I.Q., is as good as, if not better than, that of the students in the other two groups. If we assume that the two control schools represent a fair range of student quality in well-to-do suburban areas, the results indicate that conventional social studies knowledge, as measured by the ITED No. 1, was conveyed to Project students by the experimental curriculum well enough to enable them to keep pace with the students in the better control school.

Principles of American Citizenship Test. The results with this test are presented in Table 31 and are similar to the findings with the ITED No. 1. When required to demonstrate a more detailed knowledge of American government, the experimental students showed an average growth that compared favorably with that of the better control group.

TABLE 31

Comparison of Experimental Group with Control Schools on Principles of American Citizenship Test with Means Adjusted for Pretest Score and Intelligence

School	N	Pretest Mean	Pretest S.D.	I.Q. Mean	I.Q. S.D.	Posttest Mean	Posttest S.D.	Adjusted Mean
Experimental	108	24.71	8.93	113.54	12.36	34.23	7.98	34.76
West	128	21.35	5.75	118.51	14.73	28.59	6.59	29.35
Wheat	174	26.48	6.18	116.61	10.55	35.05	6.90	34.17

Test of Differences Between Means

Degrees of Freedom	F-Ratio	Probability Level
2/405	35.74	P < .001

California American History Test. The data from this test bear on two important questions: (1) Would students who studied the experimental curriculum do as well on a comprehensive and intensive history examination as students who studied a conventional United States history course? (2) How would the experimental students' scores compare with the scores of students exposed to a conventional curriculum one year *after* completion of the course? Analysis of covariance was used employing the following control variables: (1) the Kuhlman-Anderson Intelligence Test, given in Grade 6 in the experimental district; (2) the Stanford Reading Test, given in Grade 7, and (3) the seventh-grade social studies grade point average. The groups are compared on these control measures in Table 32, and correlations between the control measures and the total score on the California American History Test are given in Table 33.

TABLE 32

Means and Standard Deviations of Control Measures Used in Comparing Students Taught by Experimental Curriculum and Conventional American History Curriculum on California American History Test

Group	N	K-A I.Q. Mean	K-A I.Q. S.D.	Reading Test Mean	Reading Test S.D.	G.P.A. Mean	G.P.A. S.D.
Experimental	56	108.67	11.89	59.27	15.92	3.05	0.90
Conventional Group A	31	112.32	11.34	60.90	15.20	3.35	0.61
Conventional Group B[a]	59	110.54	12.04	59.91	17.11	2.97	0.74

[a] Conventional Group B was tested only at the end of Grade 9 during the first testing period.

TABLE 33

Correlations of Measures Used in Comparing Students Taught by Experimental Curriculum and Conventional American History Course

	1	2	3
1. California History Test (Parts I and II)			
2. I.Q.	.56		
3. Reading Test Score	.71	.61	
4. G.P.A.	.62	.52	.53

Results bearing on the first question above are presented in the first three rows of Table 34.[1] They clearly indicate that by the end of the eighth grade, students who had studied a conventional course in United States history gained no advantage on the California American History Test over students who participated in the experimental curriculum.[2]

TABLE 34

Comparison of Conventional and Experimental Groups on California American History Test: Immediate Testing at End of Seventh- and Eighth-Grade Sequence

California History Subtest	Number of Items	Experimental Group (N=56)		Conventional Group (N=31)		F=Ratio (d.f. = 1/81)
		Mean	S.D.	Mean	S.D.	
Part I (pre-Civil War)	115	51.52	12.04	54.03	12.88	0.37
Part II (post-Civil War)	120	53.16	13.61	52.03	13.94	1.96
Total I and II	235	104.66	24.14	106.06	24.92	0.34
Items not studied in experimental curriculum	73	27.46	6.41	28.13	7.33	0.00
Items treated only historically in experimental curriculum	91	43.98	10.24	46.94	10.38	1.39
Items treated only topically in experimental curriculum	49	24.32	6.86	23.26	6.45	3.60
Items treated both historically and topically in experimental curriculum	18	8.98 (9.19)[a]	3.36	7.71 (7.34)[b]	2.61	12.87[b]

[a] Adjusted means.
[b] Significant at the .001 level.

The results reported in the first three rows of Table 35 indicate the same conclusion in regard to the second question about retention one year later. The experimental group mean scores are not significantly different from those

TABLE 35

Comparison of Conventional and Experimental Groups on California American History Test: One-Year Delay at End of Grade 9

California History Subtest	Number of Items	Experimental Group (N=56)		Conventional Group A(N=31)		Conventional Group B(N=51)		F-Ratio[a]
		Mean	S.D.	Mean	S.D.	Mean	S.D.	
Part I (pre-Civil War)	115	54.20	12.44	54.74	14.21	54.71	14.16	0.91
Part II (post-Civil War)	120	50.82	13.67	54.67	13.65	52.15	16.13	0.23
Total I and II	235	105.02	24.36	109.42	26.43	106.86	28.70	0.30
Items not studied in experimental curriculum	73	26.39	6.84	29.77	7.54			2.70
Items treated only historically in experimental curriculum	91	46.16	10.45	48.48	12.45			0.03
Items treated only topically in experimental curriculum	49	23.91	6.97	23.26	6.41			2.07
Items treated both historically and topically in experimental curriculum	18	8.55 (8.73)[a]	3.00	7.90 (7.58)[b]	2.49			4.33[c]

[a] The first three F-Ratios have 2/140 degrees of freedom; the last four have 1/81 degrees of freedom.
[b] Adjusted means.
[c] Significant at the .05 level.

of the other groups after a year's delay in testing. It should be noted that "Conventional Group A" was made up of students who completed the eighth grade at the same time as the experimental group, and Group B was made up of students who had completed the conventional seventh- and eighth-grade social studies curriculum one year before. In this school district, students ordinarily take either ancient history or civics in grade 9. Neither of these courses would be expected to contribute to competence on an American history test.

There is actually a second set of data bearing on the question of information loss with delayed testing. The material on which Part I of the California American History Test is based was covered primarily during the seventh-grade social studies program. Consequently, by the end of the eighth grade, it had been a year since this information had been studied. Inspection of the first line of Table 34 indicates there was no significant difference in mean scores for experimental and conventional students on this part of the test at the end of the eighth grade.

In order to derive additional meaning from the results of this test, we classified items according to their relevance to the experimental curriculum and compared students on four subgroupings of items: (1) items not studied in the experimental curriculum but usually included in a conventional American history course; (2) items treated only in a conventional way in the experimental curriculum, i.e., reading and discussion based on the textbook; (3) items treated only topically in one of the problem units developed especially for the experimental curriculum; and (4) items treated both as part of the conventional coverage and topically in the experimental curriculum.

The results with these classes of items are presented in the last four rows of Tables 34 and 35. They shed some light on the effectiveness of various ways of organizing a history curriculum. Experimental students tend, on the average, to score higher than the conventional students on items covered in that part of the curriculum organized topically, but the advantage does not reach statistical significance. However, with items studied both as part of the conventional historical framework and in connection with topic-problems, the experimental students show a *statistically* significant advantage, both at the end of the eighth grade and one year later.

An examination of Tables 34 and 35 indicates that there was little loss of information for either the experimental or control groups during the year between test administrations. This surprising stability in mean scores might be explained in a number of ways. It is possible, for example, that the California American History Test, intended for Grades 9 through 12, was too difficult for our sample of students. The data from each administration, then, might simply reflect chance scores, resulting in greater consistency than one would expect from one administration to the next if a systematic forgetting effect were operating. Using, as the California Test does, a set of multiple-choice items with four alternatives, students would be expected to select about one-fourth of the correct answers by chance. The mean score on the total test for our sample, however, was 107, or slightly less than one-half of the total number of items. With a standard error of 6.6 for the theoretical sampling distribution, the scores can hardly be attributed to chance. Actually, a comparison of the mean score of students in the Project sample with the norms given in the test manual indicates that they performed relatively well. A score of 110 on the total test yields a percentile rank of 50 with a norms group consisting largely of eleventh- and twelfth-grade students who have completed a senior high school course in United States history. The overall mean of 107 for the post-eighth-grade data is very close to the median for this norm group.

An alternative explanation for the stability of the scores is related to the sequence of history experiences provided students in and out of the schools. It is likely that a sizable proportion of the items on the test cover information that students study a number of times before the end of the eighth grade, and that has, as well, become a part of the lore of our culture. To the extent that scores on the California Test reflect such a basic core of common information rather than knowledge recently acquired in a particular course, one would expect the kind of stability reported above. This "lore" hypothesis is further supported by the lack of significant differences between the experimental and control groups on the subgroup of items based on information not studied in the experimental curriculum but usually included in a conventional United States history course.

In general, these findings should help allay the fears of those who would restrict the discussion of contemporary societal issues to civics and problems of democracy courses for fear of inadequate time to cover historical content. The experimental curriculum, which excluded or compressed large areas of history in order to teach students to apply a framework for the analysis of political controversy to a limited set of societal problems, proved itself as effective as a conventional history curriculum in conveying knowledge about American history. Moreover, when students studied problem-topics both within an historical context and within the framework of general societal problems, they tended to retain more historical knowledge than when they studied the information only as conventional history. We would conclude that the burden of proof now rests with those who claim that historical content is sacrificed in a curriculum that stresses the reflective rather than the fact-accumulating process.

STUDENT INTEREST IN CONTEMPORARY ISSUES

An attempt was made to measure interest using an instrument similar to one developed by the Columbia University Citizenship Education Project — the Newspaper Headlines Test. The Headline Test is a relatively simple device that asks the student to rank newspaper headlines presented in sets of three according to how interested he would be in reading each of the three articles.

The directions given to the student are essentially as follows:

There are thirty sets of headlines. For each set put on your answer sheet a plus (+) beside the letter of the headline that seems most interesting to you, a minus (—) beside the headline that seems least interesting, and leave the line beside the letter of the third headline blank.

Following is an example of an item:

_____a. New Church Dedicated on Park Avenue
_____b. Many Miners Jobless, Families Suffer
_____c. Four French Dressmakers Design Original Styles

The Headlines Test developed by the Harvard Project contained three types of items: (1) "Project Items" consisted of a set of headlines one of which was closely related to a topic studied in the experimental curriculum. (2) "General Items" were made up of sets of headlines each of which contained one headline based on a problem-topic *not* studied as part of the experimental curriculum, e.g., crime, the financing of education, and the Berlin issue. (3) "Dummy Items" consisted of human interest stories, e.g., "Twenty Men Saved After Seven Hours Among Sharks," "Children Escape Falling Brick Wall by Inches." These three types of items were then randomly ordered in a single questionnaire. It was administered to the experimental group and the West and

Wheat control groups at the beginning and end of the two-year experimental period. Split-half reliability estimates were obtained using the data available from the latter administration for 103 of the experimental students. Corrected with the Spearman-Brown Formula, the reliability coefficients were .73 for Subtest P (Project Items) and .55 for Subtest G (General Items).

The findings with the two subtests of the Headlines Test, presented in Tables 36 and 37, are somewhat difficult to interpret. It appears that the experimental group gained little interest in topics studied as part of the experimental curriculum (Subtest P), while the control groups not only gained in interest as measured by the subtest, but significantly so when compared with the experimental group.

TABLE 36

Comparison of Experimental Group with Control Groups on Subtest P of Headlines Test with Means Adjusted for Pretest Score and Intelligence

| | | Pretest | | I.Q. | | Posttest | | Adjusted |
School	N	Mean	S.D.	Mean	S.D.	Mean	S.D.	Mean
Experimental	102	22.93	4.30	131.38	12.26	23.93	4.45	23.75
West	126	20.67	3.44	118.55	14.84	24.36	3.59	24.82
Wheat	187	22.64	3.71	116.66	10.83	26.73	4.06	26.51

Test of Differences Between Means

	Degrees of Freedom	F-Ratio	Probability Level
Total	2/410	19.56	$P < .001$
Experimental v. West	1/223	4.62	$P < .05 > .01$

TABLE 37

Comparison of Experimental Group with Control Groups on Subtest G of Headlines Test with Means Adjusted for Pretest Score and Intelligence

| | | Pretest | | I.Q. | | Posttest | | Adjusted |
School	N	Mean	S.D.	Mean	S.D.	Mean	S.D.	Mean
Experimental	102	25.75	4.10	113.38	12.26	26.66	4.08	26.50
West	126	23.29	3.57	118.55	14.84	21.17	3.58	21.63
Wheat	185	25.51	4.52	116.76	10.79	23.74	4.11	23.53

Test of Differences Between Means

	Degrees of Freedom	F-Ratio	Probability Level
Total	2/408	46.67	$P < .001$
Experimental	1/282	41.65	$P < .001$

The results obtained with Subtest G, presented in Table 37, are likewise perplexing. The control groups actually lost interest in the topics assessed by the subtest, while the experimental group's slight mean gain was significant by comparison. *General* interest in important national issues, as measured by this test, was enhanced rather than suppressed by the experimental curriculum. Possibly these results with the P Subtest can be interpreted as a satiation phenomenon, i.e., as reflecting the immediate effects of intensive treatment of these particular issues. It would be interesting to determine the interest of the experimental students in the Project topics one or two years hence, as compared with that of the control groups. Would the more intensive study of these issues lead experimental students to enter more readily into discussions of them, or would they tend to avoid debates involving these controversies?

SUMMARY

Coupled with the positive findings on Project measures of analytic competence reported in the previous section, the results obtained on measures of social studies content and interest in public issues are encouraging to those who would like to see a framework for the analysis of public controversy included as an important element in the social studies curriculum. The findings indicate that the experimental group's knowledge of social studies content — as measured by ITED No. 1, the Principles of American Citizenship Test, and the California American History test — kept pace with that of the control students. Moreover, historical knowledge studied within the context of both conventional history and the problem-topic unit was better retained. The effect of the experimental curriculum on student interest in societal issues was in general positive, although in comparison with the control group there was less gain in areas studied intensively and greater gain in areas not studied at all.

The overall results reported in these two sections are positive but need to be carefully qualified. The experimental school was located in a suburban community in which nearly 45 per cent of the breadwinners held "managerial, professional and technical" positions; the teachers were selected for their teaching skill and their interest in developing the experimental curriculum; the teachers and students were aware that they were part of an experimental program, although the time span of the Project should have mitigated the Hawthorne effect; and about one-third of the class discussions were carried on with the students split into groups of ten to thirteen students. All these factors theoretically gave the experimental group an advantage over control groups. Nevertheless, these results might well warrant the substitution of such an experimental curriculum for a conventional two-year United States history course in schools where receptive and capable teachers could implement the program.

References

1. Without pretest scores to include in the analysis of covariance it was necessary to assume that the experimental and control groups would have had equivalent mean scores had the test been administered at the beginning of the seventh grade and/or that the three control measures used are so highly correlated to the acquisition of knowledge about American history in earlier grades that their use would control for any slight difference that might have been present at the beginning of

the seventh grade. Both assumptions are plausible. The students in the seventh grade had, for the most part, come from the district's elementary schools, so probably had similar educational experiences in elementary school. No systematic differences could be predicted, and the assignment of students to classes in the junior high school was not contingent upon the particular elementary school attended. Also, general intelligence, reading ability, and motivation, as measured by grade point average, probably are extremely good predictors of knowledge about United States history acquired during the elementary school years (see Table 33).

2. This result is supported by results obtained in a study by Arnold Rothstein, "An Experiment in Developing Critical Thinking Through the Teaching of American History," *Dissertation Abstracts* (1960), Vol. 21, No. 5.

Two Styles of Classroom Discourse in the Teaching of Public Issues

In Chapter Nine we described briefly two styles of teaching — recitation-analytic (RA) and socratic-analytic (SA). These two styles became the basis of an experimental study of three related questions: (1) Can a reliable content analysis system be developed which will differentiate between these teacher styles? (2) Can teachers systematically vary teaching style? (3) Will radically different teaching styles have a differential effect on learning outcomes? In carrying out the study, we assumed that style description and differentiation take place at three levels of precision: the *theoretical rationale* of classroom interaction, which provides a basis for behavioral description of the styles; the *operational prescription* given to the teacher (behave in this or that way during discussions); and the selection of *behavioral categories* in a schema to provide a quantitative summary of classroom discourse. Chapter Nine developed the theoretical groundwork for a way of looking at classroom interaction. Now our task is to elaborate the operational description of the two styles under investigation and present the quantitative methodology for testing the exent to which the prescription has been successfully followed.

OPERATIONAL DESCRIPTION OF TWO STYLES OF DISCOURSE

Recitation-Analysis

A recitation-analysis discussion, as we defined it, would involve the following steps:

1. A controversial case is read aloud.

2. The students are first asked to describe in their own words what took place in the case.

3. Students are then asked to tell why the situation in the case might be considered either good or bad (they are not asked to give a personal evaluative reaction). Next they are asked to analyze the case by answering questions based on the thought process concepts. This involves the students in:

a. Describing the conflict in the case according to general social and political values.

b. Telling what policy decisions might be made in regard to the conflict and what important factual assumptions relate to each decision.

c. Telling what analogies one might use to put the values in this particular case in perspective.

d. Telling what consequences one might anticipate if any of the possible decisions were carried out.

e. Telling whether any words in the case might create special definitional problems and how one might go about dealing with these problems.

f. Telling, if there are questionable factual assumptions in the case, what evidence might be gathered to support a particular claim, and what evidence already in the case supports any particular claim.

g. Telling whether there are any rhetorical devices, such as the use of loaded words, which might influence one's judgment.

4. The students then are asked to summarize the alternative decisions available in the particular case, and the important considerations one might take into account in arriving at an intelligent qualified decision.

In the initial stages of RA teaching, much of the analysis and application is simply explained to the students by the teacher. After several class periods the students begin to carry out more of the analysis in response to the teacher's questions. They are told whether or not they have correctly applied the analytic concepts, and, in the case of an incorrect application, an explanation is given.

Socratic-Analysis

A socratic-analysis (SA) discussion involves the following steps:

1. A controversial case is read aloud to the students (as with the RA discussion).

2. The teacher first asks the student to answer questions about the events in the case to insure that they have understood the major points.

3. The teacher next asks the student to propose a policy, i.e., make a decision, in regard to the situation presented in the case. This is usually in the form of a "What should be done?" type of question.

4. After several students have given their evaluative reactions and justifications of their positions without being challenged, the teacher begins a period

of intensive questioning, concentrating on individual students for lengthy periods of time.

a. A student is asked, as he or others were before, what policy he would support in regard to the situation presented in the controversial case. And he is asked to justify this position: The question is basically "Why?"

b. The student may respond in various ways: He may just repeat his position; he may defend it explicitly in terms of a value or values in the Creed; or he may say he favors his position because certain consequences will fol· low from it, with the implicit assumption that these consequences are "good," usually in terms of a general social value or values.

c. The teacher appears enlightened; i.e., he "accepts" the justification. He then verbalises for the student, if he didn't do so for himself, a general social value that supports his position or the violation of which disturbs him. In effect, he is tying the student's position explicitly to a value in the Creed.

d. The teacher may then attempt to persuade the whole class to agree with the student's position. Usually, most students will agree, since the controversial cases tend to be loaded in one direction (which determines to some extent the initial positions taken by students) and the statement of a general value supporting the position is persuasive.

e. The teacher then presents, usually to the individual student again, a second situation or analogy (telling it as an informal story) that illustrates the value that was verbalized in conflict with another value also embedded in the controversial case. But in the analogy, the value loadings are reversed. For example, if the controversial case involved Negro restaurant sit-ins, with equality of opportunity stressed as good while de-emphasizing property rights, the analogy used might deal with the confiscation of American property in Cuba, making property rights more salient.

f. The student is then asked to reconsider his position. If he maintains it, he is asked to deal with the value reversal in the analogy, or with another analogy with the same reversal of value loadings. If the student changes his decision, the negative consequences of his new position are pointed out, again through an analogy which emphasizes a value in conflict with the one he has chosen to support. In the sit-in situation, for example, he might be referred back to the controversial case or to an analogy in which equal opportunity is even more salient.

4. Students usually are unable to resolve the inconsistency between their feelings about the case brought out by the teacher's analogies. This is especially likely because they are not allowed the easy and superficial out of simply switching positions. Instead, they are faced with another horn of the dilemma. When the student seems to have become fully aware of the dilemma in which he is caught, the teacher may either switch the dialogue to another student, i.e., ask him to state a position and defend it, or move to an analytical phase of the discussion. Being forced to deal with inconsistencies in such a manner can be very trying for students, and the cues that indicate to the teacher that it is time to let the student "off the hook" are often signs of tension or tension release.

5. When the students generally seem aware of the dilemma and consequently

have become agitated about it, the teacher suspends the intensive socratic dialogue and asks the student with whom he has been interacting to deal with the value inconsistency analytically. Here the teacher shows the student how to deal with the definitional licenses taken by the teacher, how to question the factual assumptions commonly made by the teacher, how to construct appropriate analogies of his own to clarify the situation, and how to qualify his position. As students become alert to the application of analytic concepts, the intensive socratic questioning is often suspended, not because of the frustrations, but because the student has taken a reasonable position, i.e., a qualified position, clearly defined, with factual assumptions tested or taken into account.

SA teaching, then, is an attempt to teach the student to think on two levels simultaneously while he is discussing a case. The student must deal with the problem of persuading the teacher that he is taking a reasonable position with respect to the problem presented in the case. This is the *argumentative* level. At the same time, he must see that it can be done more effectively by using the political values and critical thinking concepts taught earlier. This is the *analytic* level. Initially, even after the students are taught the analytic concepts, few see their relevance to the controversial discussion. They tend to argue "blindly," in the sense that they have no conscious framework by which to analyze the nature of the problem. The teacher can argue more forcefully because he can anticipate how to maneuver the student into unavoidable inconsistencies. As noted above, we have attempted to teach this two-level consciousness to the student by bringing the argument to a halt after a period of frustration and asking the student to apply the analytic concepts to this particular argument. If the student is unable to do so, the teacher "explains" the argument in terms of the analytic concepts. ("I am attacking your value by the use of this analogy. You could counter the analogy with one of your own, qualify your position and make the analogy less relevant, or find some important difference between the situation in the analogy and the situation in the case, which also makes the analogy less relevant.")

6. After some analysis, the argument may or may not resume. This depends on the timing and the enthusiasm of the class. While initially the class is a patchwork of two phases: socratic questioning ⟶ analysis, and application of concepts ⟶ socratic questioning, the teacher works in the direction of less and less explicit analysis as the students become more proficient in using the concepts to guide their arguments. The tone of the class theoretically should move from a strictly adversarial one to one of a mutual search between teacher and students for an intelligent position in the case.

In comparing the *socratic* element of SA teaching with RA teaching, there are two striking differences. First, socratic teaching demands relatively long interchanges between student and teacher. The student cannot be led into an evaluative or definitional inconsistency in one or two statements. The teacher must first establish what the student's position is, suggest exceptions through analogies or contradictory evidence, and counter the student's defense. RA teaching, on the other hand, deals with the problem presented in the case only from an abstract position, never from the point of view of the student's personal commitment. The teacher would ask, for example, "What are some of the ways we might deal with the problem presented in this case?" Several different students might summarize alternative positions in a sentence or two. The teacher might then ask, "What is the relative importance of the two conflicting values in this case when we consider this particular position . . . ?" Although one position may be given sustained analysis in RA teaching, no person is asked to defend the position. Thus, usually no one student becomes involved in a protracted dialogue with the teacher.

Second, as we have already noted, the level of affect in socratic teaching tends to be high. In RA teaching the student is asked only to apply a set of analytic concepts to a particular case. He has no commitment to the analytic content other than its existence as something that the teacher has taught him. Nor is he asked to state a commitment to a position in the case. Misapplication of a concept requires an immediate corrective response from the teacher. In a socratic discussion, however, the teacher has no immediate responsibility for the inconsistencies or "holes" in the student's position in the argument. The student has autonomy to accept any position he chooses as long as he can withstand the teacher's probing. The student becomes excited and often agitated because he sees that two values, which he himself holds and is committed to in the argument, conflict with each other. It seems to be this dissonance in his own position which provokes affective responses, rather than the student's particular commitment to one position or another, or the disagreement between himself and the teacher. However, the impact of the latter cannot be discounted.

EXPERIMENTAL STYLE CONFIRMATION

Our first systematic experiment in teaching style was set up to investigate two major questions:

1. Is it possible for individual teachers to manipulate their behavior and play either a socratic or a recitation role when called upon to do so, or must we identify teachers who have natural socratic and recitation styles?

2. If it is possible for teachers to manipulate their general style of teaching, what variations occur within a single style? Are there overlapping areas in which one style cannot be differentiated from another?

An instrument was developed to provide quantitative evidence bearing on these questions.

In order to develop an observational system for quantifying teacher behavior, a set of categories must be created which will have meaning in terms of the specific teaching styles to which it is applied. Our first experimental instrument (called Form A)[1] was composed of two sets of categories (as shown in Table 38). Categories 1 through 6 are affective categories;[2] categories 7 through 12 are cognitive categories; and categories 13 and 14 are procedural. Using this instrument, the observer must infer the cognitive or procedural significance of each statement, as well as its affective implications. Each scorable act is categorized in a cognitive or procedural category *and* in an affective category.

TABLE 38

Brief Definitions on the Categories in a Preliminary Observational System for the Description of Teacher Style

Affective or Socio-emotional Categories

1. *Solidarity* — Status-raising language or tone of voice; strong approval or acceptance of another person. Often indicated by enthusiastic acceptance of another's ideas.
2. *Low Positive Affect* — Signs of mild approval or acceptance of another person, or of his ideas.
3. *Tension Release* — Action interpreted as tension reducing or attempting tension reduction, e.g., laughing or telling a joke.
4. *Tension* — Behavior indicative of a state of tension, such as stuttering or becoming tongue-tied.
5. *Low Negative Affect* — Statements or acts indicating mild disapproval or rejection of another person, e.g., disbelief of, skepticism about, a statement by the other person.
6. *Antagonism* — Deflating, derogatory, or highly negative statements or actions.

   Neutral — Acts or statements with no affective message discriminable by the observer.

Cognitive Categories

7. *Suggests Inconsistency* — An attempt to lead another person to see inconsistencies in his values, claims, or definitions.
8. *Descriptive* — Statements which describe events, i.e., make claims about what reality is like, was like, or will be like.
9. *Evaluative* — Statements which evaluate events, i.e., statements of like or dislike, right or wrong, good or bad.
10. *Repeats, Summarizes, Focuses* — Statements that restate what has happened during the discussion, or bring attention to what is happening or going to happen.
11. *Clarification* — Statements that attempt to clarify the content of the discussion, i.e., clear up the meanings of statemens or specific words.
12. *Analogy* — Statements setting up for consideration a situation similar to the one under discussion. The situation set up may be hypothetical or one which it is claimed existed, exists, or will exist.

    Non-cognitive — Acts with no cognitive (including procedural) message discriminable by the observer.

Procedural Categories

13. *Directs Task-Oriented Behavior* — Statements directed at controlling behavior which is in line with the task of the group, or at delineating what that behavior will be.
14. *Controls Deviant Behavior* — Statements directed at controlling behavior which detracts from the accomplishment of the group task.

The primary function of the cognitive categories (7–12) is to answer questions about differences between the intellectual or logical content of discussions led by teachers using the two teaching styles. Central to the distinction between the two styles is the extent to which teachers deal with *descriptive information* in the controversial case as opposed to *value judgments* arising from the cases. Categories 8 and 9 are set up specifically to identify differences of this kind. Category 7 (Suggests Inconsistency) is meant to identify attempts by the teacher to arouse personal value conflicts on the part of the student by suggesting that he is making contradictory judgments in similar situations (the case and an anology). Category 12 (Analogy) thus has obvious significance. Categories 10 and 11 were included to make the cognitive subsystem exhaustive. Categories 13 and 14 allowed us to gather data about possible procedural problems incidental to the two styles.

Two other points should be mentioned. Unitization, i.e., the breaking of behavior into scorable elements, was based, in general, on the simple sentence or "single item of thought." Complex sentences were usually each scored as one unit, and compound sentences were broken into their component parts. Also, symbols were used within each cognitive category to indicate whether or not the speaker was giving, asking for, or disagreeing with a statement.

Observer Reliability

Two statistical techniques, a variation of Chi-Square[3] and binomial probability paper,[4] were used to assess interobserver agreement. During the initial part of a four-week training period two observers worked together under supervision from one to four hours a day scoring tape-recorded discussions. Once they became familiar with the categories, the observers scored discussions independently for ten-minute periods, and their agreement was checked immediately using binomial probability paper.[5] Then Bales' adaptation of Chi-Square was used to estimate reliability for the study to be discussed next. All of the Chi-Square values were well below the .50 probability level criterion, suggested by Bales, which we adopted.

The Study

In the first year of the curriculum experiment the Form A observational instrument was used to determine the extent to which the four Project teachers could systematically carry on discussions based on the two quite different styles of teaching described above.[6] It was during these discussions, based on ten controversial Supreme Court cases, that the experimental students were first exposed to a sustained application of the ethical-legal model presented in Part Two of this book. The first twenty-five minutes of each discussion were tape-recorded. A sample of twelve discussions — six for each style — was selected for each teacher, and these were scored with the Form A instrument.

In analyzing the data obtained from the tape-recorded discussions, we first determined whether there were overall differences in behavior patterns when the two styles were in use. Did the teachers in fact succeed in carrying on significantly different types of classroom discourse? To answer this question, we classified interacts scored from the discussions by teaching style and by category (for example, an interact might be classified as a value judgment occurring in a socratic discussion) and tested the interactions between the *styles* and the *categories* using analysis of variance. If these interactions were significant, it would indicate that different patterns of behavior in fact characterized the two styles.[7]

The results of this analysis are presented in Tables 39 and 40. For Table 39 the data for all the teachers were pooled for the two styles; for Table 40 the data were broken down to provide a comparison for each teacher. In each case, the ratio testing the interaction between style and category is significant beyond the .001 level. The use of different styles produced dramatically different frequencies of scores in at least some of the categories in Form A. Considered both as a group and individually, the teachers were able to carry on two quite different kinds of classroom dialogue.

TABLE 39

Tests of Interaction Between Category and Style for Transformed Proportions[a] of Teachers' Acts

Categories	Mean Square		d.f.	Ratio
	R x C	Remainder		
Effective	745.654	11.304	6/322	65.99[b]
Cognitive	259.894	5.131	13/644	50.66[b]

[a] In using parametric statistics the researcher always faces the problem of meeting the assumptions under which underlie the particular model to be applied. Analysis of variance, and the *t* test, which will be reported in following tables, assume that the data come from normally distributed populations and that the variances are homogeneous. These assumptions become untenable when results are expressed in proportions. One way of meeting this problem is to transform the proportions to angles using an inverse sine transformation, then use these figures as a basis for computation. This is the procedure followed for Tables 39–46. For those who would like to look at the following tables in terms of proportions, Table 47 provides the information for quick transformation. For discussions of the assumptions mentioned above and of the appropriateness of using the inverse sine transformation, the interested reader is referred to the following sources: Virginia L. Senders, *Measurement and Statistics* (New York: Oxford University Press, 1958), p. 498; Helen M. Walker and Joseph Lev, *Statistical Inference* (New York: Henry Holt & Co., Inc., 1953), p. 424; Quinn McNemar, *Psychological Statistics* (New York: John Wiley & Sons, Inc., 1955), p. 255; and Allen Lewis Edwards, *Experimental Design in Psychological Research* (New York: Holt, Rinehart & Winston, Inc., 1950), p. 203.

[b] P. < .001.

TABLE 40

Tests of Interaction Between Category and Style for Transformed Proportions of Acts of Individual Teachers

Teacher	Category	Mean Square		d.f.	Ratio
		R x C	Remainder		
A	Affective	402.841	16.950	5/60	23.77[a]
	Cognitive	154.975	5.080	9/100	30.51[a]
B	Affective	185.825	13.132	5/60	14.15[a]
	Cognitive	49.200	3.300	9/100	14.91[a]
C	Affective	275.538	10.699	5/60	25.75[a]
	Cognitive	228.292	6.082	9/100	37.54[a]
D	Affective	113.829	7.434	5/60	15.31[a]
	Cognitive	24.546	4.744	9/100	5.17[a]

[a] P < .001.

With overall differences in style established, a second question became pertinent: Which of the specific categories were contributing to the overall differences? The following generally stated hypotheses, in conjunction with Table 41, suggest the categories in which one might expect to find differences.

TABLE 41

Predicted Differences in Categorizations of Behavior for Teachers Attempting to Use the Two Styles

Category[a]	Style for Which Greater Proportion Predicted	Fate of Hypothesis
Solidarity	No difference	Rejected
Low Positive	Recitation	Accepted
Tension Release	Socratic	Rejected
Low Negative	Socratic	Accepted
Antagonism	Socratic	Accepted
Neutral	Recitation	Accepted
Evaluative, Gives	No difference	Rejected
Evaluative, Asks For	Socratic	Accepted
Suggests Inconsistency, Evaluative	Socratic	Accepted
Descriptive	Recitation	Accepted
Disagreement with Description	No difference	Rejected
Repeats, Summarizes, Focuses	Recitation	Accepted
Clarification	Recitation	Rejected
Analogy	Socratic	Accepted
Directs Task-Oriented Behavior	Recitation	Accepted

[a] Categories are not included in which there were insufficient frequencies for analysis or which were not considered central to the styles.

1. While recitation teaching tends to produce much low positive affect by reinforcing correct responses, there is no reason to expect a high frequency of enthusiastic praise or solidarity. The socratic dialogue, on the other hand, should reflect a greater amount of both low negative affect and antagonism than recitation. Here teachers would also be expected to use more tension release — telling of jokes and laughing — in order to reduce tension. The affect-laden socratic situation also would lead to a prediction of fewer affectively neutral acts.

2. Because of the socratic's focus on the student's personal reaction to the controversial case, there should be more evaluative statements with this style and proportionately fewer descriptive statements. Moreover, since socratic teaching attempts to expose inconsistencies in the student's position, teachers would be expected to suggest more evaluative inconsistencies with this style and avoid a statement of their own value judgments.

3. Two categories seem rather directly related to the different nature of lesson organization for the two teaching styles. While socratic teaching involves an intensive and lengthy interchange with individual students centered around

the values they have expressed, recitation teaching is organized around the teacher's conception of the adequate treatment of the problem. It is necessary, as the recitation moves from one student to another and as each responds to the teacher's queries, that this organizational structure be maintained. We therefore would expect recitation teaching to result in a greater proportion of acts in the Repeats, Summarizes, Focuses category. The same factor might well have a similar effect on the Clarification category.

4. It is obvious from our teaching style models that socratic teaching should result in many more analogies than would be the case with recitation teaching, since this is a major device for revealing value inconsistencies.

5. Calling on students is categorized as Directs Task-Oriented Behavior. Because of the difference in duration of periods of student-teacher interaction, a higher frequency can be expected in this category when the recitation style is used.

Tables 41 and 42 indicate the fate of these hypotheses when related to specific categories. Ten of the sixteen predictions were confirmed. Those that were rejected provide some interesting insights into the use of the two styles. For example, the tendency of the recitation teacher to move through a *sequence* of planned questions means more expressions of solidarity — i.e., reinforcement

TABLE 42

Comparison of Mean Interacts for Teachers
Attempting to Use the Two Styles

| Category | Style | | Difference | t^a |
	Socratic	Recitation		
Solidarity	.641	1.406	.765	4.35[d]
Low Positive	4.576	9.539	4.963	10.28[b]
Tension Release	.495	.465	.030	.25
Low Negative	10.517	2.326	8.192	34.42[b]
Antagonism	8.879	.151	8.729	6.32[b]
Neutral	34.624	48.970	14.346	7.82[b]
Suggests Evaluative Inconsistency	5.492	.161	5.331	7.50[b]
Descriptive	21.231	34.930	13.699	7.66[b]
Specific Disagreement	.904	.489	.415	2.40[c]
Evaluative	1.484	.500	.983	6.22[d]
Evaluative, Asks For	8.239	3.085	5.154	7.16[b]
Repeats, Summarizes, Focuses	5.512	7.770	2.258	4.76[b]
Clarification	2.064	2.336	.272	1.01
Analogy	6.871	1.362	5.508	5.84[b]
Directs	4.374	6.879	2.505	6.77[b]
Non-Cognitive	1.456	1.672	.216	1.15

Note: In Tables 42 through 46 interaction frequencies have been converted to proportions and transformed to inverse sine values for statistical purposes.

[a] d.f. = 23 for all computations.
[b] $P < .001$ one-tailed test.
[c] $P < .05$ two-tailed test.
[d] $P < .001$ two-tailed test.

of student responses — as well as less need to disagree with student claims. These results also indicate the more argumentative nature of socratic discourse. Also, in using the value-centered socratic style, the teacher is more likely to make value judgments himself — possibly because of the need to draw out evaluative statements from his students.

Variations in Behavior Within Teaching Styles

Despite some errors in prediction regarding individual categories, as indicated in Table 41, it seems safe to conclude that the experimental teachers

TABLE 43

Interaction Between Category and Teacher for the Two Styles

Style	Category	Mean Square		d.f.	Ratio
		R x C	Remainder		
Socratic	Affective	42.218	20.172	12/120	2.09ᵃ
	Cognitive	36.646	6.298	27/200	5.82ᶜ
Recitation	Affective	7.350	3.101	15/120	2.37ᵇ
	Cognitive	8.578	3.304	27/200	2.60ᶜ

ᵃ P < .05.
ᵇ P < .01.
ᶜ P < .001.

TABLE 44

Comparison of Means of Interacts for Teachers Attempting to Use the Socratic Style

Category	Teacher				F-Ratioᵃ
	A	B	C	D	
Solidarity	.44	.69	.24	1.19	5.09ᶜ
Low Positive	3.59	5.03	4.09	5.62	.19
Tension Release	.31	.27	1.03	.36	4.17ᵇ
Low Negative	10.18	8.10	14.09	9.69	4.25ᵇ
Antagonism	14.40	9.02	6.75	5.34	2.50
Neutral	30.52	36.86	33.14	37.97	—ᵈ
Evaluative	1.68	1.83	1.03	1.39	1.20
Evaluative, Asks For	10.31	6.75	8.97	6.93	2.44
Suggests Evaluative Inconsistency	7.59	3.64	8.21	2.53	7.03ᶜ
Descriptive	16.57	25.81	16.03	26.51	7.73ᶜ
Descriptive, Disagreement	.52	.83	1.20	1.08	1.32
Repeats, Summarizes, Focuses	4.95	7.16	3.78	6.21	5.34ᶜ
Clarification	1.31	2.57	2.38	2.00	4.70ᵇ
Analogy	9.88	4.56	8.56	4.48	2.61
Directs Task-Oriented Behavior	3.69	3.50	5.50	4.80	3.31ᵇ

ᵃ d.f. = 3/20 for all categories.
ᵇ P < .05.
ᶜ P < .01.
ᵈ Ratio not computed because within-rows variance larger than between-rows variance.

were able to manipulate their style of teaching with considerable facility. This brings us to a third question: Did significant variations in behavior occur among teachers when the same style was prescribed? Table 43 indicates the results of classifying interacts on the basis of category and teacher and then testing the significance of interaction using the two-way analysis of variance model. This tells us whether significantly different patterns of behavior were categorized from teacher to teacher when presumably they were all using the same style. The results would indicate that such is the case — with levels of significance ranging from .05 to .001. Considering educational claims about the impact of teacher personality, it is not surprising that with both styles there is considerable variation among individual teachers.

Tables 44 and 45 tell which categories account for these within-style differences. Here a simple one-way analysis of variance was used to test the significance of differences among multiple means. Differences significant beyond the .05 level are indicated for four categories when the recitation style was prescribed, and for eight categories when the socratic style was prescribed.

TABLE 45

Comparison of Means of Interacts for Teachers Attempting to Use the Recitation Style

Category	Teacher				F-Ratio[a]
	A	*B*	*C*	*D*	
Solidarity	.61	1.42	1.02	2.56	6.02[c]
Low Positive	8.51	8.39	10.39	10.87	2.55
Tension Release	.81	.28	.70	.08	3.50[b]
Low Negative	2.76	2.57	2.11	1.87	—[d]
Antagonism	.18	.07	.09	.26	1.14
Neutral	50.32	50.61	46.39	46.56	1.84
Evaluative	.43	.72	.51	.34	3.77[b]
Evaluative, Asks For	3.31	3.26	1.81	3.96	1.39
Suggests Evaluative Inconsistency	.06	.15	.34	.11	—[d]
Descriptive	32.67	36.12	38.67	32.25	2.63
Descriptive, Disagreement	.56	.40	.56	.44	—[d]
Repeats, Summarizes, Focuses	8.57	8.28	6.43	7.80	2.81
Clarification	2.15	2.36	2.76	2.08	—[d]
Analogy	1.56	1.52	1.36	1.01	—[d]
Directs Task-Oriented Behavior	7.61	5.76	6.28	7.88	4.01[b]

[a] d.f. $= 3/20$ for all categories.
[b] $P < .05$.
[c] $P < .01$.
[d] Ratio not computed because within-rows variance larger than between-rows variance.

We might now ask to what extent these differences within style resulted in overlap between styles. Table 46 reveals that in two instances in categories for which differences were predicted between styles and which reflected differences

TABLE 46

Distributions of Means of Transformed Proportions for Categories for Which Differences were Predicted Between Styles and in Which There Were Significant Differences Among Teachers Within Either the Socratic or the Recitation Style

	Low Negative				Suggests Evaluative Inconsistency		
Teacher	Socratic	Teacher	Recitation	Teacher	Socratic	Teacher	Recitation
C	14.09	A	2.76	C	8.21	C	.34
A	10.18	B	2.57	A	7.59	B	.15
D	9.69	C	2.11	B	3.64	D	.11
B	8.10	D	1.87	D	3.53	A	.06

	Descriptive[a]				Repeats, Summarizes, Focuses		
Teacher	Socratic	Teacher	Recitation	Teacher	Socratic	Teacher	Recitation
D	26.51	C	38.67	B	7.16	A	8.57
B	25.81	B	36.12	D	6.21	B	8.28
A	16.57	A	32.67	A	4.95	D	7.80
C	16.03	D	32.25	C	3.78	C	6.43

	Directs Task-Oriented Behavior[a]		
Teacher	Socratic	Teacher	Recitation
C	5.50	D	7.88
D	4.80	A	7.61
A	3.69	C	6.28
B	3.50	B	5.76

[a] Difference between the two means each of which is most extreme from the predicted direction for each style is not significant at the .05 level, *t* test.

TABLE 47

Values Resulting from the Transformation of Some Proportions with the Inverse Sine Transformation[a]

Proportion	Degrees	Proportion	Degrees
.01	.567	.25	14.483
.02	1.150	.30	17.450
.03	1.717	.35	20.483
.04	2.300	.40	23.583
.05	2.867	.45	26.750
.06	3.433	.50	30.000
.07	4.017	.60	36.867
.08	4.583	.70	44.433
.09	5.167	.80	53.133
.10	5.733	.90	64.150
.15	8.633	1.00	90.000
.20	11.533		

[a] This table is included to assist readers who wish to estimate the proportions represented by the transformed figures presented in the preceding tables.

within style the differences between the mean proportions most extreme from the predicted directions were not significant at the .05 level.

In summary, the size of the F-Ratios that resulted when differences in behavior between styles were tested undoubtedly reflects the extent to which at least some teachers can vary their own teaching style when it is their intention to do so. This indicates that in some major respects groups of experimental students received systematically different treatment.

Two Styles Experimentally Compared

As a result of the systematic attempt to describe and quantify differences between the two styles described above, we gained considerable confidence in the consistency with which Project teachers could effect socratic and recitation prescriptions. Our next goal was to investigate the relative effectiveness of the two styles. The general design for this research was introduced earlier. Each of the five regular class sections which were taught the experimental program was divided into two groups matched as closely as possible on sex, intelligence test scores available in the school records, scores on the Wagmis Test, scores on the ITED No. 5, and ratings by the experimental teachers on rate of oral participation. Since the regular class size ranged from twenty-three to twenty-six, each matched group contained from eleven to thirteen students. Characteristics of the ten instructional groups resulting from the splitting are presented in Table 48. Whenever a controversial case was discussed, the sections were split into the matched subgroups, and the RA style was used with one and the SA style with the other of each pair. About fifty controversial cases were used over the two-year experimental period.

Splitting the five regular class sections into matched groups thus resulted in ten subgroups for the discussion of the controversial cases — five SA and five RA groups. With four teachers available, two teachers taught two subgroups and two teachers taught three subgroups. Since students in the school were

TABLE 48

Selected Variables Describing Ten Matched Groups

Group	N	Number of Boys	ITED No. 5		Wagmis		I.Q.	
			Mean	S.D.	Mean	S.D.	Mean	S.D.
R-6[a]	13	5	28.08	7.40	44.50	7.25	124.67	6.90
S-6	12	6	27.17	6.09	42.00	7.98	126.91	9.64
R-4	13	7	23.83	7.54	37.83	6.11	116.83	8.32
S-4	13	5	23.46	4.50	39.53	4.52	116.00	8.71
R-7	11	4	25.00	3.81	37.64	5.20	112.80	7.25
S-7	12	8	25.33	7.65	35.69	7.20	114.15	8.05
R-3	13	8	16.11	3.17	32.44	4.65	105.11	7.42
S-3	11	7	16.50	4.49	30.92	4.72	105.00	8.79
R-5	13	8	16.25	5.13	28.58	6.40	101.81	12.76
S-5	13	6	18.30	4.22	33.20	5.31	99.50	12.21

[a] Numbers correspond to those assigned to the regular class groups for identification.
R = Recitation; S = Socratic.

grouped on the basis of general scholastic ability, there were available two very able subgroups, four subgroups of average and above average students, and four subgroups of average and below average ability.

Ideally, the research design would have been set up to allow the investigation of not only the effect of teacher style on learning, but also the effects on learning of interactions between style and teacher, style and student ability, and teacher and student ability. Unfortunately, we had neither the number of groups nor the number of teachers for such an elegant design.

Results of Comparing Socratic and Recitation Teaching

The relative effectiveness of recitation-analytic and socratic-analytic teaching are presented in Table 49. The tests listed in the table have been described in previous chapters, except the Unit Test. This test is the sum of scores from four teacher-made paper-and-pencil tests administered at the end of each of the major experimental topical units. Each test contained a section demanding simple recall of factual material, a section requiring the student to apply the analytic concepts to a particular aspect of the unit topic, and one or two open-ended essay questions. While the tests were constructed and scored under the pressures of regular school business, the total score was based on so many items

TABLE 49

Comparison of Experimental Groups Taught by Socratic and Recitation Styles During Discussions of Controversial Cases

| Test | Recitation | | | Socratic | | | t |
	N	Mean	S.D.	N	Mean	S.D.	
Content Tests							
ITED No. 1	53	35.38	10.49	55	36.04	9.66	[F=0.03[a]]
U.S. History	52	110.88	32.62	55	109.46	28.43	0.35
Principles of American Citizenship	52	33.40	8.15	56	35.00	7.67	1.04
General Reasoning Tests							
ITED No. 5	55	32.73	10.10	52	32.93	10.36	0.10
Wagmis	53	44.25	9.82	56	45.61	9.17	0.74
Interest Tests							
Headlines							
Project Topics	55	24.00	3.79	47	23.87	4.91	0.14
General Topics	55	26.85	4.05	47	26.49	4.05	0.44
Unit Test	56	161.76	46.42	53	160.39	44.22	0.16
Project Political Analysis Tests							
SIAT No. 1	53	12.02	4.84	56	12.71	3.87	0.82
SIAT No. 2	56	39.39	8.88	52	39.23	8.95	0.09
SIAT No. 3	53	29.34	11.03	53	32.19	10.50	[F=0.52[a]]
SIAT No. 4 (Interview)	51	19.24	10.40	52	19.83	9.72	0.30

[a] Covariance used because of significant difference on pretest.

that it is probably a reliable index of immediate effects upon the students of the treatment provided in the experimental program.[8]

The most striking result presented by these data is that at the end of the experimental period the groups taught by the two styles behaved similarly on every measure of learning administered. This result is consistent with general findings in "methods" research. Few experiments, however, have operated under such carefully demonstrated and marked differences in teaching style.[9] Attempts to understand this finding led us to the following possible interpretations:

1. The instruction was probably generally effective across styles. All teachers were selected not only because they could play the two style roles well but also because of their general excellence as teachers. The materials were especially prepared to teach a particular analytic framework. The teachers were involved in the development of the materials and the preparation of lessons based on the materials, as well as in the actual teaching. With this combination of quality and involvement, it is reasonable to assume that a powerful instructional situation resulted, regardless of the particular style employed by the teacher. Thus the use of an analytic framework and the preparation of the teachers may well be more powerful components of teaching than is teaching style as defined in the experiment.

2. All measures except SIAT No. 4 (the socratic interview) assessed the student's use of analytic concepts. It is, therefore, surprising that the recitation groups did not perform consistently better than the socratic groups on all measures other than SIAT No. 4. That the socratic groups performed so well in their use of the analytic framework, at least as assessed by these measures, might well be due to the redundancy of treatment. That is, having a large number of discussions involving the use of the analytic concepts perhaps compensated for the less explicit discussion of the analytic framework in the socratic groups.

3. It is difficult to explain, however, why the socratic groups did not do better on the SIAT No. 4. Two of the most plausible explanations might be mentioned. First, the test may be inadequate. One obvious deficiency lies in the amount of behavior sampled — actually only fifteen minutes. While this time provided a great deal of behavior (about 225 acts) relative to that obtained with most paper-and-pencil tests, it constitutes a very brief period of discussion so that chance factors may outweigh the effects of systematic treatment. Whether the categories in the SIAT No. 4 scoring scheme are adequate is also a pertinent question. We have already indicated the necessity for continuing efforts to assess the measure's validity. Second, there may be something deficient in the instructional situation: The students may have been too young to gain substantial benefit from use of the analytic concepts *in a persuasive context;* or the treatment may have been too brief to have a significant impact. It is our impression that both of these factors were operative. At the end of the experimental teaching, most of the students still seemed to have difficulty translating the analytic framework into usable form when engaged in a dialectical discussion. Whether this difficulty was due to the brevity of treatment, whether it stemmed from intellectual immaturity with respect to

the socratic treatment, or whether it is a general phenomenon not affected by either is difficult to say.

4. It is possible that there is an interaction between the personality characteristics of students and their ability to benefit from a particular style of instruction. In other words, although different teaching styles may produce no overall difference among groups, some *types* of students may learn better with one style than with another. This hypothesis will be explored further in Section Five of this Appendix.

A final observation should be made regarding a comparison of all ten experimental subgroups on the learning outcome measures, and especially the SIAT measures. Table 50 leads to the rather striking conclusion that regardless of the teaching style to which various subgroups were exposed the ability of the groups seems to have had a systematic effect on learning *even after intelligence tests and pretest scores were taken into acount as statistical controls.* Two obvious explanations of this finding come to mind: (1) The intelligence test as an indicator of general intellectual ability or scholastic aptitude is not a sufficiently valid predictor of the kind of learning stressed by the Project; or (2) the classroom context for high-ability groups is qualitatively different from that for low-ability groups. Thus corrections for intelligence lose their power because they cannot take into account the interactions between the students' abilities and the instructional situation. This possibility, of course, has serious implications for both educational research design *and* public school policy which seeks to provide equal educational opportunity for all young people.

SUMMARY

Analysis of data obtained by systematic observation indicated generally that Project teachers used quite different patterns of behavior when two different teaching styles were prescribed — the socratic-analytic and the recitation-analytic. However, the analysis of learning outcomes affected by these quite different teaching styles revealed no discernable differences. We did find that the ability of the group had a systematic effect regardless of the style used by the teacher despite control on a standard aptitude test.

References

1. For a more extensive and detailed treatment of the thought behind this instrument and of the instrument itself see James P. Shaver, "A Study of Teaching Style," doctoral dissertation, Harvard Graduate School of Education, 1961.

2. The affective categories, with some renaming, are basically those of Robert F. Bales, *Interaction Process Analysis* (Reading, Mass.: Addison-Wesley Publishing Company, Inc., 1951).

3. Bales used this variation of Chi-Square as an alternative to the product-moment correlation as an estimate of reliability because it tends to be more sensitive to variations in categories containing small frequencies of interacts. Chi-Square also is easier to compute and provides a concomitant estimate of the reliability of unitization and placement in categories. See Bales, *op. cit.,* pp. 102-103. Bales

TABLE 50

Comparison of Means of the Ten Subgroups on Four Project Measures Adjusted for Pretest Score and I.Q.

		Subgroups						
		3 (Average and Low Ability)	5 (Average and Low Ability)	4 (Above Average Ability)	7 (Above Average Ability)	6 (High Ability)		
Test	Style							
							d.f.	F-Ratio	P

Test	Style	3 (Average and Low Ability)	5 (Average and Low Ability)	4 (Above Average Ability)	7 (Above Average Ability)	6 (High Ability)	d.f.	F-Ratio	P
SIAT No. 1	Rec.	10.27	8.07	11.34	13.77	16.23	9/105	6.82	< .001
	Soc.	9.70	10.34	12.53	14.85	15.11			
SIAT No. 2	Rec.	44.88	43.93	47.23	49.18	50.59	9/103	3.91	< .001
	Soc.	38.78	42.84	50.12	50.09	48.56			
SIAT No. 3	Rec.	27.64	25.08	26.44	33.69	36.65	9/101	4.02	< .001
	Soc.	25.98	25.15	33.75	40.95	29.84			
SIAT No. 4 Interview[a]	Rec.	17.38	20.20	16.64	22.30	19.50	9/98	0.84	N.S.
	Soc.	16.60	18.13	19.50	25.45	18.73			

[a] The means for SIAT No. 4 are included despite the insignificant F-ratio because of the interesting overlap of scores among groups of differing ability. *Unadjusted means* are presented because of the low correlation between posttest score and either I.Q. or pretest score.

also discusses the use of binomial probability paper to estimate interobserver agreement.

4. Frederick Mosteller and J. W. Tuckey, "The Uses and Usefulness of Binomial Probability Paper," *American Statistical Association Journal* (1949), 44:194-212. Also Bales, *op. cit.*

5. For an analysis of the possibility of introducing experimenter bias through the use of such training procedures see James P. Shaver, "Experimenter Bias: The Training of Observers," *American Educational Research Journal,* in press.

6. Actually, another preliminary study, a pilot study in the usual sense, preceded this one. Its purpose was to determine whether observers could learn to use the observational instrument and whether the quantitative data obtained with the instrument would reflect differences in discussions when they were selected on the basis of intuitive judgments that they conformed to the two models of teaching. Both questions were answered in the affirmative. This study is reported in Shaver, "A Study of Teaching Style."

7. John B. Carroll first suggested this statistical approach, and William W. Cooley provided a great deal of assistance in its application.

8. Although there were considerable lapses of time between administrations of the four subtests (they were administered in December 1960, February 1961, March 1961, and May 1961), the intercorrelations range from .30 to .55. The correlations of the subtests with the total test range from .72 to .81. If the lowest of the intercorrelations (.30) is considered as a reliability coefficient and the reliability of a test four times the length of one of the unit subtests is estimated using the Spearman-Brown Formula, we obtain .63 as a rough, *minimal* estimate of the reliability of scores on the total test. By using the next highest coefficient (.46), we raise the predicted reliability for the total scores to .77. Considering the range of coefficients, this is probably a more realistic estimate.

9. See, for example, Lauren G. Wispe, "Teaching Methods Research," *American Psychologist* (1953), 8:147-150.

Student Personality and the Analysis of Public Issues

The results of our comparison of socratic and recitation teaching are not particularly surprising in view of the large body of literature which indicates that no particular teaching style is likely to have a sufficient overall effect to produce a consistent superiority over other styles. We thought a more fruitful research approach would be to explore the possibility that the two styles would have differing effects on the learning of students with different types of personalities. There is in fact enough research of this type to suggest that it might be a fruitful line of investigation. Wispe, for example, carried out an experiment in which one group engaged in a great deal of free discussion in section meetings connected with a course in elementary psychology, while the other group had highly structured section meetings.[1] Neither method proved more effective in preparing students for a final objective examination, although it was found that students who valued personal independence were critical of the structured sessions and preferred the free discussions, whereas the converse held for students who liked organization and structure. In a related experiment, Patton obtained similar results.[2] Both experiments demonstrate, however, only that different students *like* different types of classroom environments, not that different environments have an effect on learning.

Glaser's classic study on critical thinking, while not varying teaching style, does offer some clues concerning which students can function best in a critical thinking atmosphere. Glaser administered a questionnaire to assess the "happiness" or emotional satisfaction of students who participated in a critical thinking experiment, and related their responses to gain in critical thinking ability. The questionnaire contained such items as these: Do you regard yourself as religious? Do you feel appreciated by your family? Do you feel satisfactory adjustment to the opposite sex? He found that students who made the greater gains in critical thinking more consistently answered "no" to such questions than those who made smaller gains. Glaser comments:

> This finding may perhaps be explained on the ground that the pupils who gained the most in critical thinking scores were, as a group, also found to be intellectually superior to those who gained least. Persons who possess a combination of relatively high mentality and manifest a readiness to respond to training in critical thinking may well be expected to possess greater sensitivities, subtler and more varied personality needs, a sharper awareness of the nature of their satisfactions, and more resistance to saying *yes* than persons who possess a relatively low mental level and lack of readiness to respond to instruction in critical thinking. Those who gained most, then, probably are not as easily "satisfied" as those who gained least.[3]

Glaser's finding indicates that students who tend to be more critical of themselves and their culture and/or more sensitive and intelligent respond to a "critical thinking" educational environment quite differently from those who are more conventional or less intelligent. This response, moreover, is translated into learning outcomes, suggesting that intelligence and some attitudinal factor are both related to responsiveness to a critical thinking environment.

Stern and his colleagues at Syracuse and Chicago have reported efforts to identify what attitudinal or personality factors play a key part in the student's perception of a critical thinking environment.[4] Several studies were carried out using four personality constructs: the "authoritarian," the "antiauthoritarian," the "rational," and the "irrational." These typologies were made on the basis of a self-reporting inventory of beliefs, a modified version of the Inventory of Beliefs developed for the American Council on Education Cooperative Study of Evaluation in General Education.[5] According to Stern:

> Sixty items [of the revised Inventory of Beliefs] are nativistic-fundamentalistic generalizations that are parallel to but not identical with items of the California scales. The remaining forty items are reversals obtained by writing what might be called internationalistic-relativistic generalizations, rejected by the authoritarians but acceptable to antiauthoritarians. An example of an authoritarian item would be:
> "The many different kinds of children in school these days force teachers to make a lot of rules and regulations so that things will run smoothly."
> A comparable antiauthoritarian reversal was:
> "More playgrounds and fewer strict fathers would eliminate juvenile delinquency."[6]

Students with high scores on the authoritarian scale were classified as authoritarians. Students who dogmatically embraced items on the antiauthoritarian scale were classified as antiauthoritarians. Students who tended to accept either type of item were classified as irrationals, while students who rejected both were classified as rationals. (It is interesting to note the similarity between Glaser's dissatisfied nonconformists and Stern's "rationals.")

Stern suggests that the various types of students were "evidently reared differently, and obviously have different viewpoints about a wide variety of things . . . ." He also discusses whether authoritarians, antiauthoritarians, rationals, and irrationals actually behave differently in the classroom, especially in humanities or social science classes where ideological issues might arise. An experiment carried out by Stern and Cope bears directly on this question of differential classroom behavior as well as on the possible interactions between teaching style and student personality:

> Three special classes were set up in the citizenship course taken by all liberal arts freshmen at Syracuse University. One of these sections was composed exclusively of authoritarians, the second of antiauthoritarians, and the third of rationals, as determined by scores on the Inventory of Beliefs which had been administered before registration to all incoming freshmen. All three sections were taught by the same instructor who had agreed to a special assignment of students but was otherwise unaware of the particular characteristics of the three classes.
>
> The instructor met with each of these groups once a week throughout the semester, and maintained a diary of the events taking place during these meetings. By the end of the first week he commented spontaneously on his recognition of the three groups of students as types that he had encountered before.[7]

The instructor's impressions of the three classes were what one would have predicted and constitute a striking validation of the measure. The authoritarians were described as "interested in religion," "lacking in curiosity or initiative," and reticent about getting into class discussions. The antiauthoritarians were hypercritical, even going so far as to question procedures and readings used in the course. The rationals were described as polite and friendly, the obvious "future campus leaders." The instructor's general impression of the three groups remained very much the same over the whole semester, although a breakthrough with the authoritarians and the rationals was apparently achieved during the seventh week when the instructor defended the institution of slavery. At this time both groups became sufficiently indignant to "fight back."

In the context of our research, this experiment is important for at least two reasons. First, the explicit objective of the instructor was to teach the students to deal with ethical and political controversy. Second, authoritarians who were assigned to a group composed entirely of authoritarians and therefore treated in a special way by the instructor did considerably better on an objective examination than their authoritarian counterparts who were assigned randomly to control sections. Moreover, the superiority did not seem due to the quality of the particular instructor involved because the other two sections (rationals and antiauthoritarians) did no better than those in regular sections. Stern points out:

The significance of this study does not lie in the use of the discussion method as an educational panacea, but rather in the effect that the persistent application of particular discussion techniques had in helping a group of authoritarian students increase their knowledge in an area to which they are usually resistant.[8]

A productive line of attack on the analysis of the classroom would seem, then, to involve three major factors: the particular type of content which the teacher wants to handle, the discussion procedure used by the instructor, *and* the personality of the student. In the experiment described in Section Four, teachers handled the same content with quite different styles and came up with no measurable overall differences in learning between groups. This provides support for the speculation that the interaction between teacher style (or discussion method) and student personality is of critical importance. Stern's work suggests that the ideological aspect of the student's belief system is an important dimension of personality related to classroom learning.

McKeachie reported a series of experiments explicitly investigating the interaction between personality and teacher style as they affect school achievement.[9] Using the McClellan-Atkinson motivation theory as his major point of departure, he found a significant three-way interaction among need for affiliation, warmth of the instructor as perceived by the student, and grades in an elementary psychology course. He found a similar relationship among achievement cues in the classroom, need for achievement, and grades. Like relationships were found in other courses, but only for men. While from our point of view the substance of McKeachie's work is less relevant than that of Stern's, the orientation is similar and the results important.

THE INVESTIGATION OF PERSONALITY, TEACHING STYLE, AND LEARNING BY THE PROJECT

We have already emphasized the basic lack of fruitfulness of educational research designs involving simple comparisons between teaching methods. In our own work we have also used a simple correlational approach to explore various factors which might be related to the student's ability to learn a critical approach to controversial issues. Some of the results of such an approach will be reported later in this section. But we have found that correlations between personality and learning variables, although often significant, tend to be low, particularly when the effects of intelligence are partialed out, and therefore of relatively little use in explaining differences in learning. We have come to agree with a conclusion expressed by McKeachie in regard to studies of personality and learning:

One possible partial explanation for the meager findings in both these areas [the development of measures of motivation to be used in predicting academic success and research in the relative effectiveness of teaching methods] is that teaching methods affect different students differently. Students who profit from one method may do poorly in another, while other students may do poorly in the first method and well in the second. When we average them together we find little overall difference beween methods and no overall affect of a single motivational measure.[10]

It appears more profitable to go to a more complex type of research combining the experimental and correlational approaches.

A Pilot Study

Early in the Project, prior to the two-year experimental period of the major study discussed previously, a pilot study was carried out as an initial investigation of the complex relationships among teaching style, student personality, and learning. Of the several personality measures administered in the pilot study, interesting results were obtained with three: the "general activity" scale of the Guilford-Zimmerman Temperament Survey (see pages 314-315); a measure of tendency to respond to nouns in terms of descriptive extremes, i.e., to dichotomize (see page 313); and a measure of "tough-mindedness." Three measures of learning were most productive in terms of significant results: a measure of *interest* based upon the order in which students read news items when left free to choose during a current events exercise; a measure of *sensitivity to evidence,* i.e., the extent to which students' attitudes toward racial school segregation (the topic of study during the experimental period) were influenced by the presence of positively or negatively loaded factual statements accompanying the attitudinal statement; and a multiple-choice *test of information* about school desegregation.

The design of this pilot experiment was basically the same as that used for comparing socratic and recitation teaching as reported in Section Four. The teaching treatment was of two weeks' duration and involved only one controversial unit, on the desegregation of public schools. Three regular class groups were split into six groups. Three were taught with the socratic style and three with the recitation style, although no systematic confirmation of style was carried out. Three different teachers were used, each teaching a socratic and a recitation group.

There were no significant differences in the effect of teaching method on learning, although the difference in gain on the interest measure did approach statistical significance in favor of socratic students. There were, however, some interesting differences in the correlations between personality and learning measures for the socratic and recitation groups. For example, the correlation between growth in interest and tough-mindedness was −.23 for the recitation group and .46 for the socratic group; i.e., students with a tendency toward a tough-minded approach to the desegregation issue gained significantly more interest in the school desegregation issue when taught by the socratic rather than the recitation method. An interesting related finding is that the correlation between growth in interest and the Guilford-Zimmerman General Activity score was −.36 for the recitation students but .36 for socratic students. We found the General Activity scale to be highly correlated with the Guilford-Zimmerman Ascendance" (.43) and Sociability (.57) scales. These findings suggest that the student who might be characterized as a tough-minded extrovert responded well to — perhaps even enjoyed — the socratic discussions, while less outgoing and aggressive students were more inclined to pursue a subject if exposed to it in the less threatening recitation situation.

It is also worth noting that students least prone to "dichotomize" (choose moderate adjectives to describe nouns) made greater gains in interest when in socratic groups. The correlation between scores on the dichotomization measure and gain in interest was —.61 for socratic students and .03 for recitation students. Perhaps the student who tends to see the world in highly affective or extreme terms is more threatened by the socratic teacher's avoidance of definitive answers, with the tension generalizing to the subject under discussion.

A "sensitivity to evidence" measure, i.e., the tendency to switch one's position on the desegregation issue in the light of specific loaded facts, also produced noteworthy findings. There was a positive relationship (.32) between this measure and the tough-mindedness measure for students taught in socratic groups, but a negative relationship (—.22) for students taught in recitation groups. This seemed to mean that tough-minded students tend to react differently to evidence challenging their position on the desegregation issue depending upon the kind of treatment to which they have been subjected. Tough-minded students apparently became more sensitive to contradictory evidence after experiencing the socratic treatment than when exposed to the less personal and less value-oriented recitation method.

It is also interesting that scores on the "sensitivity to evidence" measure were positively related (.47) to gain on the multiple-choice test of information for socratic students, while the relationship for recitation students was negative (—.31). Apparently students who learned more facts in the socratic discussion were also likely to become more sensitive to the relationships between the loading of a fact and an attitudinal position expressed by test items, whereas students in the recitation discussions who learned more facts were inclined to become less sensitive to these relationships.[11] It seemed to the teachers that students in the recitation groups tended not to take seriously many of the facts presented as part of the unit — e.g., the crime rate, disease rate, and illegitimate birth rate among Negroes as compared to whites — which might be construed as implying negative consequences of desegregation, at least for whites. The students taught by the socratic method, however, dealt with these stubborn facts in a controversial setting which required them to defend their own positions on desegregation and consider personally the possible relationships between factual evidence and an attitudinal position. The result seemed to be that socratic students were more likely to see the facts as related to their own framework of personal decision-making, even though the recitation students "learned" as many facts (as evidenced by scores on the multiple-choice information test). (It should be remembered that knowledge of the facts is not at issue; the facts were incorporated into the items on the "sensitivity to evidence" test.)

The findings of this pilot study seemed to indicate that McKeachie's conclusion was correct: The greatest research payoff would come from a research design in which interactions between teaching style and personality in affecting learning could be tested.

Student Reaction to a "One-Shot" Socratic Treatment

Resnick conducted a study to see whether certain personality measures could be used to predict differential student reactions to a "one-shot" socratic treatment.[12] The personality measures were in the area of cognitive style (open-mindedness, the use of broad categories rather than narrow categories, communication among analytic categories, etc.). As a result of a factor analysis of a large battery of such measures, Resnick found four interpretable factors: Factor I: desire to do well in school; Factor II: size of categories used to structure messages; Factor III: femininity; Factor IV: production of transformations.

An experimental procedure was then set up to test whether students with different factor scores would react differently on measures of learning when exposed to a socratic treatment as compared to those who had no such treatment. Specifically, students were told that the experimenter would be interested in learning about their opinions on a currently important social question, socialized medicine. To help inform them about the issue, they were to be given a paper carefully constructed by the experimenter to give a balanced presentation of arguments on both sides. The students were told that they could adopt any point of view. In the control groups — both control and experimental groups contained forty-five students in two high school classes — the paper on socialized medicine was distributed, and the students were given the remainder of the class period (twenty minutes) to read it and formulate their thoughts. In the experimental groups, however, the experimenter-teacher first asked the students to express their opinions on the subject and then conducted a brief socratic discussion based on two dilemmas: (1) In terms of medical care, are all men of "equal worth," or is the higher-status member of a community more "important"? (2) Is the man who is likely to pay for medical treatment entitled to better care than the man who is a "charity" patient? After about fifteen minutes of socratic questioning, the paper on socialized medicine was given to the students and they were allowed twenty minutes to read it. Three learning outcome instruments were administered the following day to get at a number of variables, among them the student's position on socialized medicine, open-mindedness (the ability to see both sides of the question and suspend judgment), opposition (the extent to which the student considered positive and negative statements as a unit), slant (the extent to which the student considered statements which were affectively loaded in only one direction), and the percentage of statements in an initial message contradicting the student's point of view that the student chose to answer.

One of Resnick's most interesting findings was the discovery of a significantly different relationship between Factor IV (production of transformations)[13] and several learning outcome variables for the control group as compared with the socratic group. Resnick comments on these results as follows:

> . . . it is clear that under neutral conditions, the predicted relationships held; that is, the Production of Transformations was associated with "open-mindedness." Finally, it is apparent that the experimental arousal treatment caused marked differences in the effect of the Production of Transformations factor in

cognitive behavior. In effect, the Socratic discussion seems to have made subjects who were able to produce transformations behave in "closed-minded" ways in regard to the issue of socialized medicine. It would appear that certain kinds of motivational arousal, at least, can cause generally "open-minded" individuals to turn "close-minded" with regard to the issue at hand.[14]

Resnick then goes on to suggest interpretations:

> Perhaps the Socratic discussion leads subjects with the capacity to make transformations to quickly explore a number of possible "solutions" to the problem raised. Since, both implicitly and explicitly, the Socratic procedure demonstrates the inadequacy of these solutions, subjects who have considered them may come to the conclusion that there is "no way out." As a result, when the time comes to express their opinions on paper, they may, in effect "give up" on the problem, and simply support one side or another without further attempts to consider opposing points of view. Subjects who make transformations less quickly, on the other hand, and have not yet explored all the avenues, still find the problem a real one and deal with it in a more serious manner in written form.[15]

Resnick's study is particularly significant in that, while she set out to explore both motivational and intellectual variables associated with a "critical" or "open-minded" view toward a social issue, she did *not* find an interaction between motivation and production of transformation, but rather an interaction between a type of teaching procedure (socratic teaching) and the student's ability to produce transformations as reflected on learning outcome measures related to "open-mindedness." This, in a sense, provides us with a link with the previous studies. Thus Glaser found that those high school students who tended to be dissatisfied with their surroundings were more intelligent and made greater gain as a result of a "critical thinking" treatment. Stern and Cope found that antiauthoritarians were more responsive to a socratic type of teaching, and that only after sustained treatment did the "rationals" and "authoritarians" become responsive. (Antiauthoritarians also tend to be more intelligent.) Resnick now finds that the more intelligent student, who is especially good at seeing complex verbal relationships, tends to "freeze" after an immediate one-shot socratic arousal. This finding makes sense if one distinguishes between the limited one-shot "arousal" situation and a longer educational treatment. It may well be that the person who is more sensitive to abstract relationships is also more sensitive to the genuine dilemmas posed by public issues and therefore feels more keenly his own inadequacy to deal with them. While, as Resnick's study indicates, this person may withdraw in the short run, in the long run he may be most susceptible to training in critical analysis.

Exploration of Personality Variables in the Major Study

In light of the work by Glaser, Stern, McKeachie, Resnick, and ourselves described above it seemed worthwhile to explore in the Project the relationship between selected personality factors and the student's ability to understand and apply analytic and legal-ethical concepts. We selected three types of personality measures: measures of cognitive need and cognitive flexibility; measures of ideological commitment; and comprehensive measures of temperamental or social-emotional traits.

Cognitive Need and Flexibility

1. Resnick Self-Reporting Need-Cognition Questionnaire
   Sample Item:
   If some music comes on the radio that you like, but don't recognize exactly, are you likely to: (a) just sit back and enjoy it or (b) try and figure out what it is, who might have written it, or who is performing?
2. Wesley Rigidity Measure
   Sample Item:
   When I do homework, I check each problem at least twice.
3. Berlak School Work-Habits Questionnaire (Need-Structure)
   Sample Item:
   I write down my homework assignments in all my subjects.
4. Anderson Self-Reporting Need-Achievement Questionnaire
   Sample Item:
   I would be very unhappy if I was not successful at something I had seriously started to do.

Measures 1 through 4 were scored on a seven-point Likert-type scale.[16]

5. Word Description Dichotomization Test
   This measure was patterned after Osgood's semantic differential[17] format, and the variable was obtained by counting the number of times the student chose to describe objects in extreme terms (choice of "1" and "6" responses).

   Example:

	Rope	
weak	1 2 3 4 5 6	strong
angular	1 2 3 4 5 6	rounded
rough	1 2 3 4 5 6	smooth

Half of the terms to be described were neutral and half were politically loaded, e.g., "Communist." Our findings demonstrated that whether or not the terms were politically loaded made little difference in the students' responses. Those who tended to dichotomize did so with both types of words ($r = .76$).

Social Attitudes and Ideology

1. "Have" — "Have not" questionnaire.
   An effort was made to assess to what extent students were sympathetic toward economically underprivileged groups, and to what extent they thought that existing privileged groups should maintain their present status.
   Sample Item:
   People who own a house or business are usually more responsible citizens.

2. F-Scale
   This is presumably a measure of the tendency toward authoritarian solutions to basic socialization problems and interpersonal relations.[18]
   Sample Item:
   It is only right for a person to feel that his country or religion is better than any other.

The above two measures were also scored on a seven-point Likert-type scale.

3. Opinion of Southerners
   This measure was included as a general measure of distrust of an "outgroup."
   Sample Item:
   There is nothing about southerners that I could ever like.
4. Opinion of Jews
   Sample Item:
   I suppose the Jews are all right, but I've never liked them.
5. Negro Social Distance Scale
   Sample Item:
   I would not mind playing on a team in which there were Negroes.

Measures 3 through 5 are Thurstone-type scales. That is, the items carry values based on the scale position assigned to them by judges.[19] Measures 3 and 4 contain non-cumulative or "point" items, and the person's score is the scale value of the median item he accepts (agrees with). The Negro Social Distance Scale contains cumulative items and is scored like a Guttman-type scale. The individual's score is the value of the last item he selects.

Comprehensive Personality Inventories

Two comprehensive personality inventories were administered: the Guilford-Zimmerman Temperament Survey and the Cattell High School Personality Questionnaire. Some items on the Guilford-Zimmerman Survey were modified to make them more meaningful to junior high students, and a few items which seemed out of the students' experience and not susceptible of modification were omitted. The traits presumably measured by these inventories are listed and defined briefly:

Guilford-Zimmerman Temperament Survey.
1. G — General Activity: a high score suggests a rapid pace of activities, high energy, liking for speed, quickness for action.
2. R — Restraint: a high score suggests serious-mindedness, persistent effort, and self-control.
3. A — Ascendance: a high score suggests leadership habits, speaking with individuals, non-submissiveness.
4. S — Sociability: a high score suggests that the respondent has many friends, likes entering into conversations, likes social activities.
5. E — Emotional Stability: a high score suggests evenness of moods, optimism, good composure.

6. O — Objectivity: a high score suggests that the respondent is thick-skinned: that he is not hypersensitive, self-centered, or oversuspicious.
7. F — Friendliness: a high score suggests a toleration for hostile action, and a tendency not to be belligerent, hostile, or dominating.
8. T — Thoughtfulness: a high score suggests reflectiveness, meditativeness, and a philosophical inclination.
9. P — Personal Relations: a high score suggests tolerance of people and faith in social institutions.
10. M — Masculinity: a high score suggests interest in masculine activities and vocations, resistance to fear, and a tendency to be "hard-boiled."

Cattell High School Personality Questionnaire. The following brief description of the HSPQ is taken from Table 1 of the Manual. Trait designation, as with the Guilford-Zimmerman Survey, is by letter.

1. A — Stiff, critical, aloof *versus* warm and sociable
2. B — Low general intelligence *versus* high general intelligence
3. C — Emotional, immature, unstable *versus* mature and calm
4. D — Phlegmatic and stodgy *versus* excitable and unrestrained
5. E — Submissive *versus* dominant
6. F — Sober and serious *versus* enthusiastic and happy-go-lucky
7. G — Casual and undependable *versus* conscientious and persistent
8. H — Shy and threat-sensitive *versus* adventurous and "thick-skinned"
9. I — Tough and realistic *versus* aesthetically sensitive
10. J — Liking group action *versus* fastidiously individualistic
11. Q — Confident *versus* insecure
12. Q2 — Group-dependent *versus* individually resourceful
13. Q3 — Uncontrolled and lax *versus* controlled, showing will power
14. Q4 — Relaxed and composed *versus* tense and excitable

Sociometric Status

In addition to the above measures, the students were asked six questions (three positively oriented and three negatively oriented) concerning judgments about their classmates. In summary form, the three questions were: (1) Whom would you most (or least) like to work with on a committee? (2) What person in this room would you most (or least) like to have as chairman of the committee? (3) What person in this room would be the most (or least) help in the work of such a committee? In previous studies we have found that the intercorrelations among statements on this type of measure are high, so we combined responses and used a single index of sociometric status.

Reliability of the Measures

Table 51 presents reliability coefficients for the personality measures used. The most striking aspect of these is the low reliability of the HSPQ, especially compared to the G-Z Survey, which is the same type of measure. Comparing

TABLE 51

Reliability Estimates for Personality Variables[a]

Cognitive Need and Flexibility		Social Attitudes and Ideology	
1. Resnick Need-Cognition	.67	1. "Have" — "Have Not" Questionnaire	.58
2. Wesley Rigidity	.60	2. F-Scale	.63
3. Berlak School Work-Habits	.82	3. Opinion of Southerners	.26
4. Anderson Need-Achievement	.63	4. Opinion of Jews	.53
5. S-D Dichotomization	.82	5. Negro Social Distance Scale	.66

Personality Inventories

Guilford-Zimmerman		HSPQ		
General Activity	.71	A	Aloof v. warm	.39
Restraint	.68	B	Intelligence	.56
Ascendance	.81	C	Emotional maturity	.50
Sociability	.85	D	Stodgy v. excitable	.53
Emotional Stability	.81	E	Dominance	.50
Objectivity	.83	F	Serious v. happy-go-lucky	.54
Friendliness	.83	G	Casual v. conscientious	.48
Thoughtfulness	.79	H	Shy v. adventurous	.55
Personal Relations	.35	I	Tough v. sensitive	.62
Masculinity	.91	J	Groupiness v. individualistic	.29
		Q1	Confident v. insecure	.62
		Q2	dependent v. resourceful	.16
		Q3	Lax v. controlled	.36
		Q4	Relaxed v. tense	.00

[a] All the reliability coefficients are split-half estimates corrected with the Spearman-Brown Formula. For the HPSQ, Forms A and B were used.

traits which have similar nominal constructs, we find, for example, that "ascendance" on the G-Z has a reliability of .81, while "dominance" on the HSPQ has a reliability of .50; likewise, "emotional maturity" or "emotional stability" has a reliability of .81 on the G-Z and a reliability of only .50 on the HSPQ. The differences are perhaps due in part to the modifications in the G-Z Survey to make it more consistent with the experiences of junior high students. But they also suggest that the HSPQ was inappropriate for our age group. The reliability estimates for the social attitude scales are surprisingly high. The only exception is the Opinion of Southerners measure. Undoubtedly, there are two factors at work in the discrepancy between this and the other measures: familiarity with the attitude object and the resulting specificity of meaning of the questions. Junior high school students in a Massachusetts community probably do not have a very specific concept of the term *southerner*.

Relating Personality Data to Learning Outcomes

With some thirty-five personality variables to relate to twelve learning outcome measures, the problems of analysis and interpretation are, of course, enormous. Our preliminary analysis was a straightforward test of relationships. This resulted in a correlation matrix for all the personality variables and all the learning outcome variables. There were surprisingly few high or consistent relationships between personality and learning variables, and those that did show up often seemed contaminated with the more general factor of intelligence. After preliminary analysis, the fourteen most promising personality variables were selected for additional analysis. As a first step, measures related to "general test-taking ability" were partialed out. These measures were defined as an estimate of I.Q. and three tests from the Differential Aptitude Test Battery: verbal reasoning ability, abstract reasoning ability, and clerical skill. The results of this analysis are reported in Table 52.

TABLE 52 (Key)

1. Need-Achievement
2. Need-Cognition
3. Berlak School Work Habits
4. HSPQ G (Persistence)
5. S-D Dichotomization
6. G-Z E (Emotional Stability)
7. G-Z O ("Thick-skinned")
8. G-Z F (Friendliness)
9. G-Z A (Ascendance)
10. G-Z T (Reflectiveness)
11. G-Z P (Personal Relations and Tolerance)
12. G-Z R (Restraint and Serious-Mindedness)
13. Sociometric Status
14. Opinion of Jews
15. American History

16. Principles of American Government
17. ITED No. 1 (social studies concepts)
18. ITED No. 5 (interpretation)
19. Wagmis (critical thinking)
20. Headlines H (interest in topics studied
21. Headlines G (interest in topics not studied)
22. SIAT No. 1
23. SIAT No. 2
24. SIAT No. 3
25. SIAT No. 4 (socratic interview)
26. Unit Tests
27. SIAT No. 2, gain
28. Wagmis, gain
29. Headlines H, gain
30. Headlines G, gain

Inspecting the correlations among the personality variables reveals two quite distinct clusters. The first four variables, Need-Achievement, Need-Cognition, the Berlak School Work-Habits measure (Need-Structure), and HSPQ factor G (Persistence), show significant and substantial intercorrelations, suggesting that we were tapping Factor 1 (Desire to do well in school) in Resnick's factor analysis. Interestingly, a number of temperament scales also correlate with this trait system: G-Z Ascendance, Thoughtfulness or Reflectivity, and Restraint or Serious-Mindedness. It is not surprising that these variables tend to cluster together. We get the picture of a student who is highly motivated to do well in school work and who is interested in learning in general. He tends to be systematic and persistent in what he does. He is also somewhat aggressive, thoughtful, and serious-minded. It is surprising, however, that the two traits of self-discipline (Berlak School Work-Habits) and need-cognition are highly related (.57). Speculation that the more creative individual (if he is the person who has a high need-to-know, as is often assumed) tends to be punished by the rigid institutional framework within which the school operates is not supported by our data.

The second cluster of personality variables consists of G-Z Emotional Stability, Objectivity (being thick-skinned), Friendliness, and Personal Relations (tolerance of other people and ideas). The major construct underlying these variables is apparently an ability to get along with other people without feeling personally threatened.

TABLE 52

Correlations[a] Among Selected Personality and Learning Outcomes Variables with I.Q., Verbal Reasoning Ability, Abstract Reasoning Ability, and Clerical Skill Partialed Out

	1	2	3	4	5	6	7	8	9	10	11	12	13	14	15	16	17	18	19	20	21	22	23	24	25	26	27	28	29
1																													
2	29[b]																												
3	40	57																											
4	39	61	43																										
5	03	08	08	-12																									
6	00	22	15	26	-06																								
7	10	14	08	15	-15	55																							
8	21	11	06	22	-25	19	-26																						
9	32	43	15	19	-06	30	-17	29																					
10	42	30	30	19	18	-23	-15	13	01																				
11	05	24	25	22	-04	37	49	20	13	37																			
12	16	32	33	31	01	09	58	08	13	05	21																		
13	27	15	21	16	-23	16	21	09	09	15	16	07																	
14	-20	07	-27	20	-04	04	-09	08	08	14	-12	-09	-01																
15	21	16	03	26	-02	21	03	-17	01	06	05	02	17	-30															
16	21	23	05	20	00	05	02	02	08	28	05	09	29	-35	51														
17	20	19	04	12	05	12	-02	-17	15	15	-01	04	33	-11	62	68													
18	21	17	09	23	06	16	02	-08	08	14	07	06	14	-20	70	54	60												
19	06	05	-01	17	01	10	04	04	04	00	05	12	11	-19	52	36	39	57											
20	08	35	35	41	-09	33	33	26	20	06	25	23	10	-09	27	01	08	08	00										
21	10	20	16	39	-16	34	26	15	11	-10	20	12	16	-03	33	10	08	15	07	64									
22	19	13	19	21	-22	18	21	22	04	-02	24	12	40	-17	34	46	38	43	42	03	07								
23	29	26	15	36	06	18	00	15	14	04	03	03	15	-13	21	34	30	36	26	13	12	47							
24	29	39	30	30	04	03	-04	-02	30	21	08	12	21	-24	28	49	36	33	13	08	07	42	28						
25	16	13	10	28	03	09	07	03	29	21	14	18	12	-07	05	15	11	13	13	06	06	39	06	38					
26	26	18	12	08	18	08	04	-15	21	21	02	07	28	-21	41	47	45	41	30	-08	06	13	06	35	06				
27	18	08	13	19	11	11	05	08	08	03	00	07	02	00	-17	-12	-02	06	06	-08	-09	13	49	03	12	09			
28	02	-11	-05	10	-23	10	10	28	-05	-09	06	02	06	-10	10	-02	-06	11	45	00	-11	17	23	02	05	-03	19		
29	-13	25	16	26	-28	34	25	27	04	-05	23	12	07	-11	16	-06	-03	-11	04	55	23	02	02	09	-03	-14	-19	17	
30	-04	10	00	14	-15	24	15	09	-07	-07	-02	10	10	-04	01	-05	-13	-20	-03	32	46	04	07	06	07	-07	-16	05	48

[a] With four variables eliminated, the partial *r* must reach .20 to be significant at the .05 level, and .27 to be significant at the .01 level.
[b] Decimal points omitted.

The measure of anti-Semitism is, as one might expect, significantly and negatively related ($-.27$) to reflectiveness (G-Z-T). There is, in addition, an interesting negative relationship ($-.27$) between anti-Semiticism and the Berlak School Work-Habits Questionnaire (we have called it a need-structure measure). The frequently cited relationship between ethnic prejudice and cognitive rigidity would lead one to the opposite prediction. We have found generally, however, a trend for need for structure to be positively rather than negatively related to the syndrome of the reflective student. This is borne out by the positive relationship between reflectiveness and the Berlak measure ($.30$).

Relationship of Personality Variables to Learning Outcomes

Having discovered clusters of personality variables, the question becomes: To what extent are these traits or tendencies related to the performance of individuals on learning outcome measures and to their ability to learn from instruction in the analysis of controversial public issues? The matrix presented in Table 52 indicates that the answer to this question is indeed complicated.

Performance on the measures of interest in social problems (the Headlines Tests) is related to two of the clusters of personality variables discussed above. Although the highest correlations are with the HSPQ factor G (Persistence), Headline Test scores are also related to both the "school motivation and orderliness" cluster and the "interpersonal relations" cluster. However, only the former cluster seems related to intellectual achievement as reflected in SIAT No. 2 and SIAT No. 3. The other relationships between personality and learning variables do not follow such consistent patterns. As one might expect, need-achievement is rather consistently related to learning. However, the correlations tend to be low, indicating that this is only one small factor in variability in test performance. The Guilford-Zimmerman factor T (Reflectiveness) also shows some relations to learning, which is not surprising. The several positive relationships between sociometric status and learning might also be expected. Sociometric status is probably another index of school adjustment, especially as our questions were stated.

One of the most interesting and provocative findings is the significant positive relationships between measures of persistence (HSPQ G), ascendance (G-Z A), and SIAT No. 3 and SIAT No. 4. The SIAT No. 4 is related only to SIAT No. 3 among the other measures of learning, *including* the other SIAT measures. The question then is: What do SIAT No. 3 and SIAT No. 4 have in common which is not common to any of the other SIAT measures? Two answers come to mind. Neither is as structured as the first two tests (the student is rewarded for spontaneous responses not predetermined by the test format). And both are administered in personal interviews. It seems, then, that doing well on SIAT No. 4 (interview) may well depend not only upon the student's intellectual training but also upon his tendency to be outgoing and persistent in an interpersonal setting. This, of course, raises difficult problems for the development of evaluation instruments. We have stressed throughout our work the value of measuring analytic skills in "naturalistic" settings. This may very well mean the use of oral behavior rather than written or precoded tests. But if oral behavior is significantly affected by important personality factors which may have little to do with competence in analytic thinking, we must find either a methodological or a statistical means of partialing out such effects.

Another set of interesting findings revealed by Table 52 is the number of high correlations among the learning outcome measures, with the exception of SIAT No. 4, after estimates of intelligence, verbal reasoning, abstract reasoning, and clerical skill have been partialed out. The common variance remaining suggests that a number of components are contributing to scores on the tests developed by the Project. Discovering and unraveling the various components which add up to a score on one of these tests is a major research task that still lies ahead.

To this point we have discussed only the relationship of personality variables to performance on measures of learning and have not mentioned their relationship to learning — i.e., to gain scores on the learning outcomes measures. From the partial correlation matrix presented in Table 52 we can infer a composite picture of the student who reacts favorably to sustained exposure to societal issues. He is one who has a high need for cognition, is emotionally stable, feels friendly and tolerant toward others and their ideas, but is also persistent in what he does and objective and "thick-skinned" about himself and his ideas. He also does *not* tend to dichotomize; perhaps if he did the complex, non-categorical treatment of important problems would be too uncomfortable for him. The results for the SIAT No. 2 and the Wagmis gain scores, however, reveal the difficulty of generalizing about the relationships between personality and learning.

Interaction Between Student Personality and Teaching Style

Earlier in the chapter we suggested that efforts to seek relationships between teaching style and learning outcomes or between student personality and learning outcomes are less likely to yield fruitful results than complex designs in which both factors can be taken into account simultaneously. Two-way analysis of variance provides a technique for assessing the extent to which learning is significantly affected by interactions between personality and teaching method. Specifically, two-way analysis of variance with covariance adjustments[20] was used to test whether the socratic and recitation styles produced different mean posttest scores on measures of learning (with posttest scores adjusted for I.Q. and pretest scores) depending upon the personality characteristics of the students. For this analysis we included seven learning outcomes measures and thirteen personality variables that seemed clearly related to learning. These measures, summarized in Table 53, were discussed above with the exception of the Submissiveness Test, a Project-developed measure of tendency "to conform to external authority." The distribution of scores for each of the personality measures was divided into thirds, and each student was identified by his position in the breakdown. Students' scores on the measures of learning could then be classified by the teaching method to which they had been exposed and by their position in the upper, middle, or lower third of the distribution for the personality variable. The cell entries resulting from these classifications, used as the basis for the two-way analyses of variance, were the mean scores for the students falling into each two-way classification. When an analysis yielded a

TABLE 53

Summary of Personality and Learning Outcomes Measures Involved in Significant Interactions Between Teaching Style and Student Personality

Personality Measures	Learning Outcomes Measures					
	Head-lines G	SIAT No. 4	SIAT No. 3	SIAT No. 2	SIAT No. 1	Unit
Guilford-Zimmerman						
Factor A	x					
Factor E					x	
Factor F		x				x
Factor O				x		
Need-Cognition	x			x		
Need-Structure		x				
Word Description		x	x			
Submissiveness	x					
F-Scale		x				

significant interaction effect, this was an indication that the pattern of cell means was different from what one would expect by looking at the marginal means representing the effects of the styles on one dimension or the effects of personality on the other.

Of the ninety-one interaction terms resulting from this analysis, twelve were significant at the .05 level. With this number of runs we would expect about five significant interaction effects simply by chance. While this result would seem to reveal that student personality and teaching style do work together to produce systematic effects beyond those expected by chance, we found it a surprisingly meager yield. (Table 53 indicates those tests which resulted in significant interactions.) Although it was difficult to identify interpretable patterns from either the significant or the near-significant interactions, one important trend did emerge. A careful reading of the data[21] indicated that the more closely a learning outcome measure was logically related to specific coaching or teaching, the less performance seemed to be related to personality or teaching method. The Unit Tests, for example, were given immediately after the teaching of a specific unit and were most closely tied to the content of the teaching units. Here only one personality measure interacted with method to yield a significant result. SIAT No. 1 and SIAT No. 3 were also closely related to specific skills taught in the classroom, and these also were relatively unaffected by the interaction of personality and teaching method. On the other hand, SIAT No. 4, the socratic interview, is the most complex measure of the skills we were teaching, requiring both affective and intellectual control of an argument, and here there were four significant interactions. (Table 54 presents these results in some detail.)

As one would expect, students who score high on the Guilford-Zimmerman factor F (Friendliness), which is presumably indicative of a tolerance for hostile action, learn better to analyze societal issues in a live, controversial test setting when taught by the socratic style. The more striking finding, however, is that students low on G-Z-F learn to perform in this setting much better when taught with the recitation style. This may well indicate that the "low-

TABLE 54

Summary of Significant Teacher Style-Student Personality Interaction Effects on the SIAT No. 4, Interview, Posttest Scores, Adjusted for I.Q. and Pretest Scores

Style by Guilford-Zimmerman Factor F (Friendliness)

Style	Factor F			Style	Source	d.f.	Sums of Squares	Mean Square	F-Ratio
	Low	Med.	High						
Socratic	17.25	20.10	22.74	20.03	1 x J	2	820.12	410.06	
Recitation	29.87	16.48	17.67	21.34	Within	49	4234.15	86.41	4.74
G-Z F	24.56	18.01	19.80						

Style by F-Scale (Authoritarianism)

Style	F-Scale			Style	Source	d.f.	Sums of Squares	Mean Square	F-Ratio
	Low	Med.	High						
Socratic	25.60	20.22	14.82	20.21	1 x J	2	683.70	341.85	
Recitation	17.29	24.75	18.37	20.14	Within	79	8067.44	102.12	3.34
F-Scale	21.30	22.56	16.66						

Style by Word Description Test (Dichotomization)

Style	Word Description			Style	Source	d.f.	Sums of Squares	Mean Square	F-Ratio
	Low	Med.	High						
Socratic	19.71	18.45	18.30	18.82	1 x J	2	505.64	252.82	
Recitation	12.48	22.79	20.36	18.54	Within	79	6200.43	78.49	3.22
Word Desc.	15.97	20.69	19.37						

Style by School Work-Habit Test (Need-Structure)

Style	Need-Structure			Style	Source	d.f.	Sums of Squares	Mean Square	F-Ratio
	Low	Med.	High						
Socratic	22.71	17.31	19.73	19.92	1 x J	2	728.67	364.34	
Recitation	15.94	23.73	16.83	18.83	Within	88	8714.18	99.02	3.68
Need-Struc.	19.32	20.52	18.28						

friendly" student applies himself more fully to the task at hand if he is not required to deal with the emotional overtones inherent in his relationship to the socratic teacher.

The interaction effects of teacher style and authoritarianism, as measured by the F-Scale, also seem clear. Low F students do much better on SIAT No. 4 if taught by the socratic method, while both middle and high F students learn to handle themselves better in this testing situation if taught by the recitation style. The same pattern is repeated with the Word Description Test (tendency to dichotomize), and it is, in effect, the same pattern as with the G-Z factor F. Very probably the "non-authoritarian" stance of the socratic teacher provokes considerable anxiety in the high F student, as does the complexity of issues that must be faced by the dichotomizer in the socratic discussion. These findings suggest that more authoritarian students and/or students who tend to dichotomize will learn to use the analytic concepts in the give-and-take of the SIAT No. 4 interview better when exposed to controversial social issues in the less personal recitation setting, while their opposites will learn better with the socratic dialogue.

Results with the Berlak School Work-Habits Test (need for structure) do not lend themselves to so straightforward an interpretation. It is clear that students either high or low on this measure do better on SIAT No. 4 if taught by the socratic method, while those in the middle range do better with the recitation style. Perhaps the student who feels a low need to structure his school work finds the "free-flowing" socratic less restrictive and more stimulating than the more organized recitation. Feeling less "hemmed in," he may interact more freely, or at least be less concerned about the seeming lack of structure, and thus learn to handle himself better in controversial discussions than if he were in a recitation class. On the other hand, the student with a high need for structure is more likely to be disturbed by the same characteristics of the socratic discussion that make it attractive to his low need-structure counterpart. At the same time, the very need that would cause him to be disturbed is also likely to compel him to impose his own organization upon the discussion. Consequently, his own exercise in ordering the interaction may provide the framework he needs to do well in the SIAT No. 4 interview, although not to the extent that the low need-structure student's relaxed attitude toward ambiguity enhances his learning. By the same token, it is reasonable to expect that the student who lacks the compulsion to provide his own order in the discussion, but who feels sufficient need for structure to be bothered by the seeming lack of order in socratic teaching, i.e., the middle-range person on the Berlak measure, would better learn to apply the reflective framework in the more systematic recitation discussions.

GENERAL CONCLUSIONS

With the kaleidoscopic findings emerging from our comprehensive "fishing expedition," it is difficult to draw general conclusions about how student personality relates to learning or how it interacts with teaching style to inhibit or facilitate learning. Several major points might be emphasized, however. First, certain characteristics commonly associated with the "better" student turn out to bear a relationship to learning even when the best available measures of intelligence and verbal and abstract reasoning are statistically partialed out. Need-cognition and sociometric status, for example, are both good predictors of the effective learner quite independently of intelligence. As suggested earlier, either there is an interaction between these characteristics and intelligence which makes it impossible to hold constant the full effects of intelligence, or existing intelligence tests are not adequate measures for this type of statistical control.

It is possible that they do not get at the type of academic aptitude required by the experimental curriculum.

A second important finding is the complexity of the relationships among student personality, teaching style, and assessment instruments. In our review of one set of findings relating various personality dimensions to two teaching styles with the socratic interview as the learning outcome, it became very obvious that classroom learning is indeed a highly complex event requiring more sophisticated research models than have hitherto been employed.

This leads to a final consideration: the need for carefully constructed measures to conduct educational research of this nature. The striking relationship between ascendance and sociability and the student's performance in the socratic interview emphasizes the importance of this work. We placed much reliance on the SIAT No. 4 interview as a more valid way of assessing the student's ability to state and support a decision on a public issue. Compared with the usual paper-and-pencil tests, the setting is a more "natural" one relative to the context of the political discussions the student will face as an adult. Moreover, he can score well regardless of his political-ethical choices, providing he is able to identify important issues and clarify them intelligently in relation to his decision. Our results indicate, however, that this measure is sensitive to interpersonal as well as intellectual competence. And, while the former is undoubtedly important, it is a contaminating factor in a measure of the effects of a curriculum with objectives such as ours. Either a measure must be developed which is free of extraneous interpersonal effects, or adequate measures of interpersonal competences must be developed to use in controlling for their effect on intellectual performance. The problem itself, of course, suggests an exciting area of research: To what extent do people develop persuasive arguments not because of the soundness of their logic but because of more general temperamental factors such as verbal fluency or interpersonal competence?

Perhaps the most obvious difficulty with the interpretation of the research presented in this section is the plethora of data. Had we attempted the analysis of a much more limited amount of information, especially with respect to learning outcomes, our results might well have been much "cleaner" and our conclusions and recommendations more obvious. (What one doesn't know, one doesn't have to interpret.) Our effort, however, was clearly exploratory. Had some startling and consistent pattern of findings emerged, we would, of course, have been delighted. Instead, we found but a few clues and leads for further research.

The major finding coming out of this study, it may be, is the pressing need for methodological research in the development of more valid and reliable methods of assessing learning outcomes, the teaching process, and personality.

References

1. L. G. Wispe, "Evaluating Section Teaching Methods in the Introductory Course," *Journal of Educational Research* (1951), 45:161-186.
2. J. A. Patton, "A Study of the Effects of Student Acceptance of Responsibility and Motivation on Course Behavior," unpublished doctoral dissertation, University of Michigan, 1955.

3. Edward M. Glaser, *An Experiment in the Development of Critical Thinking* (New York: Bureau of Publications, Teachers College, Columbia University, 1941), p. 158.

4. George A. Stern, "Environments for Learning," in Nevitt Sanford (ed.), *The American College* (New York: John Wiley & Sons, Inc., 1962).

5. P. L. Dressel and L. B. Mayhew, *General Education: Explorations in Evaluation* (Washington: American Council on Education, 1954).

6. Stern, *op. cit.,* pp. 692-693.

7. *Ibid.,* pp. 697-698.

8. *Ibid.,* p. 701.

9. W. J. McKeachie, "Motivation, Teaching Methods and College Learning," in Marshall Jones (ed.), *Nebraska Symposium on Motivation* (Lincoln: University of Nebraska Press, 1961).

10. *Ibid.,* pp. 111-112.

11. Either of these results — not changing one's position when presented with a piece of affectively loaded evidence or shifting one's position in the face of new evidence — might be good from a societal point of view. The "goodness" hinges on the extent to which the failure to shift positions when faced with new evidence is due to rationally disregarding negative consequences of a decision after becoming aware of them or to the operation of more subtle psychological mechanisms which cause the individual to conveniently ignore or forget such negative consequences.

12. Lauren B. Resnick, "The Handling of Contradictory Information: A Study in the Effects of Cognitive Need, Cognitive Style, and Motivational Arousal," 1962 (mimeographed).

13. The production of transformations factor seems to measure the person's ability to shift his frame of reference or "break gestalt." Loaded heavily on this factor were: the Cooperative School and College Ability Tests (SCAT), basically intelligence tests yielding quantitative and verbal ability scores combined into a total score for this analysis; a Hidden Figures Test measuring ability to find figure outlines in a complex picture: a Word Relations Test of ability to see new relations among a list of words, i.e., to create a new framework for viewing the words; and a Gestalt Transformation Test which requires solving a problem using only a part of one of the objects presented as choices.

14. Resnick, *op. cit.,* p. 25.

15. *Ibid.,* p. 27.

16. For a non-technical discussion of this type of scale see Clair Selltiz, Marie Jahoda, Morton Deutsch, and Stuart W. Cook, *Research Methods in Social Relations* (New York: Holt, Rinehart & Winston, Inc., 1960), pp. 366-369.

17. C. E. Osgood, G. J. Suci, and P. H. Tannenbaum, *The Measurement of Meaning* (Urbana: University of Illinois Press, 1957).

18. T. W. Adorno, Else Frenkel-Brunswik, Daniel J. Levinson, and R. Nevitt Sanford, *The Authoritarian Personality* (New York: Harper & Row, Publishers, 1950).

19. For a discussion of the procedures for Thurstone-type scaling, see Selltiz *et al., op. cit.,* pp. 359-365.

20. The use of the covariance technique in comparing gains on measures of learning was mentioned briefly in reference 2 of Section Two. For a good technical discussion of analysis of covariance for two-way designs see William W. Cooley and Paul R. Lohnes, *Multivariate Procedures for the Behavioral Sciences* (New York: John Wiley & Sons, Inc., 1962), chap. 5. We are indebted to William

Cooley for providing the computer program for our analysis, plus much helpful advice.

21. Full results are available in Donald W. Oliver and James P. Shaver, *The Analysis of Public Controversy: A Study in Citizenship Education.* Report of Cooperative Research Project No. 8145 (Cambridge, Mass.: The Laboratory for Research in Instruction, Harvard Graduate School of Education, 1963), chapter 13. Tables A, B, C, D, and E, which report significant interactions other than those with SIAT No. 4 (see Table 53), have also been deposited with the American Documentation Institute. Order document Number 8672 from ADI Auxiliary Publications Project, Photoduplication Service, Library of Congress, Washington, D.C. 20540. Remit in advance $1.25 for microfilm or photocopies and make checks payable to: Chief, Photoduplication Service, Library of Congress.

INDEX